Democracy
on
Purpose

Democracy

⊰ on ⊱

Purpose

Justice and the Reality of God

Franklin I. Gamwell

GEORGETOWN UNIVERSITY PRESS/WASHINGTON, D.C.

Georgetown University Press, Washington, D.C.
©2000 by Georgetown University Press. All rights reserved.
Printed in the United States of America

10 9 8 7 6 5 4 3 2 1   2000

This volume is printed on acid-free offset book paper.

Library of Congress Cataloging-in-Publication Data

Gamwell, Franklin I.
   Democracy on purpose : justice and the reality of God / Franklin
I. Gamwell
      p.   cm. — (Moral traditions and moral arguments)
   Includes index.
   ISBN 0-87840-764-2 (cloth : alk. paper)
   1. Religion and ethics. 2. Teleology. 3. Democracy—Religious
aspects. 4. Justice.   I. Title. II. Series: Moral traditions &
moral arguments.
   BJ47.G27 2000
   171'.2—dc21   99-38854
                                                          CIP

For my students
at
the Divinity School

Contents

Preface

On the Christian understanding, God is the reality from which all things come and to which all things go and, thereby, is implicated in the reality of everything else. In contrast, Western moral and political theory in the last two centuries has widely asserted that morality and politics are independent of a divine reality. On this view, there is no necessary relation between theistic faith and moral worth, however important belief in God may be to a given individual's moral life. The consensus on this understanding dominates the contemporary theoretical discussion of justice. Notwithstanding their disagreements, some of them fundamental, most recent political theories agree that democracy as the normative form of political community must be conceived without any explicit or implicit appeal to a theistic conception.

This work argues that democracy depends on a divine purpose, and therefore the dominant consensus in political theory is mistaken. The attempt to separate morality and politics from the divine reality, I am persuaded, misrepresents the distinctive character of human freedom and prevents a coherent account of our democratic commitment. In the end, democracy itself requires that account, because we humans lead our moral and political lives with understanding. I seek to articulate an alternative understanding of justice through a theistic conception of what makes life distinctively human.

Papers that advanced aspects of this work were presented and discussed at Stanford University, the Society of Christian Ethics, the Center for Process Studies, and the Midwest Region of the American Theological Society, and I am grateful for the help I received from participants in those events. In a somewhat different manner, I have benefited from discussions with my associates at Protestants for the Common Good, whom I thank for assistance often given without their knowing. The suggestions of two anonymous readers for Georgetown University Press have also influenced the outcome. I am deeply indebted and express my gratitude to Schubert M. Ogden and Philip E. Devenish, both of whom read the entire manuscript and provided me their extensive and detailed comments toward improvement of the work.

On this occasion, I wish to express my inclusive and profound sense of debt to teachers, colleagues, and students at the Divinity School of the University of Chicago. I cannot imagine reconstituting my past by substituting some other academic community in the place this one has occupied for some time without an immense loss. I take the liberty of dedicating the book to my students. During my own doctoral work at the School, I was sensible of the substantial measure in which my education was received from the larger company of students. I now know that the same is true of my time as their teacher. I wish especially to thank Francisco J. Benzoni, Ronney B. Mourad, Joseph S. Pettit, and Brett T. Wilmot for their thoughtful readings of some or all of the manuscript and for conversations that saved me from mistakes I would otherwise have made. Ron Mourad also thoughtfully prepared the index.

Introduction

Morality and politics depend on a purpose in the nature of things. I seek here to redeem this assertion and to articulate the moral and political principles it implies. In the West prior to the modern age, a work so designed would have represented the prevailing view. Summarily speaking, both medieval culture and its principal intellectual traditions were controlled by the conviction that human life relates to an all-inclusive context of importance. Virtually all differences in thought or opinion were contained within the common affirmation that all human purposes are properly directed to a comprehensive telos for which all of the world exists or was created. In marked contrast, the development of modern moral thought as a whole has fashioned a dominant consensus in moral and political theory on which moral and political activity are independent of any comprehensive purpose. I am convinced that this consensus is mistaken. This work argues that human life is constituted by an attachment to the divine good that we either embrace without evasion or corrupt by loving something else as if it, too, were God, and seeks to specify the divine good to politics through the democratic principle of justice as general emancipation.

I will use the term "comprehensive teleology" to name the view that human life is properly directed to a telos defined by reality as such. The most systematic premodern statement of this view is found in the massive achievement of Thomas Aquinas. "Every thing is directed to good as its end," he wrote, and "God is supremely the end of all things" (*Summa Contra Gentiles*: 3. 16, 17). Nothing can be properly understood independently of its specific final cause, and the divine essence is the supreme or all-inclusive final cause. Because God is, on Aquinas's account, the perfect being, all things realize their own proper ends by perfecting their own being, and the moral life consists in the perfection of the human soul. This allusion to Aquinas is enough to suggest that most other medieval thought was teleological in a similar sense, since it was typically an attempt to represent a theistic conviction. Moreover, comprehensive teleology in some form can be said to characterize the Platonic tradition in metaphysics generally, which, above all, provided the philosophical resources for theistic accounts. Summarily speaking, then, the widespread consensus developed in modern moral discussion calls for practical understandings that are independent of God because they are independent of metaphysics. This work seeks to redeem metaphysical theism as the basis for moral and political theory and, thereby, to reassert theistic teleology. Still, it is not the metaphysics of Aquinas I will defend. Convincing reassertion of a divine purpose, I will argue, depends on an understanding of ourselves and our world that departs from both the nonmetaphysical consensus of modern moral thought and the classical theism that took its bearings from Greek philosophy. Against both, I will seek to show how distinctively human existence implies a neoclassical metaphysics for which Alfred North Whitehead and Charles Hartshorne provide the primary philosophical resources.

To first appearances, the reassertion of a divine purpose may seem intellectually sterile and morally suspect, at least insofar as it purports to be pertinent to politics. The modern creation of democratic political communities is, whatever their imperfections, almost universally affirmed as a civilized advance—and, for many, it is transparent that democracy emerged because politics and political thought were separated from religious convictions. For Jürgen Habermas, to choose one prominent example, democracy is a political expression of possibilities that appeared only with the transition to modernity from the "religious and metaphysical" worldviews of medieval civilization. "What is common to religious or metaphysical worldviews," he explains, "is a more or less clearly marked, dichotomous structure" that allows thought "to relate the sociocultural world to a world behind . . . the visible world of this life, . . . a fundamental order."

Such worldviews limit social possibilities because conceptions of the metaphysical order are necessarily "immunized" against criticism (1984: 189); they cannot be validated by critical thought and, therefore, can be affirmed only by submission to the authority of some tradition or institution. In contrast, democracy is a civilized advance because it determines the legal order through full and free practical discourse and, therefore, recognizes no authority to which citizens must bow except "the sovereignty of the people."

More generally, on Habermas's reading, the transition to modernity is the emergence of a worldview that opens all thought about the world and human life within it to the possibility of critical reflection, permitting the rationalization of modern society in or through which institutions express understandings that are critically negotiated. This is not to say that modern societies have fully exploited the possibilities that the modern worldview offers. Medieval civilization included a stratified social structure that was immune to change because it was thought to be as fundamental as the order behind the world by which it was sanctioned. In contrast, the release from authoritarian forms of social life introduced a historical consciousness for which all institutions and patterns of social order are subject to deliberate change, and the changes can be and often have been irrational and demonic.

Moreover, Habermas seeks systematically to show that social rationalization in the West has been one-sided or unbalanced because it has largely proceeded as if only empirical understandings about factual states of affairs can be rationally contested and validated and, thereby, has failed fully to exploit the possibilities of rationalizing our common life morally. Practical reason has been largely reduced to instrumental calculation, and modern societies have become increasingly dominated by systems of strategic rationality, especially the economic order and the state bureaucracy. For Habermas, however, the rationalizing possibilities opened by the modern worldview, including democratic politics, are themselves the only effective antagonist to modernity's social failures. Attainment of a "postmetaphysical" worldview, which makes thought independent of a fundamental order, is—or, at least, should be—irreversible (see Habermas 1992).

Habermas's account ably represents why the reassertion of comprehensive teleology may be met with ready dismissal. However different their details, religious and metaphysical convictions are widely thought to be immune to critical validation or beyond the under-standings of ourselves and our world that can be assessed by argu-ment. While beliefs of this kind may be appropriate insofar as human life is a matter of personal or private decision, no such conviction may properly control our common understandings of the world or set the terms of our common life. Whatever the failures of modernity, its commitment to the autonomy of reason is itself non-negotiable, pre-cisely because, wherever it has been effective, its consequence has been emancipation from authority or heteronomous control.

But surely it is one thing to insist that political claims should be subject to argumentative assessment and something else to dismiss theistic teleology. To identify the two uncritically is merely to assume that the assertion of a divine purpose cannot be rationally redeemed, and this contradicts the modern commitment to critical reflection. Even if we grant that medieval religious and metaphysical worldviews were explicitly thought to transcend the power of natural reason and, therefore, were sustained by submission to authority, it does not follow that theism cannot be rationally redeemed. To the contrary, I will argue, modernity's deepest mistakes include its pervasive assump-tion that liberation from authority requires the separation of morality and politics from a comprehensive purpose—even if I will also defend an understanding of that purpose significantly different from the metaphysics of the medieval consensus.

With Habermas, Whitehead identifies democratic politics as a sin-gular achievement. On Whitehead's reading, democracy culminates, in the sense that it socially embodies, the adventure of freedom as an idea and ideal within Western history—the humanitarian ideal, which "haunted the ancient Mediterranean world" as "the faint light of the dawn of a new order of life" and, through the Middle Ages, promoted "the gradual growth of the requisite communal customs" (1961: 15, 22). We can also say that, for Whitehead as for Habermas, democracy represents the rationalization of society, because human freedom is measured by the extent to which purpose becomes intelligent and, therefore, is controlled by what Whitehead calls "a sense of criticism, founded on appreciations of beauty, and of intellectual distinction, and of duty" (1961: 11). Again with Habermas, Whitehead associates the full release of critical reflection and, therefore, the possibilities of rationalization with modernity. "The great minds who laid the foundations of our modern mentality" had as "their true enemy . . . the doctrine of dogmatic finality." Modernity, on its most important meaning, is distinguished by the measure in which it affirms reason as the "ultimate judge, universal and yet individual to each, to which all authority must bow" (1961: 162).

In his own way, Whitehead, too, is sensible of distinctively modern forms of social evil. In this regard, he comments especially on theories of political economy in which individualism and competition are said to be sufficient for social coordination. "It was believed that the laws of the Universe were such that the strife of individuals issued in the progressive realization of a harmonious society" (1961: 33). If we take into account the institutionalization of this belief, it seems clear that Whitehead has in view the same one-sided or unbalanced development that Habermas describes in extensive detail. For all his agreement with Habermas, however, Whitehead's account differs fundamentally because, for him, the humanitarian ideal has been threatened by the modern renunciation of metaphysics. Having followed the idea of freedom to its democratic culmination, he adds: "This success came only just in time. For before and during the nineteenth century, several strands of thought emerged whose combined effect was in direct opposition to the humanitarian ideal" (1961: 28). In their concurrence, democracy "lost its security of intellectual justification" (1961: 36).

The hostile "strands of thought" were both theoretical and practical and expressed what Whitehead elsewhere calls the "historical revolt" of modernity. Theoretically, the modern mind turned from the view that each thing has its place within a comprehensive order to "the contemplation of brute fact" (1963: 15). The stunning development of modern empirical science widely displayed and quickened the historical revolt and, insofar, banished final causes from the world, seeking explanation solely in terms of efficient causation. The culmination in philosophy, Whitehead comments, was "Hume's criticism of the doctrine of the soul" (1961: 36). Wherever the absence of final causes invaded practical thought, each individual became the definer of her or his own happiness, so that principles of moral and political obligation could only be nonteleological.

As J. B. Schneewind documents in detail, early modern moral theory included the beginnings of a natural law tradition that sought empirical principles for solving problems of living together and separated these principles from any conception of the highest good—and Hobbes famously formulated the point: "Good, evil, and contemptible are ever used with relation to the person that useth them: there being nothing simply and absolutely so; nor any common rule of good and evil, to be taken from the nature of the objects themselves" (1962: 48–49). Still, it is probably wrong to say that moral nonteleology developed in a manner that correlates with the empirical scientific concentration on efficient causation. The natural law tradition was attacked by a wide range of thinkers, including metaphysical theists of whom Leibniz and, later, Hegel were preeminent representatives. "Whatever the fate of teleology in physics," Schneewind writes, "Christian teleology was widely used by seventeenth-century thinkers to explain the point of the various dispositions, feelings, and abilities that go to make up our nature as moral beings, and sometimes to show our true goal or our function in the universe as well. That sort of teleology did not disappear in the eighteenth century, nor did the belief that without knowledge of God's ends we could not know how to direct our actions" (1998: 286).

With the critical achievement of Kant, however, metaphysical teleology became at best a minority report in practical philosophy. Notwithstanding his own practical theism, Kant's arguments against the traditional metaphysical enterprise have, on my reading, controlled the development of subsequent modern moral and political theory. In this broad sense, the dominant consensus on which practical principles are independent of a comprehensive telos may be called a Kantian consensus. Nothing more confirms the point than the fact that teleological forms of moral theory with persisting influence in the twentieth century—the utilitarian theories of Bentham and Mill, the transformation of Hegel by Marx, and the development of empirical pragmatism by John Dewey—are all nonmetaphysical. It is this separation of moral principles from the nature of things that, for Whitehead, stands "in direct opposition to the humanitarian ideal" and withdraws from democracy "its security of intellectual justification." He means that our ideals for human life and society either have the backing of rational insight into the larger reality in which we are set, or they become arbitrary when confronted with threatening alternatives.

Summarily speaking, the loss Whitehead describes can be traced to the character of medieval civilization from which modern thought emerged. Ironically, the dominant modern consensus, which asserts that full critical reflection requires independence from a comprehensive purpose, simply reverses and, in that sense, is tied to the dominant medieval consensus, on which metaphysical theism is redeemed by appeal to an authoritative tradition. If modern thought has been a "flight from authority" (Stout 1981), its culmination in a flight from comprehensive teleology betrays in part a failure to criticize the terms on which authority and teleology had been for so long united in medieval thought. In any event, if democracy or the humanitarian ideal is intellectually insecure without a metaphysical backing, then perhaps neither the medieval nor the modern consensus represents our most adequate self-understanding. I seek to present a third alternative, namely, a comprehensive teleology that can be redeemed by argument.

This work argues that our distinctively human life implies an affirmation of God's reality and that the divine purpose for human life implies a democratic principle I will call "justice as general emancipation." The work has, therefore, two principal parts. In the first part, I seek to develop and defend a conception of distinctively human existence, in which human activity as such is constituted by its relation to a divine reality and, therefore, by a moral decision in relation to the divine good. In the second part, I seek to develop and defend a conception of justice as democratic, in which the divine good is specified to the political community. Accordingly, the work pursues the relation between philosophical theology and political theory and argues that the two are inseparable.

I recognize that this pursuit includes asking and answering a range of philosophical questions, each of which is addressed by a considerable literature and any one of which could itself occupy an extended work. I am also acutely aware that my treatment of the relevant controversies is often less complete that it could be in a more circumscribed context. Still, I am convinced that contemporary democratic theory is profoundly burdened by the assumption that comprehensive or metaphysical teleology is not credible. The nature of that burden is best disclosed through a clear and compelling case for the discredited alternative, and, in making that case, it is not enough simply to argue for the divine context of human life or merely to assert a theistic metaphysics and derive from it certain political principles. The first would leave the moral discussion at such a general level as to invite the judgment of political irrelevance, and the second would refuse to engage the dominant consensus of modern moral theory. Thus, I have chosen to do what I can toward both redeeming a theistic affirmation and articulating the conception of justice that depends on it.

As already noted, the revolt against metaphysics by which contemporary democratic thought remains pervasively informed is given its preeminent statement in the work of Immanuel Kant. His arguments against the possibility of knowing God's existence and, correspondingly, his formulation and defense of a nonteleological conception of practical reason remain the most profound challenge to the reassertion of comprehensive teleology. On my reading, Kant was lucid about the alternatives for moral and political thought: Because the moral law must be rationally necessary, it either derives from the metaphysical character of existence or it consists solely in the formal universality of practical reason. Given Kant's conviction that metaphysics is impossible, it follows that "an action . . . derives its moral worth, *not from the purpose* which is to be attained by it" (1949: 17) or, to say the same thing, that "nothing can possibly be conceived in the world, or even out of it, which can be called good without qualification, except a *good will*" (1949: 11). Since I seek here to redeem the alternative Kant rejected, I will not pursue an extended interpretation of his critical philosophy. Still, attention to his arguments and those of subsequent thinkers who can, in relevant respects, be called Kantians will be present throughout.

Although this is not a work in Christian theology, I believe that the theism for which I will argue is an appropriate formulation of the self-understanding to which Christians are called in their experience of Jesus. Subject to confirmation of that judgment, I hope that this work may be of interest and importance to Christian theology in its reflection on the contemporary political vocation of Christians. My conversation partners also include especially Reinhold Niebuhr. On my accounting, his thought remains the most thorough and important twentieth-century statement of the relation between Christianity and politics. Notwithstanding disagreements I have with some of his interpretations, I also hope that this work may make a modest contribution to his project.

In Niebuhr's terms and those of the Christian theological tradition generally, the question addressed here asks about love and justice. As

I understand these terms, "love" designates the proper relation of human life to the primal source and final end of its activity and, therefore, to self and all others, and "justice" designates the proper ordering of the political community. To ask about love and justice, then, is to ask whether there is some primal source and final end of human existence that ought to be loved and, if so, what such love implies with respect to the political order. Perhaps one way to characterize political theory without comprehensive teleology is to say that it separates justice from love, in dramatic contrast to the premodern Christian theological tradition in which Augustine and Aquinas are the towering figures and that Luther, Calvin, and modern Christian theology generally have sought to reinterpret. In any event, I will argue that politics is bound by the principle of justice as general emancipation because human authenticity is the love of God and of all others in God.

I

THE DIVINE PURPOSE

1

The Freedom We Ourselves Are

"Our wisdom, in so far as it ought to be deemed true and solid wisdom, consists almost entirely of two parts: the knowledge of God and of ourselves. But as these are connected together by many ties, it is not easy to determine which of the two precedes, and gives birth to the other" (Calvin 1989: 37). If these famous opening sentences in Calvin's *Institutes of the Christian Religion* assert that knowing ourselves depends on knowing God, they also suggest that we can know God if we truly understand ourselves. This suggestion becomes the more provocative if we can say that humans are creatures who not only exist but also understand that they exist, so that living in the distinctively human way is always marked by a self-understanding. Calvin's sentences then serve to raise the following question: Does human life necessarily include an understanding of God?

Whatever may have been Calvin's own response to that question, many modern theologians have, in one way or another, sought to answer it by showing philosophically how the essential nature of our self-consciousness or self-understanding implicates the reality of God. Indeed, we might say that this approach defines summarily the tradition of theological liberalism. Friedrich Schleiermacher, generally acknowledged as "the father of liberal theology," asserted that human life is constituted by an "immediate self-consciousness" (1989: 5, emphasis deleted) that includes a "consciousness of being absolutely dependent, or, which is the same thing, of being in relation with God" (1989: 12, emphasis deleted). In the twentieth century, to choose two

13

other examples, both Paul Tillich and Reinhold Niebuhr maintained that self-awareness is a transcendence of both self and world and, therefore, simultaneously an awareness of the unconditioned or divine reality.

On some accounts, this modern theological focus on self-consciousness has been largely conditioned by pervasive challenges to the credibility of theism that culminated in or have followed on Kant's critical philosophy. Although Kant himself affirmed theism as a postulate of practical reason, his defense of this moral conclusion has not been widely accepted. But his arguments against theoretical knowledge of God have been massively influential. In response, many liberal theologians have sought to show philosophically that awareness of God is prior to any distinction between theoretical and practical reason. In its own way, then, this theological tradition has participated in the "turn to the subject" so widely characteristic of modern thought and has sought to exploit that turn, against many others who share it, in order to make the point of Christian theism. The consequence is that this focus on the human subject also differentiates the liberal project from most previous theology. For the Christian tradition as a whole, God can only be the source and end of strictly all existence, and earlier theologians often explicitly said what this seems to imply, namely, that awareness of God cannot be absent from an awareness of one's own existence. In the theological project beginning with Schleiermacher, however, that statement becomes central to the formulation and defense of the Christian faith. On this conception of the theological task, the valid answer to the theistic question is properly pursued through a philosophical analysis of human subjectivity.

My interest here is directed to this project in philosophical theology. I believe that its purpose can be achieved. But I also believe that success has been denied to most theologians in the liberal tradition. Notwithstanding their intent to argue for theism philosophically, they also typically assert that our knowledge of God is deficient in some manner or measure without God's special self-disclosure, above all in or through Jesus as the Christ. This position is sometimes formulated by saying that God's "original" or "general" revelation to human subjectivity or human experience as such must be completed by God's special act—or, again, that our constitutive awareness of God's "reality" must be completed by a special disclosure of God's "nature" or "character" (see, e.g., Niebuhr 1941–43, 1: chap. 5). Within modern theology, this putative limitation on our inescapable awareness of God is typically associated with the statement that God cannot be objectified or cannot be an object to the subject of thought. Although we must speak as if God were an object in order to speak of God at all, such speaking must be distinguished from all literal designation of objects.

On Schleiermacher's account, for instance, the "feeling of absolute dependence" has as its "corresponding co-determinant" the infinite "Whence" of all, which cannot itself be the term of a subject-object relation (1989: 16–21). Speaking of God is always the use of objectivating thought to express and, thereby, to cultivate the piety or "religious emotions" with which we relate to what is nonobjective. This speaking, therefore, cannot be separated from the distinctive language of some or other religious communion. In a similar way, both Tillich and Niebuhr deny that any positive statement about God is properly literal, so that proper speaking of the divine either predicates by negating the characteristics of worldly things or is mythological or symbolic.[1] In the last analysis, then, both Tillich and Niebuhr assert that positive predication of God cannot be valid independently of the symbolic expressions that derive from God's special revelation.

The conviction that positive theistic predication must be symbolic is, so far as I can see, inconsistent with the project in philosophical theology it is meant to advance. If the divine reality cannot literally be an object of thought, then it is not clear how the subjective turn can redeem the credibility of theism. The analysis of our own subjectivity seeks a second-order understanding of what is present in first-order self-consciousness, and if the latter cannot have the thought of God, how can knowledge of God appear through the analysis? To assert that what appears is the consciousness of something nonobjective is to say that the concept "consciousness of something nonobjective" is a sensible one, and this implies that "nonobjective" designates an object of thought. It does not help to insist, as Schleiermacher does, that the unconditioned appears only to "immediate" consciousness, because this statement assumes that immediate consciousness and,

---

[1]Tillich, of course, famously said that "God is being-itself is a nonsymbolic statement" (1951: 238), but the literal meaning of the statement is, on my reading, negative, equivalent to "God is not a being."

therefore, its content can become an object of thought. Hence, to say that God is nonobjective is simultaneously to say that we cannot speak about God at all—and thus to offer an account of subjectivity that implicitly denies the divine reality. In that way, modern theology gives unwitting support to the explicit denial of theism that is so pervasive elsewhere in modern thinking.

In contrast to most liberal theologians, then, a convincing refutation of this denial requires a formulation of the subjective turn that includes a sound argument for theism. On that argument, the only divine nature special revelation could disclose is the character originally revealed to all human subjects, and God is shown to be an object of thought or understanding that can be designated in literal terms. The first part of this work will develop such an argument and, in the course of doing so, will seek to clarify the implications of God's original revelation for the moral character of human existence.

This first chapter seeks to show that every act of human subjectivity becomes what it is through a decision, which may be called an exercise of "original freedom" or "the freedom we ourselves are," and that this decision is a responsible or moral one because it includes knowledge of a comprehensive purpose or comprehensive telos. Chapter 2 will seek to extend an appreciation of our original freedom by attention to its misuse or duplicitous exercise and, in that context, will defend comprehensive teleology against Kant's conviction that this kind of moral theory is inconsistent with our awareness of the moral law. Chapter 3 will argue for a substantive conception of the comprehensive purpose, that is, will seek to explicate the character of worth or the good that all human activity ought to pursue, and will argue that our inescapable understanding of this good is our knowledge of a divine individual. In sum, Part One argues that human existence as such is constituted by a relation to the divine purpose that defines us as moral individuals because we must decide whether this relation is authentic or duplicitous.[2] Part Two will seek to develop a theory of democratic justice that specifies this decision to the political community.

As the first step in this larger task, the discussion in this chapter of our distinctive freedom will proceed through an analysis of our

---

[2]The Appendix to Part One seeks to confirm this conclusion by formulating a theory of belief and showing why every belief implies a belief in God.

capacity for self-understanding. I recognize that this capacity is itself a difficult thing to understand, however impossible it may also be to deny. This means that the argument will not successfully show how and why human subjectivity always includes knowledge of a comprehensive purpose unless it also clarifies the nature of self-understanding. I will seek to articulate this capacity by showing that a subject who understands anything at all must also understand itself. Thus, the discussion will assume only that we humans live with understanding, and the present chapter will also proceed through a series of steps. It will begin with the nature of understanding in order subsequently to explicate self-understanding. Having clarified both, I will then be in a position to show why a self-understanding is a decision that includes knowledge of a comprehensive purpose.

Understanding

Let us begin with the commonplace that we humans live with understanding. This beginning could itself occupy the work as a whole, since the attempt to understand understanding has, in some form or other, always been a part of the Western philosophical project and might well be said to define the modern turn to the subject. On one formulation, for instance, the process or product of understanding understandings is called "hermeneutics," and those who make this term central to their thought often conclude that "philosophical hermeneutics" is nothing other than an address to all philosophical questions. My intent here is far more limited. Whatever else might be said about understanding, I seek to interpret its character only in the measure required to show why the self who understands must also be one of the things understood—and to show how self-understanding differs from the understanding of anything else.

The assumption that we live with understanding should be formulated more precisely. Human beings are sometimes in a state of unconsciousness or dreamless sleep, and, clearly, understanding is a state that includes consciousness. I will use the terms "human activity" and, for emphasis, "distinctively human activity" to mean one of our conscious states, where "conscious" means "fully conscious." The term "fully conscious" is used to acknowledge that we also experience states of semi-consciousness, often just before sleeping or just on emerging from it. I will not speculate about whether or in what measure such semi-conscious moments include understanding, because it will suffice for present purposes to confine the analysis to our distinctively human activities. Still, "fully conscious" might also have another meaning that does not designate some concrete states in distinction from others but, rather, an abstract aspect of any human activity. Phenomenologically, it seems apparent that our consciousness includes a focus of attention in which something is plainly or perspicuously understood, and this may be distinguished from the dim apprehension of a vast background in which the focal region is embraced.

We can speak of this as a difference between the *explicit* and *implicit* understandings of a human activity. On one of its definitions, the term "implicit" means "contained in the nature of something although not readily apparent" (*American College Dictionary*), and this is precisely the sense of the term I intend. The vague background belongs to the nature of any act of understanding in the sense that explicit or focused understanding could not be what it is without the simultaneous presence of what is only dimly apprehended. For instance, a given moment of human activity typically includes implicit understandings previously learned by the individual in question. In some previous moment or moments of her or his life, attention was focused on those understandings, and they are now included, "although not readily apparent," as necessary conditions for what is now perspicuous. Suppose an informed citizen explicitly attends to a Supreme Court decision about prayer in the public schools. Her or his understanding could not be what it is without an immense context of acquired understandings of the Constitution, the legal system, public education, religious activities, and so forth. Even our explicit attention to mundane matters, say, writing and mailing a check in order to subscribe to a particular newspaper, depends on a vast background of previously learned understandings, in this case regarding finances, delivery schedules, and institutional commitments, among others.

John Searle speaks of "the Network" in order to designate this context of implicit understandings (1983: 141f.; see also 1992: 175f.). Jürgen Habermas, among many others, refers to this network as part of an individual's participation in a "lifeworld" that is "taken-for-granted" (1984: 335), and the same point is sometimes expressed in the notion that understanding is holistic in character. The abiding fact that these formulations severally express is the fragmentariness of human understanding. We are by nature limited in the sense that a human activity does not understand all things in complete detail; in fact, we are in any given moment conscious of very few things in any significant measure, and the same can be said about a human life as the sum of all its moments or activities. Among other consequences, this limitation makes our beliefs fallible. If we did apprehend all things completely, each thing and its relations to everything else would be included in our consciousness exactly as they are, and our capacity to affirm misunderstandings or to confuse some things with others derives from our merely partial apprehension of the entirety. Fragmentariness is also the reason for a dim background of consciousness in support of the center of attention. In this way, human subjectivity minimizes its limitation or increases the scope of understanding. Were our consciousness confined to what in the given moment we explicitly apprehend, we could not begin to understand a Supreme Court decision or, for that matter, most of the simple facts about our world, if indeed we could understand anything at all.

We can say that explicit consciousness is a fragment of our fragmentary understanding. What that fragment includes becomes significant insofar as there is a correlative significance to what is in the background. The extension of explicit understanding depends on greater complexity in what we take for granted, and, as a consequence, the measure of explicit understanding in a given activity depends on the previous learning of the individual in question that is now implicitly remembered. Given that learning largely depends on communication among individuals, we can also say that understanding is a thoroughly communal matter, and this means that language is important to distinctively human subjectivity. Because the communication of understandings among individuals is also fragmentary, it is mediated by conventional or publicly fixed symbols, and the development of our life with understanding beyond rudimentary forms is inseparable from participation in a rich and complex language. Beyond their most incipient appearance, then, the possibilities for explicit consciousness in a present human activity depend on the measure in which understandings previously given in linguistic form are now implicit. "The account of the sixth day should be written, He gave them speech, and they became souls" (Whitehead 1938: 57).

I will not here pursue further the communal nature of our consciousness, although it will reappear, especially in the discussion of human duplicity the next chapter will offer and in the later account of the human good. In the present context, the previous summary description of subjectivity is pertinent principally for its distinction between explicit and implicit understanding. Whatever else might be included in an account of our consciousness, we will be misled if we take the features of our plain or perspicuous apprehension to define understanding generally, and the recognition that understanding may include something on which we do not explicitly focus will be important throughout the argument for our inescapable apprehension of a comprehensive purpose. With this distinction in place, we can now seek to add greater detail to the analysis of any understanding at all.

As already mentioned, the significance of implicit to explicit consciousness helps to explain how the understanding of a given individual may grow. A person who at one point in her or his life could not possibly understand a Supreme Court decision may subsequently become sophisticated in its interpretation because she or he has acquired a vast background that is then implicitly effective. This does not mean that every subsequent occasion in one's life is an activity of greater understanding than all previous ones. To all appearances, at least, there are times when the content of consciousness lessens, perhaps especially when we become fatigued. More generally, in any event, it is transparent that the content of consciousness changes as the center of attention shifts and, therefore, the implicit understandings without which explicit attention could not be what it is are correspondingly different. It follows that distinctively human life is a series or succession of differing occasions of understanding. To say this is not to deny that the successive occasions are activities of the same individual. Individuality will be maintained if each of the successive activities includes some common characteristic or set of characteristics that distinguishes the individual from all others. But this abiding characteristic does not exhaust the nature of any given occasion, since that activity also includes understandings that are different from other activities of the same individual.

Summarily, then, I propose to think of a human individual as a career of distinctively human activities. Abraham Lincoln, for instance, was the career of activities that began in Hardin County, Kentucky, and ended with the assassination in Ford's Theater. Notwithstanding the immense diversity among the occasions of this career, all of them shared some identifying characteristic or set of characteristics, perhaps largely derived from the particular body in which they occurred, that made them Lincoln's activities and not those of any other individual. In addition, other enduring characteristics arose in the course of this career and were shared by member activities over a greater or lesser sequence, some from the time they emerged until Lincoln's death. As the reference to Lincoln's body suggests, I will understand the career of distinctively human activities to be a "stream of experiences" or series of psychic states that is, to all appearances, located somewhere in the brain and that may be distinguished from the human body. In other words, I mean by human "individual" what has traditionally been called the human soul, and I take the human body to be that part of the world with which the human individual most intimately interacts. Because this interaction is so intimate, Alfred North Whitehead notes, we are not accustomed to saying, "Here am I, and I have brought my body with me" (1938: 156); but this would be an accurate statement, assuming the meaning of "individual" I intend.

On this account, the soul as a succession of activities relates to and acts on the larger world at least primarily through being influenced by and influencing the human body. Each occasion of the soul or the human individual is constituted by relations to the past, including the body and, through the body, the larger world—and including past occasions of the soul itself. Insofar, distinctively human activities are products of efficient causation; aspects of the past are repeated or reenacted in the present. In turn, each activity becomes an efficient cause of the future, affecting the body, the larger world, and subsequent activities of the individual in question. Relations of efficient causation between or among occasions of the soul are the way in which the distinguishing features or characteristics of the individual persist throughout the succession of occasions.[3]

It follows that the concrete subject of understanding is properly conceived as a given human activity, rather than the individual to whose career that occasion belongs—at least if we assume that the subject is inseparable from its particular understandings. Since the latter change from activity to activity, the subject itself must also change. The individual, in distinction from any one of its successive activities, is identified by more or less enduring characteristics that are common to the succession. Were these characteristics themselves the concrete subject of understanding, it would be separate from the particular understandings of which it is the subject. Of course, we can say that an individual understands, and for many purposes this is not only a permissible but also the preferred way of speaking. Strictly construed, however, it is an elliptical description of the fact that one or more of a succession of activities is distinctively human, and understanding, strictly speaking, is a feature or characteristic of a concrete activity.

What is this feature or characteristic? In some sense, it must be a relation by which the subject of understanding is constituted; that is, understanding always has some content and, therefore, makes the subject what it is by relating it to some object. Nonetheless, the concept "relation" is not sufficient to define distinctively human subjectivity, because all relations are not understandings. What, then, is the specific difference that distinguishes the latter? Understanding, we have noted, is at least a kind of consciousness, and it seems apparent phenomenologically that consciousness involves discrimination. To be conscious of something is to be related to it in a manner that

---

[3]To prevent misunderstanding, I should note here that this distinction between soul and body does not imply a metaphysically dualistic solution to the problem of mind and body. Nor does the denial of dualism imply a materialistic account. The assumption that these two interpretations exhaust our metaphysical options is, I think, fallacious. The more convincing alternative to both is the metaphysics of activities that is most systematically developed by Whitehead and Hartshorne and is, I will argue in chapter 3, implied by our capacity for self-understanding. On this alternative, the difference between soul and body consists in consciousness or the capacity for consciousness, but both soul and body are composites of activities that may be identified metaphysically. For a treatment of the mind-body problem within this metaphysical account, see Griffin (1998).

discriminates it from other things, that marks it off. Moreover, the consciousness in which we understand somehow involves the discrimination of universals. Suppose, for instance, that the object of our awareness is some particular thing as perceived. Human perception is not typically mere awareness of a particular but, rather, the consciousness of it *as* an instance of some universal or universals. If we see or smell a yellow rose, for example, we see it as an instance of the universals "yellow" and "rose" or smell it as an instance of the universals "fragrant" and "rose." Accordingly, we discriminate or mark off not only the particular thing but also the universals that we perceive it to exemplify.[4]

We may well doubt that human activities alone are conscious and readily suppose that some nonhuman animals enjoy awareness, even though we are reluctant to say that they live with understanding. I propose that the distinguishing feature of understanding is the consciousness of universals. If there is consciousness without understanding, the creatures in whom it occurs are aware solely of particulars. It may be impossible for us to intuit such nonhuman subjectivity, since every moment of our consciousness seems to be distinctively human or to include understanding. Still, there are occasions when aspects of our perception afford some sense of what mere awareness might be like. I have in mind moments when something unexpected enters our consciousness, perhaps a flash of color or a sudden movement in our peripheral vision or a smell foreign to us. These experiences at least suggest an awareness before we are able to understand its content. But I will not speculate further

---

[4]I do not suggest that the discrimination by which understanding is distinguished is limited to explicit consciousness. If understanding a Supreme Court decision involves understandings of the Constitution, the legal system, and so forth, that were previously learned and are now implicitly remembered, then we must say that these background understandings implicitly discriminate their objects. We should distinguish, in other words, between a discrimination that is dim or vague because the subject's consciousness of that object is in the background, and a discrimination that is indefinite because the object discriminated is general. In contrast to its dim consciousness of previous learning, for instance, an act of subjectivity may have an indefinite consciousness of the human body on which it is dependent; that is, the particular parts of the body (or, at least, most of them) are not themselves discriminated and are understood only as they commonly belong to the body.

about consciousness without understanding, because I mention it only to contrast the conscious relation to universals that is constitutive of understanding.

Recognizing that human activity involves the consciousness of universals, we can say that understanding relates a subject to actual and possible realities by discriminating them through the discrimination of universals—or, more concisely, that understanding discriminates realities through universals. "Actual and possible realities" designates whatever might be understood as the instantiation of universals or the possible instantiation of universals. On my usage, universals are characteristics, so that the instantiation of a universal is the same as the exemplification of a characteristic. Hence, we may also say that understanding relates a subject to characteristics, since they, too, must be discriminated.[5] So far as I can see, however, there is no understanding of a universal or characteristic independently of the understanding that something may or must instantiate or exemplify it. To be sure, merely possible realities do not in fact exemplify any characteristics. To understand these realities is to discriminate something that is more or less indeterminate and, therefore, to discriminate nothing more determinate than the relevant universals. A merely possible yellow rose is not a particular rose but, rather, is exhausted by the universals "yellow" and "rose" (and perhaps others) as characteristics that may be exemplified in some way or other. Assuming that characteristics cannot exemplify characteristics, however, we may still distinguish between a universal and a possible reality as some or other instantiation of it. Absent this distinction, it would not make sense to speak of a possibility as something that may or must be actualized, since actualization is something more than a set of universals or characteristics. Hence, a possible reality is an indeterminate reality, meaning that some set of universals or characteristics may or must be instantiated or exemplified in some way or other. As the discrimination of realities through universals, under-

---

[5]I use "object of understanding" and "content of understanding" as more general terms. Depending on context, they may designate a reality discriminated, a universal discriminated, or, in contrast to both of the former, an intentional object, that is, a reality or universal or some integration of the two as discriminated. The terms "concept" and "conception" are used to designate epistemic contents or intentional objects.

standings may also be called representations of realities through universals. The discrimination of a reality "presents it again," where this capacity to represent includes the capacity to misrepresent, that is, to present again as an actual or possible exemplification of the wrong universals.[6]

Many have noted that our capacity to discriminate realities through universals is a necessary condition of participation in language, which makes understanding a thoroughly communal enterprise. As suggested above, participation in language here means the relation to conventional or publicly fixed symbols by which understandings are mediated, and we can now say that these are symbols for the conscious relation to realities through universals. The symbols are frequently sounds or marks on paper, but they might be most anything, including actions, in accord with the saying "actions speak louder than words." Perhaps some of the higher nonhuman animals have flashes of understanding, and perhaps even fewer have developed a rudimentary or primitive language. In any event, the distinctive complexity of human understanding is inseparable from participation in a rich and complex language because such participation facilitates the retention and ready recall of conscious relations through universals and, thereby, enhances the distinctions among realities that the given subject can understand. We have already noted that learned participation in a linguistically structured "network" (Searle) or "lifeworld" (Habermas) is what creates the kind of implicit understanding that so vastly extends the possibilities for our explicit focus of attention.

[6]Searle has commented that "there is probably no more abused a term in the history of philosophy than 'representation'" (1983: 11). In some epistemological discussions, the term is used to identify the view that states of the mind are "self-enclosed, in the sense that they can be accurately identified and described in abstraction from the 'outside' world," even while they also somehow "represent things in the outside world" (Taylor 1995: 9), and this view has been heavily criticized. I do not mean to imply this view. I use the term "representation" to mean solely the discrimination of some actual or possible reality. What is thereby presented again may not be an outside world from which the subject is separated but, rather, some actual or possible reality as the object of the subject's nonconscious relation to it, recognizing that some of the realities to which a subject might relate are other subjects of understanding. On that account, the subject is constituted by internal relations to other realities, and understanding involves consciousness of a world from which it could not be separated.

I have proposed that the concrete subject of understanding, strictly speaking, is not an individual but one of its activities or occasions, which is influenced by the past and becomes an influence on the future. Given that account, we can now say that discrimination through universals means a consciousness not only of the past but also of the future. In itself, a universal is indeterminate, a mere characteristic that diverse realities may or must exemplify, and there are no indeterminate realities in the past. To the contrary, the past is fully determinate or includes only the exemplifications of characteristics, having already actualized previously possible realities. The realm of indeterminate realities is the future, in which possible realities wait to be actualized, and it is for this reason that we do not have perceptions of the future. Thus, to see a particular yellow rose with understanding is to discriminate an actual or determinate reality and, simultaneously, to discriminate the universals "yellow" and "rose" as characteristics that may be exemplified in the future—and thereby to see the particular rose in question as an exemplification of those characteristics. Searle has asserted that "the philosophy of language is a branch of the philosophy of mind" (1983: vii), and, on my account, this is exactly right.[7] Without the conscious relation to the future and thereby to universals, we could not participate in the symbolizing of language.[8]

[7]Although I have been instructed by Searle's philosophy of mind, I do not mean to imply my agreement with it in all respects. In contrast to the metaphysical account I will present in chapter 3, his theory of mind is, on my reading, physicalist; it seeks to fit "a world of consciousness, . . . into a world consisting entirely of physical particles in a field of force" (Searle 1995: xi).

[8]Some may object that this conclusion can be avoided because there are counterfactual possibilities, that is, alternatives to what in fact has occurred. In this sense, the possibility that Robert Dole might have been elected president of the United States in 1996 is counterfactual. Strictly speaking, then, possible realities include those that might have instantiated universals. Since these are not future possibilities, it seems that there are indeterminate objects in the past, so that a consciousness of universals does not require a consciousness of the future. But being aware of a counterfactual possibility is, so far as I can see, a consciousness of the past as if it were still future. Being aware of the possibility that Robert Dole, rather than William Clinton, might have been elected president of the United States is conceiving of November 1996 as still future. What are now counterfactual possibilities were at one time future possibilities, and only a subject conscious of the difference between past and future could be conscious of what might have been.

The Understanding of Reality as Such

We have explicated understanding as the discrimination of realities through universals, but discrimination has not yet been discussed. Can its character, as this is exemplified in our experience, be more fully articulated? Whitehead says that consciousness differs from nonconscious relations because the content of the former is an "affirmation-negation contrast" (1978: 243), and this reformulates the idea of discrimination. Unlike a mere relation to x, consciousness of x involves the contrast between x and the negation of x, and it is this contrast that discriminates or marks off the reality. A particular rose is consciously apprehended because it is discriminated from what is not that particular rose. If we say that the term of a mere relation to x is x, then this reality is discriminated in a conscious relation to x as *not (not x)*—for instance, *not (not a yellow rose)*. So formulated, the discrimination includes an affirmation of a yellow rose and the contrast with its negation. What is affirmed depends on what is negated, and discrimination, we can say, is an affirmation mediated by its negation.[9]

The purposes of this chapter will now be served by directing our attention to this affirmation-negation contrast. If a representation of x involves or is mediated by a contrast with what is not x, there could be no discriminated reality unless what is negated has some positive content. To contrast something with sheer nothing is, in truth, not to discriminate; that is, sheer nothing adds nothing to a relation or provides no contrast. To this, some may say that sheer nothing does provide a contrast to "sheer something," that is, discriminates "completely indeterminate something," the common character of all actual and possible realities. But this character is not discriminated by contrast with sheer nothing, since the former is completely general, and discrimination of it requires a contrast with every determination of it, that is, with everything that differentiates some actual or possible realities from others. Moreover, discrimination from every such deter-

---

[9]As may be apparent from the context, the term "affirmation" as used in this account of discrimination has a different meaning than the term as used to designate a subject's assent to some understanding. On the former usage, "affirmation" designates the positive content discriminated; on the latter usage, some understanding is taken as true. Aside from reference to Whitehead's account of consciousness, I use "affirmation" to mean assent.

mination is sufficient to discriminate "sheer something," precisely because sheer nothing has no positive content and, therefore, is not something with which anything needs to be contrasted.[10] This is, I believe, one way to reach the conclusion that completely negative statements about realities, such as "nothing exists" or "there might have been nothing," do not designate the content of a possible understanding and, therefore, are not sensible statements at all.

In noting this conclusion, I have in mind especially Kant's conviction that the things humans understand positively are "phenomena" in distinction from "noumena," or "things-as-they-appear" in distinction from "things-in-themselves" (1965). On Kant's account, if I read it correctly, these positive objects of human understanding are constituted by the synthesis of sensations or sense-data in accord with a priori categories, such that knowledge of reality in itself is impossible. This commits Kant to the notion that a completely negative object of understanding provides a contrast to positive objects of understanding as such, since, without that contrast, he could not discriminate appearances from things-in-themselves. Moreover, the same contrast must discriminate noumena. The understanding of noumena as *not (not noumena)* can only mean "not any positive object of understanding."

But we may now ask: What is the difference between a completely negative object of understanding and a putative object that is in truth no object at all? If we are told that the question itself is senseless because there are no such putative objects, we need only mention putative objects that are designated by self-contradictory descriptions, for instance, "a colorless yellow rose." Such descriptions do not designate any possible object of thought. To the best of my reasoning, there can be no distinction that is more than merely verbal between putative objects whose descriptions are self-contradictory and objects that are completely negative—because, in both cases, the supposed objects are completely negative. Thus, a completely negative object cannot be dis-

---

[10]It might be said that "sheer nothing" contrasts with "all positive things in their entirety." Hence, if an omniscient individual is possible, its understanding requires sheer nothing. But consciousness of all (positive) realities in their entirety requires only that each be discriminated from the others, not that all together be discriminated from sheer nothing—and, indeed, the latter would add nothing to the former. Given that sheer nothing adds nothing to a contrast, it cannot be discriminated.

criminated or provides no contrast. "Objects of understanding as such" can only mean "sheer something," which is discriminated by contrast with every determination of it that differentiates some actual or possible realities from others, and the contrast with which understanding discriminates can only be a contrast between positive objects.

What, then, is the positive content of *not x* in an understanding of *x*? So far as I can see, this content must be "all realities other than *x*." In discriminating some actual or possible reality, understanding contrasts it with every reality that might be understood other than the object in question. This follows because marking it off from merely some other realities would not discriminate it. "Not a red rose," for instance, fails to be a contrast that discriminates a yellow rose, because a yellow rose is only one of many things that is not a red rose. "Not a reality south of the equator" does not discriminate something north of the equator, since anything in the larger cosmos is also not something south of the equator. A contrast with some but not all other realities would not discriminate a given reality but, rather, a class of realities to which the given reality belongs. Hence, *not (not x)* can be reformulated as *not any reality other than x*. It is important to recognize that "all realities other than *x*" must include all future possibilities as well as all past actualities, because an understanding includes the discrimination of universals. The discrimination of "yellow," for instance, involves the contrast "not any universal other than 'yellow.'"[11] Moreover, this

---

[11]If what is understood is, say, a particular yellow rose, the discrimination of it is the contrast *not any reality other than* that *as an instance of "yellow" and "rose"* and, therefore, includes *not any universal other than "yellow"* and *not any universal other than "rose."* I recognize that my account raises the question of what it might mean to speak of consciousness without understanding, since discrimination of all other realities means discrimination of future or possible realities, and consciousness of the future is consciousness of universals. It is not my concern here to make sense of consciousness without understanding; if it makes no sense, I believe that the distinction between human and subhuman consciousness can be drawn in terms of the extent to which consciousness can be retained and, at higher levels, the extent of a capacity for language. For whatever it is worth, however, my hunch is that consciousness without understanding is possible and can be conceived as a subjective relation whose object is something actual mediated by the negation of everything else in the past. Since nothing in the future is actual, this negation is sufficient to discriminate something actual, and this was my point in suggesting earlier that consciousness without understanding, if it exists, discriminates merely a particular.

contrast with all other realities is quite independent of whether the understanding is or is not a misunderstanding. Even an incorrect understanding discriminates its content.

If this reasoning is sound, a subject that has any understanding at all simultaneously understands all actual and possible realities; discrimination of anything requires somehow an understanding of everything else.[12] Perhaps this conclusion will seem implausible because it appears to mean that understanding requires omniscience. But the argument does not imply that the contrast with everything else requires a *complete* understanding of each and every other reality. To the contrary, the discrimination of x may occur if only one understands at least most other realities simply as realities other

---

[12]One might resist this conclusion by objecting that I have merely posited discrimination by way of negation as the character of consciousness and that consciousness might be adequately conceived in some other way. As I mentioned, my account begins with a phenomenological appeal. Attending to any given understanding of something, we can recognize, I think, that our consciousness involves discrimination of it as nothing other than what it is. For instance, understanding a particular yellow rose in one's path is consciousness of it as here-now, that is, involves its setting in time and space and, therefore, its difference from all other things—and this is so even when we do not focus on that all-inclusive setting. Tillich expresses this point by saying that human subjects have not only an environment but also a world (see 1951: 170).

To be sure, this phenomenological description may be unconvincing, at least as a description of understanding as such—perhaps because of other theoretical commitments with which one works. Even then, however, I find the following consideration pertinent: Take as the hypothesis to be tested that discrimination by way of negation is not the character of understanding as such. It is transparent nonetheless that at least some humans have the possibility of this kind of understanding, because they are able to think about all things or reality as such. Moreover, that capacity seems so dramatically different than anything else that might be called understanding as to constitute a dramatically different kind of subject—rather analogous to the difference between having and not having a capacity to participate in language. Hence, the hypothesis seems to contradict our intuitions about the similarity of all human subjects. Although I have no doubt that the development of explicit thought about all things involves learning, the more apparent account of this learning is that it brings to explicit consciousness something of which the individual was always implicitly aware.

Still, I grant that, in the end, other theories of understanding cannot be refuted in the absence of a more or less complete discussion with them. For a contribution to that discussion, see the Appendix to Part One, which includes at least a summary argument that a subject could not take any understanding to be true without a consciousness of the universal character of true understandings.

than x. The point might be clarified by analogy. Suppose that one is conscious of Socrates as a given human individual. This discrimination does not demand that one understand all other human individuals completely. What one requires is an understanding of "human individual as such" in distinction from nonhuman individuals, and the individuality of Socrates is then marked off as just this instance of "human individual as such" in distinction from any other instance. Similarly, one can discriminate any actual or possible reality from all other realities if only one has an understanding of "reality as such" or, to repeat the earlier phrase, "sheer something."

The term "reality as such" designates the character common to all possible realities or, alternatively, all possible realities themselves in the respect that they are actual or possible exemplifications of this common character. In a similar way, "human individual as such" designates the common character of all possible humans or, alternatively, all possible humans themselves in the respect that they are actual or possible exemplifications of this common character. In what follows, however, I will sometimes use the phrase "the character of reality as such," notwithstanding its redundancy, in order to help keep clear that the discussion concerns all possible realities only in the respect that they are actual or possible exemplifications of what is common to them. A discrimination of any actual or possible reality, then, does not require a complete understanding of each and every other reality but, rather, a consciousness of reality as such. Given this apprehension, understanding of x, so far from implying omniscience, may mean only that all (or most) realities other than x are discriminated as other possible exemplifications of the character common to all possible realities.[13]

---

[13]If this common character is always included in the content of understanding, then it, too, must be discriminated by negating its negation. That implication may raise the following objection: By hypothesis, the negation of the character common to all possible realities must have some positive content; at the same time, this is impossible because the common character of all possible realities is the object discriminated. Hence, an understanding of "reality as such" and, on the account I have given, any understanding at all are impossible. But this attempted *reductio ad absurdum* confuses the character of reality as such with all actual and possible realities in all of their detail. A subject may discriminate "reality as such" because what is negated is every particular or specific determination of it. It

The conclusion we have reached is not that every activity is explicitly conscious of reality as such. Our attention is typically focused on representations of particular things and specific possibilities. But understandings at the center of attention do not exhaust the understandings contained in the nature of a particular subject. To the contrary, the former depend on others that are implicit or not readily apparent. This distinction was introduced earlier by pointing to our reliance on a "network" or "lifeworld" of understandings that were previously learned and some of which, implicitly remembered, make possible the greater significance of our present explicit attention. Given the distinction, we can now add, nothing said in drawing it implies that everything implicitly understood must have been previously learned. If representation occurs by way of negation, then all human subjectivity, whatever the past of the individual in question, includes at least an implicit awareness of reality as such, because this background is a necessary condition for any other understanding.

Still, some may reject this conclusion as counterintuitive, because it implies that small children (and, perhaps, some nonhuman animals) understand the common character of all possible realities as soon as they come to any understanding at all. That implication, we may be told, attributes a kind of high-grade awareness to the first emergence of understanding and contradicts its obvious simplicity. I expect that those for whom the conclusion seems odd confuse an awareness of reality as such with the extent to which a subject understands particular things and specific possibilities. It is the latter that varies immensely in human subjects. The difference between emergent and more mature understanding consists in the diversity included or the more or less determinate realities that are simultaneously understood, and it is the

---

follows, I think, that there cannot be an understanding of "reality as such" independently of understanding some determination of it (for instance, a yellow rose or a human individual), with which it is contrasted. In this broad sense, human understanding is inescapably empirical. However free it may be to range among possibilities, it requires a contrast with something actual before the light of consciousness can be thrown on the realm of "things that never were." The contrast with any such particular determination, however, implies that there are other determinations, so that reality as such may be discriminated from this particular determination and all possible others as their common character.

relative absence of diversity that constitutes the simplistic character of consciousness in small children.

It remains, then, that any relation in which some more or less determinate reality is understood discriminates that object from the rest of the cosmos, contrasts just this part with every other actual and possible reality. Subjects of understanding are aware of reality as such; they are related, at least implicitly, to a representation of the all-inclusive context in which they are set. In this respect, there is an insight expressed in the conviction that has been widespread among modern theologians and to which I made reference at the outset of this chapter, namely, that our distinctively human subjectivity involves consciousness of something unconditioned. Whatever success these theologians may or may not enjoy in defining this something as a divine reality, we can say nonetheless that the character of reality as such is unconditioned, because there can be no conditions under which it may not be exemplified. Whitehead writes that "the primitive stage of discrimination . . . is the vague grasp of reality, dissecting it into a three-fold scheme, namely, The Whole, That Other, and This-My-Self" (1938: 150). Whatever else Whitehead means by "The Whole," our discrimination of it includes a representation of reality as such, in terms of which any given reality understood is contrasted with all possible others.

Self-understanding

The discussion to this point has characterized our understanding as the fragmentary discrimination of actual and possible realities through universals. Because understanding is fragmentary, it includes explicit and implicit aspects. Because discrimination is by way of negation, every human subject includes an understanding of reality as such. The citation from Whitehead with which the previous section closed adds another note, namely, that understanding always involves a discrimination of *self* from others as parts of the whole. On Whitehead's statement, an understanding of any reality (*x*), where this reality is other than the self, can be articulated: relation to *not the self or anything else other than x*. To understand something other than the self is always to discriminate it *as* other than the self and, therefore, also to discriminate the self. This reminds us that we pursued a summary discussion of understanding in order to prepare the way for an analysis of self-understanding, and I will now seek to show why life with understanding requires an understanding of self. Having done so, I will be in a position to argue that a self-understanding always includes the relation of the self to a comprehensive purpose.

Because understanding discriminates through universals, we have defined the subject of understanding as an activity that is conscious not only of the past by which it is affected but also of the future it will affect. Given this conception of the subject, the argument for its self-understanding may be summarily stated: Consciousness of the future requires its discrimination from the past and, therefore, a discrimination of the present, and this discrimination of the present is a discrimination of the self. The latter half of this statement may seem controversial. Perhaps the difference between future and past is understood if the self discriminates merely what it has in common with other realities that are its contemporaries, so that the self does not necessarily discriminate itself. But this alternative should be rejected, I will now argue, because a subject of understanding must be self-determining, so that the past it discriminates must be *its* past.

Self-determination is analytic of life with understanding because understanding is a relation in which something is represented. In the respect that an activity is other-determined, it is an effect of some efficient cause, and we can say that the cause "is presented" or gives to the subject some particular determination. But understanding "represents" efficient causes of which the subject is an effect, and an efficient cause cannot cause a representation of itself. A relation by which the activity is other-determined is merely "relation to x," such that the effect repeats or reenacts the cause. In contrast, understanding is "relation to *not (not x)*" or is mediated by negation. Hence, "understanding of x" can never be solely the product of other-determination, all instances of which are values of the variable "relation to x." To the contrary, then, understanding relates the subject to something other than itself in a manner that transcends the relation of other-determination, so that the subject is in some measure self-determined or constituted by its own decision. Moreover, we can say that the subject *is* its decision. As an addition to the many respects in which the subject is affected by others, this decision completes what other-determination began and, thereby, completes the activity as the one particular thing it is or becomes.

Self-determination means that a discrimination of the present must be a discrimination of self. This follows because the past as discriminated from the future consists in its particular effects on the present, and any such particular effects of which the subject might be aware begin what the subject itself must complete by its own decision. In other words, the past to which a subject relates must be *its* past. I do not mean to deny that we can think and speak of the past in the respect or respects that it has effects common to ourselves and some or all of our contemporaries. But any understanding of the past as having common effects on the self and contemporaries is a derivation from a consciousness of the past as presented to the self. Only if the subject had no part in its own determination could the present of which it is aware be merely common to itself and its contemporaries—and the absurdity of this condition is confirmed by noting that the present so understood would be indeterminate and indistinguishable from the future. Consciousness of the present is consciousness of the difference between my past and the future my decision will condition or affect. The subject's understanding of the present must be a self-understanding.

To be sure, we sometimes use the term "self-understanding" to mean the consciousness we have of ourselves as individuals. On the account given earlier, a human individual is a succession of distinctively human activities or concrete occasions of subjectivity, all of which exemplify some common character or set of characteristics that distinguishes this career—and, further, our individuality may include characteristics that have arisen in the course of that career and endure for some greater or lesser period of time. When we speak of understanding ourselves, we often have in mind an understanding of these distinguishing characteristics. Nothing I have said intends to discredit this meaning of "self-understanding." Nonetheless, use of this term to mean a subject's discrimination between past and future designates as the self understood the very activity in the present that is also the concrete subject of understanding. Indeed, this is the primary use of "self-understanding," and the other use is derivative from it. Because the concrete subject exemplifies and, thereby, includes the enduring characteristics of the individual to which it belongs, it includes or can include an understanding of them in its understanding of itself.

The notion of a human activity that is both the subject and object of understanding may seem paradoxical. We have said that understandings are relations to actual and possible realities, and this means that a self-understanding must be a relation that an act of subjectivity has to itself. But a relation to self seems to mean, absurdly, that the subject is two subjects: On the one hand, the subject is the object, or the thing understood; on the other hand, the subject is constituted by the understanding of this object and, therefore, is a different subject. Because the understanding of self belongs to or is included in the self, there now seems to be an enhanced object to be understood, and an understanding of that greater self only repeats the problem. The notion of self-understanding seems to imply an infinite regress of understandings.[14]

This apparent contradiction can be unmasked as merely apparent if, but only if, to be or become a self is an act of expression, as I will now seek to explain. "Self-expression" is a term that designates, on

---

[14]Hence, it may seem that our own acts of subjectivity can be the object of understanding only if they are already past or, perhaps, possible future activities. Self-understanding, in other words, seems to be a kind of memory or anticipation, and the remembering or anticipating activity does not remember or anticipate itself. In throwing the light of consciousness on the self, one never illumines the source of the light. But if the present is not an object of understanding, it follows that consciousness of past and/or future activities could never be an understanding that the present belongs to the career of activities in question; that is, the self could never understand the career to be its own individuality, and the understanding would not be a self-understanding. To understand the past and/or future as an individual to which the understanding subject belongs is to identify it by more or less enduring characteristics of which the present is also an exemplification, and to be conscious of the present as an exemplification of these characteristics is to have the present self as an object. More generally, a present subject that cannot make itself an object could never understand self-referential propositions, since an understanding of them includes the present subject in what is understood. "I am the individual identified by characteristics a, b, etc." is a self-referential proposition. But so too is any proposition about human subjects as such, for instance, "all human subjects are constituted by understanding." Unless the subject who understands this proposition is itself included in the object of understanding, it is not a proposition about all human subjects that is understood. If this is so, then the assertion that a present subject cannot be its own object is itself one that could never be understood.

the one hand, something that is expressed and, on the other, the expressing of that thing—and yet the two are one in the sense that expressing adds nothing to what is expressed. Offering the self to the world beyond adds nothing to what is offered. Self-understanding, I propose, is the distinctively human form of self-expression. The understanding and the self understood are one and the same because self-understanding is nothing other than our way of being or becoming an offering to the world beyond, of becoming or making a difference to others.

An activity, Whitehead writes, "arises as an effect facing its past and ends as a cause facing its future" (1961: 194)—or, again, "the self-enjoyment of an occasion of experience is initiated by the enjoyment of the past as alive in itself and is terminated by an enjoyment of itself as alive in the future" (1961: 193). To be or become a self is to be or become a cause of the future, and to understand oneself is to understand the difference to the future one is or becomes. Hence, our self-consciousness is not retrospective; its object is not something that precedes the understanding in the way that, for instance, memory is retrospective. Self-understanding is prospective; its object is the self as expressed or making a difference. To be sure, the object of self-understanding begins in relation to the past; it "arises as an effect facing its past." But what is understood is the completion of this beginning or the completion of the present, and this completion is nothing other than its relation to the future. We can also say, then, that the self *is* its purpose, and to understand oneself is to be a purpose consciously. The subject's completion is its relation to some future state of affairs as an end or telos, in pursuit of which the self is or becomes a cause, and to understand this completion of the present is to have this telos with understanding.[15]

It might still be thought that an understanding of one's relation to the future adds something to the self or to the object that is under-

---

[15]To the best of my reasoning, the specter of an infinite regress of understandings arises because consciousness of self is considered independently of this relation. In its absence, relation to self could only be another relation to the past that must be included in the self's completion and, therefore, cannot be an understanding of that completion. But a conscious relation to the future may be an understanding of the self because the complete self *is* the difference it makes to states of affairs for which it will be a part of the past.

stood and, therefore, does not escape the apparent regress of understandings. But this thought forgets that a subject with understanding is self-determining. Not just any conscious relation to the future is an understanding of self. Indeed, most discrimination of the future is not self-awareness but, rather, merely understanding of some or other possible state of affairs that will or may be actualized. "It will rain tomorrow," for instance, or "the Democrats may control the next Congress." To differentiate a self-understanding, we must underscore that being or becoming an expression or cause of the future is a free act. What is partially determined by the past is completed by a decision, and this decision *is* the activity. Hence, there is a certain understanding of the future that is also an understanding of self, namely, the future as the object of a chosen purpose. In contrast to mere discrimination of some future state of affairs, this relation is not simply conscious but, rather, is one of *conscious choice*. Self-understanding is conscious self-determination, in which the self is discriminated as the pursuit of just this future possibility rather than some relevant alternative. For instance, one consciously chooses to prepare for rain or to help realize Democratic rather than Republican control of Congress. If we call this future possibility the telos of self-determination (t), then understanding of self discriminates one's own completion as the choice of t.

In sum, a self-understanding is the choice with understanding among specific alternatives for purpose. The self is understood as the pursuit of t that might have been pursuit of t_1 or t_2. When, in his well-known poem, Robert Frost faced two roads that "diverged in a yellow wood" and chose the one "less traveled by," his activity was not merely starting down a particular road; to the contrary, his act was the conscious choice of that road rather than the well-worn path—and the fact that it was this choice between them with understanding is what the poem seeks to display. As with all other understandings of particulars, then, self-understanding discriminates through universals. A future state of affairs is in some measure indeterminate, and this means that "pursuit of t rather than t_1 or t_2" is also a universal, in the sense that more than one activity could be characterized by that pursuit. A particular human activity understands itself as this particular instance of that universal, where the particularity is given by the activity's relations to the past, through which there is just this present reality to be completed. In other words, particularity is given in the consciousness of choosing.

Throughout the Western philosophical tradition, the human capacity for self-understanding, sometimes designated by other terms, has been called a distinctive kind of freedom. Aristotle, Aquinas, and Kant, whatever their differences, all agree that the rational character of the human soul or the person is a practical capacity to choose what one is or becomes. If it is clear that understanding implies self-determination, it is the more transparent that freedom is analytic of *self*-understanding. Whatever other reality may determine or have an effect on the self, the understanding of oneself is the understanding of that effect. Another cannot cause an understanding of its effect because it would then have an effect greater than its effect. Nor will it help to say that the multiplicity of others together cause a self-understanding. The multiplicity cannot effect an understanding of the multiplicity or, what comes to the same thing, cannot effect their unity in a human activity, and this is just to repeat that the choice of a purpose with understanding completes the self.

Because it completes the self, moreover, this understanding is the inclusive understanding of any given human activity; that is, any other understandings the subject may have must somehow be a part of its decision with understanding among alternatives for purpose. Since understandings are relations to actual and possible realities, the decision with understanding that unifies all relations constituting the self must include all other understandings constituting the activity in question. One implication of this account is that classical distinctions between the intellect and the will as aspects or elements of the human subject disappear when we identify an act of subjectivity inclusively. A self-understanding is, as it were, an act in which intellect and will are identical, because this understanding is an "intellectual decision" for the future.

Notwithstanding what has been said, however, the conclusion that human activity always chooses its purpose with understanding may appear to be empirically false. Frequently, it may seem, we are not conscious of choosing among possible purposes and, therefore, can hardly be said to choose a self-understanding. But this consideration loses whatever force it may seem to have if we return again to the distinction between explicit and implicit understanding. Relations of understanding at the center of attention depend on others that are not readily apparent. Given the presence of implicit understandings in a human activity, its self-understanding may not be something on which it is explicitly focused but, rather, may be included in the background of consciousness.

This background, we have seen, is not by nature limited to understandings previously learned because the necessary condition of any understanding at all is a consciousness of the character common to all possible realities. Given that any understanding of other realities also implies a discrimination of "This-My-Self" (Whitehead), we can add that self-understanding is not a later development in a human individual or a characteristic of merely some occasions of human existence. To the contrary, it, too, is a necessary condition of understanding as such and, therefore, is always included at least implicitly wherever distinctively human activity occurs. Since an understanding of self is the choice among alternatives for purpose, it follows that this choice itself at least may be implicit. If we are told that this account is implausible ontogenetically because it attributes the choice of a self-understanding to small children, then we must repeat that the simplicity of understanding on its earliest emergence consists in the extent to which it discriminates diversity. With respect to self-understanding, the relative absence of complexity means a relatively simple range of possible ends. Just as the infant's beginning discrimination of particular things or specific possibilities is especially limited, so too are the specific alternatives for purpose among which she or he consciously chooses. But it remains that a distinctively human subject is completed by a decision with understanding about the difference it makes to the future.

Comprehensive Self-understanding

We have pursued the analysis of self-understanding in order to determine through it whether human existence as such is constituted by knowledge of a comprehensive purpose. In order to answer this question, we must now explore the relation between self-understanding and our consciousness of the character common to all possible realities. That relation, I will argue, is nothing other than our distinctive relation to the comprehensive purpose.

In the last section, we concluded that life with understanding chooses consciously among specific alternatives for purpose. Because this is a choice with understanding, we may continue, each of the possible ends or telē must be discriminated and, moreover, discriminated from the others. To understand oneself as the choice of t that might have been t_1 or t_2 is to contrast the several future possibilities one might choose to pursue. Moreover, these alternatives must be understood as possible *ends*, that is, contrasted *with respect to choosing*. The consciousness of them cannot be merely an apprehension of their descriptive differences, as, for instance, one might understand descriptively the difference between Democratic and Republican control of the next Congress. Rather, the possibilities must be compared as alternatives for purpose, because a self-understanding is an understanding of one's decision among them. The self is the *choice* of t instead of t_1 or t_2, and there can be no understanding of the self unless the several possible ends are compared with respect to the choice. In a word, a self-understanding not only describes but also *evaluates* its specific alternatives, and this means that possible ends or telē are understood as possible exemplifications of worth.

It now follows that every human activity includes, at least implicitly, some understanding of "worth" as a universal or characteristic that states of affairs may exemplify, and the choice among specific alternatives for purpose is the affirmation that the end chosen is good. To decide with understanding *is* to affirm the chosen end as good because the comparison with respect to choosing can only be an evaluation. "Every art and every inquiry, and similarly every action and pursuit," Aristotle famously wrote, "is thought to aim at some good; and for this reason the good has rightly been declared to be that at which all things aim" (1094a1–3). The long tradition that has found its bearings in Aristotle is certainly right at least in this respect: human activity pursues what it takes to be good. Moreover, "worth" as a universal through which specific alternatives for purpose are discriminated from each other must be a characteristic through which they are *inclusively* compared. Whatever other universals may be involved in understanding their similarities and differences, the evaluative understanding must include or take into account those other characteristics, because the choice is among the alternatives themselves. A comparison with respect to choosing assumes whatever descriptive similarities and differences there may be.

To be sure, many moral theories deny the inclusive character of an evaluative comparison. This is especially the case with theories in the Kantian tradition, which hold that moral worth involves a comparison in terms of certain human rights that all agents are bound to honor and that set certain limiting conditions on the purposes we choose. For instance, it might be said that alternatives are properly evaluated with respect to whether pursuit of them treats all agents as ends in themselves, although comparison in this respect does not compare possible purposes in all respects. So far as I can see, however, any theory of this kind in fact implies the inclusive comparison it denies. To restrict a moral assessment of purposes to the respect in which they honor certain human rights is to imply that the differences among possible ends in other respects make no difference with respect to moral worth. But that implication *is* a moral evaluation of those differences. In other words, the distinction between aspects of our alternatives that are relevant to evaluation and those that are not is an *evaluative* distinction. Because one can choose only between or among the alternatives inclusively, the understanding that certain features of them are irrelevant with respect to choosing is part of an inclusive comparison.[16]

This is a point emphasized by Hume: "In moral deliberations we must be acquainted beforehand with all the objects, and all their relations to each other; and from a comparison of the whole, fix our choice or approbation. No new fact to be ascertained; no new relation to be discovered. All the circumstances of the case are supposed to be laid before us, ere we can fix any sentence." Hume concludes that this "great difference between a . . . [matter] of *fact* and one of *right*" means that "after every circumstance, every relation is known, the understanding has no further room to operate, nor any object on

---

[16]Elsewhere I have said that theories in the Kantian tradition commit "the partialist fallacy." Each asserts that the principle by which alternatives for choice should be morally assessed compares the alternatives with respect to some abstract aspect they severally include. The comparison is partialist precisely because it is limited to an abstract aspect, and it is fallacious because it implies, against itself, another standard on which the aspects not compared make no difference with respect to choosing (see Gamwell 1984).

which it could employ itself. The approbation . . . which then ensues, cannot be the work of judgment, but of the heart; and is not a speculative proposition or affirmation, but an active feeling or senti- ment" (1975: 290). For Hume, in other words, the evaluation is not itself an understanding of the alternatives but, rather, a move of sentiment or "the heart"—and this account expresses his insistence that evaluative statements are separated or cannot be derived from factual statements. In this, Hume is joined by all theories of human activity on which evaluations are subrational or "emotive," and state- ments of fact are "value-free." But agreement with Hume on the inclusive character of an evaluative comparison does not bind us to the conclusion he draws.

Indeed, we cannot accept Hume's conclusion because it denies the possibility of self-understanding. An understanding of future alterna- tives becomes an understanding of self only when the decision among them is understood, and this means that the evaluation is "an object on which" understanding must "employ itself." Perhaps some will say that the choice is arbitrary and, therefore, merely a move of sentiment or merely emotive. But if the choice is made arbitrarily, the self is not understood unless the choice is understood as arbitrary, and this means that the alternatives are so compared that differences among them make no difference with respect to choosing. In other words, the alternatives are understood as equally good.

Against Hume, then, what follows from the inclusive character of "worth" is that it cannot be understood as a more or less specific characteristic or universal. The comparative worth of possible ends must be understood as their possible exemplification of the character common to all possible realities. Take any set of alternatives for purpose you please, the specific similarities and differences among them of which one is conscious are always understood as specifica- tions of this common character, because every understanding discriminates its object in contrast to all other possible realities. Each reality is understood as just this and no other instance of reality as such. Thus, an inclusive comparison cannot abstract from the fact that each alternative specifies this character; that is, "worth" must be understood as the character of reality as such because this is the only "universal of universals" (Whitehead 1978: 21) or in- clusive universal. Life with understanding not only has, at least implicitly, an awareness of reality as such but also completes itself or evaluates specific possible ends in the terms given by this awareness.

If this analysis is sound, the common character of all possible realities is always understood as a variable that differing possible ends specify in greater or lesser measure. Differences among specific possible ends with respect to this variable are differences in worth or with respect to choosing, such that greater specification is insofar a reason for choosing. Let us suppose, to illustrate the point, that an individual chooses between possible acts of kindness and cruelty toward another. In making this choice consciously, the actor compares the alternative ends inclusively. Since the understanding of each discriminates it as a specification of reality as such, the character common to all real things is the only universal with respect to which the alternatives inclusively can be compared. Thus, an understanding on which the alternatives differ with respect to choosing, such that, for instance, giving aid is more worthy, can only mean that this alternative is greater with respect to the character of reality as such.[17]

According to Aquinas, "goodness and being are really the same, and differ only in idea" (*Summa Theologica*: 1. 5. 1). Similarly, I conclude that distinctively human existence always includes, at least implicitly, an understanding of the character common to all possible realities as a variable of greater or lesser worth. Reinhold Niebuhr captures the point exactly when he writes that our freedom "forces human beings to relate their actions in the last resort to the totality of things conceived as a realm of meaning" (1942: 44). Whitehead, on my reading, implies the same thing when he writes: "At the base of our existence is the sense of 'worth'" (1938: 149). Since, for Whitehead, the "primitive stage" of our discrimination is "the vague grasp of . . . a three-fold scheme, namely, The Whole, That Other, and This-My-self" (1938: 150), the "base of our existence" as distinctively human can only be an apprehension of "that other" and "this-myself" as

---

[17]Nothing in this formulation requires that alternatives for purpose must always differ with respect to choosing. It may well be that two or more alternatives for a given choice are equally greatest as specifications of reality as such, in which case they are equally good and the choice between or among them is a matter of preference.

parts of "the whole." If this awareness is a "sense of worth," its discrimination of the whole must be, whatever else it is, "totality . . . conceived as a realm of meaning."

As these citations imply, the worth affirmed in choosing with understanding is not simply the worth to be achieved by the realization of some future possibility but also the worth of the choice itself, that is, of the present activity. The act of subjectivity is itself a greater or lesser realization of the character common to all possible realities, and, since this activity is completed in the choice of a telos, it achieves the greatest measure of worth it can achieve in deciding for the most worthy future possibility. What is expressed in a self-expression is the self's present worth. The difference one delivers to the world beyond is one's own realization of the good, and the constitutive sense of worth is our understanding that we make of our present self the best it can be by pursuit of the best possible telos.

Since the decision one makes for the future implicates an understanding of worth as coextensive with reality as such, we can now say that every human activity includes an understanding of the comprehensive purpose. As a variable with respect to which all ends or telē are evaluated, the character common to all possible realities defines a comprehensive telos. This character is necessarily understood in this way because human activity always understands itself in relation to a specific end or telos whose worth consists in its specification of reality as such. But this is just to say that the character of reality as such defines a comprehensive purpose, that is, a purpose of which all other purposes ought to be specifications. It also follows that the comprehensive purpose can be nothing other than maximizing the realization of reality as such—and, by implication, in the long run. If, with Aquinas, "goodness and being are really the same, and differ only in idea," then our telos should always be solely the maximal realization of being—and, by implication, in the long run.

To be sure, we have not yet asked about the character of "being" in the substantive sense required to clarify how realizations or exemplifications of it can be greater or less and, therefore, its maximal realization can be pursued. That question will be addressed in chapter 3. That human activities necessarily choose their completion with an understanding of the comprehensive purpose is the important conclusion of the present analysis. I will express this conclusion by saying that a self-understanding always is or includes a "comprehensive self-understanding"; that is, I will use this term to designate an understanding of the self in relation to the comprehensive purpose. A comprehensive self-understanding, then, discriminates the self as exemplifying the character of all possible human activities, at least insofar as this character is defined in relation to that purpose. Aquinas formulates this definition in theistic terms: Every human action ought to pursue the perfection of all things, where perfection means "to become like unto God" (*Summa Contra Gentiles*: 3. 19), and Aquinas equates this telos with one's own happiness. John Dewey, to select a nontheistic example, defines human activity as such in relation to what he calls the democratic ideal: All human activity ought to pursue the "all-around growth" of all human individuals (1957: 186). In each distinctively human moment of our existence, each of us includes, at least implicitly, a similar understanding of humanity as such because we discriminate ourselves as an exemplification of it.

It may seem that a subject's comprehensive self-understanding should be distinguished from the particular self-understanding with which the subject completes itself, because the latter further relates the subject to a specific end that is among the alternatives the subject's particular past makes possible. There is an obvious difference between the comprehensive purpose and any more or less specific purpose. Still, the specific choice with which a subject completes itself implies a comprehensive self-understanding, because the latter is or includes the understanding of worth as such with which specific alternatives for purpose are evaluated or understood with respect to choosing. Moreover, this comprehensive self-understanding also implies the subject's evaluation of its specific alternatives, because the former occurs within the particular situation constituted by the subject's particular past. To affirm that understanding of worth as such *is* to choose among the specific alternatives for purpose. The telos in relation to which a human activity completes itself is, we can say, systematically ambiguous. Some more or less specific purpose is consciously chosen as a specification of the purpose by which all humans ought to be directed. Thus, the choice with which a human activity completes itself is nothing other than its comprehensive self-understanding, and this is what one chooses when one is human. To say that humans live by way of a self-understanding and to say that distinctively human existence is constituted by a comprehensive self-understanding are two ways of saying the same thing.[18]

Original Freedom

Because life with understanding is fragmentary, it is also fallible, in the sense that we can confuse some things with others or assent to understandings in which realities are represented through the wrong universals. It is now important to see that a self-understanding in which the comprehensive purpose is misrepresented can only be the *choice* to affirm this misrepresentation. If a comprehensive self-understanding is false, this cannot be due to ignorance, because a subject cannot fail to understand truly the character of worth.

Our apprehension of reality as such must always include a true understanding of it because the absence of this understanding would prevent any discrimination at all. Whether they are true or false, all understandings discriminate their object from all other possible realities, and this contrast could not occur without a true understanding of reality as such. The point can be confirmed by seeing that a false understanding of reality as such could misrepresent it only as some specification of itself, as a characteristic common to some but not all possible realities, and discrimination of this more specific universal requires a true understanding of reality as such. Let us suppose, for instance, that a subject evaluates possible purposes in a chauvinistic manner; that is, all specific ends are, on this self-understanding, com-

---

[18]Some may still see a difference between one's understanding of the comprehensive telos and one's evaluation of specific alternatives for purpose because the evaluation requires a specification of worth as such to those alternatives, and the understanding required for this specification may be inadequate. On this accounting, one might have a true understanding of the comprehensive purpose and still evaluate one's possible purposes wrongly. But however apt this description may be with respect to our explicit attempts to evaluate possible ends in terms of some conception of the comprehensive purpose, the discussion in the text is about implicit choices with understanding and, therefore, about alternatives for purpose *as understood*. Hence, the specific alternatives in question are possible states of affairs or ends as discriminated or in whatever respect they are understood to specify the character of worth as such. More adequate understanding of one's specific alternatives would mean, in other words, a different set of specific alternatives.

pared with respect to choosing in terms of the advantage to people of, say, the United States. This evaluation misrepresents the comprehensive purpose by understanding it through the specific character of United States citizens. But possible exemplifications of that specific character could not themselves be discriminated or understood absent their contrast with all other possible realities and, therefore, without a true understanding of reality or worth as such. Thus, the subject who affirms a misrepresentation of the comprehensive purpose also understands it truly and, therefore, chooses the false self-understanding.[19]

[19]We can also reach this conclusion by recognizing that exclusively false understandings of worth as such would make self-understanding impossible, because a subject could not understand its specific possible ends with respect to choosing. Since a choice among these ends is a choice among alternative understandings of worth as such, a self-understanding evaluates alternative representations of the comprehensive purpose. The assumption that they are all false prevents this latter comparison, since an evaluation of alternative grounds for evaluation can only be an assessment with respect to truth. It will not do to say that the evaluation occurs in terms of what the subject takes to be true, where what is so taken may be false, because the choice of this false alternative requires its comparison with the others. In the absence of a true understanding of worth as such, the comparison of false alternatives would require an arbitrary choice of one of them, and *this* choice could not be understood. Because the object of a self-understanding is the self's relation to worth as such, a false understanding of the comprehensive purpose cannot be understood by the self except as a false alternative.

Given that every human activity understands the character of worth truly, one might be inclined to think that choosing a misunderstanding of it must be impossible. On this supposition, our fallibility or capacity to affirm misrepresentations, in which realities are discriminated through the wrong universals, does not extend to our understanding of the comprehensive purpose, and we can evaluate specific alternatives for purpose only in relation to the comprehensive telos. But understandings we cannot deny must also be understandings whose truth cannot be questioned, since asking about an understanding implies a capacity to decide whether it is true and, therefore, to decide that it is false. Were the supposition correct, in other words, we could not ask about human existence in relation to reality as such, and the supposition itself would be senseless, since it purports to be a true answer to this very question. Nor does it help to suggest that we can ask about human existence as such explicitly but not implicitly. Asking the question explicitly would be senseless if the answer to which we thereby assent can have no effect on our implicit self-understandings. Notwithstanding our true understanding of the comprehensive purpose, our self-understandings must be fallible; we can choose to evaluate specific alternatives in relation to some universal other than reality as such. Moreover, this must be a possibility for every human activity, because any other universal in relation to which we compare our alternatives for purpose can be affirmed as the variable that defines their worth.

Even with the concession that this conclusion is inescapable, one might still be puzzled. Since a true understanding of the comprehensive purpose must be present, it is implied by any false alternative for self-understanding, and this means that the latter is understood to be self-convicting or necessarily false. If we call one's self-understanding one's belief about the comprehensive purpose, then the subject who chooses wrongly must simultaneously believe that the choice is wrong. Indeed, we can say that the subject knows the choice is wrong and, therefore, knows the right alternative because it must believe that every false alternative for self-understanding is self-convicting. But if this is so, then it seems mysterious why we would ever choose a false self-understanding.[20]

These reflections pose an especially vexing question about distinctively human existence, and the next chapter is an attempt to answer it. Still, we may note here that the possibility of choosing wrongly even while knowing that the choice is wrong is precisely what makes human existence moral in character. On my usage, existence is "moral," in distinction from "nonmoral," only when it chooses between the moral and the immoral, in the sense that we choose with understanding between the good or better and the bad or worse alternatives. Moreover, we must know that the former is the good or better alternative and the latter is the bad or worse one, whatever else we may also believe; that is, a subject is not immoral unless she or he

---

[20]I distinguish beliefs from understandings because the former involve affirmation of or assent to the latter and, therefore, one may have understandings that are not believed. A self-understanding, however, is always believed because necessarily it is chosen. Since a false self-understanding includes a true understanding of the comprehensive purpose, we may say that this belief includes the belief that the choice is wrong. The distinction between understandings and beliefs is discussed in the Appendix to Part One.

Some may object to saying that a human activity "knows" the comprehensive purpose and, therefore, knows that a false self-understanding is false. On this objection, knowledge requires an understanding that is or once was explicit. If we so restrict the term "knowledge," then we can say, as the text does, that a human necessarily believes a true understanding of the comprehensive purpose. But this means that we can speak of implicit beliefs that may never have been explicit, and, having done so, I see no reason to exclude the concept of knowledge that is similarly implicit. If knowledge, as some have said, is warranted true belief (see Plantinga 1993: v), then we can say that true belief about the comprehensive purpose is warranted because no human can fail to have this belief. Hence, we can say that all humans know at least implicitly the comprehensive purpose.

knows it. When the choice is at fault, the agent was responsible for it being so, and this implies that a moral choice was both possible and known to be the right one. "Ought implies can" means not only that the moral choice was an open alternative but also, as moral theorists since Aristotle have insisted, that a choice against it cannot be ignorant. One chooses with knowledge of the right. On the account given here, life with understanding is constitutively moral because humans can choose to believe what they must also believe to be a misrepresentation of the comprehensive purpose and, thereby, choose what they know to be a false evaluation of their specific alternatives for purpose.

In calling a self-understanding a moral choice, "moral" is used in an extended sense. Some may restrict this term to the choice between more or less specific alternatives for purpose, that is, those choices in which a comprehensive self-understanding is expressed. On that restriction, the choice of a comprehensive self-understanding may be recognized in other terms, perhaps by calling it an "ultimate concern" (cf. Tillich 1951: 11–15). In contrast, I will give to "moral" a systematically ambiguous meaning, on which the moral character of human existence consists in the choice of a belief about worth as such and its expression in the choice of some more or less specific purpose. This usage is recommended because the former choice is itself the choice of a purpose, namely, the comprehensive purpose in relation to which specific alternatives for purpose are evaluated.

I will call the possibility of choosing a self-understanding the *original freedom* of human existence. Since understandings may be also be called answers to questions, we can also say that all human subjects ask the comprehensive question, What makes human life as such worth living?—and choose an answer to it in choosing the specific future they seek to help realize. Every human activity *is*, as Tillich says, an answer to the question "we ourselves" are (1951: 62), and a self-understanding is a responsible decision about totality as a realm of meaning. Because every misuse of our original freedom is believed to be self-convicting, original freedom at fault is a self-contradictory act. Because we know we have made a wrong choice, in so choosing we tell a lie to ourselves.

This account of human freedom owes a considerable debt to Kant. In every exercise of practical reason, Kant argues, a human subject chooses a fundamental maxim that her or his choice of some more or less specific maxim expresses. Either that fundamental maxim is the moral law by which all rational freedom is bound, so that one acts from duty, or the subject decides for a fundamental maxim proposed by desire. If the latter, then practical reason contradicts itself, knowing its duty when it acts against it. With Kant, the argument here concludes that the moral law is known by every human activity, and each occasion of life with understanding chooses in accord with the fundamental character of moral worth or chooses to deny what it knows.

Nonetheless, this conclusion departs from Kant's further assertion that the moral law is independent of any purpose, consisting solely in the formal universality of reason. "The purposes which we may have in view in our actions, or their effects regarded as ends or springs of the will, cannot give to actions any unconditional or moral worth" (1949: 17). On my reading, this is also what Kant means in saying that "nothing can possibly be conceived in the world, or even out of it, which can be called good without qualification, except a *good will*" (1949: 11). If I understand him rightly, Kant defines the moral law independently of any purpose because he holds that humans cannot know "things-in-themselves," in distinction from "things-as-they-appear." Convinced that knowledge of reality as such is impossible, he concludes that moral worth can be defined by nothing other than the formal universality of practical reason. In my terms, he asserts that true comprehensive self-understandings are independent of a comprehensive purpose or telos.

But this separation contradicts the fact that a decision with understanding is the distinctively human form of self-expression and, therefore, is the pursuit of some chosen end. Independently of purpose, in other words, there is no self to be understood, and a comprehensive self-understanding that is independent of a comprehensive purpose is the understanding of nothing. Against Kant, the exercise of original freedom cannot be independent of desire—assuming that we mean by desire, as Kant does, the attachment to or appetition for some telos. Human existence is constituted by an abiding desire to pursue the comprehensive telos, and our fundamental choice is whether to embrace this purpose without evasion or to corrupt it by embracing also something else.

In contrast to Kant, we can speak, with Iris Murdoch, of "metaphysics as a guide to morals" (Murdoch 1992). For Murdoch, "metaphysics" means the attempt "to promote understanding of very general features of our lives" (1992: 212), and these "very general features" define human existence as such in relation to the character of reality as such. "Good metaphysical arguments," she writes, "make models of the *deep* aspects of human life" (1992: 395, 55) and, for this reason, have a certain "circular" character; metaphysical thought "is determined to *argue* for something it already knows" (1992: 435). In my terms, metaphysics is a guide to morals because it asks critically about true self-understandings as such or about the comprehensive purpose that every human activity knows and relation to which defines the moral exercise of original freedom.

Because arguments for it are circular in the manner Murdoch describes, the constitutive moral character of human existence is also the object of transcendental philosophy, by which I mean the process or product of critical reflection that seeks to establish the truth of understandings by showing that any understanding at all presupposes them. Although she does not use the term "transcendental," Murdoch herself makes the point in saying that metaphysical argument attends to what is "essential" and, therefore, "must be built into the explanation at the start" (1992: 55). Because every human activity may choose a true understanding of itself, the true understanding of human activity as such is presupposed by any understanding that is so much as possible, and any understanding that does not consistently presuppose it cannot be true.

In modern philosophy, discussion of the transcendental project has been profoundly influenced by Kant's formulation of it. In his own way, moreover, he also spoke of "the metaphysics of morals." But the similarity is deceptive. For Kant, the transcendental or metaphysical features of our lives consist in the a priori character of reason independently of the common character of things-in-themselves. For Murdoch, as I mentioned, the "very general features" or "*deep* aspects of our lives" include the features of all possible realities, and the metaphysical attempt to clarify the moral life includes the kind of metaphysics whose possibility Kant denies. Her account, in other words, allows a transcendental project in which the true understanding of human activity as such includes an understanding of reality as such.

In the end, I do not believe that Murdoch's own metaphysical formulations best serve her intent to make metaphysics a guide to morals. If I understand her rightly, she takes her own bearings from her reading of Plato and identifies worth or *the* "Good" with an Idea or Form that is "above being" (1992: 342) or in all respects unique. Our experience of the Platonic sun, in the light of which "the whole world is revealed" (1992: 39), "leads us to place our idea of it outside the world of existent being as something of a different unique and special sort" (1992: 508). For this reason, Murdoch appreciates the theistic formulations of Tillich, who speaks of "the God above the God of theism" (see Murdoch 1992: 391–92 and Tillich 1952: 186). In her own way, then, she joins those modern theologians for whom the divine reality cannot be an object of thought or is nonobjective, so that all speaking of God must be symbolic or metaphorical. To the best of my reasoning, that conclusion contradicts the transcendental character of worth or the good, because self-understanding cannot include or presuppose something with which it has nothing in common. But I will not here pursue this discussion with Murdoch (see Gamwell 1996), since this first part of the present work seeks to present its own metaphysical or transcendental account. That account shares with her the conviction that our distinctive consciousness of self includes knowledge of reality as such, even if, against her, I conclude that the transcendental character of the good cannot be a form "above being" but only the common character of all possible realities itself.

For the sake of clarity, I repeat that our exercise of original freedom and thus our knowledge of the comprehensive purpose do not require an explicit taking of the choice. The focus of consciousness is one thing, and the understandings contained in the subject but not readily apparent are something else. This distinction between explicit and implicit understanding is involved in the "circular" character, as Murdoch calls it, of metaphysical or transcendental thought. It would be unnecessary for metaphysics to argue for something that "must be built into the explanation at the start" if we explicitly apprehended what is essential prior to pursuit of the metaphysical task. To the contrary, then, this task is to achieve explicit and convincing formulation of knowledge that is always at least implicit.

If I see the matter rightly, moreover, a subject's self-understanding cannot be the explicit focus of its attention. The exercise of original freedom must be implicit. This is because that decision constitutes the subject or completes what begins as an effect facing the past. To make the choice with explicit understanding would require explicit awareness of all our understandings, since they are included in the completion. But the fragmentariness of human understanding means that our focus of consciousness is a fragment of this fragment or always depends on understandings that are implicit. Hence, the choice with understanding of our comprehensive telos must always be among the latter. This can be confirmed by recognizing that explicit attention to the character of worth as such is a specific activity that depends on a specific purpose, while the exercise of original freedom is a decision about the comprehensive purpose expressed in that specific purpose. A person who chooses to engage in, say, metaphysical reflection rather than some other specific pursuit may or may not thereby express the understanding of worth as such that occupies her or his explicit attention.

This difference can be formulated in the existentialist distinction between an "existential" self-understanding and an "existentialist" understanding of it. In an existentialist understanding, the character of existential self-understandings as such is given explicit formulation—for instance, to recall earlier illustrations, "all human activity ought to pursue happiness" or "all human activity ought to pursue the democratic ideal." An existential self-understanding, then, is the implicit decision of a given human activity constituting it as just this particular pursuit of a comprehensive telos. An existential decision is the free and responsible creation of oneself as nothing other than the comprehensive self-understanding chosen. To be sure, one can speak of an existentialist self-understanding, since any explicit representation of the character common to all existential self-understandings includes the self within its designation. In other words, one can speak of an explicit self-understanding, meaning thereby an understanding of some possibility for which original freedom might decide. In order to recognize this distinction, we might call the self-understanding that completes a human activity its constitutive self-understanding. Henceforth, however, I will reserve the term "self-understanding" or "comprehensive self-understanding" for this constitutive exercise of original freedom and speak of explicit representations of what it might be as explicit understandings of the self or of human activity as such.[21]

That our existential decisions are always implicit does not contradict our apparent capacity to focus consciousness on specific aspects of our alternatives and, insofar, to choose among them explicitly. For instance, one may choose with explicit awareness to engage in metaphysical reflection. The point is that explicit awareness of ourselves never includes the decision about the comprehensive purpose that our activity expresses—and, because this decision is implicated in the evaluation of specific alternatives, never includes full awareness of our specific choices. This is why our own motivations for the actions we explicitly choose are never fully transparent to us and is the deepest reason why moral theories have typically distinguished, in Aristotle's terms, between acting justly and being a just person or, in Kant's terms, between action in accord with the moral law and action that is morally worthy. The fragmentariness of life with understanding prevents us from knowing fully and explicitly who or what we choose to be.

To first appearances, this fact may seem to remove any explicit responsibility for the moral character of our lives. Since the exercise of original freedom is always implicit, our moral responsibility is forever hidden from our focused efforts. But that conclusion is mis-

---

[21]On the account given here, moreover, existentialist conceptions are properly pragmatic ones, precisely because the existential or constitutive decision is about one's relation to the comprehensive purpose. In this context, I mean by "pragmatism" the view that understanding as such is properly defined in terms of the purposive character of human activity. On one formulation, the pragmatic theory of meaning may be stated as follows: Any putative understanding, assent to which does not make a difference to choosing with understanding among alternatives for purpose is in truth empty, it is no understanding at all. This is the case with an understanding whose putative content is completely negative, for instance, "there might have been nothing" or "there might come to be nothing." Assent to such an understanding does not make a difference to the choice of a purpose because the putative content can in no way designate the alternatives between or among which we choose. In the end, I expect, the putative content of all understandings that violate the pragmatic theory of meaning is completely negative. Hence, to say that existentialist conceptions are properly pragmatic is to reformulate the conclusion that an understanding without positive content is no understanding at all.

leading. To complete oneself by choosing existentially is to evaluate one's specific alternatives for purpose. The decision by which an activity is constituted is one decision. Hence, it is as true to say that the specific evaluation implicates the belief about worth as such as it is to say that the latter is expressed in the former. With whatever explicit awareness we can make our specific choices, we insofar explicitly choose our moral character. Moreover, we can explicitly choose to engage in specific activities whose purpose is, as it were, to persuade our own subsequent activities and, thereby, influence their existential decisions. I take this to be the proper purpose of moral training or moral education, the cultivation of virtue, and, most especially, of religious activity, to which I will return at the close of the next chapter.

The distinction between our explicit consciousness and our always implicit existential decision is absolutely fundamental to a proper account of distinctively human existence. Without that differentiation, the interpretation of our activity typically reduces our understandings to those that are or once were explicit in our lives. Because the explicit attention of humans depends on their specific purposes, it has no necessary common content, and this reduction easily leads to the view that nothing can be said about inescapable principles of human existence or human understanding. Universal principles of truth or goodness or reality are replaced by the hegemony of culture, tradition, or social location—or by the sheer exercise of will. Notwithstanding the limits on our thought and action that our historicity entails, we cannot take the full measure of our humanity without affirming our original but always implicit freedom, in which we know the telos defined by reality as such and are bound to decide whether pursuit of it will determine what we make of ourselves.

This chapter has taken an extended journey in order to arrive at that destination, and a brief summary may be useful. The argument has sought to make explicit the character of our distinctive capacity to live with understanding. Given that this capacity belongs to fragmentary individuals, we are not always explicitly aware that its every exercise involves an apprehension of reality as such, but this understanding is always present because any understanding at all discriminates its content by contrast with all other possible realities. Since understanding discriminates through universals, every human subject must be conscious not only of the past but also of the future; since a subject must be completed by its own decision, this discrimination of the present can only be an understanding of self. But self-understanding makes sense only as our distinctive form of self-expression and, therefore, as the conscious choice of a purpose. Because the choice is understood, the alternatives for purpose are compared with respect to choosing or understood with respect to their worth; because this comparison is inclusive, the variable of worth as such can be nothing other than the common character of all possible realities. Hence, every human activity constitutes itself as an exercise of original freedom, in which it believes only the true understanding of itself in relation to the comprehensive purpose or tells a lie to itself.

We may now return to Calvin: "Our wisdom, in so far as it ought to be deemed true and solid wisdom, consists almost entirely of two parts: the knowledge of God and of ourselves. But as these are connected by many ties, it is not easy to determine which of the two precedes, and gives birth to the other" (1989: 37). For Calvin, as for theists generally, the character of worth as such is defined by the character of God. If this theistic understanding is true, then it follows from our inescapable knowledge of the comprehensive purpose that our existence is constituted by knowledge of both ourselves and God.

Whether theism is true has not yet been addressed. In using the term "God," theists typically designate a being or individual that can be distinguished from all other realities because it is their primal source and final end, and whether there is such an individual can be critically considered only in or through a metaphysical inquiry. But the term "God" might also be used in a manner that serves to formulate the question rather than the typical theistic answer. On this formulation, "God" designates ultimate reality as the ground of worth. Thus, the question theists typically answer in the affirmative may be formulated: Is God an individual that is the primal source and final end of all realities? The following chapter seeks greater clarity about the constitutive moral character of original freedom. Accordingly, it uses "God" to mean ultimate reality as the ground of worth and, thereby postpones the theistic question. I will return to that question in chapter 3.

2

The Duplicity We May Choose

On the account given above, our life with understanding is essentially moral because it is constituted by a conscious choice about ourselves in relation to reality as such. With Schubert M. Ogden, we can say that humans exist in "an emphatic sense." Our existence is "not merely . . . the actualization of essence generally" but of "the specifically human essence that can be actualized only by self-understanding" and, therefore, by responsible decision (1996: 144). This means that every human activity knows both itself and God, where "God" is used to designate ultimate reality as the ground of worth. Because our subjectivity is fragmentary, we must decide whether to affirm God alone or also to affirm something else as the comprehensive telos in relation to which we complete ourselves. I have called this existential decision the exercise of original freedom. In order to designate its two alternatives, I will henceforth say that every human activity chooses to be authentic or inauthentic.

Because it is chosen, inauthentic existence is not simply the substitution of some false understanding of worth for God. Humans can choose to be authentic or inauthentic only because every human activity knows God. Thus, the choice to be inauthentic always affirms two understandings of worth as such. An inauthentic self-understanding is duplicitous. The false understanding of worth expressed in some or other specific purpose includes knowledge of the comprehensive purpose and, therefore, knowledge that the chosen alternative is false. A decision to be inauthentic is a self-contradictory self-understanding. Duplicity, we can say, tells a lie to itself. A liar is conscious that what she or he purports to be true is not what she or he believes. Similarly, the self that chooses a false self-understanding knows that this understanding is false.

Some may object that this conclusion is counterintuitive because we cannot believe understandings that we know to be inconsistent with themselves. On this objection, knowledge of a self-contradiction is coercive, in the sense that it prevents assent to the inconsistent understanding, even if one can still pretend that one believes it by lying to someone else. Whatever may be the case with other contradictions, however, the present discussion concerns self-understandings and, therefore, the moral choice of authentic or duplicitous assent to the comprehensive purpose. It seems at least equally counterintuitive to assert that immoral choices can be made from ignorance; hence, the objection seems committed to a denial of our distinctively moral freedom. In fact, moreover, many hold that humans sometimes choose specific purposes even when they *explicitly* believe those purposes to be immoral. St. Paul's confession, "I do not do the good I want, but the evil I do not want is what I do" (Rom. 7:19 RSV), expresses something that most serious accounts of the moral life have sought to clarify and something with which at least most of us can identify, and there are many who insist that the failure can be explicitly known when the deed is done.

Whether in truth humans can make a choice that is explicitly perverse may well be subject to debate, but the apparent need for further discussion itself suggests that the possibility of affirming a known contradiction is far from being incredible on its face. In any event, the denial of this possibility is even less obvious if, as the previous chapter argued, we should distinguish between explicit and implicit understandings. Even on the concession that humans cannot explicitly affirm a self-contradiction, it remains that knowledge of one's own inauthenticity might be implicit. Indeed, I have said that the choice of a comprehensive self-understanding can only be implicit, because it includes all other understandings a human activity may have. Explicit attention is, to the contrary, focused on only some of the activity's conscious relations and is determined by the specific purpose in which the decision for or against authenticity is expressed. Given the analysis of the previous chapter, then, the more important question for inquiry is whether one can speak sensibly of an *implicit* lie to oneself.

To the best of my knowledge, no thinker of the twentieth century more profoundly analyzes the original human decision for or against authenticity than does Reinhold Niebuhr. In three chapters of his major work that surely stand among the classic theological pages of this century, Niebuhr seeks to reformulate the traditional Christian doctrine of original sin in a manner that makes sense in our century because it is more adequate to "the psychological and moral facts in human wrong-doing" (1941–43, 1: 248).[1] The relevance of his account to the present discussion is suggested when he says that sin "can only be understood as a self-contradiction, made possible by the fact of . . . freedom but not following necessarily from it" (p. 17). For many, the terms "sin" and, even more, "original sin" appear to be distinctively religious terms, in the sense that they have meaning only within the context of the concepts and symbols of a particular religion. As Niebuhr's appeal to the "facts in human wrong-doing" suggests, however, his discussion includes an attempt so to clarify the traditional Christian doctrine that one can properly speak of "sin" in the context of philosophical anthropology. In any event, his analysis has in view nothing other than what I have called the decision for duplicity open to every exercise of original freedom, and it is in this respect that his achievement is a singular resource for our present question about an implicit lie to oneself.

I propose to pursue this question through a critical conversation with relevant aspects of Niebuhr's account. The conversation must be critical not only because we seek a constructive statement but also because there are aspects of Niebuhr's achievement that are inconsistent with the analysis of our existence developed in the previous chapter. I have in mind especially Niebuhr's conviction that sin is "inevitable." Notwithstanding his insistence to the contrary, I will argue, this interpretation contradicts his equally firm conviction that our exercise of original freedom is responsible. On my reading, however, he embraces this paradox in order to protect his theistic understanding of duplicity against its most profound challenge, one that led Kant to deny that the moral life as such can be understood in relation to a divine purpose. Summarily stated, the challenge is this: If every human activity knows God as the

---

[1]Unless otherwise noted, all citations from Niebuhr in this chapter are from Niebuhr 1941–43, volume 1.

ground of worth as such, why would any human activity choose against God, that is, understand itself as if something else were God?

As this summary formulation suggests, the problem in view identifies in its most radical form the question of how to speak sensibly of a lie to oneself. Through the conversation with Niebuhr's account, I believe, we may take in full measure the challenge duplicity poses for a theistic account of human existence and, as I will seek to show, remove the inconsistency in his own proposal by exploiting the resources Niebuhr himself provides for a constructive solution. At the same time, this appropriation of Niebuhr will afford occasion to develop in greater detail the relation between human activities and the individuals of which they are members, as well as the relation between human individuals and their larger social contexts. Understandings of both will be important to the discussion of human good in chapter 3 and to the conception of justice as general emancipation that Part Two will recommend. In keeping with the larger movement of the present work, I will assume throughout this chapter that the term "God" designates ultimate reality as the ground of worth. The difference between this meaning and use of the term to designate a divine individual is unimportant to the appropriation of Niebuhr for which I will argue.

Rebellion Against God

I previously had occasion to cite Niebuhr's formulation of the constitutive moral character that distinguishes human freedom: Humans are forced "to relate their actions in the last resort to the totality of things conceived as a realm of meaning" (1942: 44). For this reason, humans properly understand themselves "primarily from the standpoint of God" (p. 13). For Niebuhr, then, duplicity is "rebellion against God" or an "effort to usurp the place of God" (p. 179) by putting the self as an individual in God's place. The understanding of worth as such that particular purposes express centers worth in the self or, at least, gives to the capacities, achievements, and interests of the self an inordinate place in the evaluation of future possibilities.

Sin, Niebuhr writes, is "occasioned" by the conditions of "finiteness and freedom" (p. 178) that define human existence. Finitude means that a human individual, like any other creature in the world, exists contingently, in the sense that her or his existence begins and ends, and, as a consequence, her or his capacity to effect the course of events is limited. "The obvious fact is that man is a child of nature, subject to its vicissitudes, compelled by its necessities, driven by its impulses, and confined within the brevity of the years which nature permits its varied organic form" (p. 3). Human freedom means that this finite creature is conscious of itself and, therefore, "stands outside both itself and the world" (p. 14).

These conditions constitute an existential problem, Niebuhr explains, because humans, "being both free and bound, both limited and limitless," are "anxious" (p. 182). In common usage, this last term is frequently associated with the feeling of fear, but Niebuhr's usage is more precise. Unlike fear, which is directed at some specific object or possibility, "anxiety is the inevitable concomitant of the paradox of freedom and finiteness in which man is involved" (p. 182); associated with the universal features of self-consciousness, anxiety is directed to nothing specific. Moreover, this feeling is not a merely negative aspect of human life, since "it is the basis of all human creativity as well as the precondition of sin" (p. 183). A human "may, in the same moment, be anxious because he has not become what he ought to be; and also anxious lest he cease to be at all" (p. 184), and Niebuhr notes that his use of "anxiety" is better expressed by the German word *Sorge* ("care") than by *Angst* (see p. 183, n. 4).

Whatever else this use includes, then, "anxiety" means the awareness or feeling that one's authenticity or the meaning of one's life is carried in one's own hands, in the sense that it depends on one's own decision. "Anxiety," Niebuhr says, with Kierkegaard, "is the dizziness of freedom" (p. 252), and our freedom makes us "dizzy" because the choice every human activity must make concerns totality as a realm of meaning. Since each must decide about the comprehensive purpose in relation to which her or his own significance is determined, every human finds that "the abyss of meaninglessness yawns on the brink of all his mighty spiritual endeavors" (p. 182). Still, Niebuhr's use of "anxiety" includes more than simply the feeling of distinctively human freedom, because "anxiety is the internal description of the state of temptation" (p. 182), the inclination to duplicity.

This inclination should not be understood as a necessary characteristic of self-conscious freedom; "the situation of finiteness and freedom . . . becomes a source of temptation only when it is falsely interpreted" (p. 180). In the "myth of the Fall" displayed in the second chapter of Genesis, Niebuhr explains, the serpent symbolizes the intro- duction of a false interpretation into the occasion for decision. Human activity, we may say, is not so much as tempted to sin unless an inauthentic possibility, a false interpretation of the worth of life or the comprehensive purpose, "is suggested to man by a force of evil which precedes his own sin" (p. 181). Thus, when Niebuhr says that "anxiety is the inevitable concomitant of the paradox of freedom and finite- ness" (p. 182), he means that the temptation to sin is universal. It is because his use of "anxiety" includes this temptation that Niebuhr can cite approvingly another of Kierkegaard's formulations: "Anxi- ety . . . . is so near, so fearfully near to sin" (p. 182, n. 2).

But however near to sin, "anxiety is not sin" (p. 183), because temptation is not itself the decision for duplicity. Niebuhr can insist on the difference because "there is always the ideal possibility that faith [in God] would purge anxiety of the tendency toward sinful self-assertion" (pp. 182–83; see also p. 252). As with so many modern theologians indebted to Schleiermacher, Niebuhr holds that self-con- sciousness necessarily includes, at least in some sense, a consciousness of God.[2] In understanding anything at all and thus being free to choose an understanding of herself or himself, a human always knows the divine reality or what Niebuhr typically calls the "centre" or "source" of meaning (p. 16) or worth, so that the self "which it asserts [in sin] is less than the true self" (p. 252). "The experience of God," Niebuhr writes, "is . . . an overtone implied in all experience. The soul which reaches the outermost rims of its own consciousness, must also come in contact with God, for He impinges upon that conscious- ness" (p. 127). Although he agrees that this experience includes the

---

[2]The qualifying phrase "at least in some sense" is required in order to recognize Niebuhr's account of the difference between general and special revelation. On his formulation, as I mentioned in the previous chapter, God's revelation to self-consciousness generally is partial or deficient. In the absence of God's special self-disclosure, which is complete only in the event of Jesus as the Christ, humans know the reality but not the character of God (see chapter 5). My discussion in this chapter abstracts from the relation between Niebuhr's interpretation of sin and his understanding of revelation. I believe that one can account for the central features of the former independently of the latter, and my purpose here is to elicit Niebuhr's help in clarifying the decision for or against authenticity that consti- tutes human activity as such.

sense of absolute dependence with which Schleiermacher equated it, Niebuhr insists that it also includes "the sense of being seen, commanded, judged and known from beyond ourselves" (p. 128). Thereby, he confirms that the universal experience of God identifies an "ideal possibility" for the choice of self-understanding.

Throughout Niebuhr's analysis of human fault, it is obvious that he is not describing an explicit "rebellion against God" (p. 179). That alternative interpretation is, for him, the Pelagian view and is clearly inadequate to the facts in human wrong-doing. On Pelagian accounts, as Niebuhr depicts them, "actual sin is . . . regarded as more unqualifiedly a conscious defiance of God's will and an explicit preference of evil, despite the knowledge of the good" (p. 245). The credible purpose of such accounts, he allows, is to protect "the idea of responsibility" (p. 248). But the Pelagian view also implies that we are not responsible for ourselves in respects that we do not explicitly choose and, therefore, fails to appreciate the complexity of human fault. "There is, . . . , less freedom in the actual sin and more responsibility for the bias toward sin (original sin) than moralistic interpretations can understand" (p. 250). As we will see, the term "bias toward sin" introduces into his indictment of Pelagianism Niebuhr's own conviction that sin is inevitable. But whatever we should make of that conviction, it is also clear that he is working with the distinction between explicit and implicit consciousness we have previously discussed—even if he more frequently speaks of the distinction between conscious and unconscious aspects of the subject and, thereby, generally reserves the term "conscious" for explicit understanding. "Sin is . . . both unconscious and conscious. The degree of conscious choice may vary in specific instances of course. Yet even the more conscious choices do not come completely into the category of conscious perversity" (p. 250).[3]

---

[3]It might be noted that the rejection of sin as an explicit choice does not entail the acceptance of sin as inevitable. Niebuhr himself offers the terms for a third alternative in the distinction between explicit and implicit consciousness or between conscious and unconscious choices; that is, sin may be an implicit but not inevitable choice. Thus, it might be said that Niebuhr has characterized Pelagianism tendentiously. I take this to show how thoroughly Niebuhr associates the implicit character of sin with its being inevitable; that is, sin must be implicit or largely so *because* it involves a bias toward sin. Hence, we may surmise, Niebuhr is led to think that a Pelagian denial of inevitability can only mean that sin is an explicit choice.

Just as the experience of God is "an overtone implied in all experience," in other words, the exercise of original freedom occurs, at least principally, as an implicit choice, even if the decision for duplicity is invariably felt as the "overtone" of an "uneasy conscience" (see p. 267). Nothing more confirms this reading than Niebuhr's insistence that "an element of deceit" is "a concomitant, . . . , of self-love" (p. 203). In choosing self-centeredness while knowing simultaneously the "ideal possibility" of faith in God, we can live with this lie only if we hide it from ourselves. "Man loves himself inordinately. Since his determinate existence does not deserve the devotion lavished upon it, it is obviously necessary to practice some deception in order to justify such excessive devotion" (p. 203). To be sure, the deception is directed to others, as the self seeks to convince them that it serves a more inclusive understanding of worth, but "the desperate effort to deceive others must, . . . , be regarded as, on the whole, an attempt to aid the self in believing a pretension it cannot easily believe because it was itself the author of the deception" (p. 206). In self-deception, as this last citation makes clear, the self in some sense knows the truth, else it would not be the deceiver; yet, in another sense, it does not know the truth, else it would not be deceived (see p. 204, n. 2). The concept is saved from inherent inconsistency only by a difference between the aspect of the self that deceives and the aspect that is deceived, and it is just this difference that the distinction between implicit and explicit understanding allows. The duplicitous choice and, therefore, the lie to oneself are implicit, and the explicit understanding is deceived. "The dishonesty which is an inevitable concomitant of sin must be regarded neither as purely ignorance, nor as yet involving a conscious [that is, explicit] lie in each individual instance. The mechanism of deception is too complicated to fit into the category of either pure ignorance or pure dishonesty" (p. 204).

What a human activity may be self-deceived about is the moral quality of its specific purpose. Every duplicitous choice expresses itself in an act that "disturb[s] the harmony of creation" or an act of "injustice" (p. 179), and it is this act that may be explicitly understood and misrepresented to ourselves. Niebuhr often speaks of a distinction between the "vertical" and "horizontal" dimensions of human life, the former identifying "the soul's relation to God" in distinction from its relations to others in the world (see pp. 257, 269). On my reading, this may be taken as his formulation of the difference and relation between a decision about the comprehensive purpose and the specific purpose in which the exercise of original freedom is expressed. "The real essence of sin can be understood only in the vertical dimension" (p. 257). But God constitutes or is totality as a realm of meaning, so that the "vertical" choice for duplicity cannot be separated from a specific or "horizontal" purpose that violates the order of worth among future possibilities and, thereby, disturbs the harmony of creation.

Niebuhr makes the same point when he says that the content of our "ideal possibility" or "original righteousness" consists in "a harmony between the soul and God . . . , a harmony within the soul . . . , and a harmony between the self and the neighbor"—and therefore this content is summarized in the biblical statement of the "law of love": "Thou shalt love the Lord thy God with all thy heart, with all thy soul, and all thy mind. This is the first and great commandment. And the second is like unto it, Thou shalt love thy neighbor as thyself" (p. 286). At least on Niebuhr's usage here, the term "neighbor" stands for all other creatures, so that harmony with God and with the order of worth among specific possibilities for the creation are distinct but coincident; rebellion against God simultaneously violates the future of the world. That "harmony within the soul" also coincides with a proper relation to God and neighbor underscores the duplicity or self-contradiction that marks the actualization of the sinner, so that "no man, however deeply involved in sin, is able to regard the misery of sin as normal . . . .; some echo of the law he has violated seems to resound in his conscience" (p. 265). When an individual "falsely makes itself the centre of existence" (p. 179), the offense against self "points to the . . . lack of trust in God" (p. 252) and also violates the future of the world.

Temptation

In seeking a critical and constructive engagement with Niebuhr's proposal, we may begin with his account of temptation, the experience of which is internally described as anxiety. A false interpretation of worth, Niebuhr says, "is suggested . . . by a force of evil" (p. 181). He does not mean simply that the choice of a self-understanding is presented with one or more alternatives to the "ideal possibility" of faith in God. Since being finite and free necessitates a moral decision, the mere possibility of a duplicitous choice cannot itself be evil. "Suggested . . . by a force of evil" implies not only a false alternative but also its commendation. Temptation occurs because something attracts the self to a duplicitous interpretation, and this is why temptation makes human freedom anxious. One knows that the tempting alternative is false, and the attraction to it is, therefore, felt as a threat to one's worth.

Niebuhr calls this force of evil a "mystery" (p. 181), and, in the end, this term represents his conviction that sin is inevitable. At the same time, the term expresses his belief that the more or less obvious exhibition of moral fault throughout the human adventure cannot be explained. To be sure, if "explanation" means that one identifies why an event occurred by appeal to other events that caused it, then an exercise of freedom, by definition, cannot be explained. The moral or immoral character of a human activity must be its own cause. But this conceptual necessity does not account for the fact that sin so pervades the human community, a fact Niebuhr thinks can be readily confirmed. "By methods of ordinary objective analyses of human history," we can recognize "the problematic character of all human virtue and the ambiguous character of all historic achievements" (1949: 198). If we grant that we do not have to look far to find the moral weakness of the human spirit and, moreover, that we will find it however far we look, we can pose on empirical grounds alone a question about human fault that the conceptual impossibility of explaining a choice does not itself answer. In Niebuhr's mind, if I read it rightly, the inevitability of sin is the only way to account for what is empirically apparent.

In any event, the mysterious force of evil is "perhaps" best described "in the statement that sin posits itself" (p. 181) or "sin presupposes itself" (p. 251). Niebuhr means the same when he speaks of a "defect of the will" (p. 242) or a "bias toward sin" (p. 250) by which human existence is characterized. "Anxiety . . . leads to sin only if the prior sin of unbelief is assumed" (p. 252). The reference here to "unbelief" does not mean that freedom leads to sin when one chooses a false interpretation. On that formulation, the statement is true by definition and trivial. Niebuhr points instead to a *prior* sin of unbelief; that is, a false understanding of the comprehensive purpose is attractive to the chooser because the self's fault is already implicated in its attention to the alternatives. A human "could not be tempted if he had not already sinned" (p. 251), and this is why temptation itself is mysterious. It is also why yielding to temptation is inevitable.

"Responsibility despite inevitability" is Niebuhr's summary phrase for this interpretation. Inevitability does not compromise responsibility because duplicity is not "a necessity of man's nature"; "sin is natural for man in the sense that it is universal but not in the sense that it is necessary" (p. 242). Given this last distinction by itself, one might ask whether Niebuhr's use of "universal" intends a strict or, rather, a statistical universality. Does he mean to assert that every human activity is at fault, such that, given any human activity past or future, the assertion that it was or will be duplicitous is valid? Or is the universality statistical, so that Niebuhr's statement is simply an empirical generalization that, at least in principle, admits of exceptions? To the best of my reading, Niebuhr never directly asks and answers this question. But we can be sufficiently confident that he intends strict universality, precisely because the temptation to sin, which "lies, . . . , in the human situation itself" (p. 251), already implicates the self's fault. "The actual sin is the consequence of temptation to anxiety in which all life stands. But anxiety alone is neither actual nor original sin. Sin does not flow necessarily from it. Consequently the bias toward sin from which actual sin flows is anxiety plus sin" (pp. 250–51). In so making the point, Niebuhr places the inevitability of sin within the categorical conditions of finiteness and freedom "in which all life stands," so that the universality must be strict.

For Niebuhr, in other words, the "force of evil" to which original freedom is subject accounts for *both* temptation and actual sin. On the one hand, it suggests or commends a false interpretation of life's meaning or the self's authenticity, so that sin itself is a decision for which the self is responsible. On the other hand, this duplicitous choice would not be attractive except that the "bias toward sin" is a prior unbelief that makes duplicity unavoidable. Given the distinction between temptation and sin, one is led to ask why Niebuhr believes that the two are inseparable or, to pose the same question, why he thinks that human decision could not be tempted unless the success of temptation were not already implicated. In the remainder of this section, I will develop one proposal on which temptation is understood without assuming that it controls the exercise of freedom. In the next section, I will seek to show why Niebuhr believes that this proposal, however valid as far as it goes, is inadequate, and the two sections together will help prepare us for a critical appropriation of his account.

The proposal to separate temptation from the inevitability of sin may be approached by first attending to a distinction Niebuhr draws in several contexts between "the self in contemplation and the self in action" (p. 259).

> The self in the moment of transcending itself exercises the self's capacity for infinite regression and makes the previous concretion of will its object. . . . The self-as-transcendent always assumes, mistakenly, that its present ability to judge and criticize the undue or unjust claims of the self in a previous action is a guarantee of its virtue in a subsequent action. This is not the case, for when the self acts it always uses the previous transcendent perspective partly as a "rationalization" and "false front" for its interested action (pp. 277–78).

This citation might be read to suggest that moments of contemplation and moments of action are discrete moments in the life of a human individual, such that life does or could alternate from the one to the other. But other citations are inconsistent with that interpretation. "*In every moment of existence* there is a tension between the self as it looks out upon the world from the perspective of its values and necessities and the self as it looks at both the world and itself, and is disquieted by the undue claims of the self in action" (p. 278, emphasis added)—and Niebuhr also says of the self-as-transcendent that it occurs "in a moment of the self which transcends history, though not outside of the self which is in history" (p. 272).

To the best of my reading, Niebuhr's meaning is this: There is "contemplation" and "action" in every moment of human existence, so that these may be understood as differing "moments" in the sense that they are aspects of each human activity. But the action "contemplated" and criticized as inauthentic is not the activity of which the contemplation is an aspect. One contemplates and criticizes the unjust claims of a previous action, and therefore the judgment does not prevent the present action from making a false choice. Indeed, the present action deceives itself by using the judgment as a "false front" for its own inauthenticity. If this is correct, then the "contemplation" in which previous action is criticized must be a more or less explicit consciousness, because its use as a "false front" refers to the self-deception of which human fault is capable, and the understanding that is deceived is explicit.[4]

[4]This reading coheres with Niebuhr's apparent belief that a given human activity or concrete moment of human life cannot "contemplate" its own exercise of original freedom, that is, cannot explicitly choose its own self-understanding. Of course, a sinful activity will know *implicitly* that it is inauthentic, because duplicitous choice is an implicit lie to oneself. As we have mentioned, Niebuhr expresses this point in saying that inauthentic activity never completely escapes an "uneasy conscience." But explicit reflection on our own self-understanding can have as its object only the authenticity or duplicity of our previous activities, now remembered. "The self in the moment of transcending itself exercises the self's capacity for infinite regression and makes the *previous* concretion of its will its [explicit] object" (p. 277, emphasis added).

Even this retrospective assessment, we should note, must be burdened by the fact that the choice of faith expressed in "the previous concretion of will" was only implicitly understood by that activity. Our present judgment on it can be aided by focus on the sense of conscience that was experienced, but the assessment is largely inferential from what was more or less clearly discriminated and, therefore, can be more or less clearly remembered. Thus, even our past self-understandings are never apparent to explicit awareness. Still, this is not inconsistent with Niebuhr's saying that the self-as-transcendent has "the present ability to judge and criticize the undue or unjust claims of the self in a previous action." What is more or less perspicuously remembered may indeed be more or less sufficient to know that past actions were inauthentic. That some specific purpose other than the one chosen would have been more worthy and was within the open alternatives is a judgment humans frequently deliver against themselves, especially when they have been subjects of significant moral education. This ability explicitly to know we have been at fault is the more pronounced because our specific failings often fall so far short of the mark set by significant standards that the inference to duplicity is highly secure. Still, this knowledge of moral failure is not knowledge of our own hearts in the sense that we can see with equal confidence *what* self-understanding was chosen by the past activity. Our failing, so far as we know it, may be consistent with several false interpretations of the comprehensive purpose. Even if Niebuhr is right that all false interpretations center worth in the self, just what is taken to benefit the future self is less open to subsequent reflection because an inference to that conclusion, in contrast to the simple fact of failure, would require more or less complete awareness of the past activity's understandings.

For similar reasons, subsequent reflection on previous activities could never provide explicit knowledge of their authenticity, assuming for the moment that authentic self-understandings are possible. To know that a specific purpose was the best or among the best of the alternatives does not imply that the activity in question was authentic because the same specific action can be taken for different reasons or with different beliefs about the comprehensive purpose. Moreover, the case of authenticity is the more problematic because the problems of inference are compounded by the fact that subsequent activities are prone to the deception intended by earlier ones.

But if an individual may be self-deceived in her or his present choice notwithstanding a simultaneous judgment on past fault, the dynamic of self-deception may also affect the present belief about the past, that is, the moment of contemplation. When Niebuhr writes that we often attempt to deceive others in order "to aid the self in believing a pretension it cannot easily believe because it was the author of the deception" (pp. 206-07), he calls to mind our characteristic attempts falsely to justify past actions and, therefore, hide their faults from explicit awareness. In this case, moreover, deception of our present moment of contemplation may be a part of the duplicitous purpose we chose in the past, because that purpose cannot be achieved if we subsequently become critical of it. In other words, self-deception may also be a practice in which a previous activity deceives a subsequent activity or activities in an individual's life, and we can use self-deception in this sense to introduce by way of illustration the proposal in which temptation is separated from the inevitability of sin.

Consider self-deception, then, as it occurs in the relation between an individual's activities. Because an activity *is* its choice with understanding among alternatives for purpose, the deception of one's own subsequent reflection or future "contemplation" may be a part of that purpose. Let us suppose that I choose to exploit a neighbor for my own selfish advantage and, therefore, choose an understanding of the comprehensive purpose in which my own advantage occupies an inordinate place. In this expression of duplicity, I include in my purpose the intent that my own future activities, insofar as they explicitly reflect on this choice, will understand it to be considerate or helpful to the neighbor, so that my duplicity will seem to be a commitment to more inclusive values. The lie that I tell to myself in the decision to exploit includes the intent to prevent my subsequent self-consciousness from explicitly recognizing what I have done, because that recognition would compromise the advantage I seek to realize.

What now becomes apparent is that, in many cases, self-deception in this sense cannot be described simply in terms of the previous activity's purpose. Presumably, the deception is required because, in its absence, the subsequent activity would be likely to see more or less clearly that the previous activity was at fault, and preventing this recognition will, in many cases, require that the subsequent activity participate in the pretense. Having been duplicitous and having included the intent to deceive my subsequent assessment, I will be unsuccessful unless the purpose of my present activity is consistent with the deception, and that may require that my present activity is also duplicitous. If my present "contemplation" of the past is controlled by present authenticity, then I may see clearly and condemn what I have done, and my past intent will fail.

I do not mean to assert that self-deception between activities always requires duplicity in the activity deceived. Modern psychology, in many of its forms, holds that one's own past beliefs can be repressed, in the sense that they cannot subsequently enter explicit consciousness without the assistance of other individuals or, perhaps, an unusual turn in one's life. Allowing that this is so, we may also recognize that repressed beliefs are in some cases a consequence of the individual's past duplicity and, therefore, may speak of deception in which the past *coerces* subsequent activity. The purpose chosen in the past so sets the conditions for the future that the possible purposes open in the present do not include the explicit understanding required for self-criticism. But it remains that, in many cases, our past can only persuade our present, and the intent to deceive will be successful only if present activity conspires with it.

The past intent to persuade, we can say, suggests a false interpretation and, thereby, tempts the present activity. "Suggested . . . by a force of evil," we have noted, means that an alternative to authenticity is presented with a commendation, so that something attracts the self to a duplicitous alternative for self-understanding. If my past intent to deceive my subsequent self cannot be successful without the complicity of my present self-understanding, then the past activity included in its purpose a "suggestion" for my subsequent decision, and this suggestion was presented with a commendation. In choosing its own purpose, the past activity did so with a sense of worth; when the subsequent activity relates to or remembers the suggestion, it feels or entertains the sense of worth included in the past. It is this sense of worth with which the past commends a purpose or seeks to persuade present decision that makes the intent to deceive an instance of temptation.

Perhaps we can more readily pursue this proposal if we note the importance of persuasion by our own past in abstraction from the question of authenticity. Whitehead discusses the example of someone whose conscious activity is such that she or he speaks the phrase "the United States." By the time the speaker's consciousness leads to the utterance "States," the conscious moment with which she or he began the phrase is in the past—and the point may be more apparent if we consider a longer phrase, such as "the United States of America." How, Whitehead asks, shall we account for the fact that the earlier utterance "the United" was not followed by "Fruit Company" rather than "States of America"? Clearly, the purpose of the earlier conscious activity, which included utterance of "the United," also included purposes suggested to subsequent activities, namely, that they should intend the utterance "States of America," and it is the sense of worth with which these suggestions are commended that attracts or persuades subsequent activities to complete the phrase (see 1961: 181–83).

This is, moreover, simply a microscopic example of something fundamental to human existence. We consistently pursue a given telos through an extended series of activities and their particular choices because a common purpose is continually commended by past activities to present ones. An individual completes tasks or fulfills projects—writing a book, building a house, raising a child, participating in an association—*because* she or he has begun them. The common purpose was chosen with a sense of worth and thus an intent for one's own future activities, and it is the continual memory of this intent with its sense of worth, generally enhanced insofar as pursuit of the task or project proceeds, that orders the series of momentary activities. The identity of a human individual in the respect that it results from her or his own freedom consists in such general purposes and, at its most inclusive, can be defined by a purpose or set of purposes for life as a whole, a "life-plan," that the individual has chosen and continually presents to its own future with the sense of worth.

Still, purposes commended to the future can only be, as Niebuhr says, "suggested." Each moment of human activity chooses its own self-understanding and, therefore, its own purpose. With respect to that choice, the past can only be suggestive rather than coercive. Thus, we must distinguish in principle, as the earlier discussion of self-deception mentioned, between the way an individual's activity can *determine* and the way it can seek to *persuade* her or his subsequent activity. If I presently divorce my spouse, then I determine that my immediate future activity cannot be participation in that marriage, at least not without a reuniting. But if I presently quit smoking, then I can only seek to persuade my future activity, each future moment having the choice to reaffirm or to break this resolution. In particular cases, the distinction may be difficult to apply. Assuming successful self-deception between an individual's activities, for instance, it may be impossible to determine whether this required the complicity of her or his present activity or whether she or he had so repressed the truth that it could not enter explicit consciousness without the assistance of other people—since we may not be able to pursue the matter without engaging in conversation with the individual in question. But difficulty in application does not compromise the clarity and importance of the distinction in principle, as is apparent when criminal courts must decide whether the particular deed was or was not something the defendant chose to do.

Granting that persuasion is fundamental within the life of an individual, we can also see that the future one might seek to persuade is not necessarily limited to activities of the individual in question. We also commend purposes to other individuals, not only directly through verbal or other forms of symbolic communication but also through choosing those purposes in a context that makes them an example to others. Human life is steeped with persuasion of this kind. We all, in some respects, "take our cues" from other individuals. This is especially the case when the others are, for some reason, especially important to us and, perhaps, reaches its greatest extent in the developing freedom of a young child in relation to the purposes suggested by adults who care for her or him. Moreover, all individuals in some measure are successfully persuaded by purposes that are pervasive in communities in which they participate, perhaps especially including larger communities defined by some more or less distinct cultural tradition, even if the measure in which communities are successfully persuasive appears to be historically or culturally variable, depending on the respects in which the culture is or is not "individualistic." With respect to any given individual, however, the effect of the community may be coercive as well as persuasive, in the sense that she or he has been so conditioned that, at present, a choice against some of the interpretations presented by the community is not possible.

Niebuhr's well-known discussion of "group pride" or "the egotism of racial, national and socio-economic groups" (pp. 208, 209) might be understood to identify immoral communal purposes, transmitted to individuals simply through general interaction or also reinforced by the communication of leaders and symbolic communal events, that are successfully persuasive among large numbers of members. On Niebuhr's account, this persuasion is the more successful because the immoral purposes of larger groups can be more readily accepted as consistent with or in service to universal values than purposes that are individually self-interested or egotistical. The pride of a nation "is plausible, though hardly credible," because "the nation, . . . , transcends the individual life to such a degree in power, majesty, and pseudo-immortality that the claim of unconditioned value can be made for it with a degree of plausibility" (p. 212).

Whatever successful persuasion individuals exercise on each other or communities exercise on their members, however, the difference between this and successful persuasion within an individual life seems transparently dramatic. Collective purposes that are successful are decidedly general in contrast to the specific detail with which an individual can plan and execute projects. The individual, in other words, remembers the particularity of its own past activities and, therefore, anticipates its own future in a measure that, except perhaps in rare circumstances, dramatically exceeds the capacity of one individual to appreciate or anticipate the activities of another. For this reason, the individual can feel more intensely the sense of worth with which its own past decisions make suggestions to the present, and those suggestions can be designed in a more specific manner—and the use of persuasion can be the detailed capacity for continuous purpose that individuals uniquely enjoy.

This difference illustrates the general fact that the sense of worth with which suggestions for one's purpose are implicitly entertained may vary greatly in intensity, depending on the particular context in which they are received. Habitual dispositions to purpose that the individual has developed, her or his virtues and vices, will be profoundly attractive, especially when the practice is long-standing in the individual's past. Certain other individuals who are especially important to the person in question will have special influence. More general understandings of oneself that are widely shared in one's community or in established cultural and institutional structures can have persuasive effect that borders on coercion when an individual has never encountered other people who criticize them. Let us call this varying intensity with which suggestions for purpose carry a sense of worth their greater or lesser persuasive power.

We may also describe greater persuasive power as a greater probability that persuasion will be successful, and statistical probabilities regarding the exercise of human freedom are summary statements of the persuasive power of the past. The statistical probabilities that an individual will in the present act in accord with a long-standing habit are, barring unusual circumstances, very high. So, too, are the probabilities that an individual who is raised in a more or less closed cultural context will share its values. All prediction of human choices, from our trust in the promises of another individual to the sophisticated prediction of election results, is an analysis of these statistical probabilities.

The proposal for understanding temptation should now be clear: The "force of evil" commending false interpretations to the self consists in the fault of the past. Purposes previously chosen by the individual in question or inherited from the larger social context either included duplicitous intentions for the present choice or merely exemplified inauthentic alternatives for self-understanding. If I have been cruel to a neighbor and included in my past purpose the intent to deceive my subsequent reflection, then the sense of worth attached to that intention is felt in the present and tempts me now to choose in conspiracy with my past. If, for whatever reasons, I admire a certain individual, and she or he lives a promiscuous life, then I may be tempted to choose a similar course. If I am raised in a racist community, where people of color are thought to be inferior and treated accordingly, then I can be tempted to choose an understanding of worth that authorizes similar purposes. If generally respected leaders of my nation characterize its unjust aggression as advancing the good of humankind, I can be tempted to choose a self-understanding that includes action in support of this injustice. In every case, we must remember the distinction between coercion and persuasion by the past. Some past effects on the present activity—of one's culture or society, significant others in one's life, or one's own past deeds—merely limit the present alternatives for purpose, and insofar there is no effect on the present choice of authenticity or inauthenticity. But insofar as the effect on the present is a suggestion with persuasive power or attaches a sense of worth to purposes within the range of present choice, the sin or duplicity we inherit may be called a force of evil that is experienced as temptation.

Let us summarize this latter effect of the past by saying that temptation has a social character. At least in this sense, there is every reason to accept Niebuhr's phrase "sin posits itself," because the temptation in question is a consequence of temporally prior fault to which the present activity relates. Whatever else should be said, so far as I can see, an account of sin will not approach adequacy without recognition of the way in which duplicity can be a submission to lures from the past. Indeed, if one assumes that the past is pervaded by false interpretations—culturally formulated, institutionally ordered, individually exemplified and articulated—one might conclude that the social character of temptation is sufficient to account for something like a statistical universality of human fault.

The Radical Problem

But there is no mystery in the proposal that has been given, and, as we have seen, Niebuhr's insistence that the "force of evil" is mysterious expresses his conviction that the universality of human fault is strict. "Sin posits itself" means not merely that temptation requires a temporally prior sin but also that the present activity is characterized by "a defect of the will," such that "the bias toward sin from which actual sin flows" is not simply the anxiety temptation causes but, rather, "anxiety plus sin" (pp. 250–51). This is not to say that Niebuhr has any reason to reject the social character of temptation. It is merely to say that, for him, the proposal on which temptation is exhausted by that character is inadequate, so that duplicity cannot be understood unless temptation itself is inseparable from something more, namely, the present self's own fault.

In this insistence, I believe, Niebuhr expresses a profound insight, because one cannot make sense of human duplicity if the account of temptation is exhausted by its social character. There is a radical problem with respect to the nature of original freedom that persuasion from the past is not sufficient to resolve, and this problem is, I think, Niebuhr's deepest reason for recourse to mystery or a defect of the will. This problem led Kant, if I understand him rightly, to deny that moral worth can be defined in terms of a telos or comprehensive purpose, and a brief review of Kant's argument will help to clarify why Niebuhr thought that a human "could not be tempted if he had not already sinned" (p. 251).

In the previous chapter, I noted in passing that Kant separated the moral law from "the purposes which we may have in view in our actions" (Kant 1949: 17) because he believed that humans cannot understand "things-in-themselves" and, therefore, cannot know reality as such. Moral principles, then, "contain the determining grounds of the will because of their form and not because of their matter" (1956: 26)—that is, solely because of the form of universality and not because of a telos to be pursued. Since one of the central conclusions defended in the *Critique of Pure Reason* is the limitation on our knowledge, this conclusion might be called the premise the first critique delivers to the *Critique of Practical Reason*. The strictly non-teleological character of Kant's ethic displays the coherence of the two critiques, notwithstanding that it also asserts the independence of pure practical reason from all knowledge of actual and possible states of affairs. But if Kant's ethic depends in this way on his conviction about the limits of our knowledge, it is also the case that his moral theory includes an independent argument for the formal or nonteleological character of the moral law.

On this argument, a comprehensive purpose would imply that the moral law is derived from some object of inclination or desire, because a state of affairs one might choose to pursue or seek to realize can be related to the will only as such an object; but derivation of the moral law from a prior object of desire contradicts the freedom of humans to be immoral. Kant's point can be explicated by considering the following passage, in which he speaks about the relation between feeling and the moral law:

> I am far from denying that frequent practice in accordance with this determining ground [the moral law] can itself finally cause a subjective feeling of satisfaction. Indeed, it is a duty to establish and cultivate this feeling, which alone deserves to be called the moral

feeling. But the concept of duty cannot be derived from it, for we would have to presuppose a feeling for law as such and regard as an object of sensation what can only be thought through reason. If this did not end up in the flattest contradiction, it would destroy every concept of duty and fill its place with a merely mechanical play of refined inclinations, sometimes contending with the coarser (1956: 40–41).

To derive the concept of duty from a moral feeling would mean that the will is exhausted by a supposed choice among objects of inclination. Just because a prior feeling would then be attached to the moral good, or humans would have as an object of inclination what is really worthy of their choice, this would necessarily be the most refined feeling, and the "choice" among inclinations would be "merely mechanical." The feeling for moral worth would necessarily control the choice, and thus it would not be a moral choice at all. But the concept of duty presupposes moral freedom or the possibility of immoral choice.

It follows, Kant holds, that our freedom presupposes a moral law independent of objects of inclination or desire and, therefore, of any purpose. Humans experience freedom because they experience obligation, and the moral law confronts them as an imperative or obligates because it identifies a different object than those of inclination or desire. Duty must mean the relation to an object that "can only be thought by reason"; that is, the categorical imperative is nothing other than reason's form of universality, and duty requires that the will be determined by the formal self-legislation of reason in the choice among possible purposes. Thus, the possibility of both moral and immoral choice derives from the fact that humans are both rational and sensual creatures. Reason adds to inclination the relation to universals or concepts that permits understanding of possible purposes and, therefore, choice among them—and reason does this because it also adds the form of universality prescribing how this choice should be made. Precisely because the law of reason is not itself derived from a feeling or is independent of inclination, there can be no "mechanical play" between reason and sensuality, and the choice among possible purposes is also the choice *whether* to be determined by some object of inclination or desire, that is, whether to be moral or immoral. Given that the formal law can only be a priori or rationally necessary, it follows that all possible objects of purpose must be empirical. No such object could be defined by the character of reality as such, and this argument may be said to confirm the limitation on our knowledge that is defended in the *Critique of Pure Reason*.[5]

The formal character of Kant's moral law is, we can say, his solution to a problem that had long occupied the development of modern moral theory and was implicated in what J. B. Schneewind calls the fundamental division between "intellectualism" and "voluntarism" (1998: 21). In brief, the division occurs within a common conviction that God is essential to morality and concerns the relation between God's nature and the divine commandments. For the intellectualists, God's purpose "is guided by his intellect's knowledge of eternal standards" (1998: 9) that, because eternal, belong to God's own nature—and thus God's will could not be other than it is. For the voluntarists, the intellectualist account leads to a view of the human soul or human action on which the will is subordinate to the intellect, such that we desire and will whatever the intellect identifies as the greatest good to be pursued, and this "seems to imply that we can act wrongly only if we fail to know what is good" (1998: 21). Hence, intellectualists seemingly cannot explain how immorality is possible; the relation between reason and will seems to be, in Kant's words, "a merely mechanical play."

On the voluntarist account, then, the moral will is not moved by knowledge of the greatest good but solely by the voluntary or arbitrary commandments of an omnipotent God, by which we are bound simply because they are divine commands. For the intellectualists, however, "the moral gulf that voluntarism sets between God and us" (1998: 250) is unacceptable. On this last point, Kant is an intellectualist. But he seeks to transcend the previous debate by making God and the moral law noumenal and our knowledge phenomenal. Hence, the moral will is not moved by knowledge of the greatest good or a merely mechanical play but solely by the formal universality of reason, and the God whose nature authorizes the moral law can only be a

---

[5]In reaching this understanding of Kant, I have been instructed by Silber 1959, 1960.

postulate of practical reason. Thereby, the will is free to be moral or immoral without denying the moral holiness of God.

Whether Kant's own account of human freedom avoids the problem with which he indicts teleological accounts of the moral law is an important question. Granting the independence of reason and inclination he asserts, one might still ask how a choice against one's knowledge of the moral law or one's own rational nature makes sense. That Kant himself was troubled by this question is one reason for his reflections on "radical evil in human nature," presented in Book One of *Religion Within the Limits of Reason Alone*, and we may note that he there calls the "ultimate ground" for good and evil in a human person "inscrutable to us" (1960: 17). But further pursuit of Kant is not necessary here. Whatever should be said about his own resolution, the problem he has identified is a challenge to the conception of human freedom this work has developed, which, with regard to this issue, might be called a recurrence to the intellectualist tradition prior to Kant. The challenge may be formulated as follows: If the constitutive moral character of human activity is self-determination by our knowledge of the comprehensive purpose alone or by a duplicitous understanding of it, how is it possible to account for a choice of the latter?

To be sure, one can respond that self-understandings must be chosen, but this response misses the point. What is called into question by Kant's argument is whether the analysis destroys the possibility of choice. Given that original freedom includes a true understanding of worth or the good as such, what prevents this "refined inclination" from merely mechanical control? Once this problem is clear, we can also see that it cannot be solved by the proposal that humans are subject to temptations from the past. Recourse to the social character of temptation also begs the question, as becomes the more apparent if we restate it: Why should duplicitous suggestions from the past be tempting; that is, how could they have any persuasive power for a present activity that knows the comprehensive purpose?

This is, on my accounting, the most profound form of the objection to original freedom I cited at the outset of this chapter, namely, that humans cannot affirm understandings they know to be self-contradictory and, therefore, cannot lie to themselves. In this form, I consider it a radical problem for moral anthropology, and it may also be stated in Niebuhr's terms: If human existence is constituted by the general revelation of God, how could any false interpretation be tempting? If our consciousness always includes the sense of God's presence, how can this be moral freedom; that is, how can something else tempt the self to choose immorally, so that the "law of love" is experienced as obligatory? For Niebuhr, I am inclined to think, it is this question that takes us to the limits of reason and requires that we posit a defect of the will. If so, then his doctrine of original sin seeks above all to protect the theistic affirmation, namely, that God is present in every exercise of original freedom.

We can now see the deepest connection in Niebuhr's mind between the inevitability and the empirical pervasiveness of sin. The point is not simply that the former is an empirical hypothesis required to account for the latter. To the contrary, the deepest truth is that sin could not be at all were it not strictly universal. Only the paradoxical understanding of original freedom can account for any single instance of duplicitous choice. Were it the case that most humans most of the time live authentically, one would still be required to give an account of human freedom on which humans can choose otherwise. Since this account requires the defect of the will that makes sin strictly universal, the supposed possibility of widespread or even exceptional human authenticity is no possibility at all. Hence, the logic is not empirical, in the sense that the doctrine of original sin must be true because human fault is empirically pervasive. To the contrary, human fault must be empirically pervasive because the mere possibility of wrong-doing means that the doctrine of original sin is true.

But if Niebuhr's account displays a profound insight, I also believe that his solution to the radical problem cannot be correct. If I have read him rightly, we are bound to say that his account is conceptually impossible. "Sin posits itself," in his sense, could only say that a human activity decides before it decides, and, since the prior decision was sinful, it posits another decision prior to itself, and the choice of a self-understanding becomes an infinite regress of duplicitous decisions. On this meaning, in other words, Niebuhr labors without success to distinguish between what is inevitable and what is necessary in human existence, so that his formula "responsibility despite inevitability" (p. 255) asserts the conceptual or logical contradiction that humans as such choose between alternatives one of which cannot be chosen. Calling the will's defect a "mystery" does nothing to change the matter, and his persistent reference to authentic faith as an "ideal possibility" rather than a real alternative characterizing "the situation of freedom and finiteness" (pp. 182–83) is simply an attempt to have it both ways.

Indeed, nothing more fully confirms that Niebuhr intends to say what I have read him as saying than his candid recognition that his account is self-contradictory. "It expresses a relation between fate and freedom which cannot be fully rationalized, unless the paradox be accepted as a rational understanding of the limits of rationality and as an expression of faith that a rationally irresolvable contradiction may point to a truth which logic cannot contain" (p. 262). He himself is immediately troubled by this conclusion. "Formally," he says, "there can be of course no conflict between logic and truth. The laws of logic are reason's guard against chaos in the realm of truth. They eliminate contradictory assertions" (pp. 262–63). When he then attempts to reconcile the conclusion with this affirmation of rational consistency, Niebuhr in effect throws up his hands: "There is no resource in logical rules to help us understand complex phenomena, exhibiting characteristics which *seem* to require that they be placed in contradictory categories of reason. Loyalty to all the facts may require a *provisional* defiance of logic, lest complexity in the facts of experience be denied for the sake of a *premature* logical consistency" (pp. 262–63, emphasis added). The implied assertion that his understanding of sin is a provisional or premature and, therefore, not final defiance of logic cannot be true unless the account finally is not the "rationally irresolvable contradiction" that, as Niebuhr concedes, it is.

Self-assertion

In contrast to Niebuhr, I believe that the radical problem can be given a theistic resolution without appeal to paradox or self-contradiction and, further, that he himself provides or at least suggests the resources with which to secure such an interpretation. These resources are found within his discussion of self-love as the duplicitous form of human existence. As is well-known, Niebuhr takes pride to be the primary form of sin, although he also identifies a secondary form, which he calls sensuality and treats as "a derivative of the more primal sin of self-love" (p. 233). There is, I think, something right about Niebuhr's focus on selfishness or self-centeredness, as I will try to show in the constructive formulation I offer. At the same time, there is something mistaken about his analysis of the forms of sin. Hence, a successful appropriation of it in order to resolve the radical problem requires that we first submit this analysis to a brief review.

Although "pride" is Niebuhr's principal term for the primary form of rebellion against God, he can also call it "self-assertion" (p. 201), "egotism" (p. 208), and "self-deification" (p. 200). In this form, as the last term underscores, duplicity centers the comprehensive telos in the self—at least in the sense that the capacities, achievements, and interests of the self as an individual are given an inordinate place in the evaluation of future possibilities. Humans are tempted by false interpretations of this form, Niebuhr explains, because they are both finite and free. Since humans are "capable in some sense of evisaging the whole" (p. 181), they are aware of their own finitude or fragmentariness, and this awareness provides, for Niebuhr, another way to characterize the anxiety that is universal to human existence. "Since . . . [a human] is involved in the contingencies and necessities of the natural process on the one hand and since, on the other, he stands outside of them and foresees their caprices and perils, he is anxious" (p. 251).

This formulation may appear to contradict Niebuhr's assertion, noted earlier, that "the situation of finiteness and freedom . . . becomes a source of temptation [and therefore anxiety] only when it is falsely interpreted" (p. 180). But the inconsistency disappears if one takes him to mean that awareness of our finitude is inevitably anxious because our bias toward sin is already implicated. Given the defect of our will, "the temptation to sin, . . . , lies in the human situation itself" (p. 251). Since the human situation is an awareness of one's limitations, the primary temptation is presented by prideful interpretations that appear to offer an escape from the "caprices and perils" of one's finitude (p. 251). But a person cannot seek this escape "without transgressing the limits which have been set for his life. Therefore, all human life is involved in the sin of seeking security at the expense of other life" (p. 182). In transgressing human limits, one rebels against God, and "the moral and social dimension" of this rebellion "is injustice" (p. 179).

Niebuhr's assertion that self-love is the primary form of sin has been heavily criticized.[6] On this criticism, injustice has victims as well as perpetrators, and, typically, the false interpretation tempting to the oppressed is not self-assertion. However lucid Niebuhr's analysis of it may be, pride is the duplicity characteristically found among those who dominate human communities or specific relationships. Niebuhr himself suggests this connection: "This proud pretension . . . rises to greater heights among those individuals and classes who have a more than ordinary degree of social power." Still, he holds that the same pretension "is present in an inchoate form in all human life" (pp. 188–89). To the contrary, some critics insist, submission to the inordinate self-assertion of others is not itself assertion but, rather, debasement of the self, and Niebuhr ignores the way in which oppressed individuals internalize the understandings that are suggested to them by their oppressors. Indeed, Niebuhr's one-sided account is pernicious, because it counsels those who devalue themselves to even greater self-sacrifice. So far as I know, feminist theologians, pursuing an account of sin consistent with insidious cultural and institutional distinctions between genders, have most forcefully articulated this indictment (see Plaskow).

A defense of Niebuhr might appeal to his discussion of sensuality as a derivative form of sin,[7] and some of his characterizations of this secondary form do seem strikingly similar to descriptions of self-abasement. Whereas pride is an individual's attempt "to hide his finiteness," sensuality is the attempt "to hide his freedom . . . by losing himself in some aspect of the world's vitalities" (p. 179), and this latter might easily be equated with the devaluation of the self as an individual. Or, again: "Sensuality is always: (1) an extension of self-love to the point where it defeats its own ends; (2) an effort to escape the prison house of self by finding a god in a process or person outside the self; and (3) finally an effort to escape from the confusion which sin has created into some form of subconscious existence" (p.

---

[6]I will not seek to review Niebuhr's analysis of the forms pride takes, the subtleties of their expression, and their violations of the harmony of creation (pp. 186–203). One can only admire the measure in which he there achieves an account "true to the psychological and moral facts in human wrong-doing" (p. 248).

[7]Although he does so with circumspection, Robin W. Lovin chooses this course in his appropriation of Niebuhr (see Lovin 1995: 139–51).

240). The dynamic here described seems to include in its second moment the kind of escape from freedom in which one becomes an accomplice in the self-deification of others and, thereby, debases the self.

Whatever reading might be given to citations such as these, however, it seems apparent that Niebuhr thinks about sensuality principally in terms of "the self's undue identification with and devotion to particular impulses and desires within the self . . . . , as expressed for instance in sexual license, gluttony, extravagance, drunkenness and abandonment to various forms of physical desire" (p. 228). The very choice of the term "sensuality" betrays this understanding, but so, too, does the fact that Niebuhr's detailed discussion attends precisely to the kinds of behavior patterns just mentioned. The escape from freedom "by losing . . . [oneself] in some aspect of the world's vitalities" (p. 179) refers principally to the vitalities of physical nature: "The self, finding itself to be inadequate as the centre of its existence, seeks for another god amidst the various forces, processes and impulses of nature over which it ostensibly presides" (p. 234).

Even if one seeks to supplement this treatment by including self-abasement as another form of "sensuality," a response to the criticism we have in view is burdened by Niebuhr's apparent insistence on the prior actualization of pride and, in this sense, the derivative character of sensuality. Only after an individual has sought security through self-assertion and finds "itself to be inadequate as the centre of its existence" does she or he seek to escape from freedom. There is first "an extension of self-love to the point where it defeats its own ends" (p. 240), and "sensuality represents a further confusion consequent upon the original confusion of substituting the self for God as the centre of existence. Man, having lost the true centre of his life, is no longer able to maintain his own will as the centre of himself" (p. 233). Perhaps this accounting is adequate to many individuals who willingly become trapped in the destructive pursuit of physical gratification, but it is doubtful that the self-abasing beliefs displayed by some victims of injustice illustrate the dynamic Niebuhr here describes.

To the contrary, there is every reason to think that some victims of oppressive institutions, especially when they are rationalized by long-standing cultural legitimations, were introduced to self-abasing interpretations at the earliest age and, in the relevant sense, have never chosen false interpretations other than these. Many women who debase themselves were taught as soon as they could distinguish themselves from males the subservient roles that a patriarchal society assigns to them, and, in United States history, many African Americans were taught the debasing social constructs of white supremacy as soon as they could ask and answer the question of their own social status. Not the discovery through pursuit of prideful ends that one's own existence is inadequate as the source of worth but, rather, the social and cultural context accounts for the persuasive power of self-abasing alternatives. In sum, the criticism to which we have been attending does seem to have merit. Niebuhr's conviction that pride is the primary form of duplicity may be the more persuasive by virtue of his capacity to expose the subtleties of inordinate self-assertion. But it remains that something has been lost in his formulation.[8]

But if, on the whole, Niebuhr's analysis fails to credit the distinction between self-assertion and self-abasement, the loss may not display simple oversight but, rather, indicate a more fundamental mistake. To all appearances, he reasons from the fact that finite self-consciousness

---

[8]It is the more surprising that Niebuhr's account of pride and sensuality misses self-abasing interpretations because his discussion of "group pride" or "collective egoism," to which we have already had occasion to refer, so clearly describes the effectiveness with which a nation or other social group presents itself "as the source and end of existence" (p. 211) and, thereby, "achieves a certain authority over the individual" (p. 208). Given the lucidity with which he describes how dominant "racial, national and socio-economic groups" (p. 209) rationalize their oppression of others within the community by pretending that current patterns of injustice serve universal values, one might expect Niebuhr to recognize that the authority of collective egoism requires the self-abasement of some.

Instead, he generalizes over all members of the community in saying that the pretension of the group is also "a pretension which the individual makes for himself" (p. 212) and, thereby, harmonizes his insights into group pride with his claim that pride is the primary form of individual sin. "Collective egoism does indeed offer the individual an opportunity to lose himself in a larger whole; but it also offers him possibilities for self-aggrandizement beside which mere individual pretensions are implausible and incredible" (p. 212). Notwithstanding that the ambiguity of both losing and aggrandizing the self may be present when any individual accepts the inordinate importance that a collective claims for itself, the dominating side of this ambiguity would seem to differ depending on whether the group's claim legitimates one's participation among the oppressors or the oppressed within the nation or group itself.

is aware of totality to the conclusion that sin asserts the self as the center of totality. "Capable in some sense of envisaging the whole" the self commits "the error of imagining himself the whole which he envisages" (p. 181) or deifies itself. But this reasoning implies that the two choices of faith open to the self are trust in God or trust in the self, and that formulation appears to identify the self independently of the larger world in which it is set.

There is, in other words, something individualistic about this aspect of Niebuhr's proposal, as if he forgets that an understanding of the self is always also an understanding of the world. "The self knows the world, insofar as it knows the world, because it stands outside both itself and the world, which means that it cannot understand itself [and therefore the world] except as it is understood from beyond itself and the world" (p. 14). The "primitive stage" of our discrimination, to recur to the words of Whitehead, is "the vague grasp of . . . a three-fold scheme, namely, The Whole, That Other, and This-My-Self" (1938: 150), and the same three-fold character of human existence is expressed in Niebuhr's account of "original righteousness" as "a harmony between the soul and God . . . , a harmony within the soul . . . , and a harmony between the self and the neighbor" (p. 286). Given the inseparability of the three, it follows that an inauthentic self-understanding is not necessarily a deification of the self but may be instead a deification of some part of the world, and it is this latter alternative that is illustrated by the acceptance of false interpretations on which one debases oneself for the sake of some unjust community or structure of relationships.

The basic form of sin, then, is simply duplicity, the raising of some false understanding of the comprehensive telos alongside the true source of worth or the divine purpose. The capacity to understand themselves forces humans "to relate their actions in the last resort to the totality of things conceived as a realm of meaning" (1942: 44), and this self-understanding is authentic only when the ground of worth as such is ultimate reality or is "beyond" the self and the world. Anything in the world that has a future is a potential competitor to God, so that the self is, in principle, only one of the idols that the self might choose. Accordingly, the rebellion against God need not be the "effort to usurp the place of God" (p. 179) oneself but may also be the inordinate affirmation of someone or something else, and the self-abasement of which humans are so apparently capable need not wait on a prior and finally unsuccessful attempt to secure one's worth through self-centeredness or self-assertion.

I will not pursue the reasons why, notwithstanding the "three-fold scheme" he elsewhere offers, Niebuhr's account becomes individualistic when he identifies the primary form of sin. It may suffice here simply to summarize my hunch that this turn is related to the doctrine of sin as strictly universal and, therefore, to his conception of an original defect of the will. That conception leads Niebuhr to believe that our bias toward sin must itself be a form of corruption that is universal to self-consciousness or finite freedom, and the most apparent candidate is the temptation "to protect . . . [one's own existence] against nature's contingencies" (p. 182) by accepting the lie that one is not limited. Even if we allow Niebuhr's doctrine of original sin, however, his detailed analysis of original freedom does not require that one's own existence be the duplicitous source of meaning. That analysis seeks to describe the decision in any given moment of an individual's life. In this moment, the defect in our original freedom accounts for only the attraction of a false interpretation and the inevitable decision for it. So far as I can see, then, this account includes no reason in principle why this defect must express itself in the specific false interpretation that defines one's own individual future as the source of worth. Even if it is inevitable, our duplicity means in principle only that we choose to affirm something or other in addition to God as the source of our worth, and this something might also be something other than one's own existence as an individual.

But if we should reject the individualism that seems to invade Niebuhr's understanding of sin, something seems right nonetheless about his focus on self-love. To all appearances, humans have an immense capacity for selfishness. This is why Niebuhr's acute analysis of pride can, at least for those of us who are not among the oppressed, seem to cover so much of human fault that we initially overlook its one-sidedness. Although not the "primary" form of sin, in Niebuhr's sense, self-centeredness is, I will assume, so widespread that it may be called a "principal" form of sin, meaning that the decision for false interpretations of this kind is especially prominent among the facts of human life. Accordingly, the nonparadoxical account of human duplicity we are seeking here must not only resolve the radical problem but also explain why sin so widely appears as an inordinately high evaluation or undue assertion of the self.

The Fragmentary Sense of Worth

Earlier, I expressed the judgment that Niebuhr's discussion of self-love itself provides resources for this nonparadoxical account. I can begin to clarify what I have in mind through attention to the following explanation of self-centeredness:

> Man knows more than the immediate natural situation in which he stands and he constantly seeks to understand his immediate situation in terms of a total situation. Yet he is unable to define the total situation without colouring his definition with finite perspectives drawn from his immediate situation. . . . Therefore man is tempted to deny the limited character of his knowledge, and the finiteness of his perspectives (p. 182).

The first sentence of this citation might be taken as a restatement that self-understanding and, therefore, any understanding at all includes an understanding of reality as such. But this reading becomes uncertain when one adds the second sentence. In the sense that one understands reality as such, all humans are able "to define the total human situation" as it is, that is, to know the character of worth as such—at least if we assume that the possibility of centering the self in God is generally revealed to human existence.[9] But Niebuhr says that humans cannot understand the total situation without "colouring" the definition "with finite perspectives." What, then, does he mean by defining "the total situation"?

We will be aided here, I believe, by attention to another citation, drawn from a discussion in which Niebuhr seeks to show how self-centeredness prevents obedience to the "law of love": "There is no simple possibility of . . . a perfect coherence of love so that the man in China or America would affirm the interests of the man in America or China as much as he affirms his own. The human imagination is too

[9]But see chapter 2, n. 10.

limited to see and understand the interests of the other as vividly as those of the self" (p. 296). This citation explicates the fragmentary character of our contingent existence by specifying that the extent to which we can understand or appreciate the specific possibilities of other individuals is far more limited than the extent to which we can imagine our own future activities. Humans typically remember their own past activities and anticipate their own future in a measure that dramatically exceeds the capacity of one individual to appreciate the activities of another. As we have seen, it is this fact that makes consistency of detailed human purpose possible for an individual in a measure quite beyond that possible for associations. When we need to do so, therefore, we "fill in the gaps" in our knowledge of other people by assuming that their fears, hopes, and satisfactions are concretely similar to our own. More generally, when we need to specify more concretely possibilities we can only know more abstractly, we imagine them in terms of situations we more fully appreciate.

We can now return to the first citation: A human is "unable to define the total situation without coloring his definition with finite perspectives drawn from his immediate situation" (p. 182). Given that defining "the total human situation" does not mean understanding the whole in its general or abstract character, the second citation suggests that this phrase designates a definition transcending the fragmentariness of human consciousness and reaching its completeness in a fully concrete appreciation of totality. In the latter, everything that is actual would be fully appreciated as actual, and all possibilities would be appreciated with whatever specificity and probability obtains. All things would enter consciousness with full vividness. In other words, an adequate definition of the total situation is one that only a divine individual could give. It follows that any human's approach to an understanding of totality in this sense could only "colour" the definition "with finite perspectives drawn from his immediate situation."

Given the contexts in which the two citations appear, Niebuhr's references to our fragmentary powers might be read as reassertions that self-centeredness is inevitable. Because we transcend any immediate situation, our exercise of freedom includes the "ideal possibility" of understanding ourselves solely in terms of worth as such; nonetheless, the limits on our understanding mean that the total situation will always be misunderstood in a manner that gives inordinate worth to the immediate context, including especially one's own future as an individual, since this is most fully appreciated.[10] But we seek here an account of

[10]In an earlier note, I mentioned the relation between Niebuhr's discussion of sin and his discussion of revelation, on which human consciousness as such knows the reality but not the character of God (see chapter 2, n. 2). So far as I can see, there is also a systematic relation between both discussions and the limitation on human understanding—although I am not sure of the measure in which this connection is one Niebuhr himself explicitly considered and asserted. To the best of my reading, Niebuhr's conception of "totality . . . as a realm of meaning" was controlled by the classical conception of God as perfection that is eternal or changeless in all respects. In other words, there is no divine character that could be known without knowing "the total situation" in the sense that only God can know it. Thus, the constitutively human or generally revealed knowledge of God can be only knowledge of God's "reality," and Niebuhr expresses the same point in saying: "From the standpoint of human thought this unconditioned ground of existence, this God, can be defined only negatively" (p. 14). It also follows that the exercise of original freedom could be authentic only if the present act could be completed by the very understanding of "the total situation" we cannot have. In other words, the limitation on our knowledge that "colours" our definition of the total situation *implies* a false or duplicitous understanding of totality as a realm of meaning. Sin is inevitable and, indeed, seems to be necessary.

Given that God can be defined only negatively, one might conclude that Niebuhr did not in fact endorse the assumption I made a moment ago, namely, that all humans know the comprehensive character of worth because the possibility of centering the self in God is generally revealed to human existence. This returns us to the paradox expressed in Niebuhr's designation of that alternative as an "ideal possibility." He must also hold that God *is* generally revealed, because we are responsible for our sin. The dubious distinction between God's reality and God's character that marks Niebuhr's discussion of revelation seems to be systematically related to the paradox of "responsibility despite inevitability"—and, if so, then the former as the latter is simply an attempt to have it both ways.

Some might say that this relation between Niebuhr's doctrine of sin and his understanding of revelation also implies that authenticity must be possible for those who receive knowledge of God's character through special revelation. But here Niebuhr is, in his own way, consistent. Positive knowledge of God can be received only through repentance and faith when original freedom is confronted by God's special self-disclosure, and the knowledge can be formulated only in paradoxical or mythical terms. Since those who receive it must still exercise their original freedom by choosing an understanding of totality, even they cannot be released from the inevitability of sin and, for Niebuhr, this is why the gospel of Jesus Christ proclaims not the possibility of authenticity but, rather, the reality of forgiveness. If something like this reading of Niebuhr's mind is correct, then the classical conception of God he inherited and, so far as I can see, never fundamentally questioned is implicated in all of his systematic theological discussions. It will become apparent in the next chapter that my own bearings are taken from a different conception.

original freedom that does not require the paradox of "responsibility despite inevitability," and I believe that the fragmentariness of human understanding, with its special capacity to anticipate one's own subsequent activities, can be the basis for a more adequate formulation.

It is essential to recall that understanding a possible reality or state of affairs, as all understanding, includes a sense or feeling of worth. "At the base of our existence is the 'sense of worth'" (Whitehead 1938: 149). Whether positive or negative, this sense is the more intense the more we can imagine or appreciate what the realization of that possibility will or would be. The mere thought that one might receive a yellow rose, in the sense that one conceives of "yellow" and "rose" as universals that might be exemplified, is one thing; imagining the color and fragrance one would experience as being similar to past experiences is something else—and, other considerations aside, makes the prospect more attractive. The mere thought that one could have a serious automobile accident is quite different from a vivid understanding of the trauma to oneself and others it would inflict, and, other considerations aside, the latter is more likely to prevent reckless driving. An eloquent and detailed portrayal of the debasement imposed by racism is typically more effective than more abstract descriptions in keeping those of us who practice it sensible of our complicity. As the last of these examples suggests, the difference all of them illustrate is similar in principle to a distinction between artistic expressions and philosophical or scientific thought; the former have, other considerations aside, a greater capacity to represent possibilities in a manner that attracts or repels.

Let us state the principal point by saying that our sense of worth is stronger or more intense the more concretely a possibility is appreciated. Were this not the case, seeking to realize some possibilities and to prevent the realization of others would be worthless, since realization is actualizing or making concrete what previously was only possible. Thus, alternatives for purpose that are positively evaluated may differ with respect to the intensity with which one senses their worth because one appreciates them concretely in differing measure. I may, for instance, affirm conceptually that my own satisfaction and that of my neighbor are equal in worth, but I may feel the worth of my own more intensely because, with Niebuhr, "the human imagination is too limited to see and understand the interests of the other as vividly as those of the self" (p. 295). Of this example, other considerations aside, it is proper to say that pursuit of my own satisfaction in a manner contrary to the equal worth of my neighbor has greater persuasive power than the affirmation of equality, and I am tempted to think that my own future is inherently more important.

But, now, every evaluation of alternatives for purpose implicates a chosen understanding of worth as such or the comprehensive purpose. If the greater concreteness with which I appreciate my own future tempts me to give it undue regard, then it must tempt me also to an inauthentic self-understanding. Since my decision for a comprehensive self-understanding is always an evaluation of specific alternatives for purpose, the sense of worth with which the latter are felt will be included in the persuasive power of authentic and inauthentic alternatives for self-understanding. This returns us to the radical problem Kant helped us to clarify: How could any false interpretation of ourselves be tempting if we know the comprehensive purpose? If original freedom always includes the "refined" feeling of God, how could this be moral freedom; that is, how could some other feeling tempt one to choose immorally, so that human authenticity is experienced as obligatory?

The answer is this: The positive sense of worth attached to the comprehensive purpose may not be significantly strong or, to say the same, our relation to God may not be accompanied by significant persuasive power. The true understanding of worth as such defines terms for evaluation that are indifferent to the measure in which we understand possible ends concretely. Thus, a duplicitous alternative for self-understanding may be tempting because, at some level of specificity, its evaluation of our alternatives for purpose is sensed more intensely than is the possibility of an authentic self-understanding. The point is illustrated most clearly, perhaps, when a duplicitous understanding of the comprehensive purpose tempts some person to a specific purpose that differs from her or his moral responsibility. For instance, I am tempted to a self-understanding expressed in selfish deception and manipulation of other people or complicity in larger structures of injustice because I sense more strongly the worth to be gained in my own future than the worth that will be sacrificed in the lives of those whom this choice mistreats.

But the principal point does not require that temptation directs us to an obviously different purpose than does the possibility of an authentic self-understanding. I may be morally required to assist my neighbor in some specific way and may still be tempted to do so. The greater sense of worth with which I appreciate certain future possibilities may still invade the understanding of worth as such that commends this specific purpose, so that I am tempted to choose it because, say, the recipient will be indebted to me, and I will benefit in the longer run. This is the reason for saying that a duplicitous self-understanding is tempting because we sense its evaluation more intensely "at some level of specificity." I have previously distinguished within an exercise of original freedom between the understanding of worth as such and its expression in a specific purpose. But, clearly, specific purposes can include various levels of specificity. One chooses to utter "the United States of America" in order to complete a political speech in order to help elect a given candidate in order to maximize the realization of justice, and the conception of justice implicates an understanding of worth as such. Thus, some more specific purpose in which a duplicitous alternative would be expressed may, at that level of specificity, coincide with the purpose that would express an authentic self-understanding, but the former diverges from the latter in some wider context. There, the evaluation is "coloured" by the differences with which possibilities are concretely appreciated. I assist my neighbor but do so for duplicitous reasons.

Some readers of the first section in *The Fundamental Principles of the Metaphysic of Morals* have concluded that, for Kant, the difference between a good will and one determined by inclination is a specific difference in action. For this reason, he has been criticized for believing that an action cannot be morally worthy if one wants to take it. In fact, however, Kant is at pains to insist that the point lies elsewhere. Although the difference at stake may well be exhibited in differing specific maxims, he does not deny that the call to duty and the lure of inclination may coincide. Rather, he asserts that action in accord with the moral law is not necessarily a good will. Even if the specific maxim remains the same, the all important distinction is between acting *from duty* and acting *because of* inclination. My intent here is analogous: The difference between authentic and inauthentic self-understanding is most clearly illustrated when the obvious specific purposes diverge, but the difference in self-understanding is independent of this divergence because it depends on the understanding of worth as such that is implicated in the choice.

Similarly, then, the principal point is entirely consistent with the statement that we do have special moral responsibility for individuals to whom we are closely related or associations in which we are participants—those individuals and associations (for instance, family members, friends, or local communities) whose future we can appreciate more concretely than we can others more distant from us. Assuming the validity of this moral statement, it remains one thing to affirm this responsibility because the comprehensive purpose is thereby specified to our particular situation, and something else to act in a similar way because we understand the individuals and associations we can appreciate more concretely as inherently more worthy. The difference will be the more apparent should a situation arise in which we ought to turn from or qualify our attention to close relationships in order to meet a responsibility to some larger community; the duplicitous alternative will then tempt us to a specific injustice.

In giving this account, we must recognize that our constitutive knowledge of the comprehensive purpose occurs with a sense of truth, so that the possibility of authentic self-understanding is always more persuasive in this respect: It is free from the negative sense of internal dissonance or self-contradiction—or, with Niebuhr, free from the anxiety—with which every inauthentic alternative is entertained. Still, this singular advantage may have to compete with the greater intensity that characterizes duplicitous possibilities by virtue of the greater concreteness with which their specific alternatives for purposes are, at some level of specificity, appreciated. In every case of temptation, then, our fragmentary capacity to sense the worth of future possibilities gives persuasive power to alternatives for self-understanding in which the future that we appreciate more concretely is given greater inherent worth. In contrast, human authenticity understands inherent worth solely in relation to the comprehensive purpose, and to that understanding the differences with which future possibilities are more or less concretely appreciated are irrelevant. For this reason, the comprehensive purpose may not be accompanied by significant persuasive power. Hence, there is nothing contradictory in saying that duplicitous alternatives are rivals to our knowledge of God. When this occurs, the "refined" feeling of God is in conflict with temptations to immorality, and the possibility of an authentic self-understanding may be experienced as an obligation.

With respect to this experience, we are, in significant respects, better guided by Aristotle than by Kant. I have in mind Aristotle's account of moral weakness. If he was taught by Plato's thought that knowledge is virtue, Aristotle could not accept this dictum without distinguishing between knowledge of the universal and knowledge of the particular. For him, good action follows deliberation that may be summarized in a practical syllogism, which has a universal or moral rule and a particular perception as its two premises. We can illustrate the point with the following example: "Avoiding substances harmful to the body is good" is the major premise and "this particular cigarette is a substance harmful to the body" the minor premise in deliberation leading to a refusal to smoke. If I understand Aristotle rightly, the morally weak person knows the universal and even desires conformity with it; but her or his passions are poorly habituated, and perception of the particular is controlled by another desire. In perceiving the cigarette, she or he understands it in terms of another universal or general opinion, for instance, "immediate pleasure is good," and, as a consequence, smokes. Notwithstanding the desire to act in accord with the moral rule, she or he voluntarily fails to do so, and the moral rule is, we can say, experienced as an obligation that is not met. In the morally strong person, the moral rule is also known as an obligation, with the difference being that this person successfully resists the temptation. Both types, then, should be distinguished from virtuous persons, whose passions are well habituated and who, therefore, desire only to act in conformity with what is truly good (see *Nicomachean Ethics*: Book VII).

I do not mean to imply that the larger setting in which Aristotle formulates this account accords fully with the analysis of human activity in the present work. On my reading, it is doubtful that the final cause of human action in Aristotle's mature account of practical science is a telos defined by reality as such. The only telos I can find, at least in his account of moral virtue, is a happy life itself. I doubt also, although this may finally come to the same thing, whether Aristotle's understanding of human action includes anything equivalent to what I have called the exercise of original freedom, in the sense that every human activity chooses an understanding of the final cause by which all human action is properly directed. If a similar conception is absent in Aristotle, this may explain why he can say of the morally weak person that she or he is overcome by passion or is in a condition similar to those "asleep, mad, or drunk" (1147a14). But we need not pursue these differences here. In the present context, the important consideration is Aristotle's account of the conflict between desires, so that one may be tempted to act against one's knowledge of the good.

I take this account to be instructive because it may be applied to the difference between knowing the comprehensive purpose, on the one hand, and appreciating more concretely one's more or less immediate context, on the other. Perception of the cigarette, to pursue the previous example, can tempt one to disobey the moral rule because, given the fragmentariness of human understanding, one's appreciation of the more immediate pleasure is more concrete and, therefore, the sense of worth attached to this possibility is more intense. Yielding to this temptation, one chooses to act in accord with a false universal. Similarly, the more concrete appreciation of the more immediate context can tempt one to think that its inherent importance is greater and to understand the character of worth as such accordingly.

Accounting for temptation in terms of human fragmentariness is, we should note, precisely what the analysis in chapter 1 recommends. It is the fragmentary character of our understanding, I there argued, that makes us fallible subjects, capable of affirming misrepresentations of actual and possible realities, including a misrepresentation of reality as such. Although we cannot fail to know the comprehensive purpose, we can be tempted to affirm a misrepresentation of it because this same fragmentariness shapes our sense of worth. Our existence is moral because our understanding is partial. Having clarified in this way how a lie to oneself is possible, we are in a position to argue on empirical grounds that duplicitous alternatives appear in our lives with impressive power. If we are prepared to credit, as an empirical generalization, anything like Niebuhr's judgment on the extent to which sin characterizes the human adventure, we have reason to believe that the tempting power of inauthentic self-understandings is in fact massive. Moreover, resolving the radical problem in terms of human fragmentariness also explains why duplicity so widely appears as self-centeredness or as the inordinate evaluation of the self. Just because a human individual typically anticipates her or his own future far more concretely than the future of any other individual, duplicitous possibilities for self-understanding in which special worth is attributed to one's own life as an individual are, other things being equal, likely to have the greatest persuasive power. For the same reason, we are often tempted to give greater inherent importance to our own more immediate futures than to the distant moments of our lives. Other things being equal, the near future can be more concretely understood.

At the same time, we can now fully credit the social character of temptation we discussed earlier, notwithstanding that it cannot, absent something more, account for duplicity. Individuals inherit from their own past and from the larger social context suggestions for purpose that are delivered with a sense of worth. Insofar as one appreciates more concretely the past from which these suggestions come, one reenacts the sense of worth more intensely. Given an individual's dramatically intimate relation to her or his own past, one's own past duplicity may have especially strong persuasive power. But something similar may be true of suggestions made by other individuals and groups that are especially important in one's life, of suggestions made with implicit or explicit threats that can be vividly imagined, and of purposes that are widely endorsed or institutionalized in one's culture or society. Human fault is socially self-reinforcing.

The social character of temptation will be the more effective if the suggestions one inherits commend alternatives already having the advantage derived from the individual's more vivid appreciation of her or his own future. If, for instance, other individuals whose examples I desire to follow, or patterns of activity institutionalized in my society, exemplify certain general forms of undue self-assertion, the temptation to my own similar self-assertion may be all the more persuasive. This suggests that the social character of temptation not only reinforces but also shapes the content of self-assertion—*what* it is about one's own future to which one is sorely tempted to give inordinate worth. Whether one is most attracted to maximizing one's sensual pleasure, financial status, prestige, participation in a privileged class, or domination over others may be due to the suggestive power of the cultural and social context. In other words, our singular capacity to appreciate our own futures more concretely is typically given a distinct character by learning experiences in which specific evaluations are attached to the vivid understanding of self.

But this means that negative evaluations of the self's future can also be learned. Self-abasement is a duplicitous self-understanding to which individuals are tempted because they have learned to attach a negative sense of worth to the future they most concretely appreciate. This evaluation acquires persuasive power because it has been taught through vivid experiences of condemnation by the culture or society and by important individuals in one's life. Still, I am inclined to think that Niebuhr's focus on self-love as the primary form of sin can be appropriated in this respect: The temptation to duplicity in which the self is inordinately important is the principal form of temptation in the sense that it does not itself have to be learned. Unless specifically prevented by learning, this temptation will appear because it is given with the fragmentariness of human understanding itself and the dramatic appreciation of one's own past and future that characterizes human individuality. The temptation to self-abasement, on the other hand, has to be taught. Humans do not attach a negative sense of worth to the vivid sense of their own possibilities without the false interpretations suggested by others, including their culture and society. But if self-assertion is, in this sense, the principal form of temptation, it is not the "more primal" in the sense that other forms are derivative and occur when "the self, . . . [finds] itself to be inadequate as the centre of its existence" (p. 234). Learning other forms of temptation may occur as soon as one begins to understand oneself.

In sum, we can account for the consistency between our inescapable knowledge of God and our temptations to sin and, at the same time, for the pervasiveness of human fault without recourse to a mysterious defect of the will. The fragmentariness and social character of human understanding are sufficient to offer a rational account of the "facts in human wrong-doing" (p. 248). To be sure, nothing that has been said *explains* those facts, if "explains" here means giving an account of wrong-doing that is independent of the exercise of freedom. What has been explained is temptation, but however powerful may be the persuasion attached to false interpretations, no human activity is inauthentic unless it chooses a duplicitous self-understanding and, therefore, is responsible for its fault. Temptation is one thing, and the choice to sin is another. In *this* sense, one might say that there is "mystery" in the fact of sin. But there is no need to say, with Niebuhr, that a human "could not be tempted if he had not already sinned" (p. 251). We can agree that "the temptation to sin lies, . . . , in the human situation itself" (p. 251), but this fact does not itself require that a "prior sin of unbelief" already corrupts the awareness of ourselves, and therefore we have no need to assert that sin is strictly universal or inevitable. To the contrary, temptation has been explained without contradicting the original freedom of distinctively human existence and, therefore, without denying the choice between authenticity and duplicity. Because relation to God is a necessary condition of human existence, the possibility of an authentic self-understanding is always a real one, and in duplicity the self always tells a lie to itself.

In so understanding our freedom to contradict ourselves, we should recognize that the social character of persuasive power may also be used to weaken temptation. As the highest universal in an Aristotelian practical syllogism, the character of worth as such cannot, absent other considerations, have the persuasive power attaching to understandings favored by our fragmentary powers of appreciation. But learning may add other considerations. This possibility defines the proper function of religion in human life. Because our decision for a comprehensive self-understanding cannot be explicit, we humans may seek to influence our own original decisions through specific activities that are designed to increase the persuasive power of the authentic alternative. In these activities, we focus attention on concepts and symbols that present explicitly an understanding of human authenticity as such, thereby seeking to influence our implicit decisions.

As is well known, religious expressions tend to assume a highly figurative form, including symbolic actions, as in narrative or myth or ritual. In this respect, they are similar to artistic expressions, and that is because they have a similar function, namely, to represent possibilities in a manner that heightens our sensibility. Specifically religious expressions seek to focus attention on an understanding of the comprehensive purpose and to do so through a concrete experience sufficiently vivid to intensify the sense of worth with which the possibility of an authentic self-understanding is entertained. The point is, then, that this intensified sense of worth should be implicitly remembered in the other activities of life, and the power of temptation should be thereby weakened. I do not mean to deny that religious expressions also teach understandings. Were this not the case, religious practitioners would not know what understanding of reality and purpose as such is figuratively presented. Moreover, the teaching can also be for its own sake. Clear and focused affirmation of an understanding can itself heighten the sense of worth with which one relates to it. In this sense, Kant is right in saying that reason can motivate or determine the will, although, against Kant, reason does so by intensifying the desire or sense of worth without which we could not be human at all, namely, the desire for the comprehensive telos. In a typically incisive formulation, Whitehead writes that "religion should connect the rational generality of philosophy with the emotions and purposes springing out of existence in a particular society, in a particular epoch, and conditioned by particular antecedents" (1978: 15).

Whether religious activity does weaken temptation depends in part on whether its understanding of human authenticity as such is true, and it is always possible for practitioners of a particular religion to doubt the understanding whose persuasive power that religion seeks to intensify. But address to that doubt is, I think, properly distinguished from the function of religious activity itself. The latter does not question the truth of what is represented but, rather, seeks to influence the exercise of original freedom, and to ask about the validity of that influence is to engage in explicit reflection of another order, sometimes called theological or philosophical. For this reason, Ogden defines religion as "the *primary* form of culture in terms of which we human beings explicitly ask and answer" (1992: 5, emphasis added) the question of human authenticity as such. "Primary" identifies the function of religion in distinction from asking and answering that question in order to assess whether a given answer is true.

For all that, some will now object that this account of temptation and the religious response to it still fails to redeem a theistic conception of original freedom—at least if theism is now used to mean the affirmation of a divine individual that is the source and end of all things. On this objection, appeal to the fragmentary character of human understanding and, therefore, the correlation of persuasive power with concrete appreciation avoids mystery only by making God the author of temptation. Since fragmentariness is a necessary feature of human existence and the God of theism is the creator of the world, the temptation to sin must be God's own doing. We may recall that, for Niebuhr, temptation is a "force of evil" because false interpretations of our situation are thereby commended. If not responsible for duplicity, God is nonetheless responsible for the evil of temptation, and this alone compromises the perfection that theists also attribute to the divine.

Whatever force this objection may appear to have derives solely from the assumption that divine perfection implies the power to create individuals whose understanding is not fragmentary. That this assumption is at least suspect has already been suggested in noting that a nonfragmentary relation to all things is something only a divine individual could have. Given that conclusion, human understanding that is not fragmentary is not possible, and the indictment of theism is unconvincing. If we mean by an evil force an evil for which one can assign responsibility, then temptation is properly considered a "force of evil" only insofar as it displays a social character, that is, occurs as a consequence of duplicity in the human past. But the fact that temptation can occur at all only because humans are fragmentarily self-conscious individuals cannot itself be an evil in the relevant sense. If theism is true, our condition in this respect is an expression of the metaphysical fact that there can be only one God. In any event, what metaphysical understanding of reality is implicit in all human activity and, therefore, in what human authenticity consists are the questions to which I now turn.

3

The Good We Should Pursue

In the previous chapters, the exercise of original freedom has been defined as the decision for an understanding of oneself in relation to the ground of worth as such or the comprehensive purpose. Authentic and duplicitous existence are, we can say, the two possible ways of being human. But the analysis of distinctively human activity has not yet clarified the normative exercise of our original freedom because we have not addressed explicitly the substantive question about worth as such: What is the content of the comprehensive purpose? Throughout the previous discussion, moreover, we have used the term "God" to designate ultimate reality as the ground of worth. On this usage, God alone authorizes human authenticity, and the substantive question about self-understanding may be formulated: What is our authentic relation to God? In postponing this question, we have also explicitly begged heretofore the question of theism: Is God a supreme being or individual that is the primal source and final end of all realities? In this chapter, I will seek to answer the question of theism through an address to the normative question about our original freedom.

To be sure, even theists may and do disagree among themselves about the substantive character of worth and thus human authenticity because they have differing conceptions of the divine individual. But the two questions are clearly inseparable. If ultimate reality as the ground of worth is a supreme being or individual, its nature or character must imply and be implied by the substantive character of worth, precisely because both are coextensive with worth as such. Chapter 1 argued that the comprehensive telos must be the maximal realization of reality as such or the character common to all realities, and therefore worth as such must be a variable that realities or states of affairs exemplify in greater or lesser measure. Summarily stated, then, the argument for theism is this: The variable of worth as such is exemplified in a multiplicity of actualizations, and maximizing the worth of this multiplicity implies its unification by or in a supreme individual. Thus, the comprehensive purpose must be defined by the nature or distinguishing character of a comprehensive individual whose own activities include without loss every actualization. This argument, of course, begs for extended clarification, both of its terms and its logic. I will return to the logic of theism later in this chapter. I propose first to clarify the terms in which the character of God may be formulated through asking about the substantive character of worth as such and its implications for the character of human authenticity.

Because worth is defined by reality as such, a clarification of its substantive character requires a metaphysical discussion. On my intent, this statement is tautological, because "metaphysics," as here designating a kind of critical thought, means the process or product of theoretical reflection about reality as such. I recognize that the term is also used with other meanings. In the present context, the most important alternative derives from Kant, for whom the object of "metaphysics" is solely the a priori character of human reason or subjectivity. This usage is, for Kant, proper to "any future metaphysics" because, as we have noted previously, he denies that humans can know things-in-themselves. On his account, the long Western pursuit of knowledge about reality as such, beginning in classical Greece and continuing into his own time, cannot be fulfilled. Even if we do not follow Kant in that denial, we can still allow that "metaphysics" may designate reflection on the universal character of human subjectivity as well as the character of reality as such. Indeed, the analysis I have given counsels us to appropriate Kant's meaning within a systematically ambiguous use of the term. The character of human subjectivity as such includes but is not exhausted by the character of reality as such, since a human activity cannot understand itself except in relation to a comprehensive purpose and thus as an exemplification of the character common to all possible realities. "Metaphysics," then, has both a broad and a strict sense, with the former (reflection on human subjectivity as such) including the latter (reflection on reality as such), and it is this systematically ambiguous meaning of the term that I earlier endorsed in commending Iris Murdoch's phrase "metaphysics as a guide to morals." For the sake of clarity, however, I will in this chapter confine "metaphysics" to its strict sense, so that the object of metaphysical reflection is reality as such.

This chapter begins, then, with the character of reality as such that, so far as I can see, is implied by our distinctively human existence and thus defines the comprehensive purpose, and the chapter will conclude with the argument for theism. Anything approaching a more or less complete metaphysical statement is beyond my scope. But I also believe that something significantly short of this will be sufficient to clarify the basis for a substantive account of worth and its theistic implications.

Metaphysics

Chapter 1 argued that life with understanding includes self-understanding because a human activity determines itself by conscious choice. Self-understanding, then, discriminates the actual realities by which the self is other-determined from the possible realities that it will other-determine. Were there no other realities by which one is determined, there would be no self consciously to complete; were there no other realities to be determined, there could be no completion. Life with understanding, in other words, discriminates the past from the future by discriminating itself as the present. Each human activity "arises as an effect facing its past and ends as a cause facing its future" (Whitehead 1961: 194) and does so with understanding. Its past is what is actual; its future is what is possible, the actualization of which will be in part determined by present decision. The self that is understood can be nothing other than the decision completing what begins as an effect of the past by the pursuit of some future.

Life with understanding is or includes, then, an immediate awareness of time. So experienced, however, time is not properly conceived as an infinitely divisible continuum in which the "moving present" is always an instant without internal relation to past or future. Time as so conceived appears to be illustrated by the phenomenal qualities of which we are conscious in our ordinary sense experience of the external world, that is, the "sense data" that Hume took to be the primary objects of human experience. Against Hume, however, consciousness of sense data is an abstraction from an act of subjectivity that is really related to the past of which it is an effect and to the future into which it projects itself—because all other understandings are aspects of the decision for a self-understanding. Hence, the time of which we are immediately aware is this present that is inclusive of its prior causes and its telos.[1]

Given the temporal character of distinctively human activity, the character of reality as such must permit at least some actualizations to be constituted by relations to both past and future. Since it cannot exclude any possible reality, this character cannot contradict the fact that human activities are temporal. It now follows, I believe, that temporality must be a characteristic of *all* possible realities. The only metaphysical alternatives are (1) reality as such is nontemporal, and (2) reality as such includes both temporal and nontemporal specifications. The first of these alternatives implies that all possible realities are nontemporal and, therefore, contradicts the temporality of human activity. It is true that the common character of all possible realities is, in one sense, nontemporal. As the universal of universals, this character is not itself constituted by relations to past and future; to the contrary, it remains the same throughout all time. But the relevant point here is that this universal is the common character of all possible realities, and these exemplifications of it cannot all be nontemporal.

But perhaps some possible realities are nontemporal, because being temporal and being nontemporal are specifications of reality as such, so that the latter is characterized by the disjunction "temporal or nontemporal reality." But this alternative is also inconsistent with the

---

[1]For Whitehead, this distinction between the actual occurrence of time of which we are immediately aware and time as an abstracted continuum appropriate to the phenomenal data of ordinary sense experience is implied in the difference and relation between "causal efficacy" and "presentational immediacy" (see 1955; see also chapter 3, n. 6 below).

temporal character of self-understanding. Because a human activity's discrimination of itself as the present is its inclusive understanding, any other reality the self understands must be discriminated in terms of the difference between the actual past of which the present is an effect, and the merely possible future of which the present will be a cause. But a nontemporal reality could not be past or future or, to say the same, the difference would have to be indifferent to it; hence, it could not be discriminated in terms of this difference. The notion of a nontemporal reality suggests that one might pursue what is already realized or, alternatively, one might be an effect of something yet to be determined—and the disjunction "temporal or nontemporal *reality*" is senseless.

To be sure, some realities we understand have both a past and a future. For instance, we understand people and institutions as well as various other realities in the world that have existed and will or probably will continue to exist. But these are not nontemporal realities. To the contrary, each has an actual past and has or probably has a future that is at present only possible because it remains to be actualized in some way or other. In this sense, such a reality exemplifies temporality throughout its existence, just as each of us as a human individual exemplifies temporality throughout the series of activities in which her or his life consists. A nontemporal reality would be one that is in no way characterized by the difference between an actual past and a possible future, and this is the putative description that is senseless.

I recognize that this conclusion contradicts the dominant form of theistic metaphysics in Western history, for which the divine reality is a nontemporal reality because it is in all respects eternal. It is telling, however, that this metaphysical tradition has also typically allowed an understanding of God in literal terms only if they are completely negative. Thomas Aquinas, who holds that God's existence can be demonstrated by arguments from God's created effects, says that the knowledge thereby acquired is solely negative.

For by means of a demonstration many things are removed from Him, so that in consequence we understand Him as something apart from other things. . . . Now we arrive at the proper knowledge of a thing not only by affirmations but also by negations. . . . Yet there is this difference between these two modes of proper knowledge, that when we have proper knowledge of a thing by affirmations we know what that thing is, and how it is distinguished from others; whereas when we have proper knowledge of a thing by negations, we know that it is distinct from others, but remain ignorant of what it is. Such is the proper knowledge of God that can be obtained by demonstrations (*Summa Contra Gentiles*: 3. 39).

In its analysis of understanding, chapter 1 argued that a completely negative designation cannot in truth be understood. This is because the understanding of something proceeds by way of contrast with all other possible objects of understanding, and a solely negative designation adds nothing to a contrast. Summarily stated, a putative object of thought whose designation is completely negative cannot be distinguished from a putative object that is in truth no object at all, because both are completely negative. If this is so, the traditional insistence that God can be literally or univocally designated only in negative terms is a theistic affirmation that cannot be understood. On my reading, similar reasoning leads Kant to the view that all theistic arguments must fail. If conclusions are completely negative, what is the difference between demonstrating the existence of God and demonstrating nothing at all? Kant does also say that God can be conceived as a reality whose existence cannot be known. But that follows because he posits the distinction between phenomenal and noumenal things, and the same reasoning that makes knowledge of this God impossible also discredits the distinction.

To be sure, the citation from Aquinas asserts that something is being designated "by negations"; hence, "we know that it is distinct from others, but remain ignorant of what it is." On my reading, this is because Aquinas also holds that positive but nonunivocal theistic predications are possible; that is, we can also speak of God analogically. Adequate attention to his conception of a nontemporal reality would surely require an extended critical discussion of his distinction between univocal and analogical predication. So far as I can see, however, his use of theistic analogies assumes that there is a nontemporal reality to be characterized and, therefore, depends philosophically on successful demonstration of God's existence, while, at the same time, the proofs cannot successfully conclude that something is designated by negation without assuming that analogy can identify what God is. This logical circle becomes apparent when Aquinas asserts, as I think he must, that the positive term "being," with which God is designated as something, is predicated of God analogically (*Summa Theologica*: 1. 13. 5). But I will not pursue the discussion with Aquinas or with the classical theistic tradition he supremely represents. Because the notion of a nontemporal reality is inconsistent with the temporal character of self-understanding, I am convinced that this putative idea cannot be understood, and this is equivalent to saying that it is completely negative. The divine reality whose existence this chapter will seek subsequently to demonstrate is not defined by that notion. As I will try to clarify, God is properly conceived as the eminently temporal individual.

The argument for temporality as a characteristic of all possible realities helps to distinguish their characteristics generally. A feature of things characterizes all possible realities if (1) it is exemplified in some of them, and (2) a supposed reality in which the feature is absent is solely negative; that is, the supposed reality could not be an object of understanding. Temporality, for instance, is a metaphysical characteristic because it is exemplified in human activities and "nontemporal reality" designates a supposed reality that is solely negative. We can also say that a feature is metaphysical if it is exemplified in some reality and its supposed absence does not imply the presence of some other feature. If the *non*exemplification of x does not imply the exemplification of some y, then "not-x" could designate a solely negative reality. Thus, for instance, temporality is a metaphysical feature because the supposed absence of temporality does not imply the presence of any other feature, as Aquinas concedes in saying that the existence of a nontemporal reality is univocally known without positive designation. All sensible negations, in other words, are partially positive. To deny the existence of a yellow rose in one's path, for instance, is to imply that one's path is completely occupied by the existence of other things all of which have features inconsistent with being a yellow rose. Were this not the case, "not a yellow rose" could designate a solely negative reality (see Hartshorne 1970: 159–60).

The recognition that all negations must be partially positive confirms that all realities must exemplify some common character or characteristics. The negation of some feature cannot imply the presence of some other feature unless both features have something in common. To say of something, for instance, that it is not a human cannot imply that it is either something else in the world or something transcendent to the world unless all of these things exemplify something commonly. If the presence of something were implied by denying *all* the features of something else, then what is present could be designated solely by negation and would be a solely negative reality. We may conclude, in other words, that metaphysical dualism is impossible. "Dualistic metaphysics," as I intend the term, asserts that there is no character common to all possible realities. In other words, there are said to be two (or more) metaphysically different kinds of realities, in the sense that designation of one is achieved by completely negating the other (or others). In this sense, some disjunction of the form "x or *not-x*" is said to define realities metaphysically.

As an illustration of metaphysical dualism, take the assertion that all realities are either mental or nonmental, where this means that mental and nonmental realities have no common character. "Nonmental reality" is, then, a solely negative object of thought, that is, an object whose putative designation is achieved by completely negating mentality. Nor does it help to say that nonmental realities are material in character. "Material" cannot have any positive content if it is equivalent to the complete negation of "mental." Some might object that this argument begs the question, because the dualism criticized asserts that both "mental" and "material" have positive content, notwithstanding that they have nothing in common. But this assertion implies that one can think something positive by thinking the complete negation of something else, and that implication contradicts the fact that a completely negative object of understanding cannot be distinguished from a putative object that is in fact no object at all. In other words, "absolute difference" is not a genuine concept, precisely because it equates a complete negation with a positive object of thought. This is not to say that a disjunction between mental and nonmental cannot be sensible. The point is simply that it cannot be metaphysical but, rather, must be, like the disjunction between human and nonhuman, a distinction between realities that have something in common.[2]

In any event, dualism contradicts the comprehensive understanding of worth with which every human activity understands itself. "Worth," I have argued, must be a variable in terms of which all possible realities may be compared, because choice with understanding implies a comprehensive purpose in terms of which specific alternatives for purpose are evaluated. Because it is comparative, reality as such must be a character common to all realities. To this, it might be said that "worth" may have more than one metaphysical meaning, such that metaphysical evaluation does not necessarily require a single principle. Perhaps, as some moral theories have proposed, the foundation of the moral enterprise consists in two or more principles that cannot be understood as specifications of a more general one. But this proposal makes no sense because the comprehensive purpose is implicated in understanding oneself as a choice. Two or more metaphysical principles of purpose would require that the activity choose between or among them, and *that* choice could not be understood except in terms of a variable common to them.[3]

Because there must be a character common to all possible realities, there is one fundamental kind of reality. To first appearances, this

[2]The conceptual problem in dualism can also be also be disclosed by noting that, in the absence of a common metaphysical character, "all possible realities" might, absurdly, exclude some possible reality. Thus, for instance, theistic metaphysics on which God is a nontemporal reality are dualistic, because nontemporal and temporal realities have no common character. But, then, it might be the case that all possible realities are in fact temporal or, alternatively, nontemporal. In other words, the character of all possible realities might in fact exclude some possible reality or realities. For this reason, so far as I can see, classical theism cannot show why a temporal world requires a God who is in all respects eternal or show, without paradox, how a God who is in all respects eternal could create a temporal world. Of course, one can say that, as it happens, the character of all possible realities is given by the disjunction "temporal or nontemporal." But this character cannot just *happen* to be of one sort rather than another; what just happens to be the case realizes one among alternative possibilities, and the character of all possible realities must include the alternatives. Thus, classical theism implies that the character of all possible realities as temporal or nontemporal itself includes the possibility that this very character is solely temporal or solely nontemporal.

[3]For this reason, so far as I can see, classical theism cannot show without paradox how the choice between mystical union with or contemplation of the divine, on the one hand, and commitment to the affairs of this world, on the other, is properly evaluated.

conclusion may seem counterintuitive. The objects of our experience—inorganic things, plants, nonhuman and human animals—seem to be radically different and implausibly understood as instances of a single kind of thing. But this objection misunderstands the metaphysical task by assuming that the realities most commonly or obviously discriminated in our understanding are themselves metaphysically fundamental. Whether this assumption is true is precisely the question at issue, and one alternative answer is that the realities most commonly or obviously discriminated are composites or aggregates of other things that are fundamental. To be sure, this answer is bound to account for the fact that the fundamental things are not obvious. But this account can be framed in terms of the fragmentary power of consciousness. At least in our explicit consciousness, we typically discriminate composites because, with the possible exception of rare moments, our capacity to focus depends on this simplification.

I will use the term "actuality" to designate a member of this fundamental class of things. All actualities are realities; that is, the former, as the latter, are things that exemplify characteristics. But all realities are not actualities, since realities may also be composites or aggregates of the latter. An alternative for purpose, for instance, may be understood as a possible reality or state of affairs, although its realization would be the realization of many actualities. Heretofore, "reality as such" has meant the character common to all possible realities, or all possible realities themselves in the respect that they exemplify this character. Given that some realities are composites or aggregates, it is now important to refine this formulation. Metaphysical characteristics, strictly speaking, are those that define actualities as such, and these features are also common to all other realities in the sense that metaphysical characteristics must be exemplified by each of the member activities in a composite or aggregate.[4] Thus, we may

---

[4]Strictly speaking, I believe, actualities alone exemplify characteristics, and other realities do so only in a sense that is reducible to exemplification by their member actualities. This is true even when the characteristic exemplified is "being a composite" or "being an aggregate." If we say, for instance, that some multiplicity of actualities (for instance, those constituting a stone) together exemplify "being a composite," we mean that each of the member actualities exemplifies relations to the others that distinguish the composite (for instance, "being determined by other members of the stone in the respects that distinguish the stone").

henceforth understand "reality as such" to mean the character of a set of characteristics common to all possible actualities, or all possible actualities themselves in the respect that they exemplify this character, and the metaphysical attempt to define reality as such is also the attempt to define what an actuality is.

That the obvious things of our experience are composites is a commonplace of modern natural science, where, for instance, physics attends to atomic or subatomic particles and biology attends to cellular organisms. But it does not follow that we should look to the natural sciences in order to identify actualities. Each of the natural sciences has its own purpose, and in no case does the science aim at knowing the character of all possible realities. Roughly speaking, each science seeks to understand realities in some or other respect that will allow prediction, that is, to understand the regularities among those realities such that, given knowledge of particular past conditions in the relevant respect, the future can be in the same respect accurately anticipated. But we already have reason to believe that this kind of purpose cannot be metaphysically adequate, since human activities are realities, and the respects in which any human activity can be predicted exclude its distinctive choice of a self-understanding.

What does seem apparent is that each human activity must be an actuality, because it cannot be a composite. To be sure, I have said repeatedly that a human activity is composed of relations to other realities, both to actual realities of the past and to possible realities of the future. Still, it cannot be composite in the sense that it can be decomposed into two or more instances of some more fundamental kind of reality. This is precisely because a human activity completes itself by choosing among alternatives for self-understanding. A decision is singular and, therefore, determines a human activity as an irreducibly single thing. For this reason, metaphysics may seek to define the common character of all actualities by asking about the implications of distinctively human activity, as in fact we have already done in arguing that temporality is a characteristic of reality as such.

If we say that some multiplicity of actualities (for instance, all human activities of contemporary American individuals) together exemplify "being an aggregate," we mean that each of the actualities aggregated exemplifies some characteristic that distinguishes the aggregate (for instance, "being an activity of a contemporary American individual").

Clearly, the metaphysical status of temporality does not imply that all actualities understand themselves. So far as we know, the choice of a self-understanding is limited to humans (and, perhaps, some other higher animals). But if metaphysical generality abstracts from the capacity to understand, the same cannot be said of the relations to past and future, because, without these, temporality itself would be lost. Every actuality, in other words, must share with human activity relations to past actualities by which it is determined and a relation to the future that it will help to determine, even if only human activities have these relations with understanding. Since the future is, by definition, indeterminate in some measure, it follows that no actuality can be completely determined by other things. Its relation to the future requires some measure, however small or trivial, of self-determination. We should underscore that this self-determination is not self-conscious freedom. But if temporality is metaphysical, then so too is freedom. Unlike "nonconscious actuality," in other words, "nonfree actuality" is solely negative, and the metaphysical disjunction "free or nonfree actuality" is dualistic.

All of this supports the conclusion that actualities are properly understood as activities, each of which, when it occurs, becomes a single thing through a decision that completes its relations to past actualities as a condition that will affect actualization in the future. In so formulating the point, I intend that the term "activity" have a general or metaphysical designation, in contrast to its previous use to designate a human activity. On this metaphysical use, an activity is the completion of the present as a condition of the future by self-determination. Accordingly, we can also use the term "decision" in a metaphysical sense to designate self-determination and "purpose" in a metaphysical sense to designate this decision as a relation to the future. A human activity is, then, a specific kind of metaphysical activity, namely, one in which the decision that occurs is for a self-understanding and thus for a purpose that is understood. Because activities are metaphysically fundamental, all other realities are actual or possible composites or aggregates of activities. For instance, a human individual is a temporally ordered series of activities, all of which share some characteristic or set of characteristics that distinguishes that individual from any other and each of which (subsequent to the first) inherits that characteristic or set of characteristics through real relations to past member activities of the individual in question. A human being is a human individual together with its human body, which is itself an immensely complex composite of activities.

So far as I can see, then, the fact that reality includes individuals such as ourselves, who live with understanding and, therefore, ask about reality as such implies that our best guide in metaphysical reflection is the metaphysics of activities that has been most comprehensively developed by Whitehead and Hartshorne. Whitehead calls actualities "the final real things" (1978: 18), and Hartshorne calls them "concrete actualities" (1970: 172).[5] For both, these are momentary activities, each of which "arises as an effect facing its past and ends as a cause facing its future" (Whitehead 1961: 194).[6] The realities that each of us understands in understanding anything at all consist entirely in such activities or such possible activities, some of which are our own activities, and the entire cosmos is the summary adventure of the temporal process constituted by them.

On my reckoning, the most challenging conceptual objection to this metaphysics is formulated or implied in Kant's first antinomy. Because each final real thing arises from the past and ends in the future, there can be no beginning or ending to time. But Kant, on one side of his first antinomy, argues that an infinite past is impossible. To be sure, this is not an argument for a finite past. Each of Kant's antinomies is meant to show that we cannot know reality as such, so that all metaphysics is challenged by them. On one side,

---

[5]Whitehead's use of the term "real thing" is not identical to my use of "reality" because he includes characteristics or universals among "real things." Hartshorne's "concrete actualities" implies a use of "actuality" that is broader than my use of the latter term, such that his use would include composites. But what "final real thing" means for Whitehead and "concrete actuality" means for Hartshorne is what I mean by "actuality" or "activity."

[6]This formulation, as any equivalent description, implies the priority of an actuality's relations to the past and the posteriority of its relations to the future. An actuality cannot complete what was not previously begun. In turn, this priority and posteriority seem to imply a temporal passage *within* an actuality, and this apparent implication is the grounds for a criticism of a metaphysics of activities: Temporal passage internal to the actuality would mean that some of it is past before it is completed, and this contradicts the assertion that a decision in which actualization occurs is the present. On the account of actualization that has been given, in other words, time consists in the succession of actualities, and, if there is temporal passage internal to any one, the singularity of a final real thing

then, the first antinomy purports to refute Aristotle, who held that the world had no beginning. On the other side, this antinomy is an argument against any theistic metaphysics on which the past is not infinite. Aquinas, for instance, said that reason can neither prove nor disprove Aristotle's assertion, but Aquinas also believed as a revealed truth that God created time as finite. A limited or finite past, Kant argues, is also impossible because, summarily stated, a beginning implies a prior moment, and therefore a beginning to time implies a prior time. In this discussion, a metaphysics of activities rejects the creation of time and reasserts Aristotle's conviction. Hence, it is Kant's supposed disproof of a limitless past that is the pertinent challenge here.

The past cannot be infinite, Kant argues, because an infinite series cannot be completed; were the past not finite, the present could not be reached. "The true transcendental concept of infinitude is this, that the successive synthesis of units required for the enumeration of a quantum can never be completed. Hence it follows with complete certainty that an eternity of actual successive states leading up to a given (the present) moment cannot have elapsed" (1965: 401). Given that a finite past is also impossible, Kant concludes that the question answered by metaphysical understandings of time is not a sensible one because it asks about the character of things-in-themselves. Time, like

---

is denied. It will not help, the criticism continues, to suggest that the priority and posteriority internal to an actuality is logical rather than temporal in character. Logical priority and posteriority is nontemporal, and a succession of actualities characterized by this kind of beginning and ending could not constitute time. A metaphysics of activities, as Whitehead argues at length, must understand an actuality as both extended and indivisible, so that time itself passes in atomic units of finite duration (see 1978: 65–70). But, the criticism concludes, it follows that this metaphysics cannot make sense of the priority and posteriority internal to an actuality.

Although this is a significant criticism to which I cannot respond at length, I do not find it convincing because it assumes that temporal and logical priority and posteriority are the only two kinds and, moreover, does not clarify the relation between these two. A metaphysics of activities may assert that the priority and posteriority internal to an actuality is the metaphysically fundamental or concrete kind, such that the other two are abstractions from it. Temporal priority and posteriority abstract the difference between predecessors and successors from the decision that actualizes, and logical priority and posteriority abstracts certain relations between characteristics that are exemplified from the unification in which exemplification occurs.

space, can only be a form of human sensibility, characterizing things-as-they-appear, and metaphysical knowledge is impossible.

But there is good reason to doubt that Kant's solution escapes the antinomy that is said to require it. G. E. Moore argues convincingly that Kant's arguments, if they prove anything, prove that two hypotheticals are false: "(1) *If* the world exists in time at all, then it must have had a beginning; and (2) *If* the world exists in time at all, then it can have had no beginning" (1953: 166). Both are false because both a finite and an infinite past are, on the argument, impossible—and this is why the two alternatives must be stated as hypotheticals. Thus, if Kant proves anything, he proves that nothing can exist in time. From this it does not follow, Moore continues, that appearances exist in time. That inference confuses "whatever *does* exist in Time is a mere appearance," that is, what is understood to exist in time is an appearance, with "things only *appear* to exist in Time, and . . . nothing really does so," that is, what is understood to exist in time is misunderstood (1953: 171). Assuming that Kant proves something, it cannot be the case that appearances have the characteristic of being in time or that time is a form of human sensibility, because Kant proves that the notion of time is senseless. We can make the same point this way: If nothing can exist in time, we cannot coherently assert that what exists *must* appear to exist in time—because appearances are understood, and it cannot be the case that human understanding must be senseless.

Moreover, there is every reason to reject the conclusion that nothing can exist in time. Whatever may be impossible, this cannot be said of an activity that understands itself, since any understanding as such implies self-understanding. But self-understanding is a discrimination of the present. Far clearer than Kant's disproofs of the two hypotheticals, for all I can see, is the impossibility of self-understanding without a present that begins in relation to the past and is completed as the pursuit of some future. Nor can this immediate evidence of time be merely a form of sensible intuition, such that the self only appears to exist in time and in reality does not. Were our condition as Kant portrays it, the notion of a rational self independent of time would be a consistent concept; hence, self-understanding independent of the difference between past and future would be possible, even if not possible for humans. But self-understanding *is* discrimination of the present. In truth, evidence of time is inseparable from the *rational* character of the human subject, because one cannot conceive of a rational being for whom objects are not temporally ordered.[7]

To the best of my reasoning, then, both hypotheticals in Kant's first antinomy cannot be false. Since we must choose for or against a beginning to time, I think that Moore has it right: "It does seem . . . quite certain that there cannot have been a first moment of Time itself" (1953: 176). In the context of this issue, Hartshorne notes that Kant's argument against an infinite past assumes our concept of a succession *that has a beginning*. Once begun, an infinite series cannot end. In this sense, future time, which begins with the present, is "a quantum" that "cannot be completed." But a past without limit is a series without a beginning; hence, it is not transparent that the argument addresses the point (see 1970: 126). Perhaps saying this does not redeem the concept of an infinite past, but Hartshorne does give ground to doubt that this concept can be convincingly rejected. Given the inescapable temporality of human activity, our most secure conclusion, so far as I can see, is the affirmation of temporality as the common character of all possible actualities and, therefore, of a temporal adventure that is without beginning or ending.[8]

[7]In the end, I recognize, this criticism merely repeats that Kant's things-in-themselves cannot be conceived because they are solely negative objects of thought. But the point here is that Kant cannot make sense of the distinction between phenomena and noumena by way of his first antinomy. To the contrary, he can draw the conclusion he does only by assuming that there is such a distinction. Since the assumption is invalid, because one cannot distinguish a completely negative object of thought from one whose designation is self-contradictory, his argument that nothing exists in time is an argument that appearances cannot exist in time.

[8]This conclusion is the more secure if, as I expect, the only alternatives to it are represented by Aquinas's affirmation of a nontemporal creator and Kant's distinction between appearances and reality, because both of these alternatives require an object of understanding that is completely negative. But maybe what a critic asks is not how an infinite series can reach its ending but, rather, how relations to infinite past activities could become a single present. To this latter question, Hartshorne responds that the relations to be unified may be finite. This is because he holds, as discussed below, that reality as such includes a universal individual, each of whose activities is fully relative to all other things and thus all past activities. But, then, a present divine activity is constituted by relation to the immediate past divine activity and any other activities that have occurred since the previous divine unification. If space is not infinite, this set of relations is finite (see 1970: 126). Correspondingly, a nondivine activity is constituted by relations to a divine activity and to some other nondivine activities, the set of which is finite.

It seems obvious that the cosmos is vast spatially as well as temporally, and spatial difference may be understood as a distinction between or among metaphysical activities that are contemporary with each other. I will not pursue whether space as well as time is a metaphysical characteristic, although I am inclined to think so, nor whether space as well as time must be infinite, although I am inclined to think not. Questions about the relation between space and time relate a metaphysics of activities to contemporary physics in ways that require sophistication in both kinds of critical reflection. A true metaphysics must be consistent with any true theory in physics, indeed with any empirical theory that is so much as possibly true, since a true metaphysics states the character of all possible actualities. For that reason, the conversation with science is an important form of metaphysical reflection. Still, conflict between a given metaphysical proposal and a given scientific theory does not itself determine which is in need of revision. Empirical theories are themselves attempts to describe very abstract features of realities and may themselves be internally problematic, so that, in some respects, they do not successfully describe any possibility. In its own task, then, the metaphysical project is not bound to accept without criticism the reigning theoretical conclusions of this conversation partner.

Finally, the task of metaphysics is bound only by its own criteria of clarity and coherence. Since it seeks the characteristics of all possible actualities, the successful candidates are those whose exemplification somewhere can be critically affirmed and whose absence would be solely negative. This means that false metaphysical statements are necessarily false. To assert as metaphysical some characteristic that could be absent somewhere is to assert something impossible, because the feature implies characteristics more general than itself, and the assertion is self-refuting. Correspondingly, a metaphysical proposal is validated by showing that the only implications of any included characteristic are other characteristics that also imply it—and, in this sense, by its systematic coherence. If conflict with a current scientific theory is reason to reject a metaphysical proposal, then it must also be the case that this proposal is internally incoherent. The conversation with science and with itself are usefully distinct methods of metaphysical criticism, but they are logically redundant.

I cannot present the full systematic statement that validation of a metaphysics of activities finally requires, and I recognize that both Whitehead and Hartshorne, each in his own systematic context, report problems whose full resolution they do not claim to provide. In this sense, my own statement can only be provisional. But the kind of activity in which the present is determined in part by the past and is completed by a decision for the future is exemplified somewhere, because it is exemplified in our distinctively human existence. With that fact, all valid theoretical statements, empirical or metaphysical, must be consistent. So far as I can see, this requirement is violated if anything other than the character of activities in this sense is said to be the character of all possible actualities, and I have sought to present at least provisional arguments for this conclusion.

Worth

Hartshorne also calls a "concrete actuality" or activity an instance of "creative synthesis" (1970), and Whitehead calls it an instance of "creativity" (1978: 21). In either case, the term is chosen to express the unification of relations to the past by which the decision of an actuality makes it a single thing for the future. Whitehead explicates his term in a sentence that, for Hartshorne, best expresses "Whitehead's novel intuition" (Hartshorne 1972: 161f.): "The many become one, and are increased by one" (Whitehead 1978: 21). The many effects of past activities are synthesized so that one more actuality becomes a part of the past to which future activities then relate. "Creativity" is, Whitehead says, "the Category of the Ultimate" (1978: 21), meaning that this is the term he uses to name inclusively the metaphysical character of the final real things, and I will follow him in this usage.

This means that "creativity" also names the character of worth as such. Since reality as such is worth as such, creativity must be a variable that allows greater and lesser exemplifications, and these exemplifications are, respectively, instances of greater and lesser worth. Thus, the substantive character of worth can now be pursued by asking for the sense in which creativity is a variable. The answer to this question is implicit in Whitehead's formulation, "the many become one, and are increased by one." Each activity or instance of creativity is a unification of its many relations and is, therefore, a unity-in-diversity—and unity-in-diversity is a variable. The final real things may be greater or lesser unities-in-diversity, and, if the argument to this point has been sound, greater unity-in-diversity is insofar greater worth. On this account, we may say, the fully concrete character of worth is aesthetic. Unification is achieved as a consequence of the contrasts created among the diverse relations.

Our own conscious experience quite readily illustrates differing measures of aesthetic achievement. Extreme physical or mental pain, for instance, debilitates unity-in-diversity. The pain so occupies attention that the diversity of experience is enfeebled. In comparison with a moment in which we are deeply engaged in a task or in conversation with friends, to cite another example, a moment of boredom with that same task or in that same conversation is aesthetically inferior. Or again, hearing a speech or reading a book about some subject in which we are well steeped is aesthetically superior to similar attention when the subject is puzzling or foreign to us. In the former case, the immediate object of attention recalls to experience many past but different experiences with the same subject, and the present activity thereby unifies greater diversity. Also, each of us is aware that later times in our lives typically become more inclusive of diverse understandings through our learned participation in a lifeworld that is implicitly remembered, and we often speak of our later experience of things to which we also related at some earlier time as more appreciative or more profound.

If distinctively human activities display the character of creativity as a variable, even more obvious is the difference between human activity generally and what are, to all appearances, the possibilities for nonhuman creatures or individuals in the world. The capacity to live with understanding, especially when significantly developed, immensely enhances creative possibilities. Assuming that there can be consciousness without understanding, its discrimination alone adds dramatically to the diversity that is possible, as attention to the differences among nonhuman organisms suggests. But discrimination of realities through universals permits contrasts among both differing instances of the same universal and differing instances of contrasting universals. When participation in language extends this opportunity, it has in principle no limit. Our immense comparative advantage grounds the sound judgment that, among the known creatures of this world, human individuals are especially important. Still, this does not mean that other creatures and things of the world are properly understood as mere instruments for human purposes. I will return in a later chapter to the moral questions involved in human relations to the natural environment. But we can say here that answers to those questions must be consistent with this metaphysical statement: Creativity, wherever it occurs, is an aesthetic achievement, and insofar is the realization of worth.

Because it defines worth as such, creativity is the substantive character of the good, and the comprehensive purpose is the maximal realization of this good. The moral law, then, requires that humans so choose among their possible purposes as to maximize this realization, and authentic human existence is the choice without duplicity to understand oneself as a particular exemplification of that pursuit. So defined, the comprehensive telos is not the maximal good of one's own future life or the life of any other human individual or the life of a given human community. To the contrary, the moral law prescribes pursuit of maximal creativity in the future as such, precisely because all realizations of unity-in-diversity are insofar good. Sustaining this conclusion, of course, requires address to questions about its implications in moral theory. Moral teleology generally is frequently indicted for a failure to include universal human rights that must be respected whatever the consequences. An even larger company of critics persistently doubts that a metaphysical formulation of the moral law can provide guidance to specific moral decisions. Matters such as these will be discussed in the second part of this work. But there are other issues in understanding the moral character of human existence that need to be clarified prior to that discussion.

One of these issues concerns the nature of unity-in-diversity itself as a variable. As previously argued, worth as such must have a common character; alternative possible telē must be comparable in terms of a single variable because human activity understands itself as a choice. It might now be objected that the metaphysics of aesthetic achievement violates this requirement because creativity as a variable in fact implies two ways in which its exemplifications may be greater or less: They might be varying realizations, on the one hand, of unity and, on the other, of diversity. In human life, for instance, an excessive concern for diversity seems to overload experience and deprive it of unity, while an excessive pursuit of unity seems to confine our relationships and weaken the sense of contrast. Thus, the telos of maximal creativity appears to direct decision by two maxima, and the variable cannot be rescued by prescribing a "balance" between the two because identifying the proper balance requires another principle. As a definition of the good, unity-in-diversity apparently implies that maximal worth is "maximal unity or maximal diversity" and, therefore, cannot be the common character of worth.

To the contrary, I believe, unity-in-diversity is properly understood with the recognition that a loss in unity is always a loss in diversity and vice versa. Recurring to the illustrations given in human experience, we can interpret the consequence of an excess concern with diversity to be a loss of diversity in comparison with what would otherwise have been the case. The individual who seeks simply to have diverse experiences, without a steady purpose that provides some principle of selection, is in truth a series of activities, each of which may be significantly different from the others but all of which are deprived of the diversity that results from integrating the new with the old or from cumulating contrasts. Correspondingly, an excessive concern for unity, as a consequence of which an individual avoids new relationships or new opportunities, is in truth a loss of unity in comparison with what would otherwise have been the case, precisely because unity is greater or less depending on the diversity that is integrated.

Still, it may seem that something is missing in this interpretation, because the deprivation of human experience clearly occurs in two ways. As suggested in some earlier examples, some human experiences are impoverished by the presence of pain and others by boredom, and these are two different kinds of loss. Pain seems to be caused by dissonance or conflict among the things that are experienced, while boredom is so far from the sense of conflict as to be the experience of monotony. Moreover, deprivation as a consequence of painful conflict seems properly described as insufficient unity, while monotony seems to be insufficient diversity. But unfavorable dissonance and monotony are, I think, both properly understood as ways in which experience loses diversity that it might otherwise have had and, therefore, loses unity.[9] Pain, as I noted earlier, in fact so occupies attention as to block out the relations to other things that might have been included, and the effect of unfavorable dissonance generally is to prevent or impoverish the discrimination of things that would heighten the diversity of experienced contrasts. It remains that dissonance and monotony are *differing* ways to lose both diversity and unity, but the assertion that good is a single variable does not deny that evil or the loss of good can occur in different forms.

Nothing said above should be taken to mean that the extent of unity-in-diversity achieved by a given instance of creativity is solely a matter of its own choice. To the contrary, the measure of worth that any given event or activity might achieve depends on the content of the particular past to which it relates or that it inherits. Insofar as the actualities of the relevant past are, in relation with each other, unfavorably dissonant or monotonous, the possibilities of a present event are restricted; conversely, relations of aesthetic order among the actualities of the past deliver to the present greater opportunity. Activities can end or complete only what the past begins in them, and thus opportunity is created by the past. In distinctively human existence, the possible good that a given activity may realize by its choice of a self-understanding is more or less extensive depending on the context in which it occurs.

For a human individual, the most important condition is its own body. It is, at least to all appearances, the immense aesthetic order in the human body, organized in the brain, that makes self-conscious

---

[9]I speak of "unfavorable" dissonance and monotony because neither conflict nor sameness is always detrimental in human experience. As a feature of the present, either may, given certain circumstances, open the possibility of greater aesthetic achievement in the future. For instance, the struggle with a worthwhile task may be the experience of present dissonance, and rest in preparation for later effort may be the experience of present sameness—both for the sake of the future. It follows, as discussed below, that such dissonance or sameness also increases the present realization of unity-in-diversity. The struggle in a worthwhile task has its own rewards in comparison with failure to assume it, and failure to rest when one should results in the compromise of concentration or focus. Hence, the inclusion of dissonance in one's experience can be analogous to the way in which harmonic dissonance can contribute to the quality of a larger musical score and present sameness analogous to the way in which a proper background enriches the beauty of a work of art.

activity possible. Physical pain and disorder can severely limit self-conscious possibilities and, at the extreme, prevent consciousness. Assuming bodily well-being, however, the most important context controlling human opportunity is the human past itself. Because present possibilities for achievement depend on the particular past to which an activity relates, the former are extended when, other things being equal, the latter includes greater achievements—and life with understanding, in comparison with nonhuman worldly existence, involves dramatically greater creativity. The possibilities for each of us, in other words, depend especially on our own past as individuals and on the associations and communities in which we participate.

This last point is illustrated by two individuals whom we considered a moment ago, one who has no steady purpose and one who has avoided new relationships. Given a past identified by either pattern, the opportunities in the present are diminished in comparison with what they might otherwise have been. This is not to deny that an individual can change her or his ways. The opportunity to make that decision may well be among the possibilities of the present; if it is taken, the possibilities for unity-in-diversity in her or his future may, other things being equal, be increased. Still, the opportunities in the present cannot escape the consequences of what has been done. The effect of the larger human context is equally apparent. Beginning with the family or other intimate associations as the setting in which children mature, and stretching through local communities to the social and political order and the cultural inheritance, the quality of the human past to which individuals are related is profoundly important to the measure in which they have a chance to be creative.

Because unity-in-diversity is a creative achievement, the extent to which it occurs is also the measure in which an activity or an individual is distinctive. Humans are, in comparison with nonhuman worldly existence, more distinctive individuals; correspondingly, varying opportunities for good within human existence are differing chances for notable individuality. The same point can be expressed by saying that the particular past determines the measure in which a human activity or individual is free. A more favorable order increases the diversity an activity can unify and, thereby, expands the range of possible ways in which unification may occur. The immensely favorable order of the sound human body that makes life with understanding possible is the opportunity for distinctively human freedom, and the measure of distinctively human freedom itself depends on the larger context, especially the human context, in which self-understanding occurs. I will, therefore, speak of the opportunity for good received by a human from the past as the measure in which she or he is *emancipated*.

In our contemporary linguistic context, the term "emancipation," as other terms often used synonymously with "freedom," may seem to designate the removal of constraints. In this sense, one speaks naturally of emancipation "from" something, suggesting that we are free unless something in the situation intervenes. At least in classical discussions, however, freedom depends on or is increased by not only the absence of constraint but also the presence of enabling conditions. So Aristotle, for instance, speaks of citizens as free to participate in political affairs because others in the household provide for their biological necessities. On this latter usage, constraints are understood as negative aspects of one's situation that may also be formulated as the absence of enabling conditions. It is freedom in this latter sense that I intend with "emancipation." Emancipation varies with the opportunity to be creative, and may be understood as freedom "for" the realization of creativity or worth—and perhaps the point can be made by saying that emancipation is also empowerment. Insofar as the moral law requires us to pursue maximal good within the human future, our comprehensive purpose is to maximize the emancipation of human individuals.

If we assume that the decision for a self-understanding is peculiarly human, then greater or lesser realization of worth in nonhuman worldly existence depends entirely on the context in which the activities arise. To say that unity-in-diversity has been lost in, for instance, the life of a nonhuman animal is to assert that the conditions of its present activity might have been more favorable, as is the case when humans cause suffering in nonhuman animals and might have acted differently. A nonhuman worldly activity, in other words, does not have a moral choice and, therefore, cannot itself cause the loss of good that might have been realized. Human existence, I have argued in previous chapters, is specifically moral as opposed to nonmoral precisely because life with understanding chooses an understanding of worth as such in terms of which specific alternatives for purpose are compared or evaluated. This does not contradict the assertion that all actualities or final real things are in some measure free. Nonhuman worldly activities also unify themselves by a decision within a range of possibility, greater or lesser in extent. Absent self-understanding, however, any decision within that range is maximally good. In contrast, a human activity can itself cause a loss in the unity-in-diversity it achieves, and this is what occurs when it chooses to be inauthentic or to understand itself duplicitously.

Thus, there is also a sense in which human freedom as such does *not* differ in measure, namely, the sense in which original freedom is a moral choice. To be sure, having original freedom means that the individual's opportunity to be creative is dramatically greater in comparison with that of any nonhuman creature. Wherever present, however, the moral character of original freedom is always the same. The distinctive decision between authenticity and duplicity belongs equally to all human activities. This point is entirely consistent with the fact that human activities or individuals differ with respect to the measure in which they are emancipated by the past. Whatever the gift of possibility in that regard, a human activity still chooses its self-understanding, and this choice determines whether the good it might realize is fully realized or whether the activity loses unity-in-diversity it might have achieved. What varies with emancipation is the range of more or less specific purposes in which original freedom may be expressed, but being free to choose for or against the comprehensive purpose defines human existence as such.

As mentioned in the last chapter, this distinction between emancipation and original freedom seems to be absent in Aristotle's ethics. Although he clearly speaks of action as the choice that follows on practical reasoning and that involves both knowledge of a universal and perception of a particular, it is not apparent to me that, for him, the universal itself is something chosen. To the contrary, practical reasoning appears to assume an end, attachment to which expresses the individual's state of character, and this state depends on the habituation or education that has been effected by previous actions, especially through the training she or he received from parents, teachers, and the laws of the polis. Accordingly, the account of moral weakness reviewed earlier turns on the way in which differing desires that have been inadequately habituated affect the perception of the particular. On this reading, whether or not a person acts or lives virtuously is, for Aristotle, a matter of what I have called emancipation, in the sense that it depends solely on the past she or he inherits. Insofar as Aristotle was in his mind, Kant's criticism that teleological moral theories reduce human freedom to a "mechanical play" of desires is understandable. It is, then, the original freedom of human existence that so impressed Kant and that he formulated, mistakenly, in saying that rational freedom alone "has *in itself* an absolute worth" (1949: 45).

In any event, the exercise of original freedom may be responsible for a loss of creativity. Given that human activity achieves its unity with understanding, it is consciousness that suffers. Duplicity lessens the diversity received from the past that is discriminated as one becomes "a cause facing the future"; some of the contrasts among the realities of the past that might have become conscious are excluded, and this loss is a function of the conflict that occurs between one's knowledge of the good and the inauthentic purpose one chooses. Thus, we can say that immorality is experienced both as a deadening, since something is missing, and as a dissonance, since something is awry. Still, the consciousness of immorality may itself be only implicit, so that explicitly we are more or less unaware of the loss. For this reason, the analysis here is not at odds with the apparent energy and contentment that immoral people, even to their own explicit awareness, sometimes exhibit. The loss is always relative to what would have been the case had they chosen rightly, and the experience of this loss may be left in the background of consciousness. On the other hand, either the sense of deadening or that of dissonance may affect explicit awareness, and when this is the case, one is aware of guilt—of what Niebuhr calls an "uneasy conscience."

Correlative with the two respects in which humans are free, namely, the emancipation that varies in measure depending on context and the original freedom that all human activities equally share, there are two respects in which we may speak of human activity as good. In one sense, an activity is more or less good in terms of the unity-in-diversity achieved. But the measure in which that good is realized depends in part on whether the activity is good in the second or specifically moral sense of the term. Human activity is morally good when its choice of a self-understanding is authentic. In this latter sense of "good," there can be no improvement on Kant's famous opening assertion in the

Fundamental Principles of the Metaphysic of Morals: "Nothing can possibly be conceived in the world, or even out of it, which can be called [morally] good without qualification, except a *good will*" (1949: 11). As mentioned more than once already, however, Kant denied what the present argument affirms, namely, that a good will should be understood in terms of "good" in the sense defined by the comprehensive purpose. To be morally good is to maximize, given the possibilities with which one is presented, the unity-in-diversity of one's own activity.

Virtue and Happiness

The discussion to this point has offered two formulations of the morally good choice that may appear to conflict with each other. On the one hand, I have said that this choice takes as its telos maximal good or creativity in the future as such and, therefore, understands itself as this particular exemplification of the comprehensive purpose. On the other hand, the morally good choice is said to maximize the good achieved by the chooser. It may seem that attention to the future is one thing, and realization in the present is something else. But further reflection shows that the good of unity-in-diversity implies no such difference, so that both formulations should be understood to designate the same choice.

If the attempt maximally to serve the future did not or even might not maximize present creativity, then creativity could not be the character that defines the good to be pursued. On the contrary, the comprehensive purpose would require pursuit of *the maximal pursuit of* unity-in-diversity. The proper telos of a present activity would be a future in which subsequent activities maximally pursue the good, and, by hypothesis, this is not necessarily the same as seeking maximal achievement in those activities. But if achievement of unity-in-diversity does not define the good, there is no point in pursuing it. In sum, the good to be realized cannot be forever postponed without self-contradiction, and pursuit of its maximal future realization makes sense only if thereby it is maximally realized in the present.

This identity is the more apparent if we recall that a human activity *is* a decision about its purpose. Given the opportunity presented by its past, the difference between making the most of itself and failing to do so can only be a difference in alternatives for purpose. A purpose the choice of which maximizes one's own unity-in-diversity implies that creativity defines the good and, therefore, the good to be pursued. Hence, were present good maximized by a purpose other than maximizing good in the future as such, one would achieve the former only by choosing a purpose at odds with itself. But conflict in one's self-understanding lessens the unity-in-diversity achieved. Were the present in competition with the future, in other words, making the most of oneself would require a duplicitous choice. To the contrary, I conclude, authenticity realizes maximal creativity by pursuing it.

Having seen that pursuit of the best possible future makes the most of our present selves, we are in a position to discuss the relation between moral worth and happiness. This relation has attracted attention and disagreement throughout the history of Western moral theory. In the tradition of moral teleology developed by premodern thought, the two were typically united. Aristotle famously defines happiness as "activity of soul in conformity with virtue" (1098a17). For him, the meaning of "virtue" is more inclusive than most modern uses of the term, so that the happy life requires its measure of fortunate circumstances. Insofar as it depends on what an individual does with her or his circumstances, however, happiness coincides with the life of moral worth. With Aristotle, Aquinas defines the chief end or supreme final cause of a human life as one's own happiness, so that its pursuit perfects the soul. For Aquinas, however, this perfection is knowing or becoming like God in a sense foreign to Aristotle, notwithstanding Aristotle's commitment to the life of contemplation as the highest human possibility.

The utilitarian moral theories of the eighteenth and nineteenth centuries each assert some version of the "greatest happiness principle," prescribing universal pursuit of "the greatest amount of happiness altogether" (Mill 1973: 412). Contrary to both Aristotle and Aquinas, however, these utilitarian thinkers are often equivocal about the relation between conformity with this principle and pursuit of one's own happiness. John Stuart Mill, for instance, explicitly states that "the happiness which forms the utilitarian standard of what is right in conduct, is not the agent's own happiness, but that of all concerned" (1973: 418). But Mill also asserts that individuals desire virtue as an aspect of their own happiness (see 1973: 442). Kant, to choose one other prominent figure in this general discussion, holds that moral virtue is "the worthiness to be happy" and that "virtue and happiness together constitute the possession of the highest good for one person" (1956: 114, 115). But he denied a coincidence of virtue and happiness in the sense that "a person who sought his happiness found himself virtuous merely through solving his problem, or one who followed virtue found himself *ipso facto* happy in the consciousness of this conduct" (1956: 117).

As even this summary review suggests, the extended discussion of this persistent issue is complicated because fundamental differences regarding the meaning of "virtue" typically entail corresponding differences with respect to "happiness." Nonetheless, most would agree that happiness is the good *for* a human individual, with the disagreement focused on the substantive character of this good. Assuming now that this character is creativity, the good for a person is most inclusively defined as the conscious enjoyment of unity-in-diversity, and an individual is happy in the measure that this experience marks the activities constituting her or his life. From what has been established previously, it also follows that the measure of happiness experienced by any given human activity depends in part on the past, with its gift of greater or lesser opportunity. But this measure also depends on the choice for or against authenticity that the activity makes. The possibilities for present happiness are abused by immoral choice.

Given the context that the past presents, in other words, the identity between pursuing maximal good in the future as such and achieving it in the present is a coincidence of moral worth and maximal present happiness. With respect to a given human activity, "one who followed virtue" would, in Kant's terms, find herself or himself "*ipso facto* happy in the consciousness of this conduct" (Kant 1956: 117). But it must be underscored that this coincidence defines a human *activity* and is not necessarily true of a human *individual*. So far as I can see, the definition of "virtue" in terms of happiness that both Aristotle and Aquinas assert refers to the happiness of the individual in question. In each case, of course, this coincidence is articulated within an inclusive, systematic treatment of human life that would have to be taken into account in order to interpret adequately what is meant. In reading Aristotle, one must attend to the importance for both virtue and happiness of living within a good city; for Aquinas, the happiness one is always to pursue is the vision of God's essence that can occur only in eternal life. All systematic qualifications considered, however, one still might read each to say that pursuit of *the* good and pursuit of *my* good as an individual are always the same purpose (cf. MacIntyre 1967). In any event, this assertion is not implied by the comprehensive purpose I have formulated and defended above.

A given human *activity* cannot properly be said to pursue its own happiness, since the object of its purpose is some future state of affairs or telos. Its pursuit of *the* good, is coincident with the present realization, not the pursuit, of its own maximal happiness. Hence, the statement that pursuit of *the* and of *my* good are coincident must mean that maximizing creativity in the future as such is always the same purpose as maximizing creativity in the future activities of my own life, and this is the assertion that should be rejected. If we substitute "the good" for "happiness" and "metaphysical" for "utilitarian," then the statement from Mill cited earlier should be affirmed: "The good which forms the metaphysical standard of what is right in conduct is not the agent's own good, but that of all concerned." There is a real difference between the two because nothing in the metaphysical character of actualities prevents the possibility that future creativity as such may require of human individuals, as Mill puts it, a "sacrificing of their own greatest good for the good of others" (1973: 418).

Still, the coincidence of virtue and happiness in the present has important consequences for the relation between the two in the life of a human individual. This is the case, at least, if each activity in a person's career is, as a general rule, affected by her or his own past in a measure dramatically greater than the effect individuals in this world have on each other. With respect to virtue, this special intimacy has its effect in the greater or lesser integrity of a person's desires. There is every reason to appropriate Aristotle's insistence that moral virtue depends on education of the passions. Just as a past of moral failings can, to recall the previous chapter, suggest immoral purposes with immense persuasive power, so the cumulative effect of resisting temptation can weaken it. For this reason, Aristotle rightly distinguished between the virtuous person and the person who is morally strong. In the virtuous life, then, integrity is cumulative. Expressing a similar position, Iris Murdoch takes issue with those for whom the moral life is principally a matter of explicit moral choices that occur from time to time when circumstances introduce a disparity between duty and desire. "The exercise of our freedom is a small piecemeal business which goes on all the time and not a grandiose leaping about unimpeded at important moments. The moral life, on this view, is something that goes on continually, not something that is switched off in between the occurrence of explicit moral choices" (1970: 37). The response to uncommon circumstances that call for uncommon moral courage is the more likely to be truly fine action if the individual has cultivated moral virtue through many common decisions in the past.

But if the intimate relation between an individual's past and present is expressed in the cultivation of moral integrity, the same cultivation also contributes to present happiness. Temptation itself introduces its own unfavorable dissonance, the feeling of which Niebuhr calls "anxiety"—even if it is not the dissonance of duplicitous choice. Beyond this, a virtuous past means that each past activity has maximized its own achievement, and the cumulative effect is greater present emancipation. When virtue is desired for its own sake, Mill writes, "the person is made, . . . , happy by its mere possession; and is made unhappy by failure to obtain it" (1973: 441). We have ample reason to appropriate this statement also, so long as we insist that "happiness" is used in its normative sense and does not mean whatever the individual takes or believes to be her or his own good. In one sense, moreover, an individual's own happiness, properly understood, has a special place in her or his moral purposes. The highest reaches of creativity in human existence generally depend on a purpose or set of purposes that is persistent throughout a considerable period of a person's life and that cumulates achievements. The most profound friendship, the most distinctive artistic or intellectual or athletic success, the most refined performance of a craft or service, to cite a few examples, all generally require extensive cultivation. This, too, is given with the fact that the future on which each activity generally has the greatest effect is that of the individual in question. But, then, an individual's pursuit of maximal unity-in-diversity in the future as such has reason to take special account of her or his own future.

Recognizing the dramatic measure in which activities of a given human individual relate to her or his own past also allows us to address, at least summarily, the question of responsibility for past decisions. It has sometimes been charged that a metaphysics of activities cannot make sense of this responsibility. Something is amiss in a moral theory if a human individual is not accountable for immoral decisions she or he has taken and for commitments she or he has made. But if a person is a career of concrete subjects, past decisions belonged to other subjects, and this appears to release the individual's present subject from responsibility for them. On this conception, it seems, the sense of guilt for one's past misdeeds or of accountability for past commitments is merely a confusion of present and past. Some may also formulate this issue in the following way: Since the difference between my own past and the past activities of other individuals is strictly a difference in the fullness with which I presently include them, why is my past something for which I am accountable but not the past of others?

A response to this charge might begin with this last formulation. Contrary to its assumption, there are circumstances in which we may consider a given human responsible, at least in part, for the past activities of other individuals. This may be the case, for instance, when the others acted as representatives of an association of which the given person is also a member. Perhaps it will be said that the person assumes these responsibilities in choosing to be a member. But all associations are not voluntary. When a political community effects sufficiently grave injustice, we may hold the community and thus its members as citizens responsible for correcting the consequences, even if none of the citizens held responsible was a member of the community when the injustice occurred. Similarly, the present community may be held responsible for commitments that were communally made in the past. Given that the comprehensive purpose is maximizing creativity in the future as such, the point is that this telos is served if associations are in this sense held accountable for their collective misdeeds and commitments.

Return now to the difference between relations among associated individuals and those between the successive activities of a given person, namely, that the latter are dramatically more complete. Persons are especially accountable for their own past misdeeds and commitments because this is especially important to maximizing creativity in the future as such. If the special intimacy within an individual's life means that she or he has reason to take special account of her or his own future, it also means that she or he has special reason to assume responsibility for her or his own past. Perhaps it will seem that this accounting does not explain the profound human experience of guilt, in which an individual experiences the fault of her or his past as presently her or his own. Rightly conceived, however, such guilt is a judgment on past duplicity that is in service to present authenticity. Indeed, the religious idea of divine forgiveness may be taken to mean that a present activity is bound by no other obligation than the pursuit of maximal creativity, and responsibility for the past is solely in service to this end.

It is not unknown or necessarily pathological for a citizen to experience her or his present responsibility for the community's past injustice with the feeling of guilt about what was done, notwithstanding that she or he had no part in the past decision. If proper guilt about the past is typically or most apparently about an individual's own misdeeds, this is, I think, because the judgment on them must match the intensity with which they bear a moral threat to her or his present and future decisions. Precisely because the maximal good is served if correcting the consequences falls especially to the individual who was culpable, censure on them must be especially powerful. Moreover, one of the consequences is the intensity with which the duplicity in one's own past delivers temptations to the choice among present alternatives for purpose, including the temptation to comply with self-deception about what was done, and the censure is required in order to help resist this temptation. Perhaps one wishes to reserve the term "guilt" for censure on one's own misdeeds. Outside of an alternative metaphysics, however, I see no convincing reason to conclude that this feeling is not continuous with judgments on other duplicity, namely, those for whose redress the telos of maximal creativity makes one's present purpose uncommonly responsible. We can, then, summarize the present account in the following way: Special responsibility for one's own past is required by the cultivation of virtue, a formation of desires consistent with the comprehensive telos—and, insofar as this cultivation contributes to a person's own future achievements, by her or his happiness.[10]

Contrary to what was previously said, it may now seem that we have so underscored the special intimacy within a person's life as to imply a coincidence between an individual's virtue and her or his happiness. But that conclusion must still be denied. Notwithstanding that a virtuous past increases in its own way present opportunity and that increasing one's own future opportunity has a special place in moral choice, it does not follow that pursuit of *the* good and pursuit of *my* good are the same pursuit. I see no way to exclude the possibility that authenticity requires a different decision than maximizing one's own future unity-in-diversity would prescribe. This is, perhaps, especially apparent in some circumstances that call for uncommon moral courage, as, for instance, when an individual sacrifices an especially promising career in order to care for children or relatives who are in special need. Even here, of course, the virtuous alternative has its own rewards for the individual's own future, and the failure to choose that alternative has its compromising consequences. But even this consideration is excluded in those situations where the comprehensive purpose requires the sacrifice of life itself. In the end, so far as I can see, the convincing point is this: Any thorough coincidence that might obtain between a given individual's virtue and her or his own creative opportunity must finally be accidental. Whatever the contributions of

---

[10]It might now be said that this account makes an individual equally responsible in the present for the evil consequences of deeds she or he was forced to take by another. But that conclusion does not follow, because such responsibility is not required by the cultivation of virtue. Nor does the account make an individual responsible for commitments others incorrectly assume she or he has made. To ask about this matter is to reintroduce the nature of responsibility with respect to human associations. The kind of associational responsibility to which I have already referred illustrates what in chapter 4 I will call a social practice, namely, a set of constitutive norms or rules for a pattern of human interaction that is justified if it indirectly specifies the telos of maximal creativity in the future as such. It is in terms of such social practices, I believe, that we can give a credible interpretation of the justified ways in which a community holds individuals legally and socially accountable for their past decisions, including the prescription of punishments for misdeeds. Holding an individual responsible for commitments others mistakenly assume would be an unjustified social practice, because it would be inconsistent with the pursuit of maximal creativity.

the one to the other, there is no way in principle to compare pursuit of *the* good and pursuit of *my* good with respect to individuals as such and, thereby, to conclude that the two are coincident in every individual's life. Notwithstanding the profound respects in which it was closer to the truth than many more recent moral theories, the attempt in premodern teleology to identify the moral life with a pursuit of one's own happiness is, I am persuaded, mistaken, and the decision for authenticity can be defined only as the commitment to maximal good in the future as such.

Theism

We can now turn to the metaphysical question of whether this comprehensive purpose implies theism. Heretofore, the term "God" has been used to designate ultimate reality as the ground of worth. The question now is whether the reality of God in that sense implies the reality of God in the theistic sense of a supreme being or perfect individual. Henceforth, I will use the term "God" only in this theistic sense, and I will approach an answer to the question through attending to the implications of choosing a self-understanding.

Every self-understanding is the authentic or duplicitous affirmation that the present ought to be completed by pursuit of maximal creativity in the future as such. Hence, every human activity believes that the creativity of the future will, when it is realized, be unified. As the character of worth as such, unity-in-diversity is the metaphysical character of actualities, and the future, when it is realized, will be a multiplicity of actualities. It is the good so realized that one ought to pursue without duplicity, else there would be no point in pursuing it. Thus, to understand oneself is to believe, at least implicitly, that this multiplicity of creative achievements can be conceived as a whole, and in this sense human activity implies a future unification of the good to be pursued. But only something actual can unify actual achievements. Insofar as an individual's own past activities or experiences come together in her or his own life, for instance, this can occur only in a present activity that is affected by them and in which these are some of "the many become one." How, then, will the good to be realized in the multiple activities of the multiple individuals of the future become one or be unified?

In its typical form, as many have noted, classic utilitarianism has no solution to this problem. "The greatest happiness principle" prescribes pursuit of maximal happiness in human individuals or, perhaps, sentient creatures more generally, and this implies the summation of multiple realizations. But happiness, as defined by utilitarians, is an actual feeling, and a summation of such feelings could itself be only an actual feeling, that is, could occur only in some "happy" individual. It is generally recognized that the proposal of some utilitarians for a mathematical summation of realized happiness or pleasure is untenable. Conscious feelings are particular, while a mathematical measure abstracts from particularity and defines each feeling as a universal, a quantity. Hence, a mathematical summation is merely an aggregation of universals, so that the particular feelings are not in truth summated. Seeking to aggregate human happiness mathematically is rather like seeking to capture the aesthetic reality of a painting by depicting its design geometrically. The whole inclusive of the particular colors in its details is lost, and its aesthetic unity is realized only in a particular experience of the whole.

A utilitarian might propose that happiness realized is greater or less in a measure that correlates with the extent of a mathematical summation. But this proposal itself presupposes the actual unification of future particulars——because the only things with which differing mathematical sums could correlate are summations of particulars, and the latter require an actual unification. In any event, the proposal must be false precisely because the mathematical measure abstracts from particular differences. Two particulars that are equivalent in terms of this measure may yet differ with respect to happiness, just as two paintings can have the same design and differ in terms of their beauty. Hence, the proposal can only mean that the worth of an actualization is constituted by an abstract aspect of it, namely, its exemplification of quantity, and it is no longer happiness at all that ought to be maximized. The only universal that defines particulars in a manner relevant to their summation as particulars is the universal that defines them inclusively as particulars, and the unification of its instantiations is another particular.

Because multiple activities can be summed only in some activity, the future unification affirmed by every self-understanding requires an individual in whose activities all achievements of unity-in-diversity will be included. Moreover, each of the multiplicity of achievements must be fully included, since the good each realizes is its unity-in-diversity. If we now underscore that a good will pursues maximal creativity in the future as such, so that its chosen telos includes all future realizations of the good, we are bound to conclude that every human activity affirms authentically or duplicitously an individual in whose activities all achievements throughout all of the future will be completely included—or, as we may also say, an individual whose future *is* the future as such.

We can further conclude that this individual is one for whom the future as such *has always been* its future. Worth as such is the character of all possible actualities; hence, each that ever was—conscious or unconscious, significant or trivial—was a self-determination that conditioned the realization of worth in its future. Absent self-understanding, I have argued, an activity is not moral in character; that is, it does not choose whether to seek maximal future good, and its decision always makes the most of itself. Moral or nonmoral, however, every final real thing exemplifies the character of reality as such and is directed by the telos of maximal creativity, so that every activity implies a comprehensive individual in whom every realization of worth is united.

We can make the point again by noting that a multiplicity of activities, each of which actualizes some good, implies similarities and differences among their achievements. Both difference and equality of value actualized are themselves actual, facts included in the actual world, and these facts imply an actual comparison or measure of value. To be sure, human activity itself evaluates things relative to each other when it compares them—as, for instance, one might say of two individuals that one acted more courageously than another. But all worldly activities, including our own, are fragmentary. Hence, no activity in the world can fully identify a fact of relative worth between two other activities, much less all other activities. Just because creativity as the metaphysical variable implies differing exemplifications, in other words, there must be a comprehensive individual in whose all-inclusive activities the similarities and differences among all previous achievements are measured and all subsequent similarities and differences will be measured.

On my reading, Hartshorne's philosophical contribution includes the most thorough and systematic explication of the comprehensive individual, and his term "the divine relativity" (1948) is an unsurpassed formulation of this individual's character. Given that divine activities, as all metaphysical actualities, unify diverse relations to other things, each is distinguished from the activities of all other individuals by its complete relativity, even while the divine existence as an individual, which did not begin and cannot end, is absolute or relative to nothing. As the term "comprehensive" suggests, however, the divine reality is also properly called the one metaphysical individual, the one individual distinguished from all others solely by metaphysical characteristics. Since creativity is the character of actualities as such, the distinction between activities relative to some and those relative to all is itself a metaphysical distinction. In other words, the metaphysical variable of which all activities are exemplifications is self-differentiating, implying the existence of diverse fragmentary individuals, on the one hand, and, on the other, the existence of the comprehensive individual—or, in familiar terms, the differentiation between the world and God.[11]

On this theistic formulation, there could be no God without a world, no comprehensive individual without fragmentary individuals. Both God and the world are metaphysically necessary—although God is the only necessary *individual*, and the necessity of the world means only that the class of all other individuals cannot be empty. This conclusion is pertinent to the objection with which we closed the previous chapter, namely, that an interpretation of original freedom on which temptation arises from the fragmentary character of human consciousness contradicts God's perfection by making God responsible for temptation. As I

[11]I have previously said that creativity is the character common to all possible actualities, and the present paragraph may seem to contradict that assertion. If this character is self-differentiating, implying both divine and worldly concrete singulars, how can it be a character common to all? But the point is that reality as such is *self*-differentiating. Because the difference between God and the world is metaphysical, *this difference* is a character common to all final real things, both divine and worldly. Divine activities, in other words, require a world to include, and worldly activities require the divine activity in which they are completely included. We can make the same point by saying that the common character of all possible actualities is "relative to all or some other realities," with the distinction between all and some itself implied by the concept of relativity, so that "relative to all" implies "relative to any that are relative to some," and "relative to some" implies "relative to one that is relative to all."

noted, this objection assumes that divine power includes the capacity to create self-understanding individuals who are not fragmentary. But if the concept of God implies that all other individuals must be fragmentary, then the assumption is metaphysically incoherent, and the objection can be dismissed. "Perfection" as designating the character of an individual cannot be a senseless concept.

Still, to call the comprehensive individual God is to assert that it is perfect or supreme. The validity of this assertion follows from what has been said, given that "perfection" here means, as it can only mean, the best possible individual. Because divine activities are strictly relative to all, God must realize, at any moment, the greatest possible unity-in-diversity and, therefore, be the best possible individual. It does not follow that God is ever the "best possible actuality," if this term means that no future actuality could be greater. Although each divine activity is, at the moment it occurs, the greatest possible actuality, each successive divine activity is a greater unity-in-diversity than any previous one, because time is the process in which possibilities are actualized. In a later moment, the past includes a greater diversity to be unified. The existence of God, then, is an unsurpassable series of activities that necessarily surpasses itself. For this reason, Hartshorne calls it "self-surpassing" perfection (1948: 20).

In contrast to the theological tradition for which theistic predication can be only negative or nonliteral, this conception of God is formulated in positive terms that are strictly literal. Whitehead says that philosophy has insofar failed when it has paid "metaphysical compliments" (1963: 161) to God because it has "exempted [God] from all the metaphysical categories . . . applied to the individual things in this temporal world" (1961: 169). As previous comments have suggested, this exemption has occurred because speaking of God has been controlled by the metaphysical view that perfection must be in no respect dependent on others and, therefore, must be in all respects nontemporal or eternal. I am persuaded that the widespread rejection of comprehensive or theistic teleology in modern thought and especially modern moral thought is deeply conditioned by the assumption that this classical conception of the divine reality is the only possible form of metaphysical theism (see Gamwell 1990). Against both this classical conception and the modern rejection of theism, the neoclassical theism of which Hartshorne's achievement is to date the eminent statement formulates the divine character in a manner that requires no metaphysical compliments. Conceived as the supremely temporal individual distinguished solely by metaphysical categories, perfection is designated by terms that are both positive and strictly literal. To be sure, the divine individual is metaphysically unique, precisely because it is the comprehensive individual. But this does not mean that God is exempt from the most general categories of thought or is "nonobjective" in a sense that restricts theistic predication to negative or nonliteral expressions. To the contrary, "metaphysical individual" means that God is, as Whitehead puts it, the "chief exemplification" (1978: 343) of reality as such, the character common to all actualities that we presuppose in understanding anything at all.

But if the metaphysical individual should be called "God" because its activities are the greatest possible, the term is also proper because the character of this individual is nothing other than the comprehensive purpose. Since supremely relative activities are, as all actualities, unified by a decision defined by a telos, the metaphysical character of God can be formulated as a metaphysical purpose—and the only purpose that can be designated in metaphysical terms alone is maximizing creativity in the future as such. This purpose *is* God or defines God as a distinct individual. Among other things, this means that God's character is not moral, in the sense that one can choose between moral and immoral alternatives. Were it possible for a divine activity to have any purpose that is inconsistent with the telos of maximal creativity, it would be possible for God to cease being the individual whose distinct character is metaphysical. Immorality is a loss of diversity, to make the same point, and the activities of the comprehensive individual are relative to all. So far from being itself moral, God's character defines the fundamental principle of moral choice.

In the *Euthyphro*, Socrates asks whether someone is pleasing to the gods because she or he is pious or is pious because she or he is pleasing to the gods. Moral theorists have often reformulated this question as follows: Is an action moral because it is willed by God or is it willed by God because it is moral? In so presenting the question, many intend to imply that an act willed by God is not for that reason moral unless God wills what is moral, and the latter means that God's will is itself obligated by an independent moral principle. Without a logically prior standard, the reasoning goes, a theistic morality could only endorse arbitrarily the power of a divine being and, therefore, would be no morality at all. The conclusion reached is that God cannot be the ground of morality. Those who take this position frequently cite Kant, who includes "the theological view" among the moral views that are heteronomous. A notion of "the Divine perfection," he argues, can only be deduced "from our own conceptions the most important of which is that of morality," so that any attempt to derive morality from the divine perfection "would . . . be involved in a gross circle." If both an independent conception of morality and the gross circle are avoided, he continues, "the only notion of the Divine will remaining to us is a conception made up of the attributes of desire of glory and dominion, combined with the awful conceptions of might and vengeance, and any system of morals erected on this foundation would be directly opposed to morality" (1949: 60).[12]

But theism has no reason to accept the view that God's will is, in the absence of an independent moral principle, arbitrary power. Because God is the metaphysical individual, the distinguishing divine character is necessarily the comprehensive purpose affirmed authentically or duplicitously by every exercise of human freedom, and "the divine will" designates a decision that is necessarily good. Accordingly, it is proper to say that an action is moral because God wills it. To be sure, it is also proper to say that God wills it because it is moral, but this could only mean that God wills it because it is consistent with God's own character. The citation from Kant could be convincing, in other words, only to those who have already rejected moral teleology because they are persuaded by Kant's case against metaphysics. Advanced as an independent argument against a theistic ground for the moral law, the charge of arbitrariness begs the question. Given that God's "will" is metaphysical, deriving the moral law from it is so far from being a "gross circle" as to be a conceptual necessity.

Defined by maximal future creativity, the telos of divine activities is also necessarily maximal creativity in the future of God. Because the

---

[12]This issue is another aspect of the long modern debate prior to Kant between "intellectualists" and "voluntarists," which I had occasion to mention in chapter 2. Voluntarists often charged that intellectualists contradicted the sovereignty of God by making the divine reality subject to independent moral standards, while intellectualists held that the voluntarist position makes moral standards the product of an arbitrary will (see Schneewind 1998).

divine individual is supremely relative, the future as such is God's future. God is, we may say, the one individual in which pursuit of the good and pursuit of its good or, speaking symbolically, virtue and happiness necesssarily coincide. The comprehensive purpose in relation to which all human activities ought to understand themselves prescribes not simply the decision to maximize good within the world but, rather, this decision as the one that makes maximal difference to the future of God—and this repeats that the telos of good within the world would make no sense in the absence of its unification in the divine relativity. Thus, the moral law or categorical imperative may be stated: So choose as to maximize the divine good.

The divine ground of our life with understanding, then, both implies and is implied by the permanence of whatever worth we achieve. The creativity we realize by our decisions and to which they contribute could not be at all except that it makes an everlasting difference to the divine reality. "Always presupposed by even the most commonplace of moral decisions," writes Schubert M. Ogden, "is the confidence that these decisions have an unconditional significance. No matter what the content of our choices may be, whether for this course of action or for that, we can make them at all only because of our invincible faith that they somehow make a difference which no turn of events in the future has the power to annul" (1966: 36). This invincible faith is our inescapable belief, expressed authentically or duplicitously, that our decisions make a difference to the divine good, which includes them all in all of their detail throughout endless time.

The assertion that good achieved would not be good were it not permanent has, to many, seemed doubtful. Why does the temporary character of a deed's effects imply that the deed has no worth? But this way of putting the question is misleading. Nothing that has been said has denied that we make a temporary difference for better or worse to individuals in the world—to family, friends, larger associations, and the natural habitat. To the contrary, every human activity is completed by its pursuit of worth in the future as such. The issue is whether a deed can be important in the world if the difference it makes is not also permanent. Granting that temporary good is good, the statement that it is *only* temporary or not also permanent adds nothing. This statement is completely negative and, therefore, it expresses a putative understanding whose object cannot be distinguished from no object at all.

In defense of the statement, some may now assert that the absence of abiding difference is what makes decisions dear or compelling. But this assertion involves a non sequitur. That what we do here will be in the long run neither good nor bad does not imply nor is it implied by the affirmation of short-run significance. To the contrary, the thought that value is constituted by its own eventual indifference is a confusion similar to the thought that responsibility is constituted by the absence of any objective norm or principle of the good. In the absence of an objective norm, there is nothing to be responsible to, and the absence of something ultimate at stake means only that ultimately nothing is at stake. Because an exercise of original freedom understands reality as such, it evaluates in relation to the future as such—a point conceded by the supposed understanding that one's contribution is only temporary, because a temporary difference cannot be conceived except in contrast to what succeeds it. Hence, evaluating one's alternatives for purpose solely in terms of their short-run importance means that the most inclusive comparison of them marks them all as worthless or as nothing, and choice with understanding is impossible. So far as I can see, we cannot relate to the final nullity of our own decisions; it is a thought no human could have. Whitehead is eloquent on the point: "The immediate facts of present action pass into permanent significance for the universe. The insistent notions of Right and Wrong, Achievement and Failure, depend upon this background. Otherwise, every activity is merely a passing whiff of insignificance" (Whitehead 1941: 698).

Summary

Together, this and the previous chapters have recommended a conception of ourselves on which we are constituted by a moral attachment to the divine purpose. A brief summary may be useful.

The life with understanding we are given to lead allows us to discriminate realities through universals or by way of contrast with all other realities and, therefore, always includes an awareness of reality as such. However simple or complex our consciousness of the world's past actualities and future possibilities, we cannot fail to understand them in terms of the character they all have in common. But a subject of understanding is also self-determining, and this means that each moment of our existence always also understands itself, discriminating its past from the future as its present choice among alternative possible purposes. Self-understanding is the distinctively human form of self-expression, with which we complete what the past begins in us, and this can be an understanding only as an evaluation of the ends among which it chooses. Because the ends are evaluated inclusively, worth as such is understood as the character common to all possible actualities, and self-understanding is always a comprehensive self-understanding, in which a subject decides to be just this particular exemplification of what it takes to be the comprehensive purpose. Because our subjectivity is fragmentary, this constitutive or existential self-understanding is always an implicit decision and, for the same reason, is a moral one. In exercising our original freedom, we choose whether we believe only the truth about reality as such that we cannot fail to know or also affirm a misrepresentation we know to be false. In sum, humans exist in an emphatic sense. We become who we are by a responsible decision for or against the purpose that constitutes the nature of things, for or against ultimate reality as the ground of worth.

This may also be called the decision between authenticity and duplicity, where the latter is an existential lie or self-contradiction. The conversation with Reinhold Niebuhr pursued an account of duplicity, especially in view of the doubt that this choice makes sense. In differing ways, this doubt is expressed in Kant's conviction that teleology is not consistent with moral obligation and Niebuhr's conviction that the fact of human fault drives us finally to paradox. Against both, the persuasive power of false interpretations is the consequence of our limited capacity to be conscious of the past and the future. Understanding possibilities more concretely is insofar a greater sense of their worth, positive or negative. Because authenticity evaluates in relation to reality as such, duplicitous alternatives that attribute inordinate worth to something we more fully appreciate can be tempting, especially those occasioned by the special intimacy that characterizes an individual's memory and anticipation of her or his own activities. Temptation weighs more heavily and pervasively because human life is social in character; that is, individuals may inherit a "force of evil" in the form of duplicitous alternatives for purpose commended by the human past. But the social character of our lives may also serve to weaken temptation. In terms of that possibility, we may understand the distinctive function of religious activities, through which humans seek to cultivate their abiding attachment to the comprehensive good.

Chapter 3 has sought to define the substantive character of worth and, therefore, of human authenticity. Our existence in an emphatic sense, I have argued, implies that the character of reality as such is most adequately formulated in a neoclassical metaphysics on which the final real things are activities constituted by their relativity. Each unifies relations to the past by a creative decision, trivial or profound, that conditions the future. Creativity is, then, the metaphysical character of all possible actualities and the definition of the good. Because every self-understanding is the authentic or duplicitous affirmation of maximal creativity in the future as such, our relation to reality as such is our relation to a metaphysical or eminently temporal individual, all of whose activities are relative to all actuality and possibility. Every human activity is completed by an authentic or duplicitous belief in God. The comprehensive purpose is a divine purpose, and the moral law is to pursue the maximal divine good.

Part Two will seek to articulate the divine purpose in terms of principles of justice.

Appendix to Part One
On the Theistic Character of Belief

Part One argued that life with understanding is constituted by its relation to God. In reaching this conclusion, the discussion focused on the choices we make with understanding and thus on what we take to be good. Every activity that understands is completed by its decision for a self-understanding, which evaluates alternatives for purpose and, therefore, is an authentic or duplicitous affirmation of the divine good. Because affirmations may be called beliefs, I also said that every human activity is completed by an authentic or duplicitous belief in God—although the character of beliefs, in distinction from understandings, was not pursued. If the argument above is sound, it follows that every belief, as every understanding, implies a belief in God. In this Appendix, I wish to confirm the argument for theism by explicating the character of beliefs and showing that a belief in God is implied by every belief.

As the following will seek to clarify, I use "belief" to designate assent to an understanding or, more fully stated, an evaluation of an understanding as true. Both "belief" and "understanding" are ambiguous terms, in the sense that they may be used to designate respectively the content of what is believed or understood, or the subjective relation of believing or understanding. I will use both terms only in the latter sense, that is, to designate subjective relations. In chapter 1, understanding was defined as the discrimination or representation of realities through universals. For present purposes, I will stipulate that this discrimination is a subject's relation to some propositional content, so that a proposition designates some reality or realities as exemplifying some universal or universals. For instance, a representation of some roses as exemplifying the universal "yellow" is an understanding of the proposition "some roses are yellow."

Saying that "belief" designates assent to an understanding implies a distinction between beliefs and understandings. A given propositional content may be understood without the understanding being a belief because the subject may disbelieve it or, as we say, suspend belief. Believing that some roses are yellow occurs when the subject evaluates the understanding as true, in whatever sense an understanding can be true, and, in doing so, evaluates the propositional content as true, in whatever sense a proposition can be true. What the subject believes is an understanding of p and, therefore, p. Beliefs, then, can be correct or incorrect evaluations of understandings as true, and I will speak of these evaluations respectively as valid and invalid beliefs.

As already noted, the analysis of Part One argued that each occasion of human subjectivity is constituted by an inclusive belief about itself. This inclusive belief is the human activity's self-understanding, that is, its choice with understanding among its alternatives for purpose. A self-understanding is the assent to or evaluation as true of an evaluative understanding of the subject's alternative possible ends. Thus, this self-understanding is the subject's decision to believe one of its alternatives for self-understanding, that is, one of the evaluative understandings the subject has of its alternative possible ends. Since this belief is inclusive, every other belief (and every disbelief or suspension of belief) of a given subject must be inseparable from the self-expression with which that occasion of subjectivity conditions the future. Hence, the analysis developed above implies that belief cannot be adequately conceived or explicated independently of the subjective act in which a human activity expresses itself. I will call any theory that explicates belief in terms of the subject's self-expression a pragmatic theory of belief. The present discussion will seek to clarify in relevant respects a theory of this kind and to show why it implies or presupposes theism, the validity of which has already been defended on other grounds.

Because the inclusively pragmatic character of all human subjectivity has already been developed in moral terms, I will not seek to engage nonpragmatic conceptions of belief in detail, even if it will be useful toward clarifying the pragmatic theory I recommend to state the alternatives and offer summary reasons to doubt their validity. However, some philosophers who hold that moral and political theory is independent of a divine reality have also advocated "a pragmatic theory of belief." Hence, an appropriation of that term for present purposes requires a defense of its theistic implications. My own thinking about the character of beliefs has been greatly instructed by one of these philosophers, namely, Karl-Otto Apel. Accordingly, I will pursue the discussion here partly through a critical conversation with him, and I will seek to show that the "transcendental-pragmatic" theory he advocates is incomplete without a metaphysical theism he denies.

The Pragmatic Character of Beliefs

In the sense pertinent here, a "theory of belief" seeks to define the universal character of beliefs; that is, a theory of this kind seeks to clarify the implications of saying that a belief assents to an understanding. Since beliefs evaluate understandings as true, the universal character of beliefs includes or implies a universal norm of true understandings.

To be sure, some thinkers deny that true understandings have any universal norm. On one reading, this was John Dewey's intent in saying "the hypothesis that works is the *true one*; and *truth* is an abstract noun applied to the collection of cases, actual, forseen and desired, that receive confirmation in their works and consequences" (1957: 156-57). "Collection" might be read to mean that there is no characteristic all such cases have in common, so that, for any particular hypothesis, "confirmation in . . . works and consequences" is in all respects historically specific. But the denial of any universal norm of true understandings is, I hold, self-refuting, because this denial itself implies just such a norm. The denial is itself a belief about all true understandings. If this belief is valid, its understanding of all true understandings must be true irrespective of historical circumstances and, therefore, must exemplify a property that cannot be in all respects historically specific. In other words, the proposition "true as a property of understandings is a characteristic in all respects relative to varying circumstances" itself designates a universal character of true as a property of understandings.

Aware of this implication, other thinkers assert that we may simply refuse to address questions about true and false understandings as such and, thereby, neither believe nor disbelieve, explicitly or implicitly, that there is any such universal norm. Richard Rorty says that "truth is not the sort of thing one should expect to have a philosophically interesting theory about" (1982: xiii). At least if our interests are otherwise, he continues, we may simply choose to "change the subject" (1982: xiv). But the belief that this refusal is possible must be invalid if understandings do have a universal norm. On that assumption, the belief that we may neither believe nor disbelieve that there is a universal norm of true understandings could not itself be valid without presupposing the universal norm of true understandings, and thereby the putative refusal would be self-refuting. Thus, we could be permitted to "change the subject," in Rorty's sense, only if there were no universal norm of true understandings, and this means that there is no difference between a refusal and a denial of any such norm. Since the denial *is* self-refuting, a universal norm of true understandings cannot, so far as I can see, be consistently avoided.

As mentioned, the pragmatic theory of belief I seek to clarify asserts that valid and invalid beliefs cannot be explicated independently of a human activity's self-expression. Following Apel, I will formulate the point by saying that a belief cannot be explicated independently of the claim to truth or validity claim with which a subject expresses some understanding. In so appropriating the term "claim to truth" or "validity claim," however, I should note that Apel typically speaks of this claim as characterizing the speech act in or through which a human individual communicates or offers to communicate something to another human individual or individuals. On Apel's typical formulation, in other words, the subjects who make or imply validity claims are persons in relation to other persons. In distinction from that usage, I will designate by the term "claim to truth" something about the self-expression of a human activity, that is, of an occasion or act of human subjectivity. A claim to truth occurs even if there is no speech act and thus no communication or attempted communication to other human individuals. Accordingly, the recipients of a validity claim may be one or more subsequent activities in the life of the same individual, and there is a kind of communication that occurs within an individual's life with understanding. On this expanded use of "communication," intra-individual communication, on the one hand, and the communication that occurs between or among individuals, on the other, may be understood as special cases of human communication generally.[1]

This pragmatic theory of belief denies two nonpragmatic alternatives: According to one, the validity or invalidity of a belief is adequately explicated in terms of a property that characterizes the proposition believed. Let us call this the propositional theory of beliefs. According to the other alternative, the validity or invalidity of a belief

---

[1]If Apel restricts the occurrences of validity claims to the occurrences of speech acts, I believe that he also recognizes something analogous to such occurrences in all cognitive or subjective acts. He speaks of the solitary thinker as one who "is able to internalize the dialogue of a potential community . . . in the critical 'discourse of the soul with itself' (Plato)" (1980b: 258), and this at least suggests the possibility of "communication" within the life of an individual. Accordingly, when Apel also writes that "the very structure of one's meaningful thought and decision already presupposes the structure of interpersonal reciprocity, of symbolic interaction made explicit in language-communication" (1979b: 312), he seems to say that meaningful thought and decision has the structure of self-expression whether or not it is in fact expressed in a speech act. This reading seems confirmed when he says that "possible *propositions* are dependent, in principle, on possible *acts of assertion*; and correspondingly, possible *truth* is dependent on possible *truth-claims*" (1979b: 315). Understanding Apel in this way does not, so far as I can see, contradict his assertion that the structure of human cognition may be understood by reflecting on the structure of speech acts. On his account, every claim to validity is "exposed, in principle, to the possible assent or contestation of an indefinite argumentation community" (1979b: 315). This means that a meaningful thought or decision is essentially communicable to other individuals. Hence, no meaningful thought and decision, whether or not it is in fact communicated, can be explicated independently of the conditions of possibility of "illocutionary speech acts" (1979b: 315) or independently of participation in language. So, Apel writes: "Regarded empirically, some one can, of course, think for himself alone. . . . Even when he does so, however, he thinks with a *claim to intersubjective validity*, and this not only in respect of the truth of his thoughts but also in respect of their *meaning*. He must in principle be able to *share this meaning with other persons as a linguistically articulated meaning*" (1987: 21). But however Apel should be understood, I will use the term "claim to validity" to designate the constitutive self-expression of human activities, so that the validity claim proper to a speech act is a special case.

is adequately explicated as a property that characterizes the subjective form of believing. Let us call this the phenomenological theory of belief.

On the propositional theory, to say that a belief is valid is, without remainder, to say that the proposition believed is true. For instance, it might be said that a proposition is true if it has the property of corresponding with reality, so that the validity of a belief is explicated, without remainder, as the correspondence of its propositional content with reality. I will take as noncontroversial the assertion that a belief cannot be valid unless its propositional content is true. But it is something more to assert that the validity of a belief may be reduced to the truth of its propositional content. Indeed, this latter assertion must be invalid if we allow that there is a difference between a valid belief and a true understanding, because the latter may be disbelieved or belief may be suspended. If "valid belief that p" is not identical to "true understanding of p," then the validity of a belief cannot be explicated, without remainder, as a property of the proposition believed.

Given this recognition, one might be inclined to endorse the phenomenological theory of belief. The validity of a belief is adequately explicated in terms of its subjective form. Thus, "she or he believes p" means "she or he understands p with the subjective form of believing," and the difference between valid and invalid (or, at least, not valid) beliefs is adequately conceived as a difference in this subjective form. The most familiar examples of this theory, perhaps, are those that distinguish valid beliefs in some strict sense from mere opinion. For instance, it might be said, with Descartes, that a valid belief has the subjective form of indubitability or is "clear and distinct." But a phenomenological theory is open to the following objection: Let us designate as sf the preferred subjective form, so that a theory of this kind is committed to the proposition: Any belief whose subjective form is sf is valid. Since believing as such has a subjective form that characterizes both valid and invalid beliefs, sf must be a differentiation of it. But some given differentiation of the subjective form of believing as such could entail that the belief is valid only if the distinctive character of a valid belief is included in the differentiation.

In this respect, a phenomenological theory of belief is analogous to a phenomenological theory of moral choices. Since right and wrong choices are differentiations of conscious choosing, no differentiation of subjective form can entail that the choice is right unless the character of a right choice is included in the differentiation. For instance, one cannot say that a choice taken with sincerity is necessarily right unless we define "sincerity" as the subjective character of a right choice. Similarly, one cannot say that a belief having the subjective form of indubitability is necessarily valid unless we define "indubitability" as the subjective form of a valid belief. The attempt to define right choice phenomenologically is one way to commit the naturalistic fallacy, and we can say that phenomenological theories of valid belief commit an analogous fallacy.

One might now seek to deny a pragmatic theory of belief by asserting that a valid belief is adequately explicated in terms of a property of its propositional content and a property of its subjective form. Thus, to say that a belief is valid is to say that its propositional content is true and its subjective form is *sf*. But this combination of propositional and phenomenological theories must now account for the coincidence between the truth of the proposition and the specific character of the subjective form. I cannot see how this coincidence could be explicated except by saying that the subjective form is caused by the propositional content. Aside from its dubious assertion that propositions can be sensibly understood as causes, the theory now shares with propositional theories of valid belief the inability to explain how a true proposition could be disbelieved or how the subject could suspend belief.

On the pragmatic theory I seek to clarify, both propositional and phenomenological theories are inadequate because they abstract some aspect of a belief from the subjective act of self-expression. What is believed is not simply *p* but, rather, an understanding of *p*. Although a belief does evaluate some propositional content as true, in whatever sense a proposition may be true, this is because the propositional content is the object of an understanding that is evaluated as true. Moreover, this understanding is the believer's own. To believe that some roses are yellow is to assent to one's own understanding of "some roses are yellow." In other words, a belief is either the subject's inclusive belief or an aspect of a believer's evaluation of itself and, therefore, an aspect of the subject's self-expression.

We can also make the point about self-evaluation by saying that belief involves self-reference. A self-referential evaluation is an evaluation of the self as expressed; *what* one evaluates is the self as a condition of the future. A belief, therefore, evaluates as true the expression of the subject's own understanding. To believe is to claim validity. Belief that p, in distinction from understanding of p, means that one claims truth for one's understanding of p.[2] We might say that a belief is the assertion of an understanding, although in this formulation, the term "assertion" must be used in the same expanded sense I have previously given to the term "communication." I recognize that it seems natural to speak of making or implying claims for beliefs or assertions, but I take this to speak about the claims we make or imply in communication with other individuals. On my usage, then, the term "a claim to validity" is systematically ambiguous, having a general meaning, on which any assent to an understanding is such a claim, and a specific sense, on which a claim is made or implied only when assent is communicated to another or other individuals. It is in this specific sense that we can speak of making or implying claims for our beliefs or assertions.

Given that a believer's inclusive evaluation is the choice of a self-*understanding*, it follows that a belief involves an understanding of an understanding, specifically, an evaluative understanding of another understanding. The belief that some roses are yellow, for instance, involves the understanding of "my understanding of 'some roses are yellow' is true." Still, this formulation does not adequately explicate a belief. The believer understands "my understanding of p is true" whether or not she or he believes that understanding of p. Indeed, "my

---

[2]Focus on the claim to truth raises questions about possible distinctions between truth and other kinds of validity. Apel, for instance, distinguishes claims to truth from claims to meaning, to rightness, and to truthfulness. On his account, if I read him correctly, the same understanding may be the object of differing validity claims. I am inclined to think that "truth" can also be used in a broader sense, in accord with which all claims to validity may be understood as claims to truth, and, correspondingly, the understandings for which truth is claimed may be formulated in ways that allow the distinctions Apel draws in terms of differing kinds of validity. In order to avoid more complex formulations, the discussion in this appendix assumes that "claim to truth" can be used in this broader sense, although I do not mean thereby to imply that use of the term in this sense is the preferred way of speaking. If that assumption is false, then the argument here does at least pertain to belief in whatever more restricted sense we should understand the claim to truth.

understanding of p is true" is precisely what is disbelieved or what is neither believed nor disbelieved when the subject disbelieves or suspends belief. Hence, the belief that p is not identical with this evaluative understanding of an understanding but, rather, requires assent to that evaluative understanding. As an evaluative understanding, in other words, belief is either the subject's chosen self-understanding or an aspect of it, and it is the belief's implication in the choice that adds assent.[3] But, then, formulating a belief as an evaluative understanding is redundant. To assent to "my understanding of 'some roses are yellow' is true" is simply to assent to "my understanding of 'some roses are yellow.'"

Recognizing the difference between Apel's attention to communication between individuals and the analysis here of human activities, we may appropriate his formulation:

> The fact, . . . , that the predicate "is true" is implied in the very statement of a proposition simply means that truth is . . . a claim that human subjects of knowledge connect with propositions by asserting them and which they can make explicit through performative phrases like "I hereby state that . . ." (1980a: 388).

Or, again:

[3]That all of a subject's beliefs are aspects of its inclusive belief does not imply that no belief is valid unless the subject is authentic. An inauthentic self-understanding is clearly consistent with valid beliefs about the alternatives for purpose it evaluates. Because a subject's inclusive belief or self-understanding is chosen, it may seem that all beliefs are chosen. But this, too, does not follow. Indeed, most of a subject's beliefs may be inescapable given the past it inherits, including previous activities of the individual in question and the activities of other individuals to whom she or he is or has been related; that is, these beliefs must be included within whatever inclusive belief is chosen. In whatever respects this is so, an invalid belief occurs in ignorance. Still, the decision for a self-understanding may also include the choice of other beliefs. This is more likely to be so when the activity's range of specific possible purposes is about what should be believed in answer to a given question. For instance, one may choose to believe a given understanding in answer to a political question because one is specifically engaged in the process of asking and answering that question. Insofar as this is the case, the subjective act inclusive of the belief that p so chooses its self-understanding as to include the decision that its understanding of p is true.

> The *semantic* notion of *truth*, as well as that of *propositions as*
> *truth-bearers*, can be understood philosophically . . . if one reflects
> on the . . . fact . . . that there are human beings that *claim* truth
> for their knowledge and are able, in principle, to express their
> truth-claims by *performative* (and self-reflective) phrases such as,
> e.g., "I hereby state, that . . . ." through which the *propositions*
> claimed to be true are communicated as parts of illocutionary speech
> acts (1979b: 315).

This pragmatic theory of belief allows one to make sense of the
special or emphatic self-reference involved in an understanding whose
propositional content is about the universal character of understandings. In this case, the propositional content must be understood
to designate something about the understanding of it, in the sense
that this particular understanding must be understood to exemplify
what the content designates. Were this not the case, the content
would not be about the character of all understandings. If, for instance, the subject understands "all understandings have some subjective form," then it also understands "this understanding (namely,
the subject's understanding of 'all understandings have some subjective form') has some subjective form." This emphatic self-reference
cannot be explicated solely in terms of the understanding's propositional content. That content designates something as a common characteristic or property of understanding as such, while the self-reference involves the attribution of that property to a particular
understanding that exemplifies it. But the content of the universal
proposition is logically independent of any particular exemplification
and, therefore, cannot designate it. For instance, "all understandings
have some subjective form" is logically independent of this particular
subject and its understandings. The emphatic self-reference can only
be explicated pragmatically, that is, as an aspect of the self-reference
of a subject.

When the content of an understanding is a *true* proposition about
all understandings, the understanding must exemplify the character
the proposition designates. An understanding having that propositional content and not exemplifying what the content designates is
impossible. We may say, then, that any such understanding is self-referentially necessary; that is, the understanding is necessarily a true

understanding of its own character. The propositional content of a self-referentially necessary understanding, we may also say, designates a necessary condition, or condition of the possibility, of understanding as such. Apel calls such an understanding "transcendental-pragmatic" (see, e.g., 1975, 1979b) and, correspondingly, uses the same term to designate both the propositional content of such an understanding and the condition it designates. On the analysis here, the understanding is transcendental in the sense that its content designates truly the character of understanding as such; it is transcendental-pragmatic in the sense that its self-reference is an aspect of the subject's self-expression. Moreover, a true understanding of all understandings must be believed, whatever else is or is not believed. This is because a subject that evaluates its own understandings must understand itself as a subject of understandings and, in expressing itself, believe this understanding of itself. Hence, it must also believe any self-referentially necessary understandings it may have.

Simply for ease of expression, I will henceforth use the term "transcendental" to mean "transcendental-pragmatic." I will also call false understandings of or propositions about all understandings transcendental, so that we may speak of true and false transcendental understandings or propositions. Because true transcendental understandings are self-referentially necessary, false transcendental understandings are self-referentially impossible and, therefore, are merely putative understandings. An understanding whose propositional content (or putative content) negates a true proposition about all understandings is necessarily a false understanding of the subject's own understanding. This does not mean that no subject can believe a false understanding of all understandings. But it does mean that no subject can have or believe such a false understanding without also having and believing a true transcendental understanding. A false understanding of all understandings is self-referentially impossible, but a subject of understanding truly understands itself as a subject of understandings. Hence, if a subject has any understanding of transcendental characteristics, it must have and believe a true understanding of those characteristics. Given the latter, the subject can simultaneously have an invalid transcendental belief, that is, can assent to an understanding whose content negates the true proposition about all understandings that is also understood and believed. But a belief that denies the true transcendental character of understandings is necessarily self-refuting. The subject in question simultaneously believes what is denied.

Because a true transcendental understanding is self-referentially necessary, its propositional content, formulated as a proposition about understandings, is conceptually necessary; that is, a denial of any such proposition is conceptually self-contradictory. On the assumption that all understandings have a subjective form, for instance, the proposition "an understanding has a subjective form" is conceptually necessary, and "an understanding does not have a subjective form" is conceptually self-contradictory. Thus, we can also explicate in these terms the impossibility of having a merely false understanding of all understandings. Since the false proposition is conceptually self-contradictory, an understanding of it includes by implication a true proposition about all understandings. We also might make this point by saying that a true transcendental proposition is self-referentially true, in the sense that its truth is a necessary condition of its own conceptual possibility. Strictly speaking, however, only subjects are self-referential. Hence, to speak of the self-referential truth of a transcendental proposition is to speak elliptically. Fully to explicate it, one must say that the proposition cannot be understood (that is, it is not a conceptually possible proposition) without that understanding being believed.

It now follows that *every* subject has a valid belief about its own necessary conditions, whatever else it may believe. This is because every subject must have a belief about the universal norm of true understandings, in terms of which understandings are evaluated.[4] A false understanding of this norm requires a simultaneous true understanding of it—and true understandings of all understandings must be believed. Moreover, a true understanding of this norm is a true understanding of the universal character of understandings, since the content of the former implies the content of the latter. Hence, every

---

[4]Recognition that every belief includes a belief about the norm of such evaluations implies, so far as I can see, a decisive refutation of both propositional and phenomenological theories of belief. A belief about the universal norm of true understandings is self-referential, since the content believed designates something about the subject's own understandings. Hence, every belief includes a self-referential understanding, and neither the propositional nor the phenomenological theory of belief can adequately explicate this understanding of self.

subject assents to a true understanding of its own transcendental character. Every human subject is, whatever else it is, an evaluation as true of a true understanding of all human subjects.

On my reading, this is Apel's point when he says that true transcendental understandings "may be conceived of as reflective radicalization, so to speak, of that reflective knowledge that is first brought to verbal expression through the self-referential performative parts of constative speech acts. . . . [and such radicalization] takes the form of propositions that are self-referential by their universal truth-claim" (1978: 7). If I understand correctly, he means that a valid belief whose content designates the universal character of understandings is a necessary condition of believing as such, precisely because all beliefs evaluate some understanding as true and, therefore, evaluate it as an exemplification of the universal norm of true understandings. The valid belief whose content designates this universal norm and, therefore, the universal character of understandings is first brought to verbal expression through the performative parts of speech acts that claim truth for one's understandings, and an explicit understanding whose content designates this character is a "reflective radicalization" of the self-reference involved in every belief.

The analysis of understanding as such and its implications pursued throughout Part One is an attempt to argue that certain understandings of human activity in relation to the divine good are true transcendental understandings. It follows that the class of true transcendental understandings includes a class of understandings about reality as such or about the reality of God. In accord with previous usage, we may call understandings in this latter class true metaphysical understandings. Formulated as a proposition about actualities (for instance, "an actuality is a unity-in-diversity"), the content of such a true metaphysical understanding is also conceptually necessary. To first appearances, the conclusions that true transcendental understandings include true metaphysical ones may seem to contradict the statement that the former are understandings whose propositional content is about all understandings. But a subject of understanding also exemplifies metaphysical characteristics; these, too, are conditions of its possibility. Hence, the content of a true metaphysical understanding is about understandings in the respect that the latter exemplify characteristics a subject has in common with all actualities.

If the discussion to this point has been successful, it has clarified that beliefs are self-referential evaluations or claims to truth for understandings and thus for propositions. Beliefs or claims to truth are self-expressions or aspects of self-expressions. It now follows that the universal norm of true understandings in relation to which understandings are evaluated must be a norm of understandings as expressed. What one evaluates in a self-evaluation is the self as a condition for the future. With respect to each given understanding a subject has, the subject evaluates it as true (believes it) or as false (disbelieves it) or as possibly true and possibly false (suspends belief)—and does so in relation to a universal norm that defines true understandings as conditions of the future, as communicated in the subject's act of self-expression. In other words, the universal norm of true understandings is the norm of claims to validity or is pragmatic.

The Implied Belief in God

On one definition, "valid" means "well-grounded," and a claim to truth purports that the understanding for which truth is claimed is well-grounded in the sense that it conforms to the norm of true understandings. Since a "claim" is "a demand for something as one's rightful due" (American Heritage Dictionary), we can say that the subject who claims truth for an understanding calls for other subjects to accept the claim or agree that the understanding is true—and this is demanded as "one's rightful due" precisely because one claims that the understanding is well-grounded or conforms to the universal norm of true understandings. Given that the understanding is in fact well-grounded, we may say that both the understanding and the proposition understood have the validity that is claimed for them; that is, they are valid in the sense that they are true. We can also say that the claim is valid, in the sense that what is called for is in fact "one's rightful due." Given that the understanding is well-grounded, in other words, the belief is valid.

We are now in a position to pursue the theistic implications of every belief. To explicate the difference between valid and invalid beliefs and thus true and false understandings as a pragmatic difference means to define this difference in terms of the effects of self-expressions, and, since a belief or claim to truth calls for its acceptance by other subjects, the difference between valid and invalid beliefs must be explicated in terms of a subject's communicative effects or possible communicative effects. In seeking this explication, I will proceed through a consideration of Apel's account, because what I take to be the central problem in it will show why the transcendental-pragmatic theory he advocates is incomplete without a metaphysical theism he denies.

On my reading, Apel seeks to define a valid belief and thus a true understanding in terms of their communicative effects when he says that "a transcendental-pragmatic account . . . should explicate the meaning of truth in terms of the necessity and possibility of redeeming one's own truth claims" (1980a: 394). A true understanding is one "fated to be ultimately agreed to by all who investigate" (1980a: 401), and Apel also formulates the point by saying that a valid claim would be accepted by the unlimited or indefinite communication community (see, e.g., 1979b). On this account, a claim to truth includes the promise that, if contested, the claim and, therefore, the understanding as one for which truth is claimed can be redeemed or validated by argument. In other words, the universal norm of true understandings or claims to validity is the possibility of argument for the claim or understanding, such that reason commands any argumentative subject who has access to the experiential evidence and understands the argument to believe the understanding for which truth is claimed. The difference between valid and invalid beliefs is that the promise included in a valid claim to truth can be fulfilled.

For Apel, if I understand correctly, this account implies that the redemption or validation of claims is a communal practice that must be characterized in terms of a "regulative idea"—namely, the idea of an argumentation community that is indefinite because there are no constraints on time or the number of participants. "Propositions claimed to be true are communicated as parts of illocutionary speech acts and thereby exposed, in principle, to the possible assent or contestation of an indefinite argumentation community" (1979b: 315, emphasis deleted). Hence, "the possibility of creating consensus in an unrestricted communication community must, in principle, be included among the conditions of the possibility of truth" (1984: 239). Regulative ideas of this kind, Apel writes, "define obligations and provide guidance for the long-term, approximate realization of an ideal. At the same time, however, they give expression to the insight that nothing which can be experienced in time can ever fully accord with the ideal" (1987: 25).

Because the ideal cannot be realized, one might object, the assertion that a valid belief or a true understanding can be redeemed or validated is untenable. As a matter of fact, this objection notes, all argumentation is empirically constrained and can never proceed to the point where reason commands any argumentative subject who has access to the experiential evidence and understands the argument to believe the understanding for which truth is claimed. Actual arguments are always in some respects conditional, based on understandings or premises that are not themselves established by evidence and argument, and the argumentation commands agreement only on condition that certain things are uncontested. The capacity of argumentative reason to command agreement, in other words, is properly indexed to the assumption or set of assumptions of some specific argumentation community.

But this objection implies that the understanding of argument it asserts cannot itself be validated by argument. This is because the understanding for which it claims validity purports to designate the universal character of argument. On the understanding that all arguments are indexed to the assumptions of some specific argumentation community, no argument can show that the content of this understanding designates the character of all argument. Hence, this understanding of argumentative reason can only be dogmatically asserted; if contested or doubted, it can only be reasserted. More generally, this understanding of argument erases any connection between argument and valid belief. If the communal practice of argumentation always has limits in understandings that cannot themselves be validated by argument, then no argument could begin to show that some claim conforms to a universal norm of valid beliefs. Indeed, even the attempt to establish what counts as a good argument would depend on beliefs that cannot be validated, and the force of argument would dissolve into arbitrariness.

Moreover, the understanding of argument advanced by the objection is self-referentially problematic. Since the universal character of argument defines the relation of argument to the universal norm of true understandings, the true understanding of argument must itself be transcendental—even if this true understanding is that no argument can redeem a claim to truth. Were it true that all arguments are properly indexed to the assumptions of a specific argumentation community, the denial of this proposition would be necessarily self-refuting; that is, the proposition "some arguments are not indexed to the assumptions of some specific argumentation community" would be conceptually self-contradictory. But it is senseless to say that a conceptual contradiction cannot be understood to be such. Hence, it would follow that a claim for this understanding of argument could be, against itself, validated independently of any specific argumentation community by showing that its denial is necessarily self-refuting. In other words, no understanding whose content designates the universal character of argument can be true unless it includes the possibility of transcendental arguments. Through this form of argument, a claim for some understanding of the necessary conditions of understanding is redeemed by showing that its denial is necessarily self-refuting or the content of such a denial is conceptually self-contradictory, and one of the understandings that can be validated by this form of argument designates through its content the universal character of argument itself.[5]

---

[5]For this reason, I do not find convincing the theory on which a believer's proper address to contestation or doubt of her or his belief is to ask whether there are reasons that defeat the belief or require the believer to give it up. On this theory, if I understand it correctly, the absence of such reasons is always warrant for continued belief. Minor qualifications aside, writes Nicholas Wolterstorff, "a person is rationally justified in believing a certain proposition which he does believe unless he has adequate reason to cease from believing it. Our beliefs are rational unless we have reason for refraining; they are not nonrational unless we have reason *for* believing. They are innocent until proved guilty, not guilty until proved innocent" (Wolterstorff 1983: 163; see also 1996). We may readily concede that there are many situations in which asking whether one has defeating reasons may, because of specific circumstances, be a sufficient response to contestation or doubt. There is always a choice to be made about the measure in which time and energy will be committed to the practice of argumentation. To all appearances, however, Wolterstorff's statement is meant to describe what reason requires in all situations, including those in which someone engaged in the practice of philosophy seeks to respond to contestation and doubt about the theories she or he believes. So understood, the citation from Wolterstorff articulates a theory of argument as such, and it implies that contestation or doubt of the theory itself can be addressed only by showing that there are no defeating reasons, in distinction from giving reasons for believing it. But if this is the point, then the theory itself can only be dogmatically asserted, because showing the absence of defeating reasons warrants belief in the theory only on the assumption that the theory is true. In any event, the theory is in fact conceptually self-contradictory. In asserting that there cannot be reasons for a belief, one asserts the impossibility of transcendental-pragmatic argument, even while one also purports to designate the universal character of argument.

This is not to say that all beliefs are properly validated by the same form of argument. To the contrary, the universal character of argument may be self-differentiating, in a manner analogous to the self-differentiation of "true understanding" into understandings that are transcendental and those that are not. Apel holds, for instance, that argument differentiates with respect to transcendental-pragmatic, scientific, empirical-hermeneutical, and ethical kinds of true understandings (see 1979b). Against the objection, then, we require something like Apel's "regulative idea" of validation. This idea is used to make a logical, not an empirical point: Beliefs that are actually uncontested in a specific argumentation community are contestable and, therefore, subject to validation within a continuing practice of argumentation, and this possibility extends indefinitely. Validation is an ideal that the community of argumentation may approach asymptotically, and a transcendental understanding of argument, with whatever self-differentiations of argument there are, can itself be redeemed. Its content defines the regulative idea of argumentation.

I recognize that some have sought to show that transcendental argument is not possible. Rorty, for instance, reasons as follows: One cannot in fact show that the denial of an understanding is necessarily self-refuting because the denial is implied by every alternative understanding of understanding as such, and the possible formulations of alternatives are endless. Accordingly, arguments by way of self-refutation can establish only that a given alternative or set of alternatives is false, and it always remains that some alternative understanding not yet assessed may be self-referentially possible. Hence, every putative transcendental argument must be inconclusive. "All self-referential arguments are *ad hominem* arguments—arguments against a certain proposal. . . . There can be no such thing as wholesale self-referential arguments for negative conclusions" (Rorty 1979: 82)—that is, arguments for the conclusion that certain conditions of human understanding are transcendental because there are no possible competitors. The point Rorty seeks to make might also be formulated in terms of the understandings transcendental arguments seek to validate. On this formulation, the contents of true transcendental understandings, precisely because their denials are necessarily self-refuting or conceptually self-contradictory, must all imply each other. Hence, one could not show that a given transcendental understanding is true unless one could make explicit all implications of its content and show that all of these implications themselves designate necessary conditions of understanding. This task cannot be completed, since the possible formulation of implications is endless.

But this reasoning cannot be sound. Were it so, it would in fact do what it purports to show cannot be done, since it would show that transcendental arguments cannot be successful by showing that the denial of this understanding (that is, the assertion that transcendental arguments can be successful) is necessarily self-refuting. Hence, the fact that alternatives to a transcendental understanding can be formulated in endless ways or, what comes to the same thing, that the explicit formulation of its implications are endless does not mean that the understanding cannot be validated as self-referentially necessary. To the contrary, it means that the practice of transcendental argumentation, like all argumentation, is itself a communal practice characterized in terms of a regulative idea, namely, the idea of showing that all explicit reformulations of the denial are different only in a merely verbal sense or showing that all explicitly formulated implications also imply the understanding in question. But characterizing transcendental argumentation itself in terms of a regulative idea in no way denies that it is a distinct kind of reasoning.

Still, to accept Apel's assertion that argument has a transcendental character is one thing, and to accept his assertion that the validity of beliefs must be explicated "in terms of the . . . possibility of redeeming one's own truth claims" (1980a: 393-94) is something else. The former says that argumentation as such cannot be limited by beliefs that cannot be redeemed; the latter says that the validity of the belief *is* the possibility of redemption by argument. If I have understood him correctly, in other words, Apel holds that the truth of a true understanding is the property "will be agreed to in the indefinite argumentation community." This is the universal character of true understandings because only with that character so explicated is the difference between valid and invalid beliefs explicated pragmatically or in terms of a subject's communicative effects or possible effects.

So far as I can see, Apel makes just this point when he writes the following:

[The pragmatic] thesis based on a *theory of consensus* is stronger than the thesis of the classical correspondence-theory of truth, which states simply that assertions that *correspond with the facts* are, *for that reason, also intersubjectively valid.* This common way of representing the matter is not contradicted by our present considerations, but over and above it the following is being maintained: In order to bring to bear at the level of a linguistic *interpretation* or the world the *criteria* for truth that are available to us but always insufficient (phenomenological evidence for correspondence, coherence, pragmatic fruitfulness, and the like), we require the regulative idea—relevant to the pragmatics of research—of discursively building a consensus within an unlimited, ideal community of communication (1987: 39, n. 32).

If, with Peirce, "the opinion which is fated to be ultimately agreed to by all who investigate is what we mean by truth," Apel interprets this to say that the truth of a true opinion (or understanding) is its effect in the argumentation community, and, in this sense, he also endorses the completion of Peirce's statement: "and the object represented in this opinion is the real" (1980a: 401). In sum, the norm of true understandings and thus valid beliefs is properly defined as consensus in "the unlimited, ideal community of communication."

But if this is Apel's solution, then his pragmatic theory is unconvincing. For one thing, it is not apparent that all valid claims to truth can be redeemed through argumentation. As an example to the contrary, I have in mind especially the constitutive self-understandings that human activities assert. So far as I can see, a subject's inclusive belief about itself in relation to the comprehensive purpose may be valid, that is, a given human activity may be authentic, but there is in fact no possibility of redeeming this claim to truth. On some of Apel's formulations, moreover, the ideal of redemption in the indefinite argumentation community seems to mean that a valid claim to truth can be so argued as to command acceptance by all members of that community. This appears to be his meaning in speaking, for instance, of "consensus within an unlimited, ideal community of communication." If he intends his point to be so understood, I doubt its validity. As he would, I think, agree, the redemption of a belief requires that argumentative subjects have access to the relevant experiential evidence, and, in the nature of the case, this access is limited insofar as beliefs are about the concreteness or particularity of events—for instance, a belief about one's encounter with another individual or about one's own remembered past.

Naturally, Apel might deny that there are valid beliefs whose redemption is impossible, and he might hold that I have misread his intent with respect to beliefs about the concreteness of events. Moreover, revisions in his regulative idea of argumentation such as those I have implied are themselves understandings, claims for which *can* be assessed in the way Apel formulates. If valid, the belief *that* valid beliefs of certain kinds cannot be redeemed and the belief *that* the relevant argumentation community with respect to certain other types of beliefs is limited by access to the relevant experiential evidence are themselves claims to truth that can be so argued as to command consensus in the indefinite argumentation community. Assuming that they are valid, in other words, these are claims to truth for true transcendental understandings.

In any event, we can lay these matters aside, because there is a more fundamental problem in Apel's solution. "Building a consensus within an unlimited, ideal community of communication" defines the truth of an understanding and thus the validity of a belief in terms of a state of affairs that can never be realized, and this contradicts the fact that a true understanding *is* true. *Fated* to be ultimately agreed to is a present fact, that is, characterizes in some way how the future *is* conditioned. Having this property may entail that the understanding *would be* agreed to or would build consensus in the indefinite argumentation community. But an effect whose occurrence requires ideal conditions that cannot be realized cannot be an effect the understanding does have. In other words, the thought of that ideal cannot designate the character of the present fact, because one would thereby define a present fact in terms of an effect that cannot occur "on land or sea." On Apel's account, so far as I can see, the truth of a true understanding and thus the validity of a valid belief itself becomes, absurdly, an impossible property.

Given a pragmatic theory of belief, then, something different is required in order to clarify the universal norm that distinguishes a true understanding and thus a valid belief in terms of the condition it sets for the future. So far from being impossible, moreover, this distinguishing effect cannot be even a mere possibility. Because a true understanding *is* true, it can only be defined in terms of a necessary effect of the act of self-expression. If the character of an act is defined solely in terms of consequences that might or might not ensue, then one has defined an act in terms of a character it might or might not have. To say, for instance, that the eloquence Lincoln's speech does in fact have consists in the sublime feelings hearers might or might not have in listening to it is to say that Lincoln's speech has a property it might or might not have. This means that the truth of understandings and thus the validity of beliefs cannot be defined in terms of the possible agreement or acceptance of other human subjects. Their understanding is fragmentary, so that they may not understand the understanding or the argument for it, and their beliefs are fallible, so that their agreement or acceptance is merely possible.[6]

So far as I can see, then, the pragmatic character of belief implies the existence of a "subject" on which the effect of a claim is not fragmentary and whose "acceptance" of a valid claim is necessary. Since true understandings can be about anything at all, this "subject's" necessary "acceptance" of all valid claims implies that it "knows" all things completely. In other words, the "subject" implied by the pragmatic character of belief cannot be a human subject but, rather, only an activity of the metaphysical individual, whose activities are relative to all actuality as actual and all possibility as possible. A valid belief is a claim to validity that necessarily will be communicated to and "accepted" by the comprehensive individual. This conclusion does not deny but, rather, implies that at least some true understandings are "fated to be ultimately agreed to by all who investigate," in the sense that each commands the acceptance of any argumentative human subject who has experiential access to the evidence and understands the relevant argument. The point is simply that the norm of

---

[6]Similarly, a consequentialist understanding of good action is self-contradictory if it means that the goodness of the action consists in consequences that may or may not occur. This understanding makes the goodness of the action dependent on mere possibilities and, therefore, contradicts the assertion that the action *is* good. For this reason, consequentialist theories typically identify a good action as one that *intends* to have good consequences. But this makes sense only if the character of "good" that consequences may or may not exemplify is so understood that intending to have good consequences is also an exemplification of that character. Hence, the theory can be consistently consequentialist only if there is some necessary consequence that identifies the action as good.

true understandings is not itself defined by the agreement of all who investigate or by consensus in the indefinite argumentation community but, rather, by the "agreement" of the divine reality. "Will be 'agreed' to by the divine 'subject'" is the meaning of "*fated* to be ultimately agreed to by all who inquire," and "the object 'represented in the divine understanding'" is what we mean by "the real."[7]

We are now in a position to define the sense in which the propositional content of true understandings is true. Since a true understanding is one that necessarily will be communicated to and "agreed" to by the divine reality because it "knows" all actuality as actual and all possibility as possible, a true proposition is one that corresponds with reality in the all-inclusive reality. Correspondence with reality is a comparison that, strictly speaking, cannot itself be the property of a proposition. To the contrary, this comparison requires a "subject" that is internally related both to the reality in question and to the proposition. The correspondence, then, is a contrast between the two that occurs in the unification of a divine activity. Thus, to speak of a proposition as having the property "true" is to speak elliptically. It means that the proposition as an object of the divine relativity is contrasted with the relevant reality as an object of the divine relativity

---

[7]I have placed terms like "subject," "accepts," "knows," etc. in quotation marks when speaking of the divine reality because I do not believe that God is literally a subject with understanding. "Understanding" and "consciousness" are psychic terms that designate literally something specific to human existence and, perhaps, the existence of other sentient creatures. This is because each of these terms designates a kind of internal relation whose distinct character is inseparable from its exemplification in fragmentary creatures. In speaking literally of the divine reality, we must say that God is completely related to every human self-expression in being completely related to all actuality as actual and all possibility as possible. Still, we may speak symbolically of God as a subject who knows all there is to know and necessarily accepts all valid claims, and it is the symbolic character of such speaking that I intend to designate with the quotation marks.

To be sure, one might so generalize psychic terms that they are used to designate the character of all possible actualities. On this generalization, all actualities might be called subjects that experience other realities and God might be called a subject of understanding. So generalized, however, the psychic terms lose any distinctively psychic designation. Saying that all actualities are subjects of experience says only that all actualities are constituted by internal relations to other realities. Saying that God is a subject of understanding says only that God is constituted by complete relations to all actuality and possibility and, therefore, to each reality in contrast with all others.

such that the contrast is, within the divine unification, one of correspondence. Hence, to evaluate a proposition one understands as true means that it is the object of an understanding that will be "agreed" to by the divine reality.

The "truth" of a divine "understanding," we might say, is the correspondence of its propositional content with the relevant divine "experience" of reality. At the same time, however, even the "truth" of a divine "understanding" cannot be explicated independently of the divine "self-expression," because the divine unification in which the relation of correspondence occurs is itself an activity, so that the correspondence characterizes the divine activity as it conditions the future. Even the "truth" of a divine "understanding," in other words, cannot be explicated independently of the necessary "agreement" with it that will occur in all subsequent divine activities.

It is also the case that human subjects are constituted by their internal relations and, therefore, by their experience of reality as well as their relation to propositions. Although the fragmentariness of human experience means that a human subject can have many true understandings whose corresponding reality the subject does not experience, it is still possible that the propositional content of a true human understanding corresponds with the relevant reality as experienced by the subject in question. This is the case, for instance, with all true transcendental understandings, although the possibility is not limited to these. When that possibility is realized, we can say that there is a relation of correspondence within the unification of the human subject. In those cases and in that sense, we can also say that the truth of a true human understanding involves the correspondence of its propositional content to the subject's experience of reality. But this correspondence is *internal* to the subject's unification—and, because this unification *is* the choice of a self-understanding or act of self-expression, the correspondence and, therefore, the truth of the understanding characterize the subject as expressed.

While the truth of a true human understanding *may be* a correspondence internal to the subject's unification, moreover, this can never be an adequate explication of its truth. This is because no human unification can be the universal norm of true understandings, in terms of which every human subject evaluates its understandings. Hence, the sense in which the truth of a human understanding may be the correspondence of its propositional content to the subject's experience of reality depends on or is derivative from the universal character of all true understandings, namely, that they will be "agreed" to by the comprehensive individual because, in its unification, the proposition in question corresponds to reality. Similarly, then, the universal character of valid beliefs or claims to truth is that they will be "accepted" by God.

Because, as we have seen, every subject has a valid belief about the universal norm of true understandings, it now follows that every subject believes a true understanding of the divine reality. In other words, a relation to God is a transcendental condition of human activity and, therefore, every subject believes in God. Just as every choice with understanding from among alternatives for purpose implies an affirmation of the divine good, so every assent to some understanding implies assent to theism. In the last analysis, the true theory of belief is a comprehensive teleology. To believe something is to make a claim to truth that is inseparable from one's inclusive claim to authenticity, that is, the claim that one's exercise of original freedom is good because it pursues without duplicity the divine good.

II

JUSTICE

4

Democracy as a Formative Principle

A lawyer asked Jesus for "the great commandment in the law," says the New Testament, and Jesus answered: "You shall love the Lord your God with all your heart, and with all your soul, and with all your mind. This is the great and first commandment. And a second is like it, You shall love your neighbor as yourself" (Matthew 22: 35–39 RSV). If "neighbor" is taken in its most inclusive sense, so that it means any and all other individuals, human and nonhuman, with whom we are together in the world, then these two commandments express the principal conclusions of Part One: Humans are called to understand themselves in relation to the maximal divine good and, thereby, to pursue maximal good in the future as such. On this reading, moreover, the second commandment is like the first because the two imply each other. To love God with all one's heart and soul and mind *is* to pursue maximal good in the future as such or to love one's neighbor as oneself, and vice versa.

Some have said that the answer Jesus gave is paradoxical because love cannot be created by an act of will and, therefore, cannot be commanded. This observation contains a fundamental truth. *That* a human activity or individual is attached to the good is not itself open to choice. This fact is given to human existence by God's love, which precedes every activity within the world, defines the character of worth, and assures that every activity will "pass into permanent significance for the universe" (Whitehead 1941: 698). Aquinas has in mind this prior reality of God when he says that "false happiness does

179

not differ from true in an act of will; because, whatever be proposed to the will as the supreme good, whether truly or falsely, it makes no difference to the will in its desiring, loving, or enjoying that good: the difference is on the part of the intellect, as to whether the good proposed as supreme be truly so or not" (*Summa Contra Gentiles*: 3. 26). False love is possible only because a supreme good that evokes love is a prior reality, and this is why the difference consists in the understanding of this prior reality or in the intellect.

Still, the point Aquinas makes by differentiating the intellect from the will is better formulated in terms of our original freedom. For the difference in "intellect" is "willed" in the choice of a self-under-standing. Every human does decide in every moment *how* she or he will love, either authentically or inauthentically. We can say, then, that human existence is constituted by its love, which is always actualized in a decision about *what* to love. Either we love God with all our heart and soul and mind and, thereby, love our neighbor as ourselves, or our love is duplicitous, attached to some false ordering of the good. Love for God and, in God, the future as such is commanded because human activity is originally free and, therefore, moral in character. Each human activity is responsible for whether it understands itself as its own particular pursuit of the maximal divine good.

Part One offered an extended argument for this conclusion. The task of Part Two is to define the relation between love and justice. We now seek to articulate pursuit of the maximal divine good in relation to the specific purposes of politics. Stating the task in this way suggests the sense in which "justice" will be used. In both moral theory and wider discussion, the term sometimes means a broader set of normative conditions than I intend, because it designates the proper character of all institutions and cultural patterns. In contrast, the discussion here will focus on politics, and therefore "justice" will designate the conditions in or through which the divine purpose is specified to political life. To be sure, "politics" and "political" are themselves used with differing meanings, and, here also, I have in mind a more narrow sense. These terms will designate the association or associational process whose distinguishing purpose is to determine the activities of the state or the governing order of a society.

We might pursue the present task as a straightforward application of the comprehensive purpose. Beginning with the character of the divine good as developed in chapter 3, we might seek to specify that account of worth to political activity and association. But the credibility of comprehensive teleology is so widely and deeply doubted in recent discussions of justice that this doubt alone may dissuade many from the theistic conclusions previously reached, whatever the merit of the defense I have offered. Accordingly, I will pursue more indirectly the relation of justice to the divine good in order to include an argument that principles of justice depend on a comprehensive purpose. Part Two will begin without explicit appeal to the previous conclusion that human activity as such relates to a divine purpose. I will posit only, as a contribution from the earlier argument, that every exercise of human freedom is constituted by some or other moral evaluation, and thus Part Two begins without any explicit assumption about what moral claims are valid. On this basis, the present chapter will argue for a principle of democratic politics. Chapter 5 will, through a critical conversation with some recent democratic theories, seek to show that this principle is contradicted by any theory on which justice is independent of a comprehensive purpose. Only at that point will the substantive moral conclusions of Part One reappear, now as the premise that the comprehensive telos can only be the maximal divine good. Chapter 6, then, will pursue the principle of justice implied by maximizing the divine good and argue that justice so conceived is consistently democratic.

A principle of democratic politics can be defended without explicit appeal to the substantive moral conclusions reached earlier because this principle is a meta-ethical presupposition of every claim to moral validity. I will seek to show that a claim to validity for any moral prescription implies a principle for social action that is explicitly neutral to all substantive prescriptions. I will call this a "formative" principle of social action and argue that it includes the prescription of democratic politics. So understood, the argument continues, democracy implies what I will call the "compound character of justice." With this term, I designate a principle or set of principles that consistently includes a differentiation between the formative principles of a democratic constitution and a substantive principle or principles that ought to control the decisions taken in or through the democratic political process. Every attempt to separate justice from a comprehensive good, I will argue, fails to be a consistent conception of justice as compound and, therefore, as democratic. In contrast, maximizing the divine good consistently implies the compound and thus democratic character of justice, and I will seek to articulate the relevant substantive principle and its implications. If this movement of thought is successful, it will not only specify the theistic conclusions of previous chapters in a theory of justice but also confirm the comprehensive teleology they presented.

The current chapter, then, pursues the first step: an argument for democratic politics as a meta-ethical presupposition of every claim to moral validity. In order to prepare for subsequent chapters, I will keep in view the relation between this discussion and the possibility of a comprehensive teleology—although, to repeat, the argument does not explicitly depend on any substantive prescription or conception of the good. Since this argument cannot be convincing unless democracy as a formative principle is given sufficient precision, I will try to detail in some measure the proper provisions of a democratic constitution, including the rights of democratic citizens it ought legally to secure.

Anyone who is familiar with the work of Karl-Otto Apel and Jürgen Habermas will recognize that the discussion here is deeply indebted to both, notwithstanding that both are among those who doubt the credibility of comprehensive teleology. I cannot even begin to approximate the completeness with which Habermas has sought to clarify democratic politics. My discussion in this chapter will be limited by the attempt to defend a democratic constitution, and the measure of detail is determined by the need to identify what is being defended. But the direct discussion of democracy will be preceded, in the first three sections of the chapter, by the attempt to introduce and clarify a certain conception of social practices and its importance for moral theory. Democratic politics, I will then argue, is a specific social practice or set of social practices that can be defended without explicit appeal to any substantive moral prescription or conception of the good.

Social Practices

We can approach the relevant conception of social practices through attention to a common criticism of teleological ethics, which purports to show that any such ethic is self-defeating. On this indictment, a comprehensive purpose so prescribes for human action that the good cannot be maximized, and, in that sense, the purpose discredits itself.[1] This fate becomes apparent, we are told, when we take full account of the overriding status that belongs inherently to a comprehensive purpose. Any other moral norms that may be affirmed can only be guidelines or summary rules, in the sense that they hold in most cases but may always be overridden, and this means that the violation of such norms may be prescribed or permitted, depending on the particular circumstances in which one should pursue the maximal good. In the terms of a traditional distinction, there are no perfect duties, "duties not to do, or not to omit, an action of a certain [specific] kind," whatever the consequences, because all specific duties can be canceled by the imperfect duty "to promote a certain general end" (Donagan 1977: 154). But this means, the critique asserts, that the future actions of other individuals are inherently unpredictable in any significant measure, so that no given actor can take them significantly into account as she or he deliberates about the consequences of her or his choice.

Seeking to understand this assertion, one might think that the critic intends the following: Other individuals are unpredictable because their own assessment of consequences is or can be immensely complicated and, therefore, easily subject to error. But that is not the principal point. In order to clarify the more profound problem, the critic may grant that individuals both will act morally and will be informed by wise deliberation. It remains, we are told, that a present actor cannot have settled expectations about the future actions of other individuals because she or he cannot have settled expectations about the circumstances in which they will pursue the maximal good. For instance, one cannot count on another individual keeping her or his promise because circumstances at the time when the promise falls due may dictate or permit that it be broken in order to maximize the good. Moreover, the unpredictability is, as it were, cumulative. Once all actors must deliberate without settled expectations regarding the actions of others, what any given actor can expect of others becomes

---

[1]My entire discussion in this first section of the chapter is greatly indebted to Brian Barry (see Barry 1995, especially chapter 9).

even more indeterminate. If a person who makes a promise finds, at the time when keeping it arrives, that the future she or he faces is less settled, then whether keeping it will maximize the good becomes more uncertain. As Brian Barry summarizes: "The optimal course of action for me depends upon what I expect others to do, while the optimum course of action for others depends upon what they expect me to do. But the information that others are trying to bring about the best overall outcome is insufficient to enable me to predict what specifically they will do, and everybody else is in the same predicament" (1995: 220).

In contrast, maximizing the good, at least on any plausible account of it, requires a human future that is in major respects settled and, therefore, requires social cooperation or coordination. Without predictable patterns of interaction or common life, no actor can anticipate the future in the measure that permits a significant pursuit of the telos. But predictable patterns of interaction call for individuals who act in accord with them even if doing so is not, in the given circumstances, the action that maximizes the good. Institutions of social cooperation, in other words, assign specific roles to be played or duties to be honored whatever the consequences. If they are morally permissible, promises should be kept because they are made, institutional commitments fulfilled because they have been accepted, laws obeyed because they have been enacted.

This does not necessarily preclude a moral obligation to violate the usual observance of a specific norm or rule of action in extreme or unusual circumstances. The specific norms or rules of social cooperation may themselves take account of that possibility; that is, the norms are typically so qualified that they prescribe certain actions for certain people except in certain circumstances. Although promises should be kept, for instance, it is generally recognized that, with most promises, the obligation is canceled if the life of one's child depends on it. The point can also be expressed by saying that some specific norm or rule may be overridden by other specific norms or rules. One's obligation to keep a promise may be canceled by the specific norm that prescribes one's responsibilities as a parent. But the exceptions themselves are specific, and this can be true even if it is not always possible to state all of the exceptions with precision. Absent such specified circumstances, the norm should be obeyed whatever the consequences. In contrast, the critique we have here in view alleges, a teleological ethic makes social coordination impossible because it allows a *nonspecific* exception to every specific norm or rule, namely, circumstances in which an alternative action pursues the maximal good. Thus, a comprehensive teleology self-destructs because it denies the kind of moral norms without which the good, on any plausible account of it, cannot be maximized.

But this critique, as Barry points out (see 1995: 217–21), admits of a ready reply. If maximizing the good is prevented by a comprehensive purpose that may always override the norms and rules human cooperation requires, then the teleological ethic in question proscribes that understanding of its supreme principle. Insofar as social cooperation or coordination increases realization of the good, the comprehensive purpose implies specific norms or rules, observance of which is prescribed whatever the consequences. In other words, the criticism fallaciously assumes that comprehensive teleology means "looking at each calculation in isolation, and not taking adequate account of the effects on a society's capacity to function of its being known that all actions are taken on the basis of such calculations" (1995: 219); each case, it is assumed, should be "separately taken" (1995: 224). To the contrary, a teleological ethic may imply that at least some cases should *not* be separately taken, precisely for the reasons on which the criticism depends.

We can reformulate the point in a distinction between direct and indirect applications of a comprehensive purpose. The ethic may not prescribe that this principle be applied directly to every human activity; at least in some circumstances, the required application may be indirect or proceed through the specific norms and rules of social cooperation that are necessary in order to maximize the good. It is one thing teleologically to validate a particular action "separately taken" and another to validate it by appeal to a system of rules that is itself validated teleologically. Keeping a promise or obeying a law may, in some circumstances, be proscribed if the comprehensive purpose is directly applied; in the same circumstances, the action may be prescribed as conformity to a pattern of social cooperation that is itself required to maximize the good.

This distinction is drawn effectively in John Rawls's "Two Concepts of Rules," where he clarifies the difference between the "summary view" and the "practice conception" of rules. The "summary view" implies and is implied by direct applications of a teleological ethic. "Rules are regarded as reports that cases of a certain sort have been found on *other* grounds [that is, by direct application of a teleological principle] to be properly decided in a certain way," and "the point of having rules derives from the fact that similar cases tend to recur and that one can decide cases more quickly if one records past decisions in the form of rules" (1955: 19, 22). In this sense, rules are general guidelines that may be overridden in any particular case. On "the practice conception," in contrast, "rules are not generalizations from the decisions of individuals applying the utilitarian [read: teleological] principle directly and independently to recurrent particular cases. On the contrary, rules define a [social] practice and are themselves the subject of the . . . principle" (1955: 24)—and, if the practice is morally valid, actors properly "abdicate" their "title to act in accordance" with a direct appeal to consequences (1955: 16).

The two conceptions differ, then, on whether particular cases or rules are logically prior. On the summary view, any "particular case . . . may exist whether or not there is a rule covering the case." Hence, "the A's and B's" referred to "in rules of the form 'Whenever A do B' may be described as A's and B's whether or not there is the rule" (1955: 22). The particular cases are logically prior in the sense that each may be understood independently of the statement that it does or does not exemplify a specific rule. On the practice conception, however, "the rules of practices are logically prior to particular cases." With respect to "actions specified" by these rules, "it is logically impossible to perform them outside the stage-setting provided by those practices" (1955: 25) and, therefore, logically impossible to understand the actions independently of the statement that they do or do not exemplify the rules. The game of baseball illustrates the point. "One cannot steal base, or strike out, or draw a walk, or make an error, or balk" independently of the rules constituting this social practice, "although one can do certain things which appear to resemble these actions such as sliding into a bag, missing a grounder and so on" (1955: 25). Similarly, one cannot vote or run for elective office or obey or disobey a law independently of the norms constituting a political community. On the summary view, we may say, rules evaluate an independent description of particular cases, while, on the practice conception, rules regulate or constitute the descriptions, and I will henceforth call the latter constitutive rules and will call the patterns of interaction they constitute social practices.[2]

The fact that rules may constitute the description of actions is what gives to Kant's moral theory whatever moral content it may seem to have. In an earlier chapter, I argued that his categorical imperative, "act only on that maxim whereby thou canst at the same time will that it should become a universal law" (1949: 38, emphasis deleted), is empty, because Kant sought to define true self-understandings in a formal manner or independently of the choice among alternatives for purpose. In the terms of our present discussion, that conclusion may be reformulated: The imperative is empty because it purports to

---

[2]The term "constitutive rules" is taken from John Searle, who argues that all institutions require such rules (see Searle 1995: 27f.). On his account, "institutional facts exist only within systems of constitutive rules" (1995: 28), because such facts involve a status imposed on someone or something by collective agreement and in order that the person or thing may perform a function that cannot be performed by the thing independently of this agreement. Certain pieces of paper can function as money or certain individuals as citizens only because there is collective agreement that the paper "counts as" money or the people "count as" citizens—and the agreement that constitutes status is agreement on a system of rules that identifies what counts as what in what contexts. If Searle's argument is, as I take it to be, convincing, then an ethic that proscribes all constitutive rules or social practices would proscribe all institutions.

I do not mean to imply that I agree in all respects with the position Searle presents. His purpose is to understand institutional facts as a specific kind of fact in the world and, therefore, is not to give a moral account of them. So far as I can see, however, the account he does give implies that institutions are not morally valid or invalid. Searle asserts that "functions are never intrinsic to the physics of any phenomenon but are assigned from outside by conscious observers and users. *Functions, in short, are never intrinsic but always observer relative,*" that is, "relative to a system of values we hold" (1995: 14, 15). On my reading, Searle means that human existence or activity as such has no "function," that is, can be properly understood independently of any telos to which it is directed—and this account is a part of Searle's larger intent to advance a "theory of the mind" in which "a world of consciousness, . . . , fit[s] into a world consisting entirely of physical particles in fields of force" (1995: xi; see also Searle 1992). But if this is so, then "the values we hold" are never implied by the nature of consciousness or conscious activity as such; that is, there can be no transcendental moral law. On my accounting, the absence of a transcendental moral law means that no set of constitutive rules can be morally valid.

prescribe for actions that can be independently described. I assume here that "canst will that it should become a universal law" means "canst state without self-contradiction that the action so described is not immoral for any individual who might choose it." This statement cannot be self-contradictory unless the description of the action includes or implies a moral rule or principle that proscribes the action. But there can be no such implication if the action is independently described. On my reading, the independent description of actions is precisely what Kant stipulates in separating the universal form of rational freedom or the moral law from the matter or purpose that defines any given exercise of will. The maxim chosen, which ought to be chosen from duty, describes the matter or purpose of the action. This means that no description of an action implies a moral rule or principle, and any maxim can be willed as a universal law without self-contradiction—and this formulation of the categorical imperative is empty.

But our assessment of this imperative must change if the maxims in question are understood to describe actions as constituted by social practices. Since a maxim then presupposes a rule, the agent who breaks the rule both affirms and denies it and, thereby, commits a practical self-contradiction. In what may be his most famous example, Kant considers the maxim, "when in difficulty, to promise whatever one pleases, with the purpose of not keeping the promise." He argues that this maxim cannot be willed as a universal law because, were such action not immoral, "no one would consider that anything was promised to him" (1949: 40), and therefore the agent could not in truth make a promise. If "making a promise" were an independent description of the action, this argument would be unconvincing. One would then be able to make a promise without another person accepting it or considering that something was "promised to him," and making a promise would not imply the affirmation of promise keeping that the putative self-contradiction requires. But this example appears convincing because the description of one's action as making and breaking a promise presupposes the social practice of promising, in which the role of promiser requires another individual who is the promisee, and this practice is constituted by the rule that promises should be kept. So understood, the maxim cannot be willed as a universal law because it thereby contradicts the constitutive rule that makes false promising possible.[3] In other words, the maxim makes its agent a moral "free-rider." She or he cannot act in the way described without presupposing that relevantly similar individuals are morally bound by a rule that proscribes the action (see Barry 1995: 243–44).

On this reading of Kant's categorical imperative, we might say, it formulates a generalized proscription of actions that violate morally valid social practices. Having arrived at this conclusion, some may suggest, we have in fact confirmed Kant's denial of comprehensive teleology because we have shown that prescriptions like "promises should not be broken at will" can be validated by appeal to the inconsistency of their denials. But this reading of Kant gives moral content to his theory only on the assumption that there are morally valid social practices, as the phrase "generalized proscription of actions that violate morally valid social practices" suggests. With respect to the practice of promising, for instance, what the previous analysis shows is this: *If* the practice is morally valid, then promises should not be broken at will. But whether there are morally valid social practices and, if so, what they are cannot be determined without another moral principle. Kant's categorical imperative cannot also ground the moral validity of social practices unless we take it as a statement of the supreme principle or moral law. On that reading, however, the maxims of our actions describe them independently of constitutive norms or rules; hence, those maxims can-

---

[3]The point may also be formulated in terms of Kant's dictum that "ought implies can." To act on a maxim (and thus allege that one is not immoral) is to assert that the action so described is or would be a possible action (one that can be taken) under the condition that it is not immoral for any relevant individual and, by implication, known to be not immoral by all relevant individuals. But the maxim "to make a promise with the purpose of not keeping it" describes an action one cannot take under that condition, since its description presupposes the social practice constituted by the rule that promises should be kept. If promise breaking at will were not immoral, "no one would consider that anything was promised to him"; that is, there would be no social practice of promising. Moreover, the maxim "to make a promise with the purpose of breaking it should that action serve the maximal good" is also an impossible action under the condition that it is not immoral for any relevant individual. This maxim transforms promise keeping from a constitutive to a summary rule and, given the indeterminacy thereby introduced, destroys the practice without which one cannot make a promise.

not contradict themselves by presupposing a social practice. To the best of my reasoning, Kant's imperative cannot escape this dilemma: Either the imperative is empty or it should be taken as a generalized proscription of actions that violate morally valid social practices, and, in the latter case, the moral validity of practices waits on some other principle.

Whether the principle that grounds the moral validity of social practices is a comprehensive purpose is another question. The argument for a positive answer occupies the present work as a whole. The principal point here is that prescribing social coordination and cooperation in the form of social practices is not obviously inconsistent with comprehensive teleology. Given that social practices require a supreme principle by which their moral validity is grounded, a comprehensive teleology may purport to articulate this principle. To assert summarily that the grounding principle cannot be teleological is tacitly to assume that a comprehensive purpose must be directly applied to all particular choices or actions, and that assumption is one a comprehensive teleology may reject. It may prescribe certain social practices as indirect applications of a comprehensive purpose.

Perhaps the critic will now insist that the assumption of universal direct application is a necessary one. The very idea of a teleological ethic, she or he may assert, implies this prescription, and thus every such ethic is self-defeating. But the critique loses any hope of being credible once this assertion is no longer suppressed. The very idea of comprehensive teleology means only that every choice with understanding should imply without duplicity a certain understanding of the comprehensive good. This idea is not contradicted if the understanding of one's choice takes into account a set of social practices that realization of the maximal good requires, so that one acts in conformity with the constitutive rules and norms of some practice whatever the consequences of the act "separately taken." To the contrary, a comprehensive telos defines a principle in terms of which to determine which among specific purposes should be chosen, and, given that social cooperation is one of the possible purposes, the difference between direct and indirect applications of the principle marks alternatives that should themselves be evaluated in relation to the principle.

The Necessity of Common Decisions

The principal burden of the previous section was to introduce the conception of social practices. Having done this in relation to a summary criticism of teleology serves simply to prevent the untimely conclusion that teleology as such is discredited by the argument I now wish to make. On this argument, a principle constituting at least one social practice is a meta-ethical presupposition of every claim to moral validity. We can make the point by saying that a comprehensive teleology is indeed self-defeating if it purports to require universal direct application and, therefore, to proscribe all social practices, because this proscription contradicts the meta-ethical character of its own claim to validity. The clarification of this point will set the stage for presenting the argument for democracy as a formative social practice or set of social practices.

In keeping with the previous discussion, I will use the term "social practice" to mean an order or pattern of human interaction in which roles and responsibilities are coordinated by constitutive rules or norms, those meant to obligate participants whatever the consequences. The action of each participant cannot be described independently of those rules and norms. We can now add that the standard obligations of social practices are typically contingent on or assume common acceptance or general observance by the relevant individuals—as, for instance, in the game of baseball or the practice of making contracts. This point can also be formulated in terms of the constitutive rules or norms themselves. I noted in passing that the rules of social practices are typically so qualified that they identify specific circumstances in which individuals are released from the standard obligations of the practice; for instance, many morally permissible promises should be broken if the life of someone for whom one has special responsibility is at stake. Similarly, the norms of a social practice themselves typically specify when the nonobservance by others destroys the practice or releases an individual from its standard obligations, as, for instance, one may be released from a contract if the other party fails to honor it.

So understood, a social practice is a certain kind of social action. I will call a human action social in character in the respect that it affects or conditions the possible purposes of other human individuals—and, by extension, will also use the term "social action" to mean interaction between or among two or more individuals. Principles or norms that prescribe how individuals ought to treat other individuals are, then, principles or norms for social action. A comprehensive purpose is itself a principle of social action: All relations between human individuals ought to occur in accord with the principle that each person chooses to maximize the good. It is worth noting, moreover, that any such principle exemplifies the logical features of constitutive in distinction from summary norms—as one might expect given that summary norms are but guidelines. Although there are no circumstances in which an individual is released from the "standard obligations" of a comprehensive purpose, the imperative to maximize the good regulates the description of all human activity. Human activity as such can be described as a choice that exemplifies pursuit of the comprehensive telos with integrity or with duplicity, and, although there are other possible descriptions, they all imply this one. We might be tempted to say, then, that a comprehensive teleology defines social action as such as a comprehensive social practice. But this would be misleading, because it makes no sense to say that one is obligated to maximize the good whatever the consequences. Hence, I will reserve the term "social practice" for an order or structure of human interaction whose constitutive norms could be related to a comprehensive purpose only as an indirect application of it, and this is the sense in which a social practice is a certain kind of social action.

In speaking of a meta-ethical presupposition of every claim to moral validity, I use "meta-ethical" to designate a moral claim in the respect that distinguishes it from nonmoral claims. In this respect, a moral claim and thus the prescription for which validity is claimed are explicitly neutral to all moral prescriptions, that is, explicitly neutral to whether or not the prescriptions are valid.[4] Considered meta-ethically, a claim to validity for some moral prescription claims validity for some obligatory evaluation of possible purposes, that is, some designation of choices as those agents ought to make or those reason requires. It follows that a putative moral prescription is meta-ethically senseless if the individuals to whom it is said to apply cannot choose

[4]Throughout this work I use "prescription" to mean a moral prescription, and speak of prescriptions as valid or invalid in the sense that they are morally valid or invalid.

to act as it requires and do so because the prescription is valid. If we emphasize the ability to act as prescribed, this meta-ethical statement means that "ought implies can." A putative moral prescription is meta-ethically senseless if the alternatives of an agent to whom it is said to apply do not include the required action. If we emphasize the claim to validity, a putative moral prescription is meta-ethically senseless if an agent to whom it is said to apply cannot choose in a manner that expresses dissent, that is, expresses her or his decision that the prescription is not valid. The meta-ethical character of "ought," we might say, implies not only "can" but also "may not," in the sense that an agent may contest the moral claim. Some may object that judging a prescription to be invalid and expressing dissent are two different things; an agent may be able to do the former even though she or he has no opportunity to do the latter. But we are here discussing *practical* reason, that is, reason in the respect that it determines action or the choice of a purpose. If there is no possibility of a purpose that expresses dissent, then the validity of the prescription can have no part in determining action that conforms to it.

Thus, one implication of the meta-ethical character of moral claims is that moral prescriptions for social action prescribe *common* decisions, in the sense that each of the participants in the relationship or set of relationships should and thus can choose the prescribed action or actions because the prescription is valid. If I am morally required or permitted to act in a certain manner, and if that action has effects on you, then the moral validity of the prescription on which I act means that your acceptance of those effects is required by reason—and, in that sense, the prescription implies a common decision. Thus, a moral prescription for social action or, as we may also say, the social action itself is meta-ethically senseless unless each participant can choose in a manner that expresses her or his dissent. When the prescription constitutes a social practice, moreover, the expression of dissent must be possible even if the practice is otherwise observed, that is, even if all other participants adhere to the principles or norms that purport to define morally valid interaction. Every affected individual must be able to participate as an exercise of practical reason alone.

Consider in this context the social practice of slavery, where, for present purposes, this means an order of interaction whose norms prescribe that some individuals ought to have exclusive disposal over the activities of others. If slavery is in force, in the sense that slave owners adhere to its rules and the political community enforces them, then slaves cannot choose in a manner that expresses dissent from the putative validity of the practice. Having no standing in the community that creates the practice, they cannot politically or socially contest it. To be sure, slaves might seek to escape or rebel. But these ways of expressing dissent are not themselves recognized by the rules of slavery. To the contrary, the practice is meant to be so designed that such possibilities are coercively precluded, and they only betray that the practice cannot be fully established. That this social practice is meta-ethically senseless because some to whom its norms of interaction apply are denied participation in common decisions is confirmed by the fact that individuals whose service to another depends on their decision that reason so requires are not slaves.[5]

Now consider more general principles of social action. As a moral prescription, anarchy is such a principle, where, for present purposes, "anarchy" means that social action should be in no way ordered by social practices. If anarchy reigns in fact, what purpose might an individual who contests this principle choose in order to express her or his dissent? The only purpose that contests the existing anarchy would be one that affirms at least the permissibility of social practices. In the nature of the case, however, one person alone cannot constitute a social practice, since it requires rules or norms that coordinate the

---

[5]Some might say that a slave may contest the practice by committing suicide. But I assume in this analysis that the relevant moral subjects in social action are the human individuals involved rather than their member activities. To be sure, an individual may in fact choose suicide as an expression of dissent, especially in situations that allow no challenge to oppressive practices. But recognizing this fact is something different than saying that failure to commit suicide is a decision to accept as valid the social prescription or social practice in question. The latter implies that the relevant subjects are concrete activities, each of which may express dissent by terminating the individual of which it is a member. Notwithstanding the metaphysical distinction between individuals and activities, human persons are the relevant subjects of social action for the following reason: The common decisions required by social prescriptions require common understanding between or among participating individuals and, therefore, depend on participation in linguistically constituted communication—and human activities enjoy the capacity for this participation only as member activities of individuals. Hence, it is the individual understood as a subject with a future who must be able to choose a purpose that expresses dissent.

actions of several individuals or effect social cooperation through common acceptance. This means that social practices cannot be so much as permissible, because they are impossible, in the absence of a common decision-making process, an order of interaction leading to a decision by which each individual is subsequently bound. It now follows that an individual cannot choose a purpose that affirms the permissibility of social practices unless she or he can participate in such a process; that is, whether they should be permitted is itself a common decision about the general principle of social action. But a common decision-making process is itself a social practice, constituted by relevant rules or norms that define how and when a common decision is taken. Hence, an individual could not choose a purpose that expresses dissent from a reigning anarchy.

Conceivably, all individuals in a situation of anarchy might agree on the reigning principle, in the sense that the choice for it is independently taken by each. But even Hobbes, who thought that anarchy or "the war of each against all" is the "natural condition" of humankind, recognized that the decision for or against a political community requires a common decision-making procedure, in the sense that the decision is taken in or through interaction. On his account, the social contract is not something for which each individual can decide independently. To the contrary, each agrees to accept the sovereign's authority only because all others agree to do so. In other words, a social contract cannot be effected in the absence of an associational process that itself requires constitutive rules. Participating in a common decision through, for instance, discussion that leads to voting or shaking hands or signing a document is, like making a promise or stealing a base, an action whose description presupposes prescriptive rules.

Indeed, participating in a common decision about governing principles includes an exchange of promises, because there is no such common decision unless each of the parties is bound by it. For this reason, Apel argues convincingly that Hobbes's natural condition of humankind makes any social contract impossible. If the prior situation is a war of each against all, each individual who is thinking clearly would enter the supposed contract with what Apel calls a silent "criminal reservation" (1982: 88); that is, her or his interests would dictate that each individual break the contract whenever those interests were thereby best served. Whatever individuals say or do that purports to be coming to an agreement would not in fact be acts of participating in a social contract but would be, rather, further participation in the war of each against all. Barry offers a similar argument (see 1995: 33–34), and others have made the point by saying that one cannot contract to keep a contract. Only a decision-making process that already includes the moral rules of promising could bind the parties to an agreement about common principles of interaction. Thus, the question of whether or not social practices should be permitted is a sensible one only if human interaction is bound by a general moral principle that prescribes at least one social practice. Without it, an individual who contests the reigning principle of interaction could not express dissent, and, as a general principle, anarchy is meta-ethically senseless.

As may now be apparent, a comprehensive purpose that prescribes universal direct application of itself is similarly senseless, because this general principle for social action is, in the relevant sense, anarchical. It, too, prescribes that social action should be in no way ordered by social practices. Given a situation in which all other individuals choose in accord with that comprehensive purpose, no given individual could choose a purpose that expresses dissent from the reigning principle of social action. Only if the comprehensive purpose prescribes its own indirect application through a practice of common decision making, the rules of which should be observed whatever the consequences, can the general principle be contested. Because the prescription of this practice is implied by the meta-ethical character of moral claims, it sets a condition for the validity of any ethic. A general principle for human interaction must not only permit but also require the conditions of common decision making in accord with which dissent from that principle can be expressed. Absent a prescription of that practice, no individual could adhere to the general principle because it is valid, that is, no individual could act morally.

The Practice of Communicative Respect

If the preceding argument is sound, at least one social practice is prescribed as an implication of the meta-ethical character of every moral claim, namely, the practice of common decision making about contested moral prescriptions for social action. I will call this the practice of moral discourse, appropriating the term "discourse" from Habermas and meaning by it the specific social practice that suspends other purposes in order commonly to assess the validity of contested claims (see Habermas 1984: 17–18, 25, 42; 1990: 158–60). Hence, discourse may also be described as the practice of argumentation or common critical reflection in which claims are validated or invalidated by the giving of reasons. Precisely because it is about the validity of principles and norms for social action, the common decision making discussed above must be the practice of moral discourse. I recognize that the prescription of this practice remains vague until its meaning is clarified in terms of actual patterns or institutions of common decision making, and the attempt to pursue that matter will turn directly to political community. Before taking that turn, however, it is important to make explicit another implication of this prescription.

Moral discourse as a specific social practice both implies and is implied by—and therefore is inseparable from—a principle that constitutes all social action. In all human relationships, individuals are morally bound to treat each other as *potential participants in moral discourse*. This is simply to repeat that the claim to moral validity for any social action prescribes a common decision, so that every participant should be able to choose a purpose that expresses dissent from the claim. No social action can be moral if it treats another individual in a manner that denies the possibility of contestation and, therefore, of moral discourse. We can also say, then, that all human individuals always have the moral rights that define them as potential participants in moral discourse, one of which is the right to be or become an actual participant in discourse, and these moral rights articulate a universal moral principle.

This principle of social action is itself meta-ethical and, therefore, is a meta-ethical presupposition of every claim to moral validity, in the following sense: The social action prescribed is explicitly neutral to all moral disagreement.[6] On the face of it, one might object, a prescrip-

---

[6]To speak strictly, one should say that the principle is meta-ethical because the prescribed action is *insofar* or *in that respect* explicitly neutral to all moral disagreement. Any action that observes the meta-ethical principle will exemplify other characteristics in addition to its observance of the principle. But I will assume that "insofar" or "in that respect" is understood.

tion of universal rights cannot be explicitly neutral to all such disagreement, because it is not explicitly neutral to disagreement about
the principle itself. But we should distinguish between the stated or
propositional content of the principle, on the one hand, and the action
prescribed, on the other. The stated or propositional content is indeed
an explicit denial of its denial. But this is not the case with the action.
Treating all individuals as potential participants in discourse is explicitly neutral even to disagreement about whether all individuals should
be so treated, since that disagreement defines a question about what
treatment reason requires. In this sense, this meta-ethical principle
prescribes the way in which social action treats possible moral disagreement, and this is the kind of social action proper even to disagreement about the principle.

To be sure, actions are constituted by the reasons for which they are
taken or the understandings they affirm. Hence, treating others as
potential participants in discourse is or includes an affirmation of the
prescription to do so and, thereby, might seem to be an explicit denial
of its denial. But it remains that the action as constituted by this
affirmation is explicitly neutral even to its own affirmation, because
it thereby affirms argumentation as the proper treatment of moral
disagreement, even disagreement with itself. Any action that contests
this prescription asserts that the dissent is required by reason. Thus,
it, too, affirms the explicit neutrality of argumentation. Whatever the
content for which one claims validity, in other words, the taking of
any social action is also the affirmation that discourse is explicitly
neutral to moral disagreement with that action. This is what it means
to say that the principle prescribing treatment of all humans as potential participants in discourse is a meta-ethical presupposition of every
moral claim.

I will call this meta-ethical principle a *formative* principle and will
speak in the same way of the moral rights in terms of which it may
be stated. A moral principle or prescription is formative, then, if it
prescribes social action that is explicitly neutral to all moral disagreement, that is, if the action prescribed simply affirms argumentation
as the proper treatment of such disagreement. As such, the principle
is distinguished from a *substantive* principle or prescription, which
prescribes social action that is not explicitly neutral to all moral
disagreement. Thus, the distinguishing mark of a formative prescrip-

tion is its explicit neutrality to all substantive ones; that is, asserting the former does not explicitly affirm or deny the moral validity of any prescription whose prescribed social action is partisan in some or other moral disagreement. This is equivalent to saying that the action prescribed by a formative prescription is explicitly neutral even to disagreement about itself because, were this not so, it would be a substantive prescription. Using "human association" to mean all social action, I will also say that a formative prescription is explicitly neutral to all conceptions of good human association; that is, asserting the former does not explicitly affirm or deny any of the latter. To be sure, the formative principle defined above may itself be called a conception of good human association, because it means that treating all individuals as potential participants in discourse is good. But, again, the action prescribed by this principle is explicitly neutral even to disagreement about itself and, therefore, this prescription is distinguished from all conceptions of good human association whose prescribed actions are partisan in some or other possible moral disagreement. Hence, I will use "conception of good human association" to mean a substantive prescription.

Notwithstanding its universality, the formative principle we have clarified also constitutes a social practice. Here, as in all social practices, the norm or set of norms in question defines a certain kind of social action, although, in distinction from other morally valid social practices, this kind is not a specific pattern of interaction but, rather, a formative aspect of all social action. As with all constitutive norms, moreover, the principle of this universal social practice regulates the description of the relevant human actions. It is logically impossible to understand social action independently of its respect for or violation of the obligation to treat all individuals as potential participants in discourse; although social actions may be described in other ways, they all imply this one. A person cannot perform a social action independently of this principle any more than she or he can steal a base independently of the rules of baseball, and an individual who violates the principle is a moral "free-rider," presupposing it in claiming that her or his action is morally valid.

On my reading, Apel formulates just this universal principle when he asserts that every claim to validity presupposes the obligation to recognize all human individuals as persons. "All beings who are capable of linguistic communication must be recognized as persons since in all their actions and utterances they are potential participants in a discussion" (1980b: 259). Appropriating Apel (and Habermas), I will call the universal practice in question the practice of communicative action and call its constitutive principle the principle of communicative respect. Correspondingly, the rights that belong to all individuals as potential participants in moral discourse are communicative rights. On Apel's account, this conception of our communicative duty is the sense in which we may affirm Kant's categorical imperative: "So act as to treat humanity, whether in thine own person or in that of any other, in every case as an end withal, never as means only" (Kant 1949: 46, emphasis deleted).

For Apel, moreover, this imperative exhausts the supreme moral norm or "transcendental-pragmatic" moral principle, and this is one way of saying that he denies comprehensive teleology. As a consequence, he can call the "fundamental norm of an ethics of communication" (1979b: 335, emphasis deleted) a formal norm, which is independent of all material norms because it alone is universal. "Our fundamental norm is not a material norm . . . but a 'meta-norm' that prescribes the ideal procedure of . . . legitimating material norms, . . . by seeking a consensus of all affected people by an argumentative mediation of their interests" (1982: 100–101). I will subsequently argue that Apel's denial contradicts his affirmation of communicative respect, so that the "meta-norm" implies a substantive principle or set of principles that is also universal. Still, we can here agree with Apel in this: Because the principle of communicative respect is formative, it cannot be canceled by any substantive prescription or conception of good human association. Were the communicative rights of any individual subject to being canceled by a substantive prescription, the principle would not be a meta-ethical presupposition of every moral claim to validity. To the contrary, the principle would not be presupposed by a claim to validity for the conception of good human association by which those rights could be canceled. Thus, the "meta-norm" overrides, in the sense that the practice it constitutes cannot be canceled by, any other principle or norm of social action with which it conflicts. All social action always participates in the practice of communicative action and ought always to observe its constitutive prescriptions, whatever the consequences.

This does not mean that there are no conceivable circumstances in which one is morally permitted to deny another individual or other individuals the possibility of a purpose that expresses dissent. As we have seen, the norms of a social practice typically stipulate the conditions under which individuals are released from the standard obligations of the practice, including conditions when the absence of common observance cancels those obligations. In the practice of making contracts, for instance, a person may be released from keeping a contract if it is broken by another party. Similarly, the norms constituting the practice of communicative action stipulate when the failure of others to act accordingly releases an individual from communicative respect, for instance, in a situation of self-defense against an immediate threat to one's life. But this social practice differs from all others in this respect: Specific conditions under which standard obligations do not apply can be defined only as violations of those standard obligations. This is what it means to say that the norms of this practice cannot be overridden by any other prescription for social action.

A more or less complete moral theory requires a detailed treatment of these specific conditions, but I will not pursue that treatment. It depends on a prior clarification of the standard obligations that constitute the practice of communicative action, and this is the more important matter for the articulation of justice as a political principle. Because communicative rights are those that belong to each individual as a potential participant in moral discourse, the content of these rights can be derived from the necessary conditions of moral discourse as a specific social practice. As we have noted, the distinguishing purpose of moral discourse is to determine through argumentation the validity or invalidity of contested moral claims. Whether this practice achieves its common purpose, then, depends solely on the soundness of arguments, the opportunity for criticism, and common pursuit of the truth. Accordingly, its necessary conditions include equal access, that is, equal freedom for all participants to advance and contest any claim and the arguments for it; the absence of internal coercion in the form of strategic activity or, stated positively, uncompromised commitment of all participants to pursuit of the truth; and the absence of external coercion that might influence the acceptance or contestation of claims (cf. Habermas 1984: 25; 1993: 31).

With the term "external coercion," I mean coercion that is not specific to the practice of discourse. As a specific social practice, discourse occurs in the context of social action or social relationships generally. Insofar as one participant in a discourse is morally permitted to coerce another in relationships more generally, the coercion can invade the discourse and corrupt its pursuit of the truth. Let us suppose, for instance, that slavery is morally permissible, and a master and slave are to have a discourse about some matter. Under these conditions, the slave remains a slave within the discourse, and it would be morally permissible for the master to coerce the slave's acceptance of certain claims, for instance, by threatening harsh treatment once the discourse has ceased, so that agreement is not reached by the force of argument alone. Even if the master in fact treats the slave during the discourse itself as a free and equal participant, it remains that the threat of coercion is morally permissible. The master is not morally bound to treat the slave in that manner, precisely because she or he remains a slave, and the practice of slavery contradicts the necessary conditions of discourse (cf. Apel 1979b: 340–42).

In other words, the norms of a specific social practice may be a specification of those constituting a more general social practice and, in any event, are specifications of any universal principle of social action. Hence, the more general norms or principles are external normative conditions of the more specific practice, and in some situations the former may override or cancel the specific practice. For instance, norms of legal order are external conditions of the practice of baseball, and a given baseball game is canceled if a riot breaks out in the bleachers. But the external normative conditions cannot be suspended by the internal norms of the specific practice. If, for instance, norms of the legal order proscribe assault, then assault cannot be permitted within the specific practice of economic bargaining. The supposed discourse between master and slave is a more specific interaction within the more general practice of slavery, and just because the rules of slavery are external conditions that cannot be suspended, the master is permitted to control the supposed discourse by the threat of coercion. Any such threat contradicts common pursuit of the truth. Hence, discourse cannot be the specification of a more general norm or principle that permits coercion—or, to say the same thing, the necessary conditions of discourse include the absence of external coercion.

These reflections confirm that the special practice of moral discourse belongs to the universal practice constituted by the principle of communicative respect. The absence of external coercion is, in other words, the necessary condition of moral discourse that defines all individuals as always potential participants in it. The other necessary conditions mentioned above—equal freedom to advance and contest claims and arguments, and the commitment by all participants to pursuit of the truth—can only be characteristics of an actual discourse. But coercion with respect to the more general character of social action can be present or absent whether or not engagement in the practice of discourse is occurring.

To be sure, "coercion" can be present in many specific forms. Defined generally as "dominating, restraining, or controlling another forcibly" (American Heritage Dictionary), coercion involves interference with freedom, where "interference" means that the freedom in question is lessened in comparison with what it would have been had the interfering individual or group not acted at all. So defined, however, "coercion" admits of considerable controversy regarding its proper extension. It is commonly agreed that a person who is willfully killed or otherwise physically or mentally harmed or forced to act on the threat of such harm is coerced. But there is less accord that, as some have asserted, a capitalist economic system is one in which employees are or may be coerced by employers, and the involuntarily unemployed, even if they receive public welfare, suffer coerced unemployment. Moreover, "forcibly restrained or controlled" might be read to mean that an individual is coerced whenever she or he is immorally treated by others, suggesting that the meaning of "coercion" may, on some uses, depend on rather than define the content of a moral principle. Hence, "freedom from external coercion" does not help clarify the universal principle of communicative respect until the phrase is given a more precise meaning.

But the relevant meaning follows from the formative character of the principle. Because this principle is explicitly neutral to all substantive prescriptions or conceptions of good human association, the meaning of "interference" must be correspondingly neutral. It cannot be defined in a manner that explicitly answers any substantive moral question. Thus, immoral social action as such cannot be, in the relevant sense, coercive because the definition of moral treatment as such requires a substantive principle or principles. Similarly, the formative right to freedom from external coercion cannot be defined in terms of the norms of some specific social practice, other than the practice of moral discourse itself, because any such definition is a conception of good human association. The assertion, for instance, that an economic order in which some individuals suffer involuntary unemployment is insofar proscribed as coercive is not explicitly neutral to differing conceptions of a good economic order.

This means that the principle of communicative respect protects, if we abstract from the actual practice of discourse, only those freedoms that can be defined without any explicit reference to human association. Any such reference would mean either that the right in question protects the formative freedom of participants in discourse or that it depends on some conception of good human association. There is, in other words, a strictly individualistic character to the freedoms involved in the formative proscription of external coercion, and they include freedom to affirm one's own future as an individual, freedom to control one's own body, freedom to use personal property, and freedom to choose one's own conception of the good. We may speak of these as the right to life, the right to bodily integrity and movement, the right to personal property, and the right to conscience—where having the right means that all others have the duty not to interfere.

It is true that each of these freedoms can be increased by favorable participation in human association. Freedom to affirm one's own future and freedom to control one's own body can both be enhanced by the availability of resources with which to meet one's biological needs or by the availability of medical treatment, and these depend in greatest measure on social context. Similarly, freedom to control one's own body is enhanced by forms of transportation that society provides, and freedom to choose one's conception of the good is enhanced by education. But insofar as freedoms might be enhanced by human association, they cannot be defined without explicit reference to it, and the communicative rights cannot protect them. Hence, the external coercion proscribed by these rights cannot include interference with such enhancement. In one sense, of course, it is impossible to conceive of the freedoms in question in abstraction from human association. To all appearances, at least, individuals do not develop the capacity to understand and, therefore, do not become free in the human sense at all without learning, in the sense that requires human communication. But the discussion here is about proscribed coercion. Hence, the relevant rights assume that individuals have the freedoms or capacities in question, in the sense that they can be exercised in the absence of interference. Once having been acquired, in other words, the learning is an individual's own, and some of the choices it makes possible can be defined without explicit reference to human association.

Among these formative freedoms, perhaps the most difficult to clarify with precision is the freedom to use personal property. The meaning or meanings of "property" have been the subject of enduring disagreement in social and political theory. For Hobbes, the term has no meaning except that given to it by civil law. Others hold that there is a natural or moral right to property that ought to control legislative decisions, although there is disagreement about whether or in what respect property claims are individual or communal and whether or in what respects a just claim depends on meeting corresponding responsibilities. Generally speaking, this theoretical debate concerns substantive rights and responsibilities, in distinction from the formative rights we presently have in view. Still, on any account, a general view of property is about access to a shared environment. Hence, any definition of property seems to refer explicitly to human association. If so, "personal property" cannot be defined without a like reference, and we may wonder whether there can be a freedom to use personal property that is protected by the formative proscription of external coercion.

Locke, who affirms a right to property independently of the social contract, includes life among the objects of this right. In the theoretical context of the present work, we can appreciate his point, because one's own body and one's own future as an individual being belong, metaphysically speaking, to a common world. If freedom to affirm one's own future and freedom to control one's own body can be defined without explicit reference to human association, so, too, can freedom to use the "property" these freedoms involve. It is pertinent, then, that Locke also includes within the right to property a claim to things without which self-preservation is impossible. "Men, being once born, have a right to their preservation, and consequently to meat and drink, and such other things, as nature affords for their subsistence" (Locke 1952: 16). In other words, freedom to affirm one's own future and freedom to control one's own body would be meaningless in the absence of some freedom to use other things. Whatever one wishes to say about the larger theory of property Locke advances, this conclusion seems sound, and, at least in this respect, some right to use personal property can be included within the communicative rights. I am also inclined to think that this right includes exclusive disposal over whatever aspects of the shared environment the civil law has in fact defined as one's individual property. In a manner analogous to the fact that learning, once it has occurred, is the individual's own, individual property, once it has been politically defined as such, is one's own—and interference by others, for instance, through theft, is a violation of communicative respect.[7] This is not to say that the political community may not redefine property but, rather, that a change in the law violates communicative rights if it expropriates individual property or fails to provide proper compensation.[8]

I will call these formative rights to freedom from external coercion rights to *private liberties* and, thereby, distinguish them from other formative rights I will call rights to *public liberties* and will discuss presently. The term "private" here means that the freedoms in question can be defined without any explicit reference to human association. Clearly, the principle of communicative respect does not mean that the private liberties of each should be unbounded. The relevant freedoms of each are morally limited by, and can be interfered with in order to protect, the private liberties of other individuals. Moreover, each has a right to equal freedom, because equal freedom is a necessary condition of the specific practice of moral discourse. In other words, the private liberties of a given individual are protected

---

[7]Given that private property in the sense discussed here is politically defined, the last statement in the text may require qualification if political revolution and rebellion can be morally justified. I will mention revolution and rebellion below.
[8]For an informed and constructive treatment of the long discussion of "property," see Sturm 1998: chapter 5.

only to the point of consistency with the equal liberties of all individuals, and this is another way of saying that the constitutive norms of this formative social practice also specify when one is not bound by the standard obligations of the practice.

The Democratic Association

It is now important to show that the private liberties cannot exhaust the freedoms protected by the principle of communicative respect. The rights to private liberties have been derived as meta-ethical implications of any social action. Its claim to moral validity implies a common decision, and therefore every affected individual should be treated as a potential participant in a practice of common decision making. The absence of external coercion is, in other words, a necessary condition of the specific practice of moral discourse, so that the communicative rights of all individuals must include the right to participate in that discourse. This returns us to the difference between being a *potential* and being an *actual* participant in moral discourse and, therefore, to the question about actual patterns or institutions of common decision making.

In one sense, moral discourse can occur at any time and any place. This practice requires only that two or more individuals agree to suspend other purposes in order to assess the validity of contested moral claims. But it seems wrong to say that an individual is morally bound to engage in discourse whenever a recipient of her or his action contests its moral validity. This would mean, for instance, that participants in an economic transaction would be bound to halt their activity whenever any one of them or any affected individual objects to it, or a criminal court judge would be bound to halt the trial's proceedings if the accused dissents from a specific rule of the judicial system. Social action would or, at least, could be constantly disrupted. Moreover, the decision to halt other social action in order to engage in moral discourse is itself a social action, and a principle that prescribes such decisions whenever social action is contested should itself be subject to contestation and common decision. But this is not possible unless there is a particular discourse in which common decisions are taken about when and where actual moral discourse ought or is permitted to occur.

What the principle of communicative respect prescribes, then, is a particular practice of moral discourse in which the widest possible common decisions are taken. Indeed, ad hoc engagements in moral discourse always presuppose this widest possible discourse because any argument about the validity of moral prescriptions is potentially an argument about the most general principles by which all individuals are bound. Discourse about the moral validity of a particular economic transaction may become argumentation about the basic structure of the economic order. Dissent from some specific rule of the judicial system may occasion an argument about the morality of its defining principles. Whatever else is involved, in other words, the right to engage in moral discourse must prescribe the freedom to participate in a particular association constituted as the widest possible discourse and in or through which common decisions about the general principles of social action are taken. Given this association, it is not necessary that all social action be disrupted whenever any participant contests its moral validity. Whether and, if so, when more local engagement in moral discourse is required or permitted can itself be a common decision of the wider discourse, because every individual's right to participate in discourse is fulfilled by her or his opportunity to express dissent in the particular association whose common decisions are about the moral permissibility of all specific projects and practices.

In sum, the right to participate in moral discourse is the right to participate in political discourse, that is, the discourse of a particular association or social practice that has nonetheless a general character because its distinguishing purpose is to order or govern all action and association in a society. It is this peculiar character of politics, namely, that its distinguishing purpose is defined in relation to all other purposes in the society, that is sometimes formulated by calling the political association a "second-order" or "higher-order" association. Specifically political action or activity may be distinguished as participation in this second-order associational process. Political discourse, then, is discourse about the governing rules or norms that define all potential action and association in the society as morally permissible or impermissible, and this is discourse in its widest possible form. To be sure, political associations are not necessarily characterized by political discourse or, at least, not by a discourse in which all individuals have a right to participate. But our conclusion here is normative: Communicative respect as a formative principle prescribes political association of this kind. I will formulate this conclusion by saying that this formative principle prescribes a democratic political association.

It might be objected that the democratic association governing a given society cannot constitute the widest possible moral discourse because, by definition, the latter could only be a discourse among all contemporary individuals. But here, as in all cases, "ought implies can," and the pertinent question is how inclusive the political association can be and still in fact govern through discourse. Hence, the proper size of a political association or the society it governs depends on the real possibilities of having such a discourse. It is beyond serious disagreement, I expect, that differences in language and culture more generally, in addition to problems of geography, have, up to and including the present point in human history, excluded universal democracy as a real possibility. As a formative right, in any event, the right to participate in a democratic political association *assumes* that this association is possible, just as the rights to private liberties assume individuals who live with understanding. Hence, the formative principle of communicative respect does not itself provide moral guidance as to the proper size of a democratically governed society but, rather, assumes that it has been identified.[9]

The formative prescription of democracy includes grounds for the distinctively legal character of political decisions. Because the right to

---

[9]A similar response is fitting if some assert that even a nonuniversal democracy is not in fact possible in the absence of certain material and social preconditions, including education, that cannot be secured in the presence of massive and unavoidable poverty. There is, I expect, some truth in this judgment—although it is a sound maxim in such situations that the possibilities of democracy are considerably greater than those who exercise nondemocratic power would have one believe. But "ought implies can," and the principle of communicative respect assumes that democracy is possible. The argument in the present work also makes this assumption.

The general point, then, is this: A question about the real possibilities of having a democratic association cannot be properly answered without a substantive moral principle. To ask whether such possibilities obtain is to ask of a given community whether a democratic constitution is prescribed by the substantive character of good human association as such.

participate in democratic discourse cancels the right to halt at any time any social action, the principle of communicative respect implies a formative right to have democratic decisions coercively enforced. An association that makes common decisions governing all social action does not fulfill each individual's right to dissent from the moral validity of any social action unless the association prevents other individuals from violating its governing decisions. That democratic decisions are legislated means that they will be coercively enforced, and "coercion" here means interference with freedom that individuals who disobey the law would otherwise enjoy. Because its decisions are legal, a political association includes the activities of the state, the set of governing activities in which legislation is enacted, interpreted, and enforced. Accordingly, political discourse is argumentation about the activities of the state that is pursued in order commonly to decide what they will be.

We may speak of democratic political decisions as legally valid. But legal validity should not be equated with moral validity; legally valid decisions may be morally invalid. A democratic decision is morally valid only if it is consistent with a substantive principle or principles of justice that can be redeemed by argument, and this means that a legally valid decision is morally valid only if the democratic discourse through which it is taken is in fact successful, in the sense that the decision is in fact based on or, at least, consistent with sound moral arguments. Still members of a political community are morally obligated to obey legally valid laws, because democracy is a formative principle. Thus, dissent from the moral validity of a legally valid law properly takes the form of participation in the democratic process toward the end of changing the law. It follows that the laws, whatever they prescribe, should never violate the constitution of the political association as a moral discourse in or through which the widest common decisions are not only taken but also always subject to subsequent contestation and repeal.

Since the decisions of the political association have a legal character, the constitutive principles of this association must also be legal in character; that is, an institutional process in or through which the activities of the state are properly determined must itself be coercively enforced. An individual's moral obligation to obey the law and her or his right to contest its moral validity both entail that other individuals in the society, including officials of the state, should be prevented from violating the democratic determination of the state's activities. Because its principles are themselves legal in character, the constitution of a democratic association should be itself democratically decided. On my reading, this fundamental condition of democratic politics is given classic expression in the preamble to the Constitution of the United States: "We, the People of the United States, . . . , do ordain and establish this Constitution," and the same fundamental condition is reformulated in Abraham Lincoln's singular assertion that government of and for the people is also by the people.

There is an apparent paradox in the statement that a democratic constitution should be a democratic decision, since democratic decision presupposes that a democratic political association has been constituted. How a democratic political association is initially constituted in a society whose political association was not previously democratic is, in the nature of the case, historically variable. The decision may be taken by existing, nondemocratic political power or through revolution, that is, through some extra-legal process that may or may not be violent. Whatever judgment should be rendered on the Articles of Confederation, for instance, it is surely debatable whether the current Constitution of the United States was legally established in the sense that it replaced the Articles through a procedure legitimated by the Articles themselves. Still, the dictum that a democratic constitution should be a democratic decision is nonparadoxical at least in this sense: However it is initially created, a political association is not democratic unless its constitution provides the process through which democratic discourse may change the constitution. The assertion that an actual constitution is in fact or in all respects democratic itself is or implies a moral prescription that is subject to dissent.

For this reason, democracy is violated when any provision of a constitution is entrenched, that is, constitutionally protected from change through the constituted political process. The people, here understood as united in a discourse among themselves, are the sole sovereign. They authorize any actual constitution, and the only sense in which a democratic constitution can be called sovereign is the ideal sense in which that constitution does in truth establish politics by way of democratic discourse. Hence, any actual constitution is always subject to assessment by the people. Although I will not pursue the matter further, the supremacy of "we, the people" implies, so far as I can see, that they have the formative right to establish a democracy by extraconstitutional means if and when, all things considered, these are more likely to yield success than whatever legal means might be available.

The proper provisions of a democratic constitution institutionalize the formative principle of communicative respect. In sum, we can say that the political association should be constituted as a full and free political discourse. It should be full in the sense that it takes no moral principle or norm, formative or substantive, to be immune from dissent, and the discourse should be free in the sense that all individuals who are subject to the common decisions in question should have equal rights to participation.[10] That it is a discourse means that proposed principles or norms, if questioned, can be redeemed only by argument. "Full and free discourse" is, in other words, simply a summary expression of the *internal* conditions of discourse noted earlier: equal access or equal freedom of all participants to advance and contest any claim and the arguments for it, and the uncompromised commitment of all participants to pursuit of the truth. "Full and free *political* discourse" means that these internal conditions characterize the process by which the activities of the state are determined.

A democratic constitution should, therefore, institutionalize the state and stipulate the decision-making procedures through which officials of the state are selected and through which legislation, including changes in the constitution itself, is enacted, interpreted, and enforced. These general requirements do not themselves imply any specific set of political institutions, such that the constitutions of all democracies should be identical in detail. Whatever the detailed provisions, however, they are not democratic unless they allow the political association to maximize the measure in which the taking, interpretation, and enforcement of political decisions is the consequence of full and free discourse. Summarily speaking, this entails that democratic decision is taken through some form or forms of majority voting

---

[10]I will not attend to the political status of children, although I recognize that important questions are involved.

or through other procedures that are themselves subject to some form of majority voting. In a large society, the decision-making procedures can and should become highly complex, involving representative voting and delegation of authority.[11]

But size is not the only consideration that leads to complexity in the decision-making procedures. Given the temptations to immoral action discussed at length in an earlier chapter, the constitution must also do what it can to protect against the corruption of decision making by "the strategic assertion of interests." With this phrase, I mean the kind of political participation that is concerned only with the effectiveness and legality of means to one's ends and does not submit the ends themselves to criticism and validation. As an internal condition of a full and free discourse, common pursuit of the truth means the absence of coercion through strategic activity. Strategic participation in a discourse is obviously coercive when deception is included. But such participation is coercive even without the attempt to deceive, because one seeks to effect through bargaining a decision that is properly taken only by the force of the better argument. In saying this, one need not overlook that some and perhaps many conflicts the political process must adjudicate can only be decided through bargaining, that is, a process in which the ends of differing parties are not questioned and debated. But however far-reaching political bargaining must be, it remains that decisions about its use and the conditions under which

---

[11]Since empirical judgments are involved in designing a procedure through which decision making is maximally informed by full and free discourse, one might question whether the character of a democratic constitution can be prescribed solely by formative prescriptions. But, once more, "ought implies can," and the prescription that individuals have a right to participate in the widest possible discourse through which common decisions are taken cannot be observed in the absence of institutions that constitute a political association. It might seem, then, that this formative right assumes a political constitution, in a manner analogous to assuming that the relevant society has been identified and the relevant material preconditions obtain. But the present case is different. Those assumptions must be satisfied in order to constitute a democracy. Once constituted, however, its constitutional provisions are themselves subject to assessment and revision in and through discourse, and the decisions of this discourse require a principle defining the proper character of the constitution. That principle is formative: Taking empirical conditions into account, the decision-making procedure must maximize the measure in which decisions can be taken through full and free political discourse.

it occurs should be taken through discourse. Which conflicts are properly resolved through what kind of bargaining should not themselves be decisions reached through bargaining. The threat to democratic decision making consists in a withdrawal from discourse with respect to ends that are themselves contested (or with respect to withdrawals that are contested), and it is this against which the constitution, insofar as it can, must protect.

In the Constitution of the United States and in debates about it, this requirement is given extended attention. Detailed provisions regarding the selection of state officials and the separation and balance of powers within the state are attempts to minimize the measure in which the strategic assertion of interests can divorce decision-making procedures from political discourse. We may call this the political realism of the constitution, that is, its recognition that the democratic process can easily be corrupted by the absence of moral commitment. In a famous aphorism, Reinhold Niebuhr said that our "capacity for justice makes democracy possible" and our "inclination to injustice makes democracy necessary" (1960: xiii). Whatever Niebuhr may have meant, we can use the former part of this aphorism to summarize "democracy" in its ideal sense, that is, to mark the process in which full and free moral discourse determines the activities of the state; the latter part, then, means by "democracy" the realistic design of decision-making procedures that constrains the success of strategically asserted interests. Still, it should be clear that realism alone cannot create anything approaching democracy. Without some significant commitment within "we, the people" to pursuit of the truth, any pattern of decision making can be overwhelmed by strategic power.

Moreover, democracy in its ideal sense cannot be legally enforced, because a commitment to pursuit of the truth cannot be coerced. Habermas clarifies this point by noting that legal restraint controls action through sanctions on the individual in question, by the threat of interference with freedom the individual would otherwise enjoy. But observance of the law in order to avoid its sanctions is not an action taken because it is morally required; on the contrary, the law and its threat becomes one more of the given conditions in which one acts strategically or calculates means to one's ends. With respect specifically to the democratic process, this means that legislation cannot secure a democratic commitment in distinction from strategic adherence to constitutional decision-making procedures (see Habermas 1996: 30–32, 447–48). In sum, choosing an action for the right reasons is exclusively a moral matter. In an apt formulation, Habermas says that democratic constitutions "call for" the commitment to discourse (1996: 130, emphasis deleted) or, as I will say, "anticipate" it.

Constitutional Rights

What a democratic constitution properly stipulates, then, are the formative conditions of a full and free political discourse in the respect that they can be legislated. These conditions must be explicitly neutral to all substantive prescriptions precisely because the discourse is about prescriptions for social action in their pertinence to legal norms. Properly speaking, a democratic constitution provides the one set of prescriptions that all citizens should explicitly accept as participants in the political discourse, including discourse about whether the actual constitution is in fact democratic and, indeed, whether democracy itself is the proper form of political association. If any of those prescriptions are substantive, they do not constitute the special practice in which the validity of any political prescription is subject to argument for the purpose of validating or invalidating it. We might say that the constitutional provisions, properly speaking, are those that must be explicitly accepted by all participants in order to have a political discourse about what must be explicitly accepted by all participants in order to have a political discourse—and it is this character that makes the stipulated conditions formative.

Because the provisions of a democratic constitution should be explicitly accepted by all citizens, the state has a right to teach the constitution, including its anticipation of a commitment to discourse, as the set of prescriptions by which participation in the political process is morally bound. As already noted, adherence to the constitution for moral reasons cannot be coerced. But the state may seek to inculcate this moral commitment through public schools or the writings and speeches of public officials or such other means as it may design. Indeed, the state has the duty to teach its constitution, at least if this teaching is not otherwise sufficiently effected in nongovernmental associations, because the activities of the state are not legally valid unless they are democratically decided. This recognition gives other terms in which to assert that constitutional provisions must be solely formative: Were some conception of good human association included in the constitution, then the teaching of that substantive prescription by the state would bias the discourse. This teaching would contradict the teaching that democracy is a political association in which the validity of every political prescription can be contested.

In the nature of the case, the statutory legislation that governs social action and is enacted through the democratic process cannot be explicitly neutral to all substantive prescriptions. To legislate definitions of property and the organization of an economic free market or to establish systems of public education, for instance, is explicitly to endorse some conception of good human association. Because it is required to teach this legislation, the state will be teaching a substantive prescription as one all citizens should accept; that is, all citizens are morally bound to obey the law. But this statutory legislation does not stipulate a conception of good human association that citizens should explicitly accept *as participants in the political discourse*. To the contrary, the point of the discourse is that political decisions already taken and the substantive norms they prescribe are subject to contestation. Citizens are not bound to accept legally valid norms as morally valid, and political discourse is the practice in which their dissent is properly expressed. Accordingly, the constitutional provisions that can be taught by the state because they define citizens as political participants should not include any that are not formative conditions of democratic discourse itself.[12]

In addition to institutions of the state, including its procedures for enacting, interpreting, and enforcing laws, these conditions include

---

[12]Given that a democratic constitution provides for possible amendment to itself, some may argue, it is not necessary to limit constitutional stipulations to formative conditions. Substantive constitutional prescriptions do not contradict a full and free discourse because the provision for constitutional change stipulates that even these prescriptions are subject to the sovereignty of the people or to dissent. But this argument misses the point. Only constitutional conditions that are formative are consistent with a provision for constitutional change, since only formative prescriptions must be explicitly accepted by any political participant who seeks to change the constitution through discourse. In contrast, constitutional stipulations that are substantive contradict the provision for constitutional change, because they falsely assert that they must be explicitly accepted by any political participant who seeks to change them democratically.

certain formative rights that may be called rights to *public liberties* because these rights constitute inclusion within "we, the people" or participation in a democratic political association. They are distinct from the rights to private liberties because the public liberties cannot be defined without any explicit reference to human association. To the contrary, their definition explicitly refers to the specific practice of full and free political discourse. But the rights to both kinds of liberties are formative; in each case, the prescription is explicitly neutral to all substantive prescriptions. Hence, the distinction between the two kinds of rights expresses the difference between being a merely potential and being an actual participant in discourse. Among the American revolutionaries, on the account of Sidney E. Mead, it was Thomas Jefferson who most clearly understood and articulated the revolution as a political commitment to the way of reason or to democratic discourse. Jefferson, according to Mead, believed "that [political] reform depended upon the freeing of man's natural reason . . . by opening all the channels of communication through freedom of speech, freedom of the press, freedom to assemble and petition, so that every opinion could have a hearing" (1963: 46), a formulation that echoes the wording in the First Amendment to the Constitution of the United States. In addition to the franchise, then, the rights to public liberties include equal freedom to participate in the "channels of communication," without which political participants could not advance or contest in discourse claims to moral validity.[13]

There is controversy in discussions of United States constitutional law about the limits to rights such as those to freedom of speech and freedom of the press, and, specifically, whether and, if so, what distinctions should be made between political and other forms of speech (see, e.g., Sunstein 1993; Greenawalt 1995). I will not pursue that discussion. As formative prescriptions, however, rights to speech

---

[13]Akhil Reed Amar has argued that an understanding of the First Amendment and, more generally, the Bill of Rights as principally concerned to stipulate individual rights is a reconstructed reading that is legitimated by the Fourteenth Amendment (see Amar 1998). In alluding to the First Amendment, I do not mean to take issue with this argument. Whether one should say something similar about the reading of Jefferson's convictions is not pertinent here, since my point is not historical but, rather, one in political philosophy.

and the press depend on the right to democratic participation. Accordingly, the extent to which these rights should be protected constitutionally is properly determined by their status as necessary conditions of a full and free political discourse. Moreover, there is this wider principle: The exercise of any constitutional right, including the right to free speech, may be legally constrained when that exercise violates the equal right of others—or, for that matter, violates equality with respect to any other constitutional right. This is because all individuals are inherently equal in discourse, which is concerned only with the validity of claims and the soundness of arguments, whatever their source, and the only differences among individuals pertinent to discourse are those in commitment to pursuit of the truth.

Since the actual discourse in which each individual has an equal right to participate is a political process, the rights to public liberties include by extension formative rights that define an individual as the object of democratic governance. For instance, there is a set of rights that may be summarized as the right to due process in the interpretation and enforcement of the law. Due process is required in order that coercive norms do indeed regulate the actions they are intended to regulate. Further, there is a constitutional right to equal protection of the laws. This right here means that no law, constitutional or statutory, can stipulate differential treatment of individuals solely on the basis of differences between or among them that are beyond the control of the individuals in question, for instance, differences in race or sex. Whenever a law does stipulate such differential treatment, this stipulation must be required by some conception of good human association other than the differential treatment itself. Failure to meet this condition asserts that inherent differences between or among individuals are differences in worth. But a difference of that kind would also characterize individuals as participants in democratic discourse, and discourse knows no differences among individuals that are beyond their control. To legislate differential treatment solely because of inherent differences is, in other words, to contradict the fundamental condition of a democratic constitution, namely, that it is ordained and established by "we, the people." A full and free political discourse, notwithstanding that it cannot exist without a political constitution, is nonetheless sovereign over or authorizes any actual constitution.

It is true that laws frequently distinguish among individuals on the basis of differences beyond their control. The young are subject to military service but not the elderly; the victims of floods or earthquakes receive special governmental aid but not those who escape such disasters; admission to opportunities on the basis of capacity to achieve is not only a reward for past efforts but also for good fortune in the accidents of birth; and affirmative action programs distinguish on the basis of race or sex. But laws such as these do not distinguish individuals solely on the basis of these differences. In each case, the democratic process decides that the differences are pertinent to some conception of good human association other than the differential treatment itself—association that serves to protect the political community, to insure basic well-being throughout the community, to maximize achievement in the society, or to overcome the consequences of systematic discrimination. In contrast, the 1954 United States Supreme Court decision proscribing school segregation might be understood to mean that this segregation had no other purpose than asserting that a difference in race is an inherent difference in worth.

In addition to the rights to public liberties, a democratic constitution must also stipulate the rights of all citizens to private liberties. In the earlier discussion, the latter were derived from the necessary conditions of discourse, because discourse requires not only equal freedom of participation and the absence of internal coercion but also the absence of external coercion. When the norms of a specific social practice specify those of a more general social practice or specify a general principle, the more general practice or principle is an external normative condition of the specific practice, and the specific practice of discourse is inconsistent with a general practice or principle that permits violation of the rights to private liberties. Thus, the formative conditions of a democratic discourse include the right of all individuals to be treated as potential participants in that discourse, and a democratic constitution must stipulate this right. Habermas formulates a similar point by saying that "private autonomy" is an "enabling condition" of "public autonomy" (1996: 127–28). If "private autonomy" and "public autonomy" are understood as formative prescriptions, it is proper to say that a political constitution is not democratic unless it stipulates both kinds of autonomy as conditions of social action that will always be coercively enforced whatever the consequences.[14]

Conspicuously absent from the present discussion is any mention of constitutionally guaranteed substantive rights—for instance, the right to some level of health care or the right to assistance with economic necessities if one cannot provide for oneself or the right to an education. It is well known that the Universal Declaration of Human Rights includes not only political and civil rights but also social and economic rights (see Gewirth 1996: 29), and it might well be argued that the right to be an equal participant in a democratic discourse is hollow without substantive rights to certain social and economic conditions. There is something disingenuous in saying, for instance, that citizens of the United States who suffer social and economic deprivation can be nonetheless equal participants in the political process. Summarily stated, individuals who are more emancipated in certain general human ways have, other things being equal, greater opportunity to affect the decisions taken through democratic decision-making procedures. Thus, it may seem that a democratic constitution is not complete without the stipulation of certain substantive rights.

[14]The distinction between rights to private and to public liberties, it might seem, could also be stated as the difference between negative and positive rights. Both sets of terms have been used with differing meanings for differing purposes, and, in this context, clear and consistent usage is the principal criterion of propriety. Negative rights are frequently said to be rights to noninterference, and it may seem that rights to public liberties are not members of this class. In other words, these rights may seem to be positive because they prescribe freedom to participate in a kind of human association. But I am not persuaded that a difference between noninterference and its contrast usefully distinguishes the two kinds of formative rights. Rights to public liberties are themselves rights to noninterference, at least to noninterference by the state.

But if both kinds of formative rights involve rights to noninterference, perhaps the distinction between negative and positive rights will serve to distinguish the formative rights from other rights individuals may have. On this account, "positive rights" designates rights to kinds of assistance, in the sense that having such a right obligates others in a way that enhances one's opportunities beyond what they would have been had others not acted at all—and the proposal is that only substantive rights are positive. In this sense, however, the rights to public liberties are also positive, because one cannot be free to participate in the democratic discourse without the participation of others; that is, this right obligates all others to accept a democratic constitution. Thus, I doubt that the distinction between negative and positive rights can be easily appropriated in the present context. The important distinction here is between formative and substantive rights.

But it is one thing to affirm that all human individuals have certain substantive rights democratic political communities should secure and something else to assert that these rights should be stipulated in a democratic constitution. If it is true that democratic politics can be constituted only as a full and free discourse, then the constitution should be explicitly neutral to all conceptions of good human association, and constitutional rights should be restricted to those that articulate the formative principle of communicative respect. The specific social practice of discourse suspends other purposes in order to assess contested validity claims through argumentation. As a consequence, the constitution of this practice assumes that those who suspend their other purposes are able to participate in it, and this is the point in saying that its necessary conditions are equal participation, the absence of external coercion, and commitment to pursuit of the truth. In the absence of this assumption or in the presence of additional constitutive conditions, it could not be the case that all social prescriptions can be contested and subjected to discourse. Any constitutional provision of substantive rights would, in other words, arrest a full and free political discourse by stipulating that citizens as participants in it explicitly accept some conception of good human association.

One might now object that there must be something wrong with the distinction between formative and substantive rights because it puts a democratic constitution at odds with itself. In fact, the capacities of individuals to participate in and influence the outcomes of the democratic process do vary depending on their differing social, economic, and cultural circumstances. This is transparently so insofar as the process is not a genuine discourse because corrupted by the strategic assertion of interests, and the consequences can be profound when the inequalities are severe. But differing circumstances are relevant even if all citizens are committed to pursuit of the truth. Those who are more advantaged economically and educationally will, as a general rule, have greater resources in time and money to advance their claims and arguments in public debate and, perhaps, greater capacity to persuade. If the constitution does not stipulate requisite substantive rights to social and economic conditions, the objection asserts, the full and free discourse it is meant to constitute cannot occur because, as participants in the discourse, citizens are not in fact equal. In that sense, a formative constitution puts democracy at odds with itself.

Against the objection, however, a formative constitution does not implicitly deny that democratic discourse is compromised by certain inequities the political community can and should alter. The point is, rather, that a fully democratic political process is not something its constitution can guarantee. What we must say is that a democratic constitution *anticipates* substantive justice in the activities of the democratic state. Here the term "anticipates" recurs to an earlier discussion, which noted that a constitution cannot legislate commitment to full and free discourse. Although the constitution should recognize that individuals may use the political process in order to pursue their interests strategically and, therefore, should design realistic decision-making procedures, commitment to decision making maximally informed by argument can only be anticipated because commitment to pursuit of the truth cannot be coerced. Unless that anticipation is in large or, at least, tolerable measure fulfilled, the political community is at odds with its constitution.

For a differing reason, the constitution of governance by the people through discourse also can only anticipate that the constituted political process will be in large or, at least, tolerable measure successful, so that governance will in that measure legislate morally valid conceptions of good human association. If this anticipation of substantive justice is not fulfilled, the democratic community will be at odds with its constitution. In this case, however, the reason why the constitution cannot stipulate is not that the relevant substantive rights cannot be coercively secured; indeed, insofar as individuals have such rights, they should be secured by statutory legislation. But the legislation should be statutory because the constitution establishes nothing other than a political discourse about the validity of all social prescriptions.[15]

[15]This conclusion represents a change of mind from a position I took in an earlier work. I there asserted that the provisions of a democratic constitution should identify "the optimal conditions in which any political claim, including any comprehensive conviction, may be publicly assessed as a part of the political process" (Gamwell 1995: 173; see also 172–79). That position, I now believe, implies that the constitution should or, at least, may stipulate substantive principles of justice, and a constitution that does so violates a full and free discourse by stipulating that a certain conception of good human association should be explicitly accepted by all citizens as participants in democratic discourse. The proper distinction with which to define the character of a democratic constitution is that between formative and substantive principles of justice, and the constitution can only anticipate that the discourse will be successful.

It follows, I believe, that citizens of a democratically constituted association have a formative right, under certain circumstances, to alter the current regime by extra-legal means. When substantive injustice results in obstructions to a full and free political discourse, the anticipation of the constitution itself may permit activity that violates statutory law. This sets one context in which the propriety of civil disobedience, as an activity seeking to announce that certain claims and arguments have not participated or participated equally in the political process, should be considered, and more severe forms of extra-legal action cannot be excluded. But the formative right to such activity is also characterized by severe constraints. I will not attempt here a detailed discussion of the matter, but, summarily speaking, there is at least this constraint: Extra-legal attempts to establish what one takes to be the substantive conditions of a democratic discourse are not permitted unless one could argue successfully that the changes are more likely to occur or to occur more quickly in this manner than through legal activity, and that the democratic political process can be expected to sustain those changes once they are made.

Formative and Substantive Principles

This chapter has argued that the principle of communicative respect is a meta-ethical presupposition of every claim to moral validity. Because a prescription for social action purports to define choices agents ought to make, no such prescription can be valid unless individuals to whom it applies can choose a purpose that expresses dissent. Prescriptions for social action, therefore, imply common decisions and a social practice of common decision making or moral discourse. Every social action is bound to treat all affected individuals as potential participants in discourse, and this is a formative principle in the sense that the social action prescribed is explicitly neutral to all moral disagreement. This principle is, in other words, explicitly neutral to all substantive prescriptions or conceptions of good human association.

This principle constitutes a universal social practice and may be articulated as a set of formative rights. Because they belong to every individual as a potential participant in discourse, they include the right to participation in a democratic political association—the widest possible moral discourse, in or through which common decisions about the general order of social action are legislated. A democratic association is constituted as a full and free political discourse and, therefore, its constitution should not stipulate any substantive norm or conception of good human association. The political constitution should stipulate those conditions and only those conditions that all participants must explicitly accept in order to have a discourse about all political prescriptions, including the provisions of the constitution. This means that the constitution properly provides, in addition to institutions through which activities of the state are decided, rights to the private and public liberties prescribed by the principle of communicative respect.

Because it is formative, this principle overrides all substantive principles and norms. No conception of good human association can be valid unless it is consistent with the prescription of communicative respect. Contrary to a common criticism, this conclusion does not discredit teleological ethics as such, because there is nothing in the very idea of comprehensive teleology that prohibits indirect application through social practices without which the good cannot be maximized. But it does follow from the meta-ethical character of moral claims that no ethic and, therefore, no comprehensive teleology can be valid if it is inconsistent with the principle of communicative respect. We are now in a position also to say that any ethic and, therefore, any comprehensive teleology is committed to social practices beyond the formative practice of communicative respect. This is because the latter includes the practice of legislating practices in a democratic political association. In other words, the order defined by the statutory law of a democratic political community is a complex social practice or set of social practices whose norms individuals are morally obligated to obey whatever the consequences.

This is not to say that the morally valid social practices through which individuals in a society cooperate are limited to those established by legislation. Any enduring association or institution that is permitted but not required by the legal order may be morally valid—although, if it is, individuals are not bound by its rules unless they choose to be among its members. Moreover, the common decisions taken through a society-wide discourse are not limited to those that are legally enforced. We may speak of a general moral discourse that is more or less coextensive with the society as a whole and that transcends its specifically political discourse. This more inclusive discourse also defines, sustains, and alters general practices that are not legislated, although the procedure for such decisions is not institutionalized. Thus, the decisions can be enforced only through attitudes of moral approval and disapproval and through morally permissible private sanctions, and refusal to participate in the practice may be a morally permissible expression of dissent. In many societies, for instance, a general definition of immoral sexual relationships quite transcends those that are legally prohibited. Again, general rules about promising, including a specification of what kinds of promises are and are not morally permissible, are taught and upheld far beyond promises that are legally enforced. Since all enduring specific associations depend on the practice of promising, in the sense that they require common commitment to a set of constitutive rules, democratic communities also typically sustain in a nonlegal manner the following general norm: Those who choose to be members of a morally permissible voluntary association are bound by its constitutive rules, notwithstanding that they are not legally enforceable.

We can say, then, that a democratic community will have a general setting of social practices that is in part legal and part nonlegal (cf. Barry 1995: 34). Aside from the fact that nonlegal social practices must be legally permissible, the two aspects of this general setting are also related in this respect: A general moral discourse that transcends the political discourse depends on the democratic constitution, in the sense that the former cannot be an actual discourse unless the rights to private and public liberties are legally secured. It is precisely because the society is governed democratically that discourse can establish, sustain, or alter wide social practices without legislation. Indeed, the decision to have a nonlegal general practice is the decision through democratic discourse not to legislate another of its decisions. Given that marital fidelity is a social practice that belongs to the nonlegal aspect of the general setting, for instance, the democratic process may be wise to decide that state enforcement of this practice would do more harm than good. In this sense, the general setting as such is politically determined.[16]

Just insofar as the argument here for the principle of communicative respect is successful, some may suggest, it gives reason to doubt or reject comprehensive teleology. In the nature of the case, a teleological ethic asserts that no moral claim is valid independently of the telos of all human activity; that is, the comprehensive purpose is a necessary condition of all moral claims. In contradiction to that assertion, it might be said, the argument for communicative rights purports to show that the principles of a universal social practice can be validated without appeal to any comprehensive purpose. This is, on my understanding, Apel's position. On his account, as noted earlier, the principle of communicative respect is "a meta-norm for communicatively generating material norms" (1979b: 335, emphasis deleted).

Simply to state this suggestion recalls that a similar one was reviewed earlier, when Kant's categorical imperative was construed as a generalized proscription of actions that violate the norms of morally valid social practices. "When in difficulty, to promise what one pleases, with the purpose of not keeping the promise" is a self-contradictory maxim because it presupposes the practice of promising and, therefore, implicitly affirms the constitutive rule that promises should be kept. Accordingly, it might be thought that promise keeping is a valid moral prescription independently of any other principle. But I

---

[16]It might be said that there is something like a general moral discourse that is wider than any given political community because it occurs, however fitfully, between or among the nations of the world. Were this not the case, those relations would be reduced to solely strategic action. In our time, the United Nations and other world organizations provide a minimal political context for this discourse. But even if it proceeds in the absence of that context, an international moral discourse still depends on political association, in the sense that the discourse occurs among officials or members of communities that themselves have constituted conditions for moral discourse in some measure or other. The practice is possible internationally because those who participate in it consider it an extension of the moral discourse of their own political communities. If there is something like a practice of promising internationally, for instance, it depends on the similar practice internal to each of the nations, so that each has some reason to think that the other has reason to observe the relevant norms. Where the internal order of a nation does not provide this confidence, a second nation is wise to exchange "promises" with the first only in the measure that the second can secure them by strategic power.

argued that this generalized proscription does not itself ground the moral validity of any social practice. That making a promise with the intention of breaking it is a practical self-contradiction does not mean that keeping the promise is morally required unless promising is a morally valid social practice, and its moral validity cannot be redeemed without appeal to another principle.

Still, it might be thought that the practice of communicative action is different in a way that makes a difference, since the proscription of actions that violate its constitutive principle is presupposed or implied by social action as such. Because this principle is a meta-ethical presupposition of moral claims, its validity does not depend on any substantive principle, and communicative rights are independent of any comprehensive purpose. Indeed, recalling that, for Apel, his statement of the meta-norm formulates the valid meaning in Kant's categorical imperative, one might hold that Apel's argument turns aside my earlier criticism of Kant; that is, Apel shows that Kant's imperative, properly understood, is not empty but, rather, is the independent principle constituting a universal social practice.

But this reasoning ignores that the principle of communicative respect, which prescribes treatment of all individuals as potential participants in discourse, presupposes that moral discourse is possible and, therefore, that substantive moral prescriptions can be valid. A meta-ethical presupposition of claims to moral validity itself presupposes the possible validity of some such claims. If no moral claim can be valid, the supposed concept of such a claim and thus of the right to dissent from it is nonsensical, and no moral obligations, formative or substantive, follow from anything. Practical reason is forever trapped in a Hobbesian state of nature. Nor can this consequence be avoided by saying that a valid claim can be made for the principle of communicative respect itself. It cannot be the case that the only prescription from which it makes sense to dissent is a prescription about whether one has the right to dissent, because this prescription implies that there is something else one might contest. If no substantive prescription can be valid, moral discourse can only be argumentation about the conditions of argumentation—and that argument is senseless unless there is something else to argue about. In sum, a meta-ethical principle is empty without one or more ethical ones.

To be sure, Apel does not hold that there are no valid substantive prescriptions. On his account, the principle of communicative respect presupposes *that* there are such prescriptions but implies nothing about *what* they are. Hence, the principle is formal or independent of any material norm, and Apel's position is that no other valid social prescription is, like the principle of communicative respect, universal. So far as I can see, however, this position is self-contradictory. The presupposition that some or other substantive prescriptions are valid is senseless unless the meta-principle also implies the meaning of "valid substantive prescription," that is, implies the criterion in relation to which substantive prescriptions are determined to be valid or invalid. But a criterion for this determination is itself a substantive moral principle. It is, moreover, a universal substantive principle, since the implications of a universal principle are themselves universal. I recognize that, for Apel, the criterion of valid substantive prescriptions is simply that they can be redeemed by argument or in moral discourse, but the point is that this criterion is empty unless argument can show that a prescription conforms to a universal substantive principle.

Recalling the difference between constitutive and summary rules, we can also make the point this way: Were the principle of communicative respect the only universal principle, every human action could be independently described in terms of its purpose, and no human action would presuppose the constitutive norms of a universal social practice. Thus, the argument here against Apel simply reformulates in the present context earlier arguments against Kant's attempt to separate the form of practical reason from the choice among alternatives for purpose. Independently of this choice, there is no human action and, therefore, no possibility of an implied moral principle. On my understanding of him, Apel repeats Kant's attempt to separate a universal moral principle from the purposes for which moral validity might be claimed and, thereby, equally fails to formulate a coherent ethic. Just as a generalized proscription of actions that violate morally valid social practices presupposes another principle by which the moral validity of social practices is grounded, so the principle of communicative respect presupposes that the practice it constitutes is grounded by some universal substantive principle or principles of human purpose.

In the end, this is just to say that democracy makes no sense in the absence of something about which citizens may engage in full and free political discourse. The democratic discourse cannot be solely about the formative character of the discourse. This would mean that democratic politics has nothing to argue about except its own constitution, and it would be senseless to constitute a discourse for the sole purpose of constituting it. Accordingly, the Preamble to the Constitution of the United States declares that "We, the people, . . . , do ordain and establish this Constitution" in order to "insure domestic tranquility, provide for the common defense, promote the general welfare, and secure the blessings of liberty to ourselves and our posterity." The discourse is about the legislated norms by which the society will be governed. Hence, a democratic constitution presupposes a universal substantive principle to which all activities of the state ought to conform. Whether this means that democracy depends on a comprehensive purpose is another question, to which the remaining chapters of this work are addressed. But were there no such principle, political decisions could not be the consequence of discourse, and governance by the way of reason could not govern.

≈ 5 ≈

Justice as Compound

Democracy as a formative principle is a presupposition of every moral claim. On this principle, the political constitution prescribes the legal conditions and only those conditions that should be explicitly accepted by citizens as participants in a full and free political discourse. The discourse is about the activities of the state and, therefore, the formative principle itself presupposes one or more substantive principles in relation to which those activities are properly decided. To constitute politics by the way of reason is to imply that politics has something to reason about.

If these conclusions of the previous chapter are sound, it follows that the character of justice includes a similar differentiation of principles.[1] On the one hand, justice includes a formative principle or set of principles, which defines a constitution as democratic; on the other hand, justice includes a substantive principle or set of principles, which ought to control the decisions of a democratic process. This distinction cannot be a separation. To the contrary, the character of justice can only be internally coherent, in the sense that its formative and substantive principles consistently imply each other. On the one hand, the principle or set of principles specified in the constitution consistently implies the substantive principle or principles of justice, because democracy as a formative principle presupposes one or more

---

[1] As noted in the previous chapter, the argument of the present work assumes that democracy is possible, so that the character of justice is necessarily democratic.

substantive principles. On the other hand, the substantive principle or set of principles consistently implies the formative principle or principles, because any claim to validity for a moral principle implies the principle of communicative respect. The character of justice, we can say, is self-differentiating.

It now follows that the substantive principle or set of principles define justice inclusively. This is because any given moral claim includes but is not exhausted by its meta-ethical character, and similarly the life of a democratic association includes but is not exhausted by its constitution. The moral validity of democracy as a formative principle depends on the substantive principle or principles of justice. The character of justice *is* a substantive principle or set of principles that implies the formative principle of democracy as a distinct part of itself. I will call this *the compound character of justice.* Chapter 6 will argue that the divine good in its specification to politics has this character. I will there attempt to articulate the substantive principle of justice that specifies the divine purpose and to show that this principle is self-differentiating in the required sense. As noted earlier, however, the assertion that justice specifies the divine good departs from a basic consensus characterizing most recent theories of justice, on which democracy is independent of a comprehensive purpose. In the present chapter, therefore, I will seek to show that a theory of democracy cannot represent the compound character of justice unless that theory specifies to politics a comprehensive teleology.

The Principle of Religious Freedom

As preparation for this argument, it will be useful to introduce a constitutional principle that was not explicitly discussed in the previous chapter, namely, the principle of religious freedom. In its fullest sense, the meaning of this principle is precisely what is at stake in this chapter. But the discussion will be aided, I judge, if the conception of religious freedom for which I will argue is clarified at the start. For the purpose of this initial discussion, then, I will assume what the chapter is designed to confirm, namely, that valid moral prescriptions depend on a comprehensive purpose. Given this assumption, we can say that the democratic discourse about principles of justice is about the comprehensive purpose in its pertinence to the activities of the state. In other words, every conception of justice specifies to politics some or other understanding of the comprehensive telos, and a full and free political discourse includes an argument about which such understanding is valid.

At least for citizens of the United States, speaking of religious freedom brings to mind the classic formulation in the First Amendment to their political constitution: "Congress shall make no law respecting an establishment of religion, or prohibiting the free exercise thereof." In United States constitutional law and in wider public debate, the meaning or set of meanings expressed in these clauses is disputed. Among other matters of disagreement are the differences between the two clauses and whether they are in all applications consistent with each other. My purpose here is not to discuss the Constitution of the United States specifically but, rather, to define religious freedom as a formative condition of democratic politics. Whatever else this principle means, I take it to prescribe the following: All religions are legitimate, in the sense that any citizen who believes any religion does so legitimately.

How, if at all, "religion" is properly defined is immensely controversial, and this is one reason why the clauses in the First Amendment evoke persistent and varied disagreements. Still, common use of the term designates communities and traditions that are characterized by, among other things, symbolic or figurative expressions, including symbolic practices, through which some belief about human life in relation to its ultimate context is affirmed or reaffirmed. On the present account, a religion includes an explicit answer to the question we ourselves are, which every human activity answers implicitly in its choice of a self-understanding. Accordingly, Part One proposed that the function of religion in human life is so to represent explicitly an understanding of human authenticity as such and, therefore, the comprehensive purpose that the authentic exercise of original freedom is thereby cultivated. Religion is "the primary form of culture in terms of which we human beings explicitly ask and answer" the question of human authenticity as such (Ogden 1992: 5).

The principle of religious freedom prohibits the state from teaching that any given religion is invalid; doing so would deny legitimacy to that religion. Hence, the state may not teach that any given religion or set of religions is valid, because doing so would teach that a religion is invalid if it does not agree with the religion or religions the state promulgates. We may say that religious freedom proscribes to the state the explicit affirmation or denial or any religion and, in that sense, prescribes explicit state neutrality to all religions. This limitation on the state is a constitutional principle of democracy because religions are or include completely general conceptions of good human association. A claim to validity for any understanding of the comprehensive purpose is or includes the substantive prescription that all human association should be directed by that purpose. In other words, explicit state affirmation or denial of any religion would contradict the properly formative character of a democratic constitution.

To be sure, a democratic state is not barred from teaching all conceptions of good human association. Were that the case, the constitution would, absurdly, prohibit all statutory legislation. It might seem, then, that explicit constitutional endorsement or denial of a religion is one thing, and a similar activity by the state is something else. But statutory legislation, when it is legally valid, does not teach substantive prescriptions that all citizens as participants in democratic discourse should explicitly accept. To the contrary, the political discourse is full and free, so that any legislated conception of good human association is subject to contestation in and repeal through the political process. The state cannot be given statutory permission to teach the validity or invalidity of any religion precisely because a religion is or includes an understanding of the comprehensive purpose. Were it permitted explicitly to affirm or deny any religion, the state would thereby teach a conception of good human association that citizens should explicitly accept in all social action, including their participation in democratic discourse, and the solely formative character of a democratic constitution would be violated.

It follows that the principle "all religions are legitimate" must mean by "all religions" all possible religions, in the sense that any understanding of the comprehensive purpose can be called a possible religion. Clearly all such understandings are not in fact religious, because a religion is a cultural system in terms of which its adherents or members of the religious community seek to cultivate the authentic exercise of original freedom. But any understanding of the comprehensive purpose is a "possible religion" in the sense that it could be explicitly represented in symbolic expressions through which that understanding functions religiously for a community of adherents. The constitution must prohibit to the state the explicit affirmation or denial of any completely general conception of good human association and, therefore, any understanding of the comprehensive purpose because the constitution is formative. The content of such understandings in principle rather than their specifically religious functioning in fact is the basis for explicit state neutrality to all of them. Religious freedom is, we may say, the right to both a private and a public liberty —the former because potential participants in discourse have the right to freedom of conscience, and the latter because the democratic discourse is not only free but also full, in the sense that no moral claim is immune from dissent. In speaking of religious freedom as a political principle, therefore, I will henceforth use "religion" in this constitutionally relevant sense, so that "a religion" means any possible religion or any conception of the comprehensive good.

On this meaning, religious freedom is, all implications taken into account, the principle that a democratic constitution should be explicitly neutral to all substantive prescriptions. If, as this initial discussion has assumed, the validity of any moral claim depends on the comprehensive purpose, then every substantive political prescription, valid or invalid, specifies an understanding of that purpose. A substantive constitutional prescription would require that the stipulated conception of good human association be explicitly accepted by all citizens as participants in democratic discourse. The state would be authorized to teach that consistency with this prescription is a necessary condition of all valid political claims and, thereby, to teach that legitimate religions are limited to those whose understandings of the comprehensive purpose do not require a contrary prescription. Hence, explicit neutrality to all religions requires explicit neutrality to any specification of any possible religion.[2] In sum, the principle of

---

[2]It will not help to say that a substantive constitutional stipulation may not itself explicitly state an understanding of the comprehensive good and, in that sense, may be explicitly neutral to its own implications regarding the comprehensive purpose. This fact notwithstanding, a substantive prescription is not explicitly neutral to all substantive prescriptions. Hence, it is not explicitly neutral to any religion whose understanding of the comprehensive purpose requires a contrary prescription—and, in that respect, adherents of that religion are not legitimate participants in the political discourse.

religious freedom stipulates that no politically relevant claims are immune to dissent and argumentative assessment—and thereby expresses the sovereignty of "we, the people."

On my reading, no writer participating in more recent discussion of religious freedom in the United States has appreciated the relation between this principle and democratic discourse as clearly as Sidney E. Mead. I will not assess here Mead's specifically historical analysis of the events surrounding ratification of the First Amendment. On his account, however, the only consistent rationale for its religion clauses is the one more or less adequately formulated by those founders who were children of the Enlightenment and who, therefore, believed that a political community could be united by the way of reason. In their minds, Mead summarizes, religious freedom "was clearly envisaged as the deliberate creation of a situation where every religious opinion and practice, having the right to free expression, would continually contend with all others in order that error might be exposed to view and the truth be recognized" (1963: 82–83). Thereby, Mead alludes especially to the singular words in Jefferson's "Act for Establishing Religious Freedom" in Virginia: "Truth is great and will prevail if left to herself; . . . she is the proper and sufficient antagonist to error, and has nothing to fear from the conflict unless by human interposition disarmed of her natural weapon, free argument and debate; errors ceasing to be dangerous when it is permitted freely to contradict them" (cited in Mead 1963: 82).

To the best of my reasoning, the formative character of a democratic constitution sustains this view of religious freedom even against the possible objection from religious adherents for whom religious truth transcends the capacities of natural reason. On this objection, the stipulation that political decisions should be taken through full and free discourse itself denies legitimacy to the belief that ultimate reality and, therefore, human authenticity as such cannot be known or fully known without some special revelation or disclosure. This is because the state may teach its constitution or teach that politics should be by the way of reason. But if democracy is a meta-ethical presupposition of every claim to moral validity, then a democratic constitution stipulates only conditions that all citizens must explicitly accept in order to have a political discourse about any moral prescription, including the prescription that democracy itself and thus democratic discourse is the proper constitution of a political community. Those who hold on religious grounds that knowledge of the comprehensive purpose is impossible without a special revelation are legitimate participants in that discourse, in the sense that they are invited to argue for any politically relevant claims they wish to make, including a claim for that understanding of religious knowledge.[3]

In other words, the objection could be credited only if the question about human authenticity as such did not constitute a rational order of reflection, in the sense that answers to it can be validated or invalidated by argument. Given that the question is a rational one in this sense, uniting all possible religions by way of reason does not explicitly deny any religious belief, even the belief that our ultimate nature and destiny are "beyond reason," because every such belief is in truth an answer to that rational question. We might say that the principle of religious freedom legitimates all possible religions because the political community is constituted solely by the question. This initial discussion has assumed that the question is a rational one, and the first part of this work is or includes an argument for that assumption.

But this conception of democracy and, therefore, religious freedom is denied by a widespread contemporary consensus. Summarily speaking, most recent theories are, to choose the term used by Jürgen Habermas, "postmetaphysical," meaning that they deny the possibility of validating a conception of the comprehensive purpose or, at least, seek to avoid implying any such conception in formulating principles for democratic politics. Expressly or tacitly, in other words,

---

[3]John Courtney Murray, referring to the constitutive conditions of democratic politics as the truths we hold, wrote about them: "We hold certain truths; therefore we can argue about them" (1998: 10). To first appearances, this assertion seems nonsensical; if we hold these truths, then there is no argument about them. But his point, on my understanding, is this: The constitutive conditions of democracy are those presupposed by a full and free discourse about whether democracy itself is the best form of political association. This is what it means to say that a democratic constitution is formative or explicitly neutral to all understandings of the comprehensive purpose. To prevent any misunderstanding, I should say that I am not in agreement with Murray's identification of constitutive democratic conditions, specifically with his assertion that among them is the affirmation of God's sovereignty over nations. So far as I can see, the inclusion of this stipulation contradicts religious freedom. I have elsewhere discussed my agreements and disagreements with Murray (see Gamwell 1995, especially chapter 4).

these theories typically agree that a comprehensive purpose cannot or could not be understood independently of an understanding of reality as such and, with Kant, deny that metaphysical beliefs can be validated or, at least, that political principles must imply them. In that broad sense, these are theories within the Kantian tradition. At the same time, this tradition does not deny that religious freedom is a *sine qua non* of democratic politics, in the sense that a democratic constitution must legitimate diverse conceptions of a comprehensive good. For many of these theories, moreover, justice must be independent of any such good precisely because this diversity must be legitimated.

I have in mind especially recent theories commonly thought to represent the liberal political tradition. As many have said, liberalism as a specific kind of political theory may be traced to the beginnings of the modern West and the emergence of substantial religious diversity internal to political communities (see, e.g., Stout 1981: 3, 35; Toulmin 1990: 16–17; Rawls 1996: xxii-xxv). The ruinous and indecisive religious wars of the sixteenth and seventeenth centuries demonstrated to modern politics that this diversity must somehow be tolerated if politics is to avoid both the anarchy of basic civil discord and the tyranny of coerced uniformity, and liberal democratic theory is a conceptual response to this challenge. The problems that political liberalism in its diverse expressions has sought to address are, naturally, themselves diverse. Still, the distinctive task of liberal theory, all implications taken into account, has been to define the terms on which a community that legitimates religious plurality can be civilized.

Many recent liberal theories have sought to complete precisely this task by so conceiving of justice that it is independent of any comprehensive good. In order to capture the point in a phrase, we may say that these theories seek to separate justice from the good, where "the good" is used in this phrase to mean the comprehensive good. I am deeply indebted to the work of several thinkers who have pursued this conceptual strategy, notwithstanding my conviction that it is mistaken. Recognition of their importance in contemporary theoretical discussions recommends that this conviction be sustained by an internal criticism of their common approach. The remainder of this chapter will argue that separating justice from the good prevents a coherent account of religious freedom and, therefore, a coherently democratic conception of justice. Thus, the chapter seeks to argue negatively that the formative principle of democracy implies a comprehensive purpose, and the democratic discourse is about the comprehensive purpose in its pertinence to the activities of the state.

Henceforth, I will call a theory on which justice is inseparable from the comprehensive good a teleological theory of justice. Correspondingly, any theory on which justice is separated from the good is nonteleological. Following widespread usage, we might also call the latter a liberal theory. But doing so suggests that a theory of justice must be nonteleological in order to solve the modern political problematic that emerged with substantial religious diversity in the modern West, and this work argues that the solution lies elsewhere. This contemporary use of "liberal," moreover, excludes from the liberal tradition theories that claimed the name even while they were also teleological and that remain, on my accounting, important contemporary resources. I have in mind especially the political thought of John Dewey (see below, chapter 6). As an alternative to "nonteleological," then, I will also call theories of the type it designates "separationist" or theories of justice as separate. Alongside the fact that those theories seek to separate justice from the good, this alternative name alludes to the focus here on religious freedom as a *sine qua non* of democratic politics. In public discussion, "separationists" often designates those who hold that religious freedom means "the separation of church and state" in the sense that questions about justice are properly independent of any religious belief.

Among recent theories, the two most influential formulations of the separationist position are, no doubt, those of John Rawls and Habermas, and both will be used here as examples. In addition, the work of Alan Gewirth and that of Brian Barry will be important to the discussion. Since any theory of justice is or could be a contribution to the process by which democratic decisions are made, we may ask any such theory to clarify its proper place within that process. More specifically, the discussion here will put to each theory the following question: In what respect, if any, should the principle or principles of justice as separate advocated by the theory and, in that sense, the theory itself be stipulated in the constitution of a democracy? The price of separating justice from the good, I will argue, is an answer to this question that contradicts religious freedom or fails to legitimate diverse conceptions of the comprehensive good—and, therefore, a separationist theory of democracy cannot be internally consistent.

Among the thinkers who will serve as conversation partners, Rawls is, at least in his most recent work, most sensible of the problem that will focus this discussion. As a consequence, his work is, at least with respect to that problem, significantly different from the others, and the relevant difference is this: Habermas, Gewirth, and Barry defend universal principles of justice, and Rawls purports that justice is independent not only of a comprehensive good but also of any universal principles. I will call the former universalist theories of justice as separate and the latter a nonuniversalist theory of justice as separate. This reading of Rawls is itself controversial (see, e.g., Habermas 1996: 56–63), although I am not alone in thinking it correct (see, e.g., Wolterstorff 1997: 109–11). But this is the reading on which his theory adds to the present discussion a distinct alternative. The argument will first consider universalist theories of justice, and attention to Rawls will follow.

Justice as Separate: Universalist Theories

The previous chapter gives every reason to affirm, with Habermas, that valid norms for social action can be defined in relation to practical discourse. "Just those action norms are valid to which all possibly affected persons could agree as participants in rational discourse" (1996: 107). His moral theory is universalist because moral discourse is bound by a "universalization principle": "Every valid norm must satisfy the condition that the consequences and side effects its *general* observance can be anticipated to have for the satisfaction of the interests of *each* could be freely accepted by *all* affected (and be preferred to those of known alternative possibilities for regulation)" (1993: 32). The theory is also nonteleological because Habermas asserts that this universalization principle is independent of any interest or purpose.

The interests satisfied by general observance of a valid norm depend on beliefs about "the good life" (1993: 9) or express each individual's "existential self-understanding" (1993: 4), and "morality is not oriented to the *telos* of a successful life" (1993: 24). As a consequence, "the universalization principle acts like a knife that makes razor-sharp cuts between evaluative statements and strictly normative ones, be-

tween the good and the just" (1990: 104), where evaluative statements endorse or oppose some possible interest. On Habermas's
account, this is because conceptions of the good, even conceptions of
the good life as a whole, cannot transcend a specific lifeworld and the
"diverse individual life projects" (1993: 16) it makes possible.

> Postmetaphysical theories of value take into consideration the par-
> ticularity of values, the flexibility of value hierarchies, and the local
> character of value considerations. They either trace values back to
> traditions and settled value orientations of particular cultures or, if
> they want to emphasize the subjective and deliberate character of the
> choice of values, they trace them to existential decisions about
> metapreferences (1996: 257).

Thus, valid moral norms define general regulations of social action
that are "equally in the interests of all possibly affected" (1993: 29)
or "equally good for all" (1993: 34), and Habermas also formulates
the point by calling such regulations "generalizable interests" (1996:
61). It follows that the universalization principle is not itself a moral
norm but, rather, "a rule of argumentation" (1996: 109) in terms of
which moral discourse cannot reach a normative conclusion without
"contingent content" or independently identified interests "from outside" (1990: 103).[4]

In a recent revision of his previous formulations, Habermas says
that the discourse principle of practical reason should be distinguished

---

[4]Habermas allows that the discourse principle itself "has a normative content
insasmuch as it explicates the meaning of impartiality in practical judgments"
(1996: 107). But this, if I understand rightly, is consistent with his saying that
"postconventional morality provides no more than a procedure for impartially
judging disputed questions" (1996: 114) because the normative content to which
he refers consists in "the general pragmatic presuppositions that must always be
made by participants when they enter into [moral] argumentation" (1993: 31).
So far as I can see, then, Habermas's universalization principle is itself as empty
of normative content as is Kant's categorical imperative. For Habermas, however,
his account succeeds where Kant's fails because the universalization principle is
the rule of argumentation for practical discourse and, therefore, implies that
interests are to be regulated in a manner equally good for all. In the end, I doubt
that this makes any difference, because the universalization principle itself does
not define, explicitly or implicitly, what *equally* good means. For a development
of this criticism, see Gamwell 1997.

from the universalization principle of moral discourse, because the former admits of two specifications, namely, the moral principle and the principle of democracy. "In assuming a legal shape, the discourse principle is transformed into a principle of democracy" (1996: 455); that is, the latter specifies the discourse principle "for those action norms that appear in legal form" (1996: 108). Among other things, this means that democratic discourse "is not restricted to moral reasons alone" because legal norms may also call on "ethical-political" reasons (1996: 108). The term "ethical" here is not synonymous with "moral" but, rather, designates reasons dependent on some conception of the good life. Thus, legal norms may represent democratic decisions that "express an authentic, collective self-understanding" specific to the lifeworld or "form of life" of the given political community (1996: 108) and, therefore, express evaluative judgments.

But this reformulation does not alter the separationist character of Habermas's theory of justice, precisely because an authentic collective self-understanding can only be specific to a form of life, representing "a goal that is absolute *for us*" (1996: 161). The principle of democracy itself must be conceived independently of any such self-understanding. As one consequence, laws cannot violate relevant moral norms that are independent of ethical-political reasons. "Even if moral considerations are not selective enough for the legitimation of legal programs, politics and law are still supposed to be compatible with morality—on a common postmetaphysical basis of justification" (1996: 453; see also 106, 110).[5] Thus, the conception of justice itself is independent of any conception of the comprehensive good, and, we can infer, Habermas thereby purports to define justice in a manner consistent with a plurality of legitimate religions.

In contrast to that of Habermas, Gewirth's universal principle is itself a supreme moral norm. In *Reason and Morality* and, subsequently, in *The Community of Rights*, he argues for democratic

---

[5]Indeed, Habermas typically uses the term "justice" to mean the regulation of "typically recurrent action conflicts" by moral norms, so that any proper consideration of "collective goals and goods" is bound to be consistent with independent norms of justice (1996: 153). But the review and criticism of Habermas will not be affected if we continue to designate with "justice" the principle for all legal norms. The main point is that, on either meaning of the term, the theory of "justice" is separationist.

political principles as applications of the "Principle of Generic Consistency" (PGC) that obligates all human action: "Act in accord with the generic rights of your recipients as well as of yourself" (1996: 19, emphasis deleted). This categorical imperative prescribes equal "freedom and well-being" for all humans, that is, prescribes equality with respect to "the proximate necessary conditions and generic features of action and of generally successful action" (1996: 14). Justice in the specifically political sense is an indirect application of the PGC through the laws and institutions of the political order. Because the generic rights include the right to freedom, "the state in question must be democratic"; that is, there is "a political human right of persons that they be governed by democratic states" (1996: 313).

The PGC itself, Gewirth argues, is "dialectically necessary." It defines "what every agent must logically accept for herself" (1996: 16, emphasis deleted) in acting at all. To choose a purpose is always to accept "that the purpose . . . has at least some value sufficient to merit . . . trying to attain it" (1996: 17). The agent takes the purpose to be good in some moral or nonmoral sense of the term "good." This implies that every agent endorses her or his generic conditions of action and generally successful action as themselves necessarily good. As Gewirth also formulates the point, every agent accepts the statement "'I must have freedom and well-being,' where this 'must' is practical-prescriptive in that it signifies the agent's advocacy or endorsement of his having" those conditions (1996: 17). It now follows, Gewirth continues, that the agent claims both negative and positive rights to freedom and well-being: Others ought not to interfere with the agent's having those conditions and, further, ought actively to assist her or him in having freedom and well-being when the agent cannot have them by her or his own efforts, at least if the others "can give such help without comparable cost" to themselves (1996: 40). Not to claim such rights is to contradict the statement "I must have freedom and well-being." Since "the necessary as well as sufficient justifying condition" (1996: 19) for the claim to generic rights is solely that one is an agent, any agent is logically bound to affirm or accept that "the generic rights are rights had equally by all agents" (1996: 19) and, therefore, to accept as categorically obligatory the PGC.

The indirect application of this principle in or through the democratic state "is not neutral with regard to all values or conceptions of the good" (1996: 162). Because "human rights are based on the necessary goods of action and generally successful action, the state must respect these goods for all persons and help to provide them when persons' own efforts cannot do so" (1996: 162). Still, applications in or through principles and norms of justice are independent of any *comprehensive* good, precisely because the necessary goods in question are generic capacities for action. Equality in such capacities or, better, the maximization of such capacities consistent with equality is not itself a comprehensive purpose, because it is not a telos by which all exercise of those capacities should be directed. In other words, Gewirth's argument from any purpose at all to the PGC does not presuppose that any given purpose is morally required. The statement that every agent takes her or his purpose to be good "does not presuppose any moral principle" (1996: 356) because "good" here means value in some moral or nonmoral sense. At least by implication, then, Gewirth's theory purports to define justice in a manner that legitimates a plurality of religions because the conception of human rights does not presuppose any conception of the comprehensive good.

In *Justice as Impartiality*, Brian Barry also defends a separationist theory. Appropriating a formulation of T. M. Scanlon, Barry asserts that norms for the civil order should accord with the following universal principle: "An act is wrong if its performance under the circumstances would be disallowed by any system of rules for the general regulation of behavior which no one could reasonably reject as a basis for informed, unforced general agreement" (1995: 67). The phrase "no one could reasonably reject" means, at the least, that a proposed rule is unjust if it prescribes for some "a unilateral sacrifice of their interests" (1995: 70), where interests are defined by what individuals take to be good. Barry does not assert, however, that the separation of justice from a comprehensive good follows directly from this universal principle. A given individual, he recognizes, might believe that her or his conception of the comprehensive good cannot be reasonably rejected as a basis for informed, unforced general agreement because that conception is rationally compelling. But justice must be conceived nonteleologically, Barry maintains, if one adds that "no conception of the good can justifiably be held with a degree of certainty that warrants its imposition on those who reject it" (1995:

169), and therefore all conceptions of the good should be held with "moderate scepticism" (1995: 172). In saying this, Barry intends that "secular conceptions of the good and religious views are to be assimilated, . . . , because they create the same problems for the project: they give rise to conflicting practical implications and these conflicts cannot be resolved by rational argument" (1995: 30). Since all such conceptions have this character, any given one can be reasonably rejected by those who have a different one, and "the basic principles and rules" for "social cooperation" (1995: 160) in a democracy are properly independent of a comprehensive good, all conceptions of which are thereby legitimated.

If we wish to reason about justice, Barry holds, we have no alternative to democracy because the prescribed scepticism is itself the most reasonable conclusion. He thinks that there is "a strong a priori argument for the inherent uncertainty of all conceptions of the good" (1995: 169), although he does not tell us what it is. Such arguments are, he says, too easily rejected, "too speculative," and, therefore, he prefers "to appeal to experience" (1995: 169). Since the appearance of religious plurality and conflict in the sixteenth and seventeenth centuries, "the sheer weight" of historical evidence is "overwhelming" in favor of scepticism. "It is not hard to be impressed by the fact that so many people have devoted so much effort over so many centuries to a matter of the greatest moment with so little success in the way of securing rational conviction" (1995: 171). From this evidence, "it follows that reasonable terms [for the civil order] must be terms that do not presuppose the correctness of any conception of the good" (1995: 169).

It also follows, Barry concedes, that the normative force of democratic legal regulations "presupposes" what he calls "the agreement motive," that is, "the existence of a certain desire: the desire to live in a society whose members all freely accept its rules of justice and its major institutions" (1995: 164, 165). If I understand rightly, "presupposes" here means "assumes," because Barry means that this motive or desire is not prescribed by reason and, therefore, impartial justice cannot itself be validated against the refusal to regulate one's pursuits by unforced, informed general agreement. Such validation would require a conception of the comprehensive good that is rationally compelling. Whatever one's conception of the good, Barry remarks,

"I take it to be unproblematic that it has motivational force. The problem is, rather, to explain why people might do anything else" (1995: 112). Scepticism with respect to all such conceptions requires that one posit the agreement motive to explain democracy, and together they mean that the norms on which democratic citizens agree are properly separated from the good.

Universalist Theories in the Constitution

Assuming that democracy requires some written or unwritten set of legal stipulations that constitute the political community, we may address to each of these three theories the question formulated earlier: In what respect, if any, should the principle or principles of justice as separate advocated by the theory and, in that sense, the theory itself be stipulated in the constitution of a democracy? On Habermas's account, for instance, should the constitution stipulate that valid norms for the civil order are determined by practical discourse in accord with the democratic principle, including its separation of moral and evaluative statements? On Gewirth's account, should the constitution stipulate that all humans have negative and positive rights to freedom and well-being? On Barry's account, should the constitution stipulate that justice means impartiality, in the sense that basic principles and rules of the civil order should be those no one can reasonably reject, given the agreement motive and moderate scepticism about conceptions of the comprehensive good?

I am not sure how each of these theorists does or would respond. Although Habermas discusses the constitution of a democratic state extensively, he does not, to the best of my reading, specify the relation between his own theory and the democratic process. Again to the best of my reading, Barry does not offer a considered address to the question. He mentions that justice as impartiality is "a legitimate topic for debate" (1995: 123), but he also advocates "a neutral constitutional framework" (1995: 161), where "neutral," to all appearances, should be understood in his separationist sense. In contrast, Gewirth pursues at some length the relation of political decisions required by the PGC to the process of democratic decision making. In addition to articulating the "political and civil rights" (1996: 348–49) implied by the universal "right of persons that they be governed by democratic states" (1996: 313), *The Community of Rights* develops in detail the economic and social rights that may be derived from the PGC and that entail duties of the democratic state—for instance, positive rights to education, productive agency, property, and employment. Gewirth then asks whether these "economic and social rights [should] be subject for their effectuation to the consensual procedures of political democracy" (1996: 318). "Within certain important limits," he argues for "the affirmative answer" (1996: 319). But the meaning of this affirmation is not entirely clear.

The answer is affirmative at least in part because "the very meaning of 'freedom' or 'well-being' and its applications in complex areas like welfare, education, employment, or workers' control may leave open many possibilities of alternative interpretations and evaluations" (1996: 323). In other words, the implications of the PGC with respect to the positive rights involve specification in appropriate "institutional arrangements" and, in that sense, are subject to "rational discussion and debate" (1996: 323). But if effectuation through the democratic process should be affirmed because positive rights to freedom and well-being must be institutionally specified, then it remains possible that the political constitution should stipulate such rights. Indeed, democratic effectuation seems to mean, for Gewirth, "effectuation, *in a constitution* and accompanying laws, of the economic rights" (1996: 324, emphasis added), and he subsequently asserts: "The solution that is called for regarding both kinds of rights [political and economic] is a constitutional one. There should be a constitution that is initially set up by a democratic political process, but which then gives a fixed, firm status to both the political and economic rights" (1996: 326). At the least, then, he seems not to preclude the constitutional stipulation of rights to freedom and well-being.

However each thinker in fact does or would answer the question we have put, some may summarily object that placing any such theory of justice in the constitution grants unacceptable power to the judiciary, at least if the courts have responsibility to insure that laws are consistent with the constitution. But the constitutional recognition of a given theory could mean only that it should be taught to all citizens—so that the courts' powers are limited to more specific constitutional provisions. Unless nongovernmental associations sufficiently execute the task, the state has a duty to teach its constitution, because it is the set of prescriptions all citizens should explicitly accept as political participants. Including in the constitution a theory of justice could mean defining the most general political principle or principles in accord with which all citizens ought to deliberate as they participate in the process by which activities of the state are determined. To be sure, this constitutional provision could not be enforced, in the sense that deliberation in accord with the stipulated principle or principles cannot be coerced. But explicit acceptance of the conception in question would belong within the ethics of citizenship, and the state would be bound to insure that it is taught or, as I will henceforth say elliptically, to teach it. Leaving aside whether any of the theorists we have reviewed intends to prescribe an explicit constitutional endorsement of his own theory, let us consider the consequences if one or the other theory does require its own teaching by the state.

Notwithstanding that the three theories are all separationist, there are disagreements among Habermas, Barry, and Gewirth. In the end, the similarities between Habermas and Barry may be more impressive than their differences, although Barry, who simply says that conceptions of the good are rationally uncertain, does not, with Habermas, assert that existential self-understandings or conceptions of the good are in all respects specific to some lifeworld. But both clearly reject the dialectically necessary character of rights to freedom and well-being that Gewirth asserts. Further, as we will see, all three theories disagree with the conception of justice as nonuniversal proposed by Rawls. If the state's teaching should include a given separationist theory, the theory in question asserts that this governmental power should be placed behind its claims in contrast to those of competing non-teleological theories. But that assertion, it seems, should be unacceptable to all of the thinkers we have briefly reviewed. In the case of Habermas, is not practical discourse compromised if the state teaches that only his conception of justice can be redeemed in discourse? In the case of Gewirth, is not the generic right to freedom in its specifically political sense contradicted if the state teaches that the PGC is rationally necessary? In the case of Barry, is not impartiality violated if the state teaches that his conception alone cannot be reasonably rejected?

Alternatively, then, a separationist theory might assert the following: The constitution should stipulate and the state should teach only that the principle or principles of justice are independent of any comprehensive good. Citizenship is not defined by explicit acceptance of any given nonteleological theory, and differences among such theories are themselves subject to debate within the constituted democratic process. On this account, however, the constitution explicitly denies all teleological conceptions of justice. To be sure, all of the authors in question defend nonteleology. But some democratic citizens may not find those arguments convincing and may believe, to the contrary, that principles of justice are dependent on a comprehensive purpose. At least to first appearances, it would be a compromise of "practical discourse" or "political freedom" or "impartiality" were the state to take sides in this debate.

Moreover, a constitutional provision stating that justice is separate from the good is inconsistent with the legitimacy of all possible religions. As we have seen, this separation is thought to be required in order to civilize a community that legitimates diverse conceptions of the comprehensive good. At least some of these conceptions may assert that principles of justice are *inseparable* from it. If the state is constitutionally bound to teach the contrary, these religions are illegitimate. Given that all citizens should explicitly accept the separation of justice from the good, no citizen can adhere to any such religion without violating the constitution.

Still, nonteleological thinkers may insist on this constitutional provision because, they argue, its only alternative is a constitution that stipulates some or other conception of the comprehensive good. On this defense, to accept a nonteleological conception of justice is simply to believe that no religion is established. Precisely because a democratic constitution provides religious freedom, *this* condition of the political association ought to be taught to all citizens—and, we may be told, teaching that justice is separate from the good is nothing other than teaching the principle of religious freedom. But whatever force this defense may seem to have derives, I think, from a confusion between contradictories and contraries. If religious establishment and the separation of justice from the good were contradictories, then one could not consistently deny one without affirming the other. But these two alternatives are logical contraries, so that one can consistently deny both. The disestablishment of all religions does not imply that justice is independent of any one because there is another alternative.

This third option is the compound character of justice, which means that formative principles of a democratic constitution are differentiated from the substantive principle or principles that, through the democratic discourse, ought to control the decisions of the political association.

On the conception of justice as compound, the constitution may not explicitly affirm or deny any theory of justice because the political association is properly constituted as a full and free discourse among all such theories. As a political principle, religious freedom stipulates nothing more or less than this political discourse, so that other constitutional provisions properly legislate only formative conditions of it. Against the compound character of justice, even a constitutional provision *that* justice is separate from the good without an explicit statement of *what* its principles are places a substantive prescription within the constitution. Because that stipulation explicitly denies all teleological conceptions of justice, it explicitly prescribes political deliberation independently of appeal to any comprehensive good, and the prescribed action is not explicitly neutral to disagreement about it. Whether any citizen should so deliberate is itself properly subject to contestation within the democratic discourse.

I will call any theory of justice that prescribes an explicit constitutional denial of one or more other theories, teleological or non-teleological, insofar a "simple" theory of justice. In this context, the term "simple" does not mean that a theory fails to be sophisticated or to appreciate complexity; even a cursory acquaintance with any of the authors reviewed above discredits anything approaching such a judgment. "Simple" means, rather, that the theory in question fails consistently to be compound or to distinguish formative and substantive principles of justice. In the respect that it is simple, then, a given theory fails to be democratic, even if only because it asserts or implies that the constitution should explicitly endorse the separation of justice from any comprehensive good.

Universalist Theories in the Discourse

But our discussion to this point has only assumed that separationist theories and, specifically, those we have reviewed are, at least in some respect, simple theories of justice. Perhaps, to the contrary, one or more intends to assert or could assert the conception of justice as compound. On this reading, the theory in question does not prescribe an explicit constitutional endorsement of itself or even of nonteleology as such; the theory itself is placed solely within the democratic discourse. Because Habermas holds that democracy is the political form of practical discourse, it may seem that his theory not only could but also does assert that justice has a compound character; one might hold that nothing in Gewirth's moral theory requires that the constitution stipulate rights to freedom and well-being, whatever he may say explicitly about the matter; and Barry does write that justice as impartiality is itself "a legitimate topic for debate" (1995: 123), suggesting that his theory is consistent with a formative constitution.

Presenting a nonteleological theory as a substantive contribution to full and free political discourse means that its asserted separation of justice from the good is now subject to, rather than constitutive of, assessment in the democratic argument, and the theory must defend this independence as the proper basis on which citizens should deliberate about activities of the state. Each of the theories we have reviewed seeks to provide a convincing defense for that conclusion. The present section will assess those arguments and, through them, the general kind of theory they defend. Assuming that the principle or principles of justice are universal, I will seek to show that no separationist conception of them can be redeemed or, to say the same, that such principles cannot be successfully defended without validating a conception of the comprehensive good. If the criticism is sound, no theory of justice as universal and separate from the good can consistently represent the compound character of justice, because the theory cannot be redeemed in discourse without ceasing to be nonteleological.

We can begin by noting that any universalist theory of justice as separate implies the following statement about all purposes: Pursuit of what is taken to be good is morally impermissible if it violates the independent principle or principles of justice. Because there is this class of impermissible purposes, there are also impermissible conceptions of the comprehensive good, namely, those belonging to the class each member of which prescribes impermissible purposes. For instance, a conception of the comprehensive good as maximal white supremacy is morally proscribed by all three of the theories we have reviewed.[6] Correspondingly, there are conceptions of the comprehensive good that are morally permissible, meaning here only that each member of this class is consistent with the independent principle or principles of justice. Hence, a universalist nonteleology implies this universal moral difference between impermissible and permissible conceptions of the comprehensive good.

Still, any such theory must deny that its distinction between the two itself is or implies a conception of the comprehensive good, because the distinction is derived from a nonteleological principle or set of principles. In other words, the theory in question cannot assert that permissible conceptions of the comprehensive good are morally valid conceptions, because this would mean that they and the purposes they prescribe are all equally good, and that assertion contradicts nonteleology. To say that two or more such purposes are equally good is to imply a principle in relation to which they can be compared and determined to be, in the relevant sense, equal—just as, for instance, to say that two or more individuals are equally proficient at some craft implies a standard for such proficiency. Thus, a universalist nonteleology on which permissible conceptions of the comprehensive good are morally valid would imply a universal principle of the good by which their validity is grounded and would cease to separate justice from the good.

But, then, we can ask each such theory about the meaning of "permissible conception of the comprehensive good," given that it does not mean "morally valid conception," and the three theories we have briefly reviewed give, I believe, three different answers to that question: (1) A permissible conception of the comprehensive good is in a relevant sense valid or invalid, but there is no universal principle of its validity and, therefore, it is not morally valid or invalid; (2) a permissible conception of the comprehensive good is in no relevant sense valid or invalid and, therefore, is merely morally permissible; (3) whether a permissible conception of the comprehensive good is mor-

---

[6]Some nonteleologists might wish to say that conceptions of the comprehensive good are impermissible *insofar as or in the respect that* they prescribe impermissible purposes. Even the telos of maximal white supremacy might prescribe some purposes that are morally permissible. But we may take any such conception to include all of its prescriptions, so that changing some aspect of it in order to maintain consistency with independent principles of justice would be to introduce another conception of the comprehensive good.

ally valid or invalid is a question neither answer to which can be validated. So far as I can see, these exhaust the possible alternatives, and the argument here will now seek to show that each answer implies a conception of the comprehensive good, so that the theory in question could not be redeemed in democratic discourse without validating that conception and, thereby, ceasing to be separationist.

The first alternative, on which a permissible conception of the comprehensive good is in a relevant but not moral sense valid or invalid, appears to be Habermas's position. On his account, the universalization principle or rule of argumentation for moral discourse "makes razor-sharp cuts between evaluative statements and strictly normative ones, between the good and the just" (1990: 104). Conceptions of the good and thus "existential self-understanding[s]" (1993: 4) are the contingent content in moral discourse of which the universalization principle is independent. Still, legal norms, so long as they are morally valid, may also express "an authentic, collective self-understanding" specific to the "form of life" of a given political community (1996: 108). This seems to imply that permissible conceptions of the comprehensive good are subject to democratic discourse and, therefore, that each is in some relevant sense valid or invalid, even though its validity is always in all respects specific to a lifeworld.

Assuming this reading of Habermas, we can approach an assessment through recognizing that his distinction between the universal validity of moral norms and the thoroughly contextual validity of evaluative statements itself defines a universal difference. The assertion that validity as it characterizes conceptions of the comprehensive good is in all respects historically specific cannot be an assertion whose validity is itself in all respects historically specific; that is, the independence of Habermas's democratic principle from any comprehensive good cannot itself be specific to some lifeworld. To the contrary, this separation must be universally the case, as Habermas seems to concede when he says that the universalization principle is what makes the razor-sharp cuts. But, then, the assertion that validity as it characterizes conceptions of the comprehensive good is in all respects specific to historical conditions itself requires validation in universalist terms, if Habermas's separationist theory is to be redeemed.

To the best of my reading, Habermas in fact never defends this assertion. Validity as it characterizes existential self-understandings is assumed to be thoroughly contextual because he believes that meta-physical worldviews are not subject to universal discourse. Universal-ist and nonteleological moral and political theory typically agrees, as noted above, that an understanding of the comprehensive good im-plies an understanding of reality as such and, with Kant, holds that no metaphysical conception can be validated. On Habermas's ac-count, this means that full rationalization of moral norms depends on a postmetaphysical worldview or, as he also puts it, a transition to modernity. In contrast to the "religious and metaphysical" world-views characteristic of medieval civilization, in which "ontic [and] normative, . . . aspects of validity" are fused in the conception of a "fundamental order" that is "immunized against" criticism (1987: 189), the modern worldview separates assertions about what exists from moral ones and, thereby, releases both for unrestrained dis-course. Within practical discourse, then, moral norms are separated from evaluative ones, and, validity as it characterizes conceptions of the comprehensive good or existential self-understandings must be in all respects historically specific.

Quite apart from any explicit appeal to earlier arguments through which this work sought to defend metaphysics against Kant, one can show that Habermas's appropriation of Kant is untenable. If it is universally the case that evaluations can be valid, there must be a universal principle of their validity; that is, "valid" in the sense that it can characterize existential self-understandings must be a universal characteristic, precisely because the possibility is not limited to any specific historical conditions. But a universal principle of valid evalu-ations means that any one of them conforms to some standard or exemplifies some character that is not thoroughly contextual. More-over, an evaluation is valid if the telos it takes to be good is, in truth, good; hence, the universal principle of such validity is or im-plies a universal principle of good ends or a definition of the com-prehensive good.[7] On the assertion that existential self-understan-

---

[7] It will not help to say that a universal principle of the good does not require a comprehensive good because the principle may prescribe for ends merely in some respect. Insofar as the principle is said to have this character, it, too, is a nonteleological principle, and the question about permissible conceptions of the comprehensive good reappears.

dings can be valid, Habermas's separation of justice from the good implies, against itself, a comprehensive good, and his appropriation of Kant is self-refuting.

A defense of Habermas might respond that the universal principle in question is solely negative. On this response, the validity of evaluations is in all respects specific to historical conditions because a statement that this is universally so simply denies any universal character of "valid" in the relevant sense. But the denial that existential self-understandings can be valid in any universal sense does not imply that they can be valid in a thoroughly contextual sense. So far as the denial goes, a permissible conception of the comprehensive good is neither valid nor invalid. If Habermas does assert that evaluations can be valid, then this statement about evaluations universally cannot simply deny that their validity has any universal character.[8] But, then, his own theory cannot be redeemed in democratic discourse without validating a conception of the comprehensive good, and this theory cannot represent the compound character of justice without ceasing to be nonteleological.

The defense might now say that we have misread Habermas. In fact, he intends that a permissible conception of the comprehensive good is in no relevant sense valid or invalid but, rather, is merely morally permissible—the second of the alternative understandings formulated above. On this reading, his separation of moral norms from evaluations means that existential self-understandings, like metaphysical worldviews, are immune to criticism and are, therefore, nonrational decisions. Although I am not entirely clear what Habermas does intend, I doubt that this second account is consistent with democratic discourse about the collective self-understanding of a particular community. But however Habermas should be read, this second alterna-

---

[8]In a relevant sense, to restate the point, Habermas's view of existential self-understandings is analogous to the view that all cultures are historically specific. The latter cannot mean "in all respects historically specific" because it implies a universal character of cultures by which they are distinguished from other aspects of human existence. Similarly, the assertion that validity as it characterizes evaluations is always historically specific implies a universal character of valid evaluations by which an evaluation exemplifying this character is distinguished from permissible but invalid conceptions of the good, and this character defines a comprehensive good.

tive is plausibly attributed to Gewirth, and we may pursue it in terms of his nonteleological theory.

The Principle of Generic Consistency, as we have seen, is not neutral to all conceptions of the good because it is based on the necessary goods of action; in that sense, we can say that Gewirth asserts a universal principle of the good. Still, this is nothing other than the nonteleological moral principle itself, which prescribes equality with respect to the generic conditions of action and generally successful action. Conceptions of the good that are consistent with this principle and that prescribe the purposes for which an agent will exercise her or his generic capacities, that is, permissible conceptions of the comprehensive good, seem to be merely morally permissible. They are in no relevant sense valid or invalid, because the PGC is the supreme and thus complete principle of morality (see 1978: 327f.). The same conclusion is implied by Gewirth's assertion that his derivation of the PGC from a conception of human purposes "does not presuppose any moral principle" (1996: 356).

Gewirth might properly remind us that a purpose can be good in more than one sense. It might be, for instance, instrumentally good or aesthetically good as well as morally good. Accordingly, there are different senses in which one might say that a conception of the good is valid or invalid. In the present context, "a permissible conception of the comprehensive good is in no relevant sense valid or invalid" means that no such conception defines a good in relation to which agents categorically ought to evaluate their possible purposes. Although every agent, on Gewirth's account, affirms her or his purpose as good, there is no comprehensive good by which practical reason is categorically bound. Hence, "my purpose is good" may be valid in the sense that it is instrumentally good, but the agent is not rationally bound to that pursuit unless she or he chooses some other purpose to which the first is instrumental. Similarly, "my purpose is good" may be valid in the sense that it is aesthetically good or, for that matter, is consistent with some specific cultural tradition, but the agent is not rationally bound to that pursuit unless she or he chooses to evaluate her or his alternatives in relation to a standard of aesthetic goodness or, alternatively, the cultural tradition in question. On Gewirth's account, in other words, any sense in which an agent can validly assert "my purpose is good," other than the nonteleological sense defined by the PGC, must be hypothetical.

One might ask whether this second understanding of "permissible conception of the comprehensive good" is really an alternative. Is not the statement that all such conceptions are morally permissible equivalent to saying that the purposes they prescribe are all equally good and, therefore, all morally valid? If so, that reformulation implies a universal principle of the good in terms of which such equality is determined. So far as I can see, then, this second understanding implies that human agency as purposive is not itself something about which one can ask a moral question. To assert that permissible conceptions of the comprehensive good are in no relevant sense valid or invalid is to say that moral theory does not ask whether humans ought to have purposes but, rather, assumes that there are humans who do choose ends or telē. If we now ask whether moral theory can be indifferent to whether humans have purposes at all, the response may be that this is not a practical problem to be addressed, since a human cannot decide whether to have a purpose but only what it is or will be.

In truth, however, a human individual may choose whether or not to have *future* purposes. The agent's present alternatives always include the possibility of attributing no worth to her or his own future agency, and one way in which that choice might be expressed is an action that terminates her or his own life. If moral theory is indifferent to whether humans have purposes at all, it must also be indifferent, in the absence of other considerations, to whether humans value their own future agency. Naturally, a moral theory may hold that there are other considerations; for instance, action that attributes no worth to one's own future agency may violate the generic rights of others. But the theory remains indifferent to whether humans as such choose to have future purposes, since appeal to the rights of others does not imply that they ought so to choose. When the rights of others are not involved, then, the difference between a choice for or against one's own future agency must be morally indifferent.

But can the neutrality of moral theory to the differences between choices consistently mean that they are not morally evaluated? As argued in a previous chapter, moral evaluation defines the similarities and differences between alternatives for choice *with respect to choosing* and, therefore, assumes whatever descriptive similarities and differences the alternatives are understood to have. To the best of my reasoning, moral indifference to some difference between choices can only mean that the difference in question makes no difference with respect to choosing, and that assertion *is* a moral evaluation of the difference. Thus, if moral theory is neutral to an individual's decision whether to have future purposes, this cannot mean that neither choice is morally valid or invalid but, rather, that both alternatives are morally valid. Moreover, the same conclusion applies generally to indifference between conceptions of the comprehensive good. That certain such conceptions are all morally permissible cannot mean that they are morally neither valid nor invalid but only that they are all morally valid and, therefore, equally good. Accordingly, the second understanding of "permissible conception of the comprehensive good" is also self-refuting because it implies a universal principle of the good in relation to which the equality in question can be determined. On this second understanding, as on the first, a nonteleological theory cannot be redeemed in democratic discourse without validating a conception of the comprehensive good and, therefore, without ceasing to be a separationist theory of justice.

Still, this conclusion cannot be convincing unless Gewirth's dialectically necessary derivation of the PGC is unsuccessful. If his argument is sound, then he in fact redeems a nonteleological principle. In brief, he argues that every agent in choosing any purpose at all accepts the statement "I must have freedom and well-being" and, therefore, claims both negative and positive rights to these necessary conditions of her or his agency; because the necessary and sufficient justifying condition of this rights claim is solely that she or he is an agent, every agent is logically bound to accept as categorically obligatory the equal generic rights of all agents.

As Gewirth seems to concede, however, "'I must have freedom and well-being,' where this 'must' is practical-prescriptive" (1996: 17), makes no sense if the generic conditions in question are solely those of the agent's present action. Others cannot interfere with these conditions and the agent does not require assistance in having them, since her or his very exercise of agency means that she or he "already has these conditions" and is not prevented from acting (1996: 23). But this fact does not jeopardize the derivation, Gewirth argues, because "a person who is presently an agent may subsequently come to lack freedom and well-being; hence, he claims rights to freedom and well-being not only as a present agent but as a prospective or future agent" (1996: 23). So far as I can see, the success of this response depends on showing that an agent claims rights as a *future* agent. Given such a claim, one may say that she or he also claims rights "as a present agent," in the sense that every agent claims rights to her or his agency as such. At least in the context of the argument, however, the absence of a claim to rights as a prospective agent would mean that the derivation of "I must have freedom and well-being" is fallacious, since there would be no reason for the agent to be "practical-prescriptive" with respect to the conditions she or he already has.

But whether an individual claims rights to future freedom and well-being depends on whether she or he chooses to be a future agent. As already noted, an agent's present alternatives include the possibility of attributing no worth to her or his future agency; hence, every agent must choose whether or not her or his future choices are included in the telos of present action. I am not sure whether Gewirth concedes this point. "No human, . . . , can evade the context of action," he writes, "except perhaps by committing suicide; and even then the steps he takes for this purpose are themselves actions" (1996: 13). The concluding half of this citation seems to assert that even the choice not to value one's future agency requires that one value one's future agency, at least briefly. But Gewirth's theory, so far as I can see, gives him no warrant for that assertion. If the agent's choice of a purpose, from which the derivation of the PGC begins, "does not presuppose any moral principle" or any conception of the comprehensive good, then it must be possible for an individual in her or his present choice to attribute no worth to her or his future agency or to disavow the context of her or his future action.

This follows precisely because attention is here directed to the agent's own *future* agency. Present choice relates to the future because a purpose is chosen; hence, the agent's attribution of worth to future states of affairs depends on what she or he takes to be good. Every exercise of agency must, as Gewirth says, take some or other future as good, because action as such is purposive. But his argument begins without presupposing any principle of the good in relation to which morally required purposes are defined. Hence, there is no reason to assert that one's own future agency must be included in the telos that is chosen. Given where Gewirth means to begin, in other words, an agent may consistently choose as her or his telos a state of affairs that excludes the worth of her or his own future, that is, may consistently evaluate future possibilities in a manner that excludes her or his own future agency from the good to be realized. On that choice, a present act of suicide implies no moral principle. Even if future steps are needed to cease being an agent, moreover, this does not imply a rights claim because the agent in the present may be indifferent to whether others prevent the freedom and well-being required for those steps. The present denial of one's own future agency is indifferent to whether it ceases by one's own hand or by the interference of others. One simply chooses not to affirm "I must have future freedom and well-being" and, therefore, one is not necessarily committed to the rights claim that, for Gewirth, implies a categorically obligatory principle of equal rights for all agents.[9]

This means that Gewirth can derive the claim to rights from the present choice of a purpose only by presupposing that no human can consistently choose to deny the worth of her or his future agency. But, then, the concept of action from which the argument begins *does* presuppose a morally required conception of the good, since an affirmation of worth no agent can consistently deny is categorically obligatory. This is, moreover, a moral presupposition that must be validated prior to the derivation of the PGC, since the rights claim to be universalized depends on this concept of action. To be sure, the notion of a present choice that attributes no worth to the individual's own future agency seems especially odd. Perhaps this is why Gewirth says that individuals are assumed to be "conatively normal," meaning that an agent "has the self-interested motivations common to most persons and is willing to expend the effort needed to fulfill them; in

---

[9]Since suicide was mentioned in a note to the previous chapter, it may be useful to clarify the difference between the pertinence of this act in that context and in this one. I previously argued that suicide cannot be taken as a possible form of expressing dissent, in the sense that failure to commit the act is a decision to accept the moral claim in question, because the relevant subjects with respect to the formative character of every social prescription are human individuals rather than human activities (see above, chapter 4, n. 6). Consistency may seem to require that the present discussion should also take individuals as the relevant subjects. But the question here is not about the implications of a social prescription; rather, we are asking about the implications of a human choice or action, and the relevant subject of a choice or action is a human activity.

other words, he is at least a prospective agent" (1978: 90; see also 1996: 23–24). But however normal prospective agency may in fact be, Gewirth cannot assume it without introducing into the account of present action a purpose the agent might choose against and, thereby, asserting something about the good in contradiction to the supposed derivation of the PGC.

Some may object that this criticism is tendentious. Let us grant, this objection runs, that prospective agency is a present choice and, further, that a present agent who attributes no worth to her or his own future agency is not committed by dialectical necessity to the PGC. It remains that any agent who in the present does attribute worth to her or his future agency thereby claims rights to its necessary conditions and is logically committed to affirming that all other agents have the same rights. The consequence is a nonteleological moral principle for all conatively normal persons, and this is what Gewirth means in assuming that individuals are of this kind. But the PGC is derived from the claim to rights because agency itself is said to be the necessary and sufficient justifying condition of that rights claim. The argument, in other words, invokes "the logical principle of universalizability: if some predicate P belongs to some subject S because S has a certain quality Q (where the 'because' is that of *sufficient* condition), then P must belong to all other subjects . . . that also have Q" (1996: 18, emphasis added). If prospective agency is a choice, however normal this choice may be, then the sufficient condition for an agent's claim to rights is not that she or he is an agent but, rather, that she or he is an agent who chooses to affirm the worth of her or his own future agency.

Nonetheless, the objection might insist, an agent who so chooses is logically committed to the equal rights of all other agents. But Gewirth, I believe, would not endorse this assertion, because it involves a non sequitur. Absent a moral prescription, choosing a telos commits an agent practically only to the means that are both possible and necessary to her or his end. As Kant formulated the point: "Whoever wills the end wills also (so far as reason decides his conduct) the means in his power which are indispensably necessary thereto" (1949: 34). Thus, the choice to affirm *my* future agency rather than deny its worth does not imply an affirmation of any other's agency except insofar as it is a necessary means to mine. If prospective agency is chosen and that choice does not itself presuppose a moral principle, the only imperatives that follow from that choice are, to recur to Kant, hypothetical. Gewirth's attempt to derive a supreme moral principle that is nonteleological leaves human action with solely hypothetical imperatives and, therefore, with no morality at all.[10]

The conclusion reached in this review of Gewirth's argument can be generalized: Any universalist nonteleology on which all permissible conceptions of the comprehensive good are merely morally permissible is self-refuting. Purposeful action as such can be bound by a principle for human interaction only if purposes as such are bound by a prior principle of the good.[11] Hence, a nonteleological theory that seeks to formulate universal nonteleological prescriptions asserts that all permissible conceptions of the comprehensive good are morally

[10]Derek Beyleveld's defense of Gewirth argues that an agent whose present choice allows intervention with her or his future freedom and well-being is at least committed to the following rights claim: Others have a duty "to (at least) refrain from such interference with my freedom and well-being *as is against my will*" (Beyleveld 1991: 27). Hence, even this agent is bound to refrain from interfering with the freedom and well-being of other agents against their will. But this argument is, I think, unsuccessful. If "my will" means my future exercise of agency, the criticism has not been addressed, because it asserts that my present exercise of agency may or may not endorse my future "will." If, to the contrary, "my will" means my present choice, then "others ought not to interfere with my future freedom and well-being against my will" means "others ought not to interfere with my future freedom and well-being *if* I now will them." But universalizing this claim does not yield "I ought not to interfere with the future freedom and well-being of others if *they* will them but, rather, "I ought not to interfere with the future freedom and well being of others if *I* now will them." The sufficient condition of my claim to future rights is, in other words, the choice to affirm them. Since the claim is not implied by agency as such, there can be no derivation of a moral principle.

My suspicion is that those who find Gewirth's argument convincing tacitly assume an understanding of human beings in which the present "I" and the "I" that identifies the individual as a career cannot be distinguished. The concrete self is taken to be the individual as a temporally extended series of activities. On that assumption, every agent in the present is necessarily a prospective agent. So far as I can see, however, this understanding of the self commits the "fallacy of misplaced concreteness" (Whitehead 1978: 7), because it contradicts its own recognition of a difference between the self's present and future decisions.

[11]This statement reformulates the point urged in chapter 4 against both Kant and Apel, namely, that no moral principle can be derived from human action as such if every human action can be independently described in terms of its purpose.

valid or the purposes they prescribe are equally good. So generalized, the review of Gewirth confirms the earlier conclusion that moral indifference to the differences among conceptions of the good is a moral evaluation of those differences. Whether a universalist theory of justice as separate asserts, with Habermas, that a permissible conception of the comprehensive good can be valid in a relevant but nonmoral sense or, with Gewirth, that this conception is merely morally permissible, the theory itself cannot be redeemed in discourse without validating a conception of the comprehensive good. No such theory can represent the compound character of justice without contradicting its claim to be separationist.

There remains the third understanding of "permissible conception of the comprehensive good," namely, whether such a conception is morally valid or invalid is a question neither answer to which can be validated. This understanding, it might be said, is what allows Barry's theory consistently to represent the compound character of justice. On his account of impartiality, democratic principles should be independent of any comprehensive good because all conceptions of that good should be held with "moderate scepticism," which means that whether any such conception is morally valid or invalid cannot be determined, at least in a sense relevant to political decisions. The most reasonable conclusion is that "no conception of the good can justifiably be held with a degree of certainty that warrants its imposition on those who reject it" (1995: 169). Given this conclusion, reasonable terms of "informed, unforced general agreement" (1995: 67) are terms that "do not presuppose the correctness of any conception of the good" (1995: 169).

As the term "imposition" suggests, however, Barry's apparent reason for recommending scepticism and thus a nonteleological theory is that the political order is otherwise unable to legitimate a plurality of religions or conceptions of the comprehensive good. Any citizen who believes that a given such conception is the proper basis for political decisions thereby denies the legitimacy of all others that are substantively different from it. Thus, Barry's argument for moderate scepticism concludes: "Scepticism supplies the premise that is needed to get from the desire for agreement on reasonable terms to the conclusion that no conception of the good should be *built into the constitution* or the principles of justice" (1995: 172, emphasis added). The argument seems to assume, in other words, that a nonteleological conception of justice is the only alternative to the constitutional establishment of some religion, and, on that assumption, the constitution must stipulate that justice is separate from the good.

But this assumption is fallacious because it ignores the conception of justice as compound. The alternative to both religious establishment and justice as separate is a discourse in which all theories of justice are critically assessed, and we are now asking for a defense of Barry's theory as one that affirms this discourse and seeks validation within it. Considered in this context, his commendation of scepticism with respect to teleological conceptions of justice loses its apparent appeal. We can agree that democratic discourse itself requires a kind of scepticism. This is not, however, a refusal to derive principles of justice from some conception of the comprehensive good but, rather, a readiness to place claims to validity in question, as is required by all critical reflection. In this sense of the term, participants in the discourse would not exempt from "scepticism" Barry's own theory of justice, with its assertion that reasonable terms must be terms that "do not presuppose the correctness of any conception of the good."

To be sure, any theory of justice that becomes sufficiently persuasive in the discourse as to control democratic decisions will be, thereby, *implicitly* imposed on those who reject it, but this will be the case even if the persuasive theory is Barry's. Indeed, the very point of the discourse is that the valid theory of justice *should* be implicitly imposed through the activities of the state on all citizens who disagree with it. Hence, to recommend scepticism about teleological theories of justice because none can be held with a degree of certainty that warrants imposition is, in the context of a full and free political discourse, simply to assert that a separationist theory is more convincing, and it is this assertion that still requires a convincing defense. But now it might now be said that Barry provides or could provide just such a defense by showing how the "sheer weight" of historical evidence is "overwhelming" in favor of thinking that religions are, in some special way, uncertain. Hence, no conception of the comprehensive good should control democratic decisions or be implicitly imposed on those who disagree.

"It is hard not to be impressed," Barry writes, "by the fact that so many people have devoted so much effort over so many centuries to a matter of the greatest moment [that is, validating a claim to religious truth] with so little success in the way of securing rational conviction" (1995: 171). If "securing rational conviction" means "securing agreement by argument," what Barry says here about conceptions of the comprehensive good also applies to theories of justice, including separationist theories. However thorough the agreement achieved in the modern West on more or less specific norms of justice (for instance, on the abolition of slavery or on democratic decision-making procedures), there has been and remains significant and widespread disagreement about the theory by which those norms are redeemed. But even if democratic citizens widely accepted a certain theory, appeal to this historical evidence would not validate that theory. Validation requires a sound argument, and widespread agreement is not itself sufficient to redeem principles of justice in democratic discourse. To assert the contrary is to imply that relatively small minorities in the democratic process should, simply because they are relatively small, reject their own positions. Hence, Barry's historical appeal is finally misguided as a response to asking what theory of justice ought to control the democratic process.

As already noted, recent political *philosophy* in the West is marked by a widespread, although hardly unanimous, agreement that valid principles of justice are nonteleological. On my reading, this common conviction expresses the yet wider consensus that Kant decisively discredited all attempts to validate metaphysical assertions and, therefore, comprehensive teleology. It might be said, moreover, that Kant's conclusion is itself echoed in a view widely shared among democratic citizens more generally. I have in mind those who think that religious beliefs are not subject to argumentative assessment or are "solely matters of faith." As it happens, this appears also to be what Barry thinks about conceptions of the comprehensive good. "Religious beliefs," he asserts, "are not susceptible to rational proof or disproof" (1995: 30), and, as noted, he mentions without giving "a strong a priori argument for the inherent uncertainty of all conceptions of the good" (1995: 169). In the end, this understanding of religious beliefs seems to be why he recommends scepticism and is logically prior to or informs his interpretation of the historical evidence.

But if Barry's theory separates principles of justice from religious conceptions because in principle the latter cannot be assessed by argument, then he asserts that permissible conceptions of the comprehensive good are morally neither valid nor invalid. So far as I can see, this is in fact what one must mean in saying: whether a permissible conception of the comprehensive good is morally valid or invalid is a question neither answer to which can be validated. To be sure, one may insist on a difference between the validity of a belief and the possibility of validating it. But this difference is quite irrelevant when the belief in question asserts some conception of the comprehensive good. If any such conception is valid, then it designates the good that all humans in all of their activities ought to pursue, and, since "ought implies can," an understanding of this good must be included, at least implicitly, in any human activity. A comprehensive good, if there is one, must be presupposed by human choice as such, and a conception of what is so presupposed is, for that reason, "susceptible to rational proof or disproof" or can be assessed by argument.

To the best of my reasoning, then, the third understanding of "permissible conception of the comprehensive good" cannot be distinguished from the second. If the moral validity of such conceptions cannot be determined, this is because they are morally neither valid nor invalid and, therefore, are merely morally permissible. But the second understanding, as the first, is self-refuting. Moreover, these three understandings exhaust the possibilities open to a universalist theory of justice as separate. Unless I have been mistaken at some point in this critical discussion, the principles of justice any such theory advocates cannot be redeemed in democratic discourse without validating a conception of the comprehensive good, and no such theory can represent the compound character of justice without ceasing to be separationist.

Justice as Separate: Nonuniversalist Theories

Given that universalist nonteleology is inconsistent with the conception of justice as compound, universal principles of justice cannot be separated from the good unless the constitution so stipulates, and the state is bound to teach this separation. But it also follows that this stipulation will not be sensible if it merely asserts the independence of justice from all conceptions of the comprehensive good. To limit the constitutional provision in this way implies that differing conceptions of the universal principles can engage in democratic discourse in order to determine which set of nonteleological principles is valid. Since no universalist theory of justice as separate could be redeemed in discourse without validating a conception of the comprehensive good, a discourse restricted to such theories is senseless. At least if justice is articulated in universal principles, the price of being nonteleological is that a given conception of justice as separate must be explicitly endorsed by the constitution, so that the state has the duty to teach a given theory of justice. In its fullest sense, a universalist nonteleology is a simple theory of justice.

In the end, however, even a willingness to pay that price will not purchase principles of justice separate from any conception of the comprehensive good. If a given theory is stipulated in the constitution, the state makes a claim to validity for that theory. But were a universalist nonteleology valid, its understanding of "permissible conception of the comprehensive good" would be valid, and every such understanding is or implies a conception of the comprehensive good. Thus, the state cannot teach a given conception of justice as separate without teaching that conception of the good. So far from legitimating a plurality of such conceptions or prescribing religious freedom, then, universalist theories of justice as separate endorse by implication an established religion. They contradict the *sine qua non* of democracy.[12]

To my knowledge, no separationist theory is as sensible of this problem as is the most recent work of John Rawls. On Rawls's own account, the movement of his thought from his monumental *A Theory of Justice* to *Political Liberalism* exhibits his self-critical conviction that a liberal conception of justice must not present itself as part of

---

[12]It might seem that the state could teach certain universal principles of justice, for instance, those derived from the PGC, without thereby explicitly stating the implied conception of the comprehensive good, for instance, one on which all conceptions of the good consistent with the principles of justice are equally good. But the point is that teaching these universal principles *as separate* from any religion *is* the teaching of their implied conception of the comprehensive good, because the putative meaning of "separate" must be taught. One might now propose that the principles should be taught without teaching them as separate from any religion. But the point of a nonteleological theory is to offer a conception of justice that is democratic and thus consistent with religious freedom. Hence, the state would be bound to teach the principles as separate from any conception of the comprehensive good.

and, therefore, dependent on "a comprehensive philosophical doctrine." His earlier work, he says, so presents its nonteleological theory and, to this extent, is "unrealistic." The problem is precisely that modern democracy "assumes . . . a plurality of . . . incompatible comprehensive doctrines" (1996: xviii), and a theory of justice cannot be dependent on one of them without contradicting that assumption. Rawls makes essentially the same point when he writes that the second book seeks "to fix a basic inherent conflict [in the first book] . . . between the cultural conditions needed for justice as fairness to be a comprehensive doctrine and the requirements of freedom guaranteed by the two principles of justice" (1996: 388, n. 21). All implications considered, it is the guarantee of religious freedom that conflicts with the theory as presented in the earlier volume.

Rawls concludes, if I understand correctly, that nonteleological theories fail when they seek to be universalist, because universal principles of the right cannot be separated from a conception of the comprehensive good. Indeed, I am emboldened to think that my critique of Habermas, Gewirth, and Barry has merit because Rawls, in his own way, arrives at the same conclusion. But Rawls also believes that a theory of justice, at least insofar as it formulates principles for the "basic structure" of society (1996: 11), must be separationist. Thus, his later work seeks so to revise the earlier as to articulate systematically the all-important "distinction between a political conception of justice and a comprehensive philosophical doctrine" (1996: xviii). The term "distinction" must here be read to mean "separation," as Rawls confirms when he says that a political conception "is neither presented as, nor as derived from, such a [comprehensive] doctrine applied to the basic structure of society, as if this structure were simply another object to which that doctrine applied" (1996: 12).

On this separation, a political conception is independent of all conceptions of the comprehensive good because the former includes no universal principle but, rather, only practical political rules for civilizing the "diversity of opposing and irreconcilable religious, philosophical, and moral doctrines" (1996: 3–4). "The central idea is that political liberalism moves within the category of the political and leaves philosophy as it is" (1996: 375); the conception of justice is "limited to . . . 'the domain of the political'" (1996: 38). Rawls also makes this point by saying that a political conception is "presented as a freestanding view" (1996: 12); that is, its principles "stand free" from any universal moral ground because they derive solely from historically specific values that are inherent in "the public political culture of a democratic society" (1996: 13). If we do not push the comparison too far, we might say that Rawls stands Habermas on his head: For Habermas, justice has a universal principle and the good is in all respects historically specific; for Rawls, justice is in all respects historically specific, and the good is comprehensive.

On Rawls's account, then, a plurality of comprehensive doctrines or conceptions of the comprehensive good is consistently legitimated, given only that each joins in an "overlapping consensus" on justice; each affirms the nonuniversal principles of justice for its distinctive reasons. This consensus is necessary to "public justification by political society" (1996: 387). The justification of a political conception in terms of the values specific to a democratic culture is "*pro tanto* justification," which "may be overridden by citizens' comprehensive doctrines once all values are tallied up" (1996: 386). Thus, "public justification happens when all the reasonable members of political society carry out a justification of the shared political conception by embedding it in their several reasonable comprehensive views" (1996: 387). Still, a political conception presents freestanding principles in the sense that it does not depend on any particular comprehensive doctrine. "Even though our comprehensive doctrines are irreconcilable and cannot be compromised, nevertheless citizens who affirm reasonable doctrines may share reasons of another kind, namely, public reasons given in terms of political conceptions of justice" (1997: 805). That it authorizes possible participation in such an overlapping consensus is, we can say, precisely what makes a comprehensive doctrine "reasonable." "Those holding a reasonable comprehensive doctrine must ask themselves on what political terms they are ready to live with other such doctrines in an ongoing free society. Since reasonable citizens hold reasonable doctrines, they are ready to offer or endorse a political conception of justice to specify the terms of fair political cooperation" (1996: 392).

Let us now address to this proposal the question previously put to others. In what respect, if any, should the principle or principles of justice as separate advocated by the theory and, in that sense, the theory itself be stipulated in the constitution of a democracy? Rawls might answer that a constitutional separation of justice from comprehensive doctrines is consistent with religious freedom because what is thereby stipulated is not a universalist theory of justice and, therefore, not a comprehensive doctrine. This constitutional provision, moreover, need not compromise a democratic discourse because the stipulation need not include any particular set of principles. Rawls makes clear that the principles of justice for which he is famous and that are summarized in the term "justice as fairness"—those of basic liberties, fair equality of opportunity, and the "difference principle" (see 1996: 291)—exemplify but do not define political liberalism. The latter, he says, is a "kind" of political theory (1996: 226), one necessary feature of which is his distinction or separation between "a political conception of justice and a comprehensive philosophical doctrine" (1996: xviii). Or, again: In a socially unified modern democracy, "the basic structure of society is effectively regulated by one of a family of reasonable liberal conceptions of justice (or a mix thereof), which family includes the most reasonable conception" (1996: xlix). Correspondingly, Rawls affirms an idea of "public reason" (1996: l), which includes the possibility of argument among political liberals about which one of the family is most reasonable. Thus, the constitution might explicitly endorse only public reason in this sense and, thereby, constitute a discourse about the particular principles that most adequately express the political culture specific to a democratic society.

Still, a constitutional stipulation that these principles should be, in Rawls's sense, politically liberal explicitly asserts that justice is freestanding. A democratic state, then, has the duty to teach that principles for the basic structure of society are independent of any universal moral or political ground, because they are justified *pro tanto* by historically specific values and publicly justified by an overlapping consensus. But this is the teaching that no universalist conception of justice is necessary in order to validate the principles of justice that should regulate the basic structure, and, in that teaching, the state takes sides in the disagreement between Rawls and all universalist theories of justice—not only all avowedly teleological theories but also those of Habermas, Gewirth, and Barry. Notwithstanding his turn to a nonuniversalist conception of justice, Rawls cannot maintain an explicit constitutional endorsement of political liberalism, in his sense, without denying legitimacy to all universalist theories of justice. In sum, a substantive prescription has been placed in the constitution. All citizens as political participants should explicitly accept that justice is freestanding and deliberate accordingly. Dissent from this prescription violates the ethics of citizenship.

To this criticism, Rawls might respond as follows: An explicit constitutional endorsement of political liberalism in fact legitimates every reasonable comprehensive doctrine precisely because each is invited to see whether it can participate in an overlapping consensus. But precisely the statement that public justification consists in an overlapping consensus is at odds with universalist theories of justice, each of which asserts that it alone can redeem political prescriptions. Thus, when Rawls seeks to advance "the wide view of public political culture," in accord with which "reasonable comprehensive doctrines, religious or nonreligious, may be introduced into public political discussion at any time," he must add what he calls "the proviso," namely, "that in due course proper political reasons—and not reasons given solely by comprehensive doctrines—are presented that are sufficient to support whatever the comprehensive doctrines introduced are said to support" (1997: 783–84). But adherents of a universalist theory of justice cannot consistently agree that reasons sufficient to support political prescriptions can be presented independently of the universal principles in question, that is, cannot accept "the proviso," and this is another way of saying that no such theory could mean by "public justification" an overlapping consensus. In this respect, then, an explicit constitutional endorsement of political liberalism, in Rawls's sense, prescribes a discourse exclusive of universalist theories.

If Rawls intends that the constitution should stipulate the freestanding character of justice, one may suspect that he is led to his position for the same reason that Barry advocates scepticism with respect to conceptions of the comprehensive good. Each believes that separating justice from the good is the only alternative to imposing a particular religion or comprehensive doctrine. On that reading, Rawls, too, neglects the conception of justice as compound. If the freedoms constitutive of democracy, including religious freedom, entail political liberalism, then any citizen who rejects political liberalism is committed to the constitutional imposition of her or his comprehensive doctrine. Given the compound character of justice, however, opposition to freestanding principles does not imply religious establishment but, rather, that some universal principle or principles can be redeemed in the democratic discourse. The rejection of freestanding principles, in other words, is thoroughly consistent with a commitment to public reason, that is, to argument about all contested political assertions, including theories of justice.

But it may be wrong to suppose that Rawls neglects the conception of justice as compound. Perhaps he would resist the constitutional stipulation of political liberalism and thus the teaching by the state that principles for the basic structure do not depend on any universal principle. It then follows that any given proposal of freestanding principles would become one of the conceptions subject to assessment within the full and free political discourse. The adherent of a conception limited to "the domain of the political" commends it to democratic citizens by seeking to redeem its superiority relative not only to others in the "family" of political conceptions but also to all universalist theories of justice.

Rawls gives some reason to think that this is his intent. In a notable exchange of views with Habermas, Rawls begins by insisting that the two differ fundamentally because "Habermas's position . . . is comprehensive while mine is an account of the political and is limited to that" (1996: 373). "From what point of view," Rawls asks himself, "are the two . . . to be discussed? And from what point of view does the debate between them take place?" That he might be read to affirm the compound character of justice becomes apparent in his reply: "To all these questions the answer is the same: all discussions are from the point of view of citizens in the culture of civil society" (1996: 382). This answer draws on a distinction Rawls offers between "the public political forum" (1997: 767), through the discussion and debate of which public officials are selected and in which they carry on their official functions, and "civil society," which consists of discussion and debate within diverse other associations. Participation in the former is bound by "the proviso" of public reason, while participation in the latter is not so limited. In civil society, "comprehensive doctrines of all kinds . . . are taught, explained, debated one against the other, and argued about," and in its "endless political discussions of ideas and doctrines" (1996: 383), the relative merits of political liberalism and Habermas's ideal of discourse can be debated.

Assuming that, in this way, Rawls rejects a constitutional stipulation that justice is freestanding, we may now ask how, within civil society, political liberalism is redeemed as superior to universalist theories of justice, such as that of Habermas. "The argument [within civil society]," Rawls continues, "is normative and concerned with ideals and values, though in political liberalism it is limited to the political, while in . . . [Habermas's view] it is not" (1996: 384). The concluding phrases of this sentence are perplexing. On the account Rawls has given, the limits to argument set by "the political" characterize the public political forum, in distinction from civil society. Now to impose those limits on argument within the latter seems to preclude a debate *between* political liberalism and Habermas's universalist theory, that is, to beg the question.

The same perplexity reappears when Rawls says that "the overall criterion of the reasonable is general and wide reflective equilibrium; whereas we have seen that in Habermas's view the test of moral truth or validity is fully rational acceptance in the ideal discourse situation" (1996: 384–85). On Rawls's meaning, "reflective equilibrium" is itself a concept within "the domain of the political." Related to the notion of "public justification," such equilibrium is achieved when citizens affirm a "political conception on the basis of their several reasonable comprehensive doctrines," giving "weight to the considered convictions of other reasonable citizens," and "general and wide reflective equilibrium with respect to a public justification gives the best justification of the political conception that we can have at any given time" (1996: 388). In stipulating this criterion for the argument within civil society, Rawls assumes that the argument is about political conceptions of justice, in his sense, and thereby again begs the question against Habermas. Showing the superiority of political liberalism to Habermas's universalist theory requires an argument *for* the criterion of reflective equilibrium, since the choice between it and "fully rational acceptance in the ideal discourse situation" is already a choice between two views of democracy.

In sum, Rawls does not tell us how political liberalism can be redeemed within the democratic debate prescribed by the compound character of justice. So far as I can see, moreover, he cannot do so without denying the validity of every universalist theory of justice. To redeem political liberalism is to show that every universalist theory of justice is invalid, because a universalist theory asserts what political liberalism denies—namely, that justice depends on a universal principle. But if Rawls denies all universalist conceptions, the argument for political liberalism moves beyond "the domain of the political," because the denial cannot itself be redeemed by appeal to the specific political culture of a democratic society. The statement that no universalist conception of justice is valid is itself a statement about what is universally the case, since a universalist conception that is invalid anywhere is invalid everywhere. Hence, those who adhere to free-standing principles of justice could not redeem their theory in a democratic discourse without introducing a statement about principles of justice that purports to be universally true and, thereby, transforming their theory into a universalist one.

In defense of Rawls, some may say that a denial of all universalist conceptions of justice can be solely a negative assertion and, therefore, does not commit its adherent to a universalist theory. But merely to deny all universalist conceptions is insofar to say that principles of justice are neither valid nor invalid. If one also asserts a nonuniversalist conception of justice, then one implies that *all* valid principles of justice are in all respects historically specific—and, in that implication, one has affirmed both a positive and a universal principle of justice. Just as Habermas cannot assert as universally true that the validity of existential self-understandings is thoroughly contextual without implying a universal principle of their validity and thus of the good, so one cannot assert as universally true that the validity of principles of justice is thoroughly contextual without implying a universal principle of their validity and, thereby, of justice. Rawls, I believe, accepts this conclusion. A political liberal, he says, tries "neither to assert nor to deny any particular comprehensive religious, philosophical, or moral view, or its associated theory of truth and the status of values" (1996: 150). In other words, Rawls seeks simply to avoid the denial of all universal principles precisely because he agrees that this denial makes his own theory a universalist one. If political liberalism is, as Rawls also formulates the point, "political and not metaphysical" (1996: 10), this is because, as he concedes, "to deny certain metaphysical doctrines is to assert another such doctrine" (1996: 379, n. 8). Still, this attempt to avoid "metaphysics" is futile, because the denial of all universalist conceptions of justice is implied by the assertion of a nonuniversalist one.

Some neopragmatic proposals will insist that this criticism is illicit. On their account, a nonuniversalist theory of justice implies only that no universalist conception can be redeemed. I have in mind here Richard Rorty's assertion that the theories of "Philosophers" are not denied if one merely refuses them or merely chooses to "change the subject" (Rorty 1982: xiv, xv). Perhaps this is also Rawls's intent in saying that a political liberal tries "neither to assert nor to deny any particular comprehensive . . . view" (1996: 150). But the statement that no universalist conception can be redeemed does not itself imply that a nonuniversalist theory of justice is valid. So far as the negative statement goes, there may be no valid principles of justice and, therefore, no possibility of democratic discourse. As participants in that discourse, advocates of a nonuniversalist conception claim validity for it; thereby, they imply that universalist theories cannot be validated because all such theories are invalid. With that implication, the nonuniversalist theory ceases to be nonuniversalist, and that is why no such theory can be redeemed in full and free discourse.

To be sure, Rawls offers a defense of political liberalism. He argues that it alone provides a reasonable conception of democracy, that is, a conception of justice that legitimates a "diversity of opposing and irreconcilable religious, political, and moral doctrines" (1996: 3–4). But this argument cannot redeem political liberalism in discourse among both universalist and nonuniversalist theories of justice and, therefore, cannot make Rawls's theory consistent with the conception of justice as compound because the democratic discourse itself legitimates the diversity of doctrines. Given that they are all legitimate participants in the discourse, we still require some reason to believe that political liberalism is valid. To the contrary, then, Rawls finds his own case convincing because he excludes universalist theories from the search for what is "reasonable." To the best of my reading, moreover, he makes this move because he assumes at the outset that universalist or comprehensive theories of justice are not themselves subject to argumentative assessment—or, in Barry's terms, "are not susceptible to rational proof or disproof" (Barry 1995: 30).

That view is expressed in Rawls's statement that "reflective equilibrium" is "the overall criterion," and the assumption becomes the more apparent when Rawls formulates the question to which *Political Liberalism* is the answer as follows: "How is it possible for those affirming a comprehensive doctrine, religious or nonreligious, and in particular doctrines based on religious authority, such as the Church or Bible, also to hold a reasonable political conception of justice that supports a constitutional democratic society?" (1997: 807). In stipulating that a conception of justice must not contradict a religious appeal to authority or, as he also says, "can be sincerely defended before others without criticizing or rejecting their deepest religious and philosophical commitments" (1996: 390), Rawls is bound to assume that no universalist conception of justice can be redeemed by argument. It then follows that political liberalism itself cannot be convincing in a full and free discourse, because the assumption cannot be redeemed without transforming the theory into a universalist one. This implication confirms the conclusion reached at the close of the preceding chapter: Democratic discourse presupposes a substantive principle that is universal because the former is prescribed as a meta-ethical presupposition of moral claims and makes no sense in the absence of a moral principle in relation to which the validity or invalidity of moral claims is determined.

But if freestanding principles of justice are not consistent with the compound character of justice, then, against Rawls's appeal to civil society, political liberalism must be stipulated in the constitution. As noted, this constitutional provision might be taken to legitimate a discourse among advocates of differing freestanding principles. The argument would seek to determine which politically liberal theory is most reasonable because it best represents the historically specific values inherent in the public political culture of a democratic society, where "best" includes the capacity to command an overlapping consensus. Clearly a debate about principles within a common commitment to certain historically specific values is a sensible one. For instance, male supremacists might sensibly argue about the best principles for organizing a patriarchal society. In truth, however, a stipulation that principles of justice should be freestanding is itself inconsistent with the public political culture of a democratic society.

The fundamental mark of democratic politics, on Rawls's own account, is the principle of religious freedom or the legitimation of diverse comprehensive doctrines, and a theory of justice cannot be reasonable in terms of democratic political culture unless it is consistent with this principle. But stipulating that the argument appeals only to historically specific values and an overlapping consensus denies all comprehensive doctrines that include a universalist conception of justice, thereby violating the principle. In a discourse constituted by this stipulation, advocates of a given liberal theory could not argue that it is most reasonable in terms of democratic culture. To insist that the democratic principle of religious freedom legitimates only "reasonable comprehensive doctrines," in Rawls's sense, is to argue in a vicious circle. Thus, the price of being politically liberal, in Rawls's sense, is the explicit constitutional affirmation of some particular freestanding principles of justice, for instance, those Rawls calls justice as fairness. Thereby, the state has the duty to teach them as the proper grounds for all political decisions about the basic structure. Any such politically liberal theory is, in the fullest sense, a simple theory of justice.

In the end, however, even a willingness to pay that price will not purchase principles of justice separate from any conception of the comprehensive good. If the constitution stipulates certain principles as freestanding, the state makes a claim to validity for them. As we have seen, the assertion of such principles denies the validity of all universalist conceptions of justice and, with that denial, the theory asserted becomes universalist. But the previous section concluded that all universalist theories of justice include a conception of the comprehensive good and, therefore, are not consistently nonteleological. The fundamental contradiction inherent in all avowedly universalist theories of justice as separate cannot be solved by the turn to a nonuniversalist one. In either case, the separation of justice from the good implies, against itself, that some conception of the comprehensive good should be constitutionally established.

In sum, all such theories contradict the principle of religious freedom that they intend to protect as a *sine qua non* of democratic politics. So far from separating justice from the good, democracy makes sense only if justice is dependent on the comprehensive good. It then follows that religious freedom prescribes nothing other than a full and free discourse among conceptions of this good, and the purpose of democratic politics is to determine the activities of the state in accord with principles derived from the comprehensive purpose. Religious freedom constitutes the political association by the question to which every religion or conception of the comprehensive good purports to be the valid answer. In nonteleological theories, we can say, the conception of justice as separate from the good seeks to do the work that only the conception of justice as compound can do. Such theories seek to substitute that separation for the distinction between formative and substantive principles of justice. As a consequence, the distinction is collapsed, and a conception of the comprehensive good is constitutionally established. Contrary to a widespread consensus in recent liberal theory, democracy implies a comprehensive purpose because it implies the compound character of justice.

Some may now object that the conception of justice as compound also contradicts a full and free democratic discourse because it implies the explicit constitutional denial of separationist theories of justice and, thereby, fails to legitimate them. But I have argued that the term "separationist theory of justice" is self-refuting because every such theory implies a conception of the comprehensive good. Thus, to proscribe to the state the explicit affirmation or denial of any theory of justice and to disestablish all teleological theories are two ways of stipulating the same thing, and "nonteleological theory" is equivalent to "nontheoretical theory." To constitute a political community by the formative principle of religious freedom requires, in other words, some consistent meaning of "religious" in order to distinguish the class of understandings or convictions, no one of which the state is permitted explicitly to affirm or deny. On the only consistent meaning that is relevant to a democratic constitution, the term designates conceptions of the comprehensive good or comprehensive teleologies.

Moral assertions can be nonteleological, then, only in the sense that they purport to articulate the principles or norms of some social practice that applies indirectly the comprehensive purpose. The formative principles of justice properly specified in a democratic constitution are, *in this sense*, nonteleological, and, in this sense, the state has the right and the duty to teach nonteleological principles of justice. But this is not the teaching that justice is independent of religious conceptions; to the contrary, these nonteleological principles mean that activities of the state are properly determined through discourse about the good that is not only free but also full. Beyond inculcating this constitution, the teaching of the state may not include principles of justice but only those more specific norms of social practices that the democratic process legislates. In so deciding, the democratic process implies that those social practices are, at least for the political community in question, also indirect applications of the comprehensive purpose, but the state is never allowed to teach what conception of the comprehensive purpose is or is not implied by statutory law or by the social practice of democracy itself. Hence, the state may not teach that any theory of justice whose substantive principle or set of principles purports to be independent of the good is invalid. Since all such theories include some comprehensive conception of the comprehensive good, they are, like all such conceptions, protected by the constitutional guarantee of religious freedom.

Justice as General Emancipation

The previous two chapters have argued for a democratic community constituted as a discourse about the comprehensive purpose. On this argument, the principle of communicative respect is a meta-ethical presupposition of every claim to moral validity, and this principle includes the right of all individuals to participate in the widest possible discourse in or through which common decisions are taken. Democratic discourse, therefore, implies principles of two distinct kinds—formative principles specified in its constitution and substantive principles that are the object of discussion and debate and ought to control political decisions. The character of justice is compound; a substantive principle or set of principles consistently implies as an aspect of itself the formative principles constitutive of democracy. In turn, the compound character of justice implies a comprehensive purpose, of which justice is an indirect application or from which its principles are derived. Theories that seek to separate justice from the good nonetheless depend on a conception of the comprehensive good. Hence, the price of being separationist is a simple theory of justice that implies the constitutional stipulation of some substantive principle or set of principles and, thereby, an establishment of religion. Religious freedom is, all implications considered, the democratic principle that constitutes the political association as a discourse among conceptions of the comprehensive purpose in their pertinence to activities of the state.

Returning now to the substantive moral conclusions of Part One, this chapter seeks to articulate the substantive principle or set of

281

principles of justice implied by pursuit of the maximal divine good. I will argue that this pursuit is specified to politics in the principle or principles of what I will call "justice as general emancipation." If the previous argument in Part Two has been successful, it convicts not only all separationist theories of justice but also all teleological theories that are not consistently democratic. A conception of the comprehensive purpose is false if it does not consistently imply the conception of justice as compound. Hence, I will also seek to show that justice as general emancipation is consistently compound in character. Because this theory of justice is teleological, direct discussion of the principles it defends requires prior attention to the maximal divine good as a telos of human community. The initial section of this chapter will reformulate the divine purpose in terms of the good to be created by or realized in our common life, and I will call the latter "our maximal common humanity." Subsequent sections will articulate justice as general emancipation in a principle or set of principles derived from maximizing our common humanity.

Our Maximal Common Humanity

On the metaphysics of activities summarized in Part One, the character of good as such is the unity-in-diversity or creativity that is realized in greater or lesser measure by all final real things or actualities, of which all other realities are composites. In all of their decisions, therefore, humans ought to pursue maximal creativity in the future as such. This pursuit has as its telos the maximal divine good because the future as such *is* the future of the comprehensive or metaphysical individual, in whose own realizations of unity-in-diversity all other achievements are again and again unified. The creativity of an activity is its self-determined unification of its relations to past actualities. Thus, its possible measure of unity-in-diversity depends on its particular past, that is, on the measure of aesthetic achievement in and the aesthetic order among the past realizations to which the present one relates. Activities can complete only what the past begins in them, and opportunity for good varies depending on the order of creativity from which the present activity arises. Moreover, greater opportunity to be creative is greater freedom. To begin from a more favorable order is to have increased possibilities to be distinctive.

In comparison with nonhuman worldly existence, human activities enjoy a measure of freedom or opportunity for good that is vastly extended. This is because the order of creativity in the human body makes self-understanding and complex participation in language possible. The difference is finally a difference of degree, but the degree of difference is so dramatic that Whitehead can say "the Rubicon has been crossed" (1938: 38). A new world of immense opportunity appears because in this world the world as such is understood. As a consequence, realization of the good also loses its innocence. Freedom with understanding does not decide *how* pursuit of the maximal good occurs without also deciding *whether* it occurs. In contrast to nonhuman existence, human activities may fail to achieve the full creativity opened by the past because our self-determination is or includes a decision for a self-understanding and, therefore, about the comprehensive purpose itself; humans create "knowing good and evil." Hence, we must distinguish between the human freedom that varies in measure depending on the past and the moral freedom that is never a matter of degree because its exercise decides between authentic and duplicitous self-understandings. I have called the former emancipation and the latter original freedom.

Because human understanding immensely enhances the diversity that may be unified, future human creativity and thus the emancipation of humans occupy a preeminent place in our normative pursuit of the good. Accordingly, there is a summary sense in which the order of the natural world is best when it maximizes the possibilities of the human future as such. Greater present possibilities everywhere depend on greater aesthetic order in the past. Given the dramatic extension of opportunity that emerges with distinctively human existence, the aesthetic character of all achievement means that the creativity realized in the nonhuman order of the world is maximized when it maximizes the possibilities of self-understanding individuals—and, by implication, in the long run. This is emphatically not to say that worth is identical with human achievement, much less with the satisfaction of human wants and preferences. That understanding would fallaciously define good in terms of some specifically human characteristic and, thereby, reduce nonhuman existence to merely instrumental value. To the contrary, creativity or unity-in-diversity is intrinsically good wherever it is realized because every realization makes a difference to the divine individual. Hence, the summary statement relating the natural world to future human good asserts only a coincidence between maximizing the latter and maximizing creativity in the future as such. If we can assume that coincidence, the comprehensive purpose as a principle for our decisions might be reformulated: maximize creativity in the human future as such.

Granting the assumption, some may still doubt that this reformulation adequately includes our responsibilities to our natural habitat, especially responsibilities to the diversity of species in the nonhuman world and to individual animals, at least within those species whose members exhibit consciousness and the capacity to suffer. In these respects, intrinsic good within nature may seem to require protection beyond its contribution to human possibilities, and the comprehensive purpose as restated may seem to permit treatment of our natural habitat in ways that violate the maximal divine good. The issues implicit in these considerations require a longer discussion than focus here on the question of justice allows. Still, we can protect the theocentric character of justice by prescribing that pursuit of the maximal human good is always constrained by the following principle of environmental respect: Human purposes that reduce natural creativity relative to the measure that would be realized if the humans in question did not act at all are a violation of the maximal divine good unless such treatment is required in order to maximize human creativity in the long run.

In terms of this principle, I expect, one might speak of the prima facie "rights" of nonhuman animals, at least of those that are conscious, and, in a more extended sense of the term, the prima facie "right" of the natural order to its own diversity. All implications considered, I also expect that pursuit of the maximal human future itself includes this principle. Precisely because the nonhuman world and its individuals are intrinsically valuable, the good we realize is greater, other things being equal, when our relations to the natural habitat appreciate the nonhuman world for its own sake. Respect for that world of the kind prescribed by the principle is itself an enhancement of human creativity. But whether it is an implication of maximizing the human future or a prior constraint, the principle of environmental respect will be assumed in what follows. With it so included, I will also assume the coincidence of maximizing human good and maximizing the future as such.

The distinctive possibilities of human life that ground this coincidence further imply that greater or lesser emancipation depends especially on the order of creativity in the human past. The higher possibilities of human achievement are a gift from past human achievements, favorably ordered, where the human past includes both the previous activities of the individual in question and the communities of human individuals to whom she or he relates. This is not to deny that good fortune in natural and genetic endowment can make a difference. However significant natural gifts may be, development of them typically requires individual effort and the favorable support of human communities. The potential naturally given to Aristotle may have been extraordinary, but its perfection waited on his own dedication and on Plato and the Academy.

In principle, there is no distinction between one's own past activities and those of other individuals in one's communities; together they constitute the human past that is especially important to present opportunity. As discussed earlier, however, it seems clear that distinctively human creativity develops beyond rudimentary forms because a human individual relates to her or his own past with a measure of completeness or concrete appreciation far exceeding her or his appreciation of any other individual. For this reason, an individual's own past is, perhaps excepting younger children, more important to her or his present emancipation than the life of any other single person. The extent to which this is so may well vary with culture and from individual to individual within any given culture. But the bold comparison seems given with the dependence of distinctively human activity on a particular human body and, specifically, on the brain. This special intimacy with one's own past relates the development of proper dispositions and persistent, detailed purposes to the good an individual might achieve and relates virtue and happiness in an individual life. Indeed, the emancipation of human activities is, to all appearances, so dependent on the accumulation of achievement in a person's life that we may, at least in a discussion of justice, abstract from the difference between activities and individuals. In prescribing pursuit of the maximal human good, we may speak, as I will henceforth, of emancipating human individuals.

Given this abstraction, the special importance of the human past directs our attention to the distinctive character of human communities, with the essential qualification that emancipation also depends on whether the individual in question makes the most of the opportunities her or his communities present. These opportunities are created through human communication, that is, through the action or interaction by means of which understandings or conscious experiences of other individuals become a part of the diversity to which a given person relates. Just insofar as human communities are especially important to it, then, emancipation depends on the communicated order of human achievements of which an individual is the beneficiary. I will speak summarily of this distinctively human order as "our common humanity." This term can have many meanings and is often used to designate descriptively the characteristics, or normatively the rights, that are universally human. In contrast, I mean the content of human communication, so that common humanity is created whenever two or more human individuals share conscious experience by way of relationships between or among them. Insofar as human communities emancipate, an individual's creative opportunities depend on her or his participation in our common humanity.

To be sure, an individual's relations to the nonhuman world, natural and artificial, are also important. Because human activity is dependent on the human body, we are biological creatures with corresponding biological and material needs. At least as a general rule, our opportunities are severely compromised when provision for those needs is inadequate. As already noted, moreover, the nonhuman world enhances human opportunities beyond our dependence on it for survival, health, and technical resources. Because natural creativity is itself the realization of unity-in-diversity and, therefore, of intrinsic worth, our relations to other creatures and to the beauty and integrity of the nonhuman order more generally add diversity to be consciously appreciated. Further, the nonhuman world can, as it were, be taken into our common humanity, and its importance to human creativity is thereby enhanced. We can, in other words, communicate about the nonhuman world, so that its intrinsic worth becomes a part of the distinctively human order.

We are now in a position to reformulate once more the comprehensive purpose as a principle for our decisions, specifically in relation to the human order. To maximize the divine good and, therefore, creativity in the future as such is to pursue *our maximal common human-*

ity—and, by implication, in the long run. This reformulation takes into account the dependence of human good on the nonhuman world. The fulfillment of biological and material needs is a precondition of contributions to our maximal common humanity, and our appreciation of the nonhuman world, natural and artificial, is itself something that can be communicated. Moreover, the importance of order within an individual's life is also included, since the accumulation of achievement within that life increases its potential for significance to our common humanity. Although maximizing the distinctively human order may seem to imply that every human individual should seek to maximize the measure in which her or his achievements are communicated to others, that conclusion does not follow. Contributions to the content of human communication in the long run are also made by providing and caring for the nonhuman conditions in which the content can be increased. Moreover, there are some human experiences or aspects of them that should, for one or more of many reasons, remain within the privacy of an individual's life—for instance, because the individual is preparing for a later and more significant communication or because public expression would prevent others from communicating more significant content or would introduce conflict that makes no creative contribution. Our maximal common humanity is, in sum, a telos, and pursuit of it by any given human activity may take many forms other than immediate human communication.

So understood, the order created by human communication is meant to be a source of its own enhancement. Its emancipation of individuals should be the occasion for activities that pursue our maximal common humanity, so that subsequent human activities can be the more emancipated. We may call this the self-surpassing character of our common humanity. Reinhold Niebuhr summarized the point especially well: "The individual is related to the community . . . in such a way that the highest reaches of his individuality are dependent upon the social substance out of which they arise and they must find their end and fulfillment in the community" (1960: 48). As this citation suggests, the point here is a moral one. The emancipation an individual enjoys may not be directed to its proper telos. We may be duplicitous or immoral and, thereby, compromise the achievement we might have contributed or debase the human order of which we were the beneficiaries. Thus, the self-surpassing character of our common humanity is a teleological or normative rather than a descriptive feature; it identifies what is meant to be the case.

This normative feature implies another. Our common humanity will be the more self-surpassing insofar as the emancipation it creates is enjoyed by a larger number of individuals, because the possibility of diverse or distinctive achievements that contribute to the human order is thereby increased. Teleologically speaking, then, we may also say that our common humanity is self-widening. It is the greater insofar as it makes possible and benefits from the greater emancipation of a wider community of individuals. This feature expresses in terms of our common humanity the universal character of the telos by which human purpose is properly directed. We should aim at maximal good in the future as such; hence, the emancipation to be pursued is that of human individuals universally.

Still, this self-widening character is potentially in conflict with the greater emancipation of any given individual. Maximizing the opportunities for some and maximizing the number for whom opportunities are created involve two different variables. For most of us most of the time, the fragmentariness of human experience localizes possible effects that are more than trivial. In many situations, an individual can contribute significantly to the emancipation of others only if she or he limits the number of others. As a general rule, notable exceptions to this constraint occur only for the leaders of larger communities (Lincoln at Gettysburg, to choose a dramatic example) or through systems of interaction (for instance, the economic order) that can greatly extend the effects of certain pivotal decisions. Typically, however, our greatest associational effect is on those with whom we have some more immediate or local relationship or set of relationships—friends, families, work crew, neighborhood, or voluntary association. Were each individual always to choose in terms of her or his maximal contribution to the widest number of others, the emancipation of each and thus our common humanity would be greatly impoverished, because the actor's distinctiveness would be sacrificed to the width of effect.

The human order that emancipates any given individual, to reformulate the point, is not exhausted by conditions she or he shares with all others in a wide human community. Rather, our common humanity is a complex order that includes those wider conditions and is enhanced by the distinctive creativity of local associations, including especially the most intimate and enduring relationships. The social and political order, institutions of work and culture, voluntary associations, neighborhoods, families and other personal relationships are integrated in presenting to each of us our own particular range of possibilities. Summarily stated, the human order is greater when it includes the wider realization of more distinctive local and immediate associations, and therefore our maximal common humanity is not only self-widening but also self-localizing. I will call these two features together the complex character of our common humanity. But, then, pursuit of our maximal common humanity may have to choose between wider and more local contributions.

There is no universal principle of the good in terms of which these alternatives can be evaluated except pursuit of our maximal common humanity itself. The conditions common to wider communities set the larger context for the creative possibilities of more local associations, and whether an individual's action or larger project ought to be directed to wider or more local conditions of emancipation depends on her or his situation. Moreover, the choice may not be a moral one, in the sense that one alternative is better. Some classic dilemmas involve situations in which important contributions to both wider communities and more immediate relationships cannot both be achieved. Jean-Paul Sartre, for instance, posed the dilemma of a young man during World War II who faced the choice between joining the Free French Forces and staying at home to care for his dependent mother (see 1957: 24–25). In less trying circumstances, perhaps, many others have been called to choose between political activism in pursuit of what they take to be justice and attention to other careers or to the needs and possibilities of family and friendship. Our maximal common humanity does not eliminate such dilemmas precisely because it is both self-widening and self-localizing. But these situations, given that neither alternative is finally prescribed by that telos, do not imply that the comprehensive good is in conflict with itself. On the contrary, the proper conclusion is that the alternatives involved are equally good.

Nonetheless, the self-localizing character of our maximal common humanity may seem to imply that the human order as such does not exist. Distinctive human experiences or achievements are communicated between or among us in a vast multiplicity of relationships and associations that are themselves related to each other as inclusive or exclusive in an equally vast multiplicity of ways. Thus, "our common humanity" may seem to be a collective noun that designates a mere multiplicity of human orders, making senseless the notion of maximizing the whole. But this appearance repeats in terms of our common humanity the apparent impossibility, previously discussed, of maximizing creativity in the future as such, given that this future will be a multiplicity of creative activities (see chapter 3). In either case, the telos seems senseless only because one ignores the unification of all things that occurs in the divine relativity. What is, if understood solely in terms of human existence, a mere multiplicity of human orders becomes our common humanity as a whole within the divine good. The theistic character of this teleology is the necessary and sufficient condition of its conceptual coherence.

It remains, however, that maximizing the human order is an exceedingly abstract moral principle and, at least to first appearances, is exceedingly vague with respect to counsels for practice. Indeed, one might wonder whether anything is gained by restating the comprehensive purpose in terms of our common humanity. The task now is to show that the abstract character of this discussion does not make it irrelevant with respect to questions of justice.

The Principle of Justice

The political association, we have said, determines the governance of all associations in the society, and justice in its relevant sense is defined by the principle or set of principles in accord with which norms for the society as a whole are properly legislated. The principle or principles of justice are specified in the general norms constituting the widest set or general setting of morally valid social practices. To be sure, this setting includes some social practices that are nonlegal, and we may speak of a general moral discourse whose decisions may or may not be legislated (see chapter 4). But justice provides the normative ground for both kinds of the widest practices. Whether or not to legislate a general moral norm itself requires a principle, and this decision would be subject to conflicting principles were the principle or principles of justice not the normative ground for the widest set of social practices as such. For instance, it may be wrong to enforce legally all promises that should be kept, notwithstanding that promising more inclusively is properly society-wide. Since this decision requires a coherent principle for differentiating aspects of the general setting, the proper conclusion is that legal enforcement of all morally prescribed promise keeping is unjust. What follows, however, will focus on the activities of the state and thus on justice in its legal respect, thereby taking for granted that some aspects of the general setting should not be legislated.

As we have seen, a comprehensive purpose may prescribe its own indirect application in or through social practices, whose constitutive norms or rules are morally binding whatever the consequences. Indirect applications are prescribed insofar as the social coordination and cooperation such practices make possible is required in order to maximize the good. It is evident that maximizing our common humanity prescribes a wide range of social practices. The human order would be quickly reduced to triviality in the absence of constitutive rules that steady and enhance the content of human communication. All associations that are not merely transitory and all institutions, without which the content of human communication would be at best chaotic, are or involve social practices.

Previous discussion also derived the formative principle of communicative respect as constituting a universal social practice. Every claim for a social prescription implies that each individual to whom the prescription applies can accept it because it is valid and, therefore, implies her or his right to be treated as a potential participant in moral discourse. We can now show that the self-widening character of our common humanity grounds this principle teleologically; that is, this universal practice is consistently prescribed by pursuit of our maximal common humanity as an indirect application of itself. Greater emancipation means a greater range of possible purposes. Whatever other possibilities are given to an individual by morally valid social action of which she or he is a recipient, the possibility of accepting those effects because they are morally valid increases, or the absence of this freedom lessens, emancipation. Whatever social action is morally prescribed, in other words, an individual's range of purposes is greater if she of he can also choose whether to dissent from her or his social context. Being a recipient of communicative respect is, we may say, a formative condition of emancipation. Since our common humanity is self-widening, this formative condition is prescribed universally.[1]

But if our maximal common humanity grounds the principle of communicative respect teleologically, it also grounds a democratic political association, since the latter is included in the former. The right to participate in a moral discourse through which general norms are legislated is also a formative condition of emancipation. Moreover, the legal order effected through a democratic discourse is itself a part of our common humanity, in the sense that it exists and structures social action only as a complex order of human understandings that is communicated. Thus, we can say that justice is the creation of our common humanity in the respect that it ought to include legislated social practices. Legislated norms are required insofar as maximizing our common humanity depends on providing and promoting through the general practices they constitute the widest possible conditions of emancipation. The legal prescriptions and proscriptions governing a political community concern circumstances and resources that at least could be important to the creative opportunities of all individuals in the society. These conditions are the subject matter of justice, and I will call them "general conditions of emancipation."

---

[1]Because communicative rights override any other social prescription, some may object that the self-widening character of our common humanity is not sufficient to ground this formative principle. Given that the telos is also self-localizing, there could be situations in which our common humanity would be maximized by effecting the emancipation of a more narrow community through violating the communicative rights of some outside it. Hence, the formative principle has not been teleologically grounded unless adherence to it not only emancipates its recipients but also *maximizes* our common humanity. This objection has missed the point if it implies that a comprehensive purpose must always be directly applied to human activity or that each case must be "separately taken." On that implication, any comprehensive telos to which social coordination and cooperation are important is arbitrarily denied. To the contrary, pursuit of our maximal common humanity grounds social practices, and the norms of a morally valid universal practice override, by definition, any local considerations. Alternatively, then, perhaps the objection denies that maximizing our common humanity grounds any universal constitutive principle. But the moral validity of communicative rights is precisely what is validated in saying that the emancipation effected by social action is always greater if the recipient is free to accept it as morally valid. To deny the constitutive principle of communicative respect would be, in other words, to deny that the comprehensive purpose prescribes maximizing emancipation universally.

I have in mind circumstances and resources that are potentially important to an individual by virtue of her or his membership in the human community or the political community in question. So understood, general conditions of emancipation are distinguished from local ones, which are potentially important to an individual by virtue of (1) her or his membership in some more particular association or community, or (2) her or his morally permissible choices. These two alternative characteristics that define local conditions of emancipation may both be present, in the sense that a person's participation in some more particular association or community may itself be a consequence of her or his morally permissible choices. Still, there are other particular human bonds we do not choose, such as communal memberships defined in relation to race or ethnicity or cultural tradition, and there are some morally permissible choices that may not usefully be called decisions to participate in an association, for instance, certain more or less solitary leisure time activities.

If a given individual, for whatever reasons, lives in a certain town or neighborhood and, as a consequence, receives health care from a particular clinic, access to the clinic in question is a local condition of her or his emancipation. In contrast, health care from some or other competent person or group or persons could be important to all individuals in the society and, therefore, is a general condition of emancipation. If an individual works for a particular business firm, a share in the income of that organization and, arguably, some form of participation in its organizational decisions are local conditions of her or his emancipation. On the other hand, access to income and decision-making participation in the relevant association could be generally important. Participation in the patterns of life distinctive to a given racial or ethnic group may be locally important to many of its members, while an opportunity to cultivate one's own cultural identity, whatever that is, is potentially important to any human individual. Local conditions of emancipation that depend on morally permissible choices are related in part to vocational and avocational decisions. The conditions important to artists are different from those important to scientists or construction workers, and all three are different from those important to sports enthusiasts or lovers of music. But there are conditions that could be important to any such choice—for instance, income with which to acquire resources peculiar to one's vocation or avocation; access to education on the basis of which to make the choice and, having made it, pursue it; and freedom of association that allows engagement in differing vocations and avocations with others who make the same choice.

Although much more needs to be said if this distinction between general and local conditions of emancipation is to serve particular political decisions, I will assume that it can be sustained in a more extensive discussion. I am encouraged to do so because virtually all theories of justice are driven to a similar distinction. Rawls introduces the concept of "primary goods," Gewirth the concept of "generic capacities for action and generally successful action," and Habermas the concept of "generalizable interests." To be sure, in all of these theories the distinction depends on a nonteleological conception of justice, and the "goods" or "capacities" or "interests" with which justice is concerned are putatively independent of any comprehensive good. But if in truth every such theory implies a conception of that good, there can be no such independence, and the only relevant question is what conception of the comprehensive good is in effect. On the telos of our maximal common humanity, I will also assume, general conditions of emancipation include conditions of health, economic provision, education, cultural context, beauty and integrity in the nonhuman world (both natural and artificial), and the general pattern of associational life itself.

Because our maximal common humanity is self-widening, justice consists in maximizing the emancipation of all individuals insofar as emancipation depends on these general conditions. More precisely, the substantive principle of justice implied by the divine purpose may be formulated as follows: Maximize the measure of the general conditions of emancipation to which there is equal access. But the phrase "the measure of" is redundant, given the term "maximize," so that we may reformulate the principle more concisely: *Maximize the general conditions of emancipation to which there is equal access.* The integrity of the legal order consists in maximizing the extent of these conditions that is equally available to all individuals who are subject to the legislation. I will call this the principle of *justice as general emancipation*, using the term "general" to express not only the kind of emancipatory conditions with which justice is concerned but also the prescription to maximize the measure of them that is generally available or equally available to all. Within the limits it imposes, the remainder of this chapter will seek to unpack this principle.

The initial point to underscore is that justice as general emancipation has a compound character. Our maximal common humanity, we have seen, grounds teleologically the principle of communicative respect and, therefore, a democratic political association. Because this telos is specified to politics in or through the principle of justice as general emancipation, that principle also implies the formative norms that constitute social action. In other words, the substantive principle of justice is self-differentiating. It is the inclusive principle for democratic legislation that implies the formative principles of a democratic constitution as an aspect of itself. We can also make the point by saying that the rights to private and public liberties properly stipulated by the constitution are themselves general conditions of emancipation. Whatever legal norms increase the measure of general emancipation to which there is equal access, it is greater if individuals have the freedoms that can be defined without any explicit reference to human association (private liberties) and the formative freedoms that define participation in a democratic association (public liberties). Thus, the political duty to secure these rights overrides any other duties justice may prescribe. This is simply to repeat that these rights should be protected by the democratic constitution, with which all other political decisions should be consistent.

Because our maximal common humanity grounds teleologically the principle of communicative respect, it also follows that the formative principles specified in a democratic constitution imply the substantive principle of justice as general emancipation. This simply repeats that a democratic constitution presupposes the substantive principle that can be convincing in discourse so constituted and, through the discourse, can control democratic legislation. Still, it is no business of the constitution to stipulate the substantive principle by which the constitution itself is grounded. Precisely because the principle of communicative respect and thus the right of every individual to dissent from any social prescription is overriding, the integrity of the legal order beyond its constitution depends on the democratic process. It is the business of this discourse to determine whether justice as general emancipation will control the activities of the state. But only a state so controlled has the following character: The principle exemplified in its activities is consistently democratic.

Refining the Principle

Although its compound character has been clarified, justice as general emancipation still begs for articulation because there are many general conditions of emancipation beyond the formative rights, and maximizing the opportunity that is equally available to all must, among other things, relate these several conditions to each other. The next section will attend to those relations. Prior to that discussion, however, it will be useful further to refine the principle itself by making explicit several of its other implications. Some of these can be formulated as limits on political achievement or on justice. Summarily, there are such limits because the legal order is subservient to the comprehensive telos that grounds it; that is, achieving justice is not equivalent to maximizing our common humanity. The latter has a complex character, and the legal order properly provides and promotes the context for distinctive local and personal associations. The point can also be expressed by saying that freedom from legal or coercively enforced norms and, therefore, freedom of association are among the most important general conditions of emancipation.

In this setting, we may reassert the responsibility of individuals to make the most of the possibilities their communities present. Given the importance to an individual's present emancipation of accumulated achievements in her or his past life, justice itself is not served if the state's activities ignore whether individuals exercise the abilities they have to emancipate themselves. For instance, our maximal common humanity would be compromised if the state were to insure the requisite equality in economic resources notwithstanding that individuals who can contribute to economic production choose not to work. Again, it would be unjust for the state to insure the requisite education notwithstanding that some individuals are undisciplined in pursuing the opportunities provided. On the other hand, capacities to be productive or disciplined can themselves be crippled by personal or social or cultural circumstances that were not chosen, and it is also unjust to require that individuals assume responsibilities they cannot meet. Summarily and insofar as possible, then, general conditions of emancipation include those that cultivate and support in each individual the capacity to be increasingly responsible in relevant respects for her or his own emancipation. But this means that conditions of emancipation for any given individual include her or his own choices, and, in this sense, the achievement of justice is limited.

In this setting also, we may address in principle the difficult question of whether justice requires compensation for naturally caused inequalities—for instance, inequalities in natural talent and inequalities due to natural disablement. Similar access to educational institutions or associations does not equally emancipate those who bring to their participation differences in ability, and access to the same measure of supportive resources does not equally emancipate those whom nature has treated differently with respect to health or physical handicap. If the equal access prescribed by justice as general emancipation includes compensation for natural inequalities, then plausibly the legal order is bound to effect such massive transfers of resources to those who are most unfortunate that the possibilities for our common humanity are dramatically less than they otherwise would be. As this consequence suggests, however, to construe the equality justice requires in this manner is to abstract it from the telos that grounds it. Naturally created differences are inescapable because human beings are constituted by fragmentary relations to a world all of whose realities are also fragmentary. Pursuit of maximal creativity in the human future must take those differences into account. The general fact of natural inequalities, in distinction from those created by human action itself, is a given for the legal order, and its service to our maximal common humanity properly assumes this general fact. Hence, the meaning of "equality" with respect to general conditions of emancipation should not be defined as equality after compensation for natural differences. For instance, equality in education cannot mean equal opportunity for achievement regardless of natural capacity but, rather, must mean equal opportunity to be educated in the measure that natural ability allows.

This limitation on the equality justice effects in no way exempts the political community from special responsibility to individuals whom nature has treated less favorably or who suffer from natural handicaps. Humane treatment for those mentally afflicted, special educational efforts for those who learn more slowly, uncommon medical and other services for those physically disabled, and the pursuit of advances in medicine or technology that will lessen or prevent illness or handicap, to choose a few examples, are all properly subjects of political decision because compensation for natural created disabilities is itself a general condition of emancipation. Precisely because natural inequalities are a part of the human condition, compensation for them is potentially important to any individual by virtue of her or his membership in the human community. But it remains that this is *one* of the general conditions of emancipation and, accordingly, the resources properly given to it must be determined in relation to the many other general conditions that maximize the wider context for distinctive local and personal achievement.[2]

Again, focus on the limits of justice provides the setting in which to connect with recent discussion about the contrast between an "ethics of justice" and an "ethics of care." Disagreement in that discussion is many-sided and, naturally, depends on what each party takes the principal terms to mean (see Gilligan 1992; Held 1995; Barry 1995: 246–57; Kymlicka 1990: 262–86). For some, the terms identify inclusive alternatives in moral theory or in the moral orientation of individuals, so that a person whose activity is just cannot simultaneously be caring and vice versa (see, e.g., Noddings 1984). Summarily speaking, however, writers who have introduced the term "ethics of care" and advocated its importance use it to affirm the moral significance of more personal and particular human relationships in which an individ-

---

[2]At best, these comments merely suggest the general terms in which to seek a solution to this problem. Although I cannot pursue that solution, I have been instructed by Ronald Dworkin's detailed attempt to provide direction for political decision. The political community may calculate the proper level of compensation, he proposes, by conceiving a hypothetical measure of insurance against natural handicaps that citizens would, prior to knowing their own place in the natural lottery, be willing to purchase. The equivalent of premiums, then, are collected through the tax structure, and the equivalent of insurance payments are effected through redistributive mechanisms (see Dworkin 1981; see also the discussion of Dworkin in Kymlicka 1990: 76–85). Dworkin's theory of justice is nonteleological in character, and an attempt to appropriate it within the teleological context of this work would require an accounting of the differences this difference makes. But I take his solution to be generally similar to my suggestion in this: Although justice requires compensation for natural inequalities, this imperative is constrained by the larger purpose of justice, namely, to provide the widest communal context in which individuals live valuable lives.

ual has special responsibilities. On this account, for instance, one is morally permitted or required to give greater moral weight to the good of one's family or friends or vocational associates and thus to treat them differently, at least in some contexts, than others to whom one does not have such relationships. Correspondingly, then, this view criticizes moral theories or principles of moral obligation that require treatment of all individuals as if the only relevant considerations were features that are independent of the actor's special relationships to them. Brian Barry notes, for instance, that impartiality is such a principle if it means, as for him it does not, that we should always consider all other humans in abstraction from our own personal attachments or associational involvements (see Barry 1995: 194–216; 246–57).

Justice as general emancipation is not consistent with an ethics of care on which the personal or particular features of an actor's relationships to others are the only or always overriding determinants of moral obligation. To the contrary, all individuals are morally bound whatever the consequences or particular context to obey the laws, at least if they have been democratically enacted. This does not deny the possibility of extreme situations in which one is released from these general obligations. Perhaps someone whose family is starving and who has no other recourse is permitted to violate the law against theft, at least if her or his circumstance is the consequence of an invalid legal regime and the victim of theft is someone who has benefited from that injustice. But specific exceptions of this order, even if not included in the legislation and difficult to formulate, are themselves identified by general rules and do not establish the particular context as overriding. Nonetheless, justice is limited because our maximal common humanity is complex in character, self-localizing as well as self-widening. Our common humanity would be debilitated to the point of near impotence if individuals did not assume special responsibility for their own families, enduring attachments, and local communities and associations. This is, on my accounting, the meaning of an "ethics of care" that should be zealously protected against every attempt to expand the legal order beyond its mandate to provide and promote general conditions of emancipation.

If justice is, in the ways we have summarily reviewed, limited in its achievement, there are also, as it were, limits to these limits. In some libertarian theories, justice is severely circumscribed because the political principle is defined simply as freedom from coercion, in the sense that the legal order is properly designed to maximize such freedom. To be sure, any such proposal is vague until the term "coercion" is given precise meaning, and it is possible so to use the term that it does not define but, rather, depends on the meaning of justice. On that usage, any individual who suffers injustice is thereby coerced. But the term "libertarian" commonly designates theories on which freedom from coercion is so defined that it prohibits political attention to many of the general conditions of emancipation. Notwithstanding that justice as general emancipation is limited, then, it is not "libertarian" in the current sense of that term. A legal order is prescribed insofar as it is required to maximize the measure of *all* general conditions of emancipation that is equally available.

Still, justice is also not equalitarian, in the sense that it does not prescribe maximizing equality of access to the general conditions of emancipation. Equality in itself is without content, and there can be equality in want as well as in plenty. Nor does justice prescribe maximizing the general conditions of emancipation consistent with equality, such that the maximizing is constrained by equality of access or that the latter prescription overrides the former. Equality is not a prior principle but, rather, is important because and in the measure that it serves our maximal common humanity or maximizes human creativity in the future as such. Hence, justice prescribes maximizing the measure of general emancipatory conditions that is equally shared. This means that a just political community will prescribe some inequalities and permit others if doing so in fact increases the general conditions of emancipation that are equally available to all. Clearly, some in a political community must enjoy a greater opportunity to affect the decisions of the state, at least insofar as there is representative government and all cannot take a turn at being a state official. In addition, some inequalities in wealth, income, and access to education beyond those determined solely by the choices of the individuals in question may well be required in order to maximize the measure of general emancipatory conditions to which there is equal access. By the same principle, such inequalities are unjust if this measure might otherwise be increased.

Although justice as general emancipation is neither "libertarian" nor "equalitarian" within some understandings of these terms, there is also a sense in which it is both, namely, the sense in which both terms are defined by its principle. Justice is libertarian if "liberty" is used broadly enough to mean emancipation, and justice is equalitarian because it maximizes the general emancipatory conditions to which there is equal access. In a similar way, this principle may be used to define "the common good" as a politically relevant term. So intended, this term designates the distinctively human order in the respect that it provides or promotes general conditions of emancipation that are equally available to all. In this sense, the economic order, the wider social and cultural order, the legal order, the administration of the state, and the political discourse itself are the common good insofar as they are associational conditions for general emancipation, and the common good is an aspect of our common humanity. Justice, then, maximizes the common good insofar as the legal order may do so.

This conception of justice may also be expressed in terms of a universal human right that I will call *the right to general emancipation*. In contrast to the formative rights to private and public liberties that articulate the principle of communicative respect, this is a substantive right, and it may be formulated as follows: Human individuals as such have a right to the greatest measure of general emancipatory conditions that a legal order can provide or promote equally for all. The associational order or set of social practices that is legislated by a political association has as its specific purpose nothing other than securing for all this universal right.

It is, I will assume, beyond informed dissent that the extent to which general conditions of emancipation are equally available in contemporary United States society falls far short of what justice as here defined requires. Inequalities between, on the one hand, the deprived in both our cities and our rural areas, and, on the other, the advantaged classes, sometimes made the more severe because of persisting structures of racial and sexual inequality, are transparently inconsistent with the right of all to general emancipation. Some may object, then, that this right implies for individuals who are not among the most deprived an overwhelming duty to give of their own resources, insofar as they can, to the least advantaged. As long as the substantive right of each has not been secured, it might seem, individuals should, so far as they can, transfer their advantage voluntarily to the most deprived. But the right to general emancipation is to general conditions *that a legal order can provide or promote.* Hence, the duties correlative with this right are those of a political association, and they fall to individuals as citizens or participants in the political process.

Still, this clarification may seem simply to relocate the problem. So long as injustice or, at least, severe injustice prevails, individuals ought to be consumed by political activity that seeks to reform the legal order. Accordingly, all other creative projects of individuals and associations ought to be postponed until justice is secured—or, at least, other projects should be pursued only insofar as they are necessary to effective political activity. But this conclusion neglects that politics is one of many kinds of activity through which individuals properly pursue our maximal common humanity. The same pursuit may occur in family life and personal relationships and through participation in economic, educational, cultural, religious, and other forms of social action. There is no principle for the measure in which each individual's contribution should occur through one or another form except that defined by our maximal common humanity itself, and there is every reason to think that individuals have alternatives in this regard that are equally good. Whether, for instance, one's vocation should focus on politics or education or art, economic production or religious activity, health delivery or child care, may not be a moral question for a given individual.

These considerations reflect again the complex character of our common humanity; it is both self-widening and self-localizing. Hence, maximizing it provides no principled ranking of vocations that focus on wider or more local contributions to it. Still, we may affirm a summary rule, applicable in most cases, prescribing political participation in some measure as an important part of each individual's life. Because decisions of the political association determine what vocations and associations are permitted to create our common humanity, participation in political decisions is not simply one more vocation but, rather, has special importance as an aspect of them all. Moreover, the democratic discourse through which political decisions are taken itself creates a human order that is, in a unique way, emancipating for those who relate to it, because it integrates in the fullest possible manner the widest possible human diversity. These distinctive features of politics give reason to appropriate the long tradition of political thought, stretching back at least to Aristotle, that prescribes political participation as essential to a full human life.

Because universally human, the right to general emancipation apparently implies that the human community as such ought to be so ordered that it maximizes the general conditions of emancipation to which there is equal access. The massive disparities in opportunity among humans in the contemporary world display a massive failure if they are judged by that prescription. In this context, one might conclude that more favored political communities face an overwhelming duty to transfer resources, insofar as possible, to societies that are severely disadvantaged. That conclusion is the more problematic because a political association also seems bound to establish justice within the society it governs. In coordinating associational life, a democratic legal order can maximize the general conditions of emancipation to which there is equal access only for individuals who participate in its decisions and its legislated set of social practices. This vexing issue arises because the right to general emancipation requires a legal order, and the political institutions requisite for justice in the world community do not exist. If we assume that democratic governance of the whole human community is not presently a real possibility, the formative right to participate in the widest possible discourse can be actualized only in societies that are not universal. In the first instance, then, the duties correlative to an individual's right to general emancipation can only belong to the political association of which she or he is a member.

But if democratic governance of the world community is not a real possibility, it remains that political associations interact. Because the telos of our maximal common humanity is universal, justice cannot be separated from these interactions. Thus, the moral responsibility of a political association to maximize general emancipation among individuals subject to its legal order must be qualified by the association's responsibility in the community of political communities. So far as I can see, the latter obligation can only mean so interacting with other political associations as to pursue those conditions in which ever wider communities can be governed democratically, and this prescription has both negative and positive aspects. Negatively, a given state may not use the superiorities it enjoys to exploit other political communities. The relations among nations are, in other words, bound by the principle of communicative respect, in the sense that individuals of other political communities ought to be treated as potential participants in discourse. Positively, given states should seek, where possible, international political institutions that relate nations to each other in something analogous to democratic forms. It also follows that a political community in which individuals enjoy substantially greater emancipation should assume some responsibility to assist political communities in which individuals are severely disadvantaged, since the conditions for international democracy will be more closely approached insofar as humans universally are more emancipated.

Calling for a political community to pursue wider democracy and assume some responsibility to assist severely disadvantaged societies is, clearly, an indeterminate prescription. It is not within my purpose here to achieve a more detailed statement, and, in any case, I believe that a more precise principle is not possible. The issue again illustrates the complex character of the distinctively human order. Present limitations on the scope of democratic communities exemplify the self-localizing character of our common humanity; its self-widening character is expressed in the responsibility that particular political associations have to the universal human community. The formulation of our substantive human right, namely, a right to the greatest measure of general emancipatory conditions that a legal order can provide or promote equally for all, leaves ambiguous the meaning of "all"—and therefore affirms that our common humanity is universal even while a universal democracy is not presently possible. So far as I can see, this ambiguity cannot presently be removed.

The Principles of Justice

Those familiar with the work of Rawls will recognize the debt that previous sections of this chapter owe to his achievement and, specifically, to his "general conception of justice": "All social primary goods—liberty and opportunity, income and wealth, and the bases of self-respect—are to be distributed equally unless an unequal distribution of any or all of these goods is to the advantage of the least favored" (1971: 303). Notwithstanding Rawls's conviction that principles for the basic structure are separate from the good[3], my thinking

---

[3]As discussed in chapter 4, Rawls's earlier essay, "Two Concepts of Rules," can be read as a formal defense of teleology against the charge that it is inconsistent with constitutive norms or social practices that are morally binding whatever the consequences. Assuming that this defense is sound, we might ask why the theory Rawls later develops rejects teleology as the basis for constitutive principles of

about justice as general emancipation has been further aided by his articulation of this general conception in a threefold differentiation. Rawls formulates principles of basic liberties, fair equality of opportunity, and the "difference principle" and argues that these are lexically ordered, such that the first overrides the other two and the second overrides the third (see 1971: 42f., 61f.; 1996: 291f.).

The differentiation of lexically ordered or, as I will say, democratically ordered principles is important because it relates differing general conditions of emancipation to each other. On the summary above, general emancipation is greater or less depending on conditions of health, economic provision, education, cultural context, beauty and integrity in the nonhuman world (both natural and artificial),[4] and the general pattern of associational life itself. Prescribing the largest possible measure of these conditions that is equally available is insofar to beg questions about their internal connections. In some respects or circumstances, these connections are not problematic, because the

---

justice. Some might propose the following answer: Because his thought came to focus on the democratic legitimation of diverse comprehensive doctrines, none of which is rationally compelling, Rawls concluded that democratic principles must be politically liberal in the sense clarified by *Political Liberalism*. But this answer does not explain the nonteleological character of *A Theory of Justice*, which, on Rawls's own account, presents its conception of justice as part of a comprehensive doctrine. I am not familiar with any writing in which Rawls relates *A Theory of Justice* to his earlier essay. But the two are consistent in his mind, I expect, because Rawls shares the Kantian conviction that moral and political theory must be independent of a metaphysical telos. In *A Theory of Justice*, the candidate form of teleology is utilitarianism, and in fact, the earlier essay discusses the relation between social practices and "what we may call the utilitarian view" (Rawls 1955: 3). Without contradicting the formal distinction between two kinds of rules, then, Rawls also holds that the material telos asserted by utilitarianism cannot ground a constitutive principle for the distribution of utility. Thus, he concludes that constitutive principles of justice must be nonteleological.

[4]Promoting natural beauty and integrity as a general condition of emancipation is distinct from observing the principle of environmental respect, which was discussed earlier. This is especially apparent if the principle is understood as a prior constraint. In that case, the principle protects the natural world *unless* action to the contrary is necessary to maximize our common humanity, while the prescription to promote environmental beauty and integrity protects the natural world *as* necessary to that pursuit. But even if the principle is itself implied by maximizing our common humanity, the present discussion adds something to the earlier one. The principle protects intrinsic value in the natural world that would be realized if the humans in question did not act at all. In contrast, natural beauty and integrity as a general condition of emancipation may mean that intrinsic value in the natural world should be increased by human intervention.

conditions are mutually reinforcing. For instance, greater availability of health care may increase the possibilities of economic provision, as may the greater availability of education, and greater economic provision may increase the possibilities of free association. Designing the legal order in a manner that exploits and promotes such mutual reinforcement wherever possible is a prescribed aspect of creative politics. But the relations may be competitive. Economic provision may be lessened by the enhancement of environmental beauty or integrity or by a commitment to maintaining local patterns of community; the resources with which to educate all members of the society may be lessened by an increased measure of health care; and the extent to which freedom of association is present may at some point be decreased by increasing the measure of any other general condition of emancipation that is equally available. Democratic politics, then, cannot avoid decisions about how these competitive relations should be evaluated. We must now ask whether and, if so, in what respects the principle of justice derived from maximizing our common humanity implies differentiations that serve these decisions.

Since these must be differentiations in principle, they can only be "self-differentiations" of the substantive principle of justice. Recurrence to this term recalls that justice as general emancipation is self-differentiating because it is compound in character. Its inclusive principle implies and is implied by the formative principles specified in a democratic constitution; that is, the latter define the formative aspect of maximizing general emancipation. This means that securing the rights to private and public liberties is democratically prior to any other political duties. Although substantive justice may prescribe or permit some inequalities in order to maximize general emancipation, there is no proper inequality with respect to the formative rights. The only limit to those of any individual are the equal rights of all other individuals because equality is a formative condition of discourse. Indeed, were there any grounds for inequality in the democratically prior principles of the constitution, the substantive principle of justice could not control other inequalities by the prescription that they maximize the general conditions of emancipation to which there is equal access. Formative differences would imply that the substantive principle prescribe access to these conditions in a manner consistent with that inequality.

Because the formative rights are to public as well as private liberties, one of the conditions of emancipation is access to the democratic process. In its formative sense, as argued earlier, discourse assumes that individuals have the capacity to participate in it. This means that individuals in any actual discourse require certain substantive conditions. It is transparent that substantive injustice can mean a correlative inequality in access to the political discourse. As a general rule, for instance, individuals who suffer beyond their control from the absence of basic health care, economic security, or education do not have the same opportunity to participate as those who enjoy a substantially greater measure of these conditions of emancipation. This is more the case insofar as the political process is also corrupted by the strategic assertion of interests in distinction from pursuit of the common good. But inequality in political access may be present even without this corruption. Those who are more advantaged economically and educationally will, as a general rule, have greater resources with which to advance their claims and arguments in public discussion and debate and, perhaps, greater capacity to persuade.

For this reason, the constitution of a democracy as a full and free political discourse anticipates that the constituted political process will be in large or, at least, tolerable measure successful, so that governance will be in that measure substantively just. But substantive justice may prescribe or permit inequalities in the general conditions of emancipation in order to maximize the measure of those conditions that is equally available, and even these inequalities could affect the democratic process. They should not. The legal validity of the state's activities, including any inequalities they prescribe or permit, depends on determination through full and free discourse, and a free political discourse is one in which all individuals governed by the law are equal participants. The constitution's anticipation of substantive justice, therefore, includes the anticipation of maximal political equality, so understood as to include whatever special consideration must be given to officials of the state in order to effect the taking, interpretation, and enforcement of decisions through the discourse. Given that substantive equality is defined in terms of emancipation, a democratic constitution anticipates or implicitly prescribes maximal equality of political emancipation or, as I will say, of public access. In addition to the democratic priority of the constitution, then, maximal equality in public access is democratically prior to any inequalities that might otherwise serve to maximize general emancipation. We may also say that all individuals have a right to maximal equality of public access or, for short, a right to public access. This right constitutes the substantive character of institutionalized democratic discourse, just as its formative character is defined by the equal right to public liberties.[5]

That all have the right to maximal equality of public access may seem to imply that justice prescribes maximal equality with respect to all general conditions of emancipation, such that maximizing those conditions is always constrained by a principle of equality. On this reading, inequalities in, say, wealth and income or educational opportunity, even if they would otherwise increase the measure of general emancipation available to all, would cause inequality in public access, and the right to public access is overriding. Accordingly, the latter so transforms the principle of justice that it should be stated: Maximize the general conditions of emancipation consistent with equal access. But this conclusion is avoidable, because substantive access to the democratic process may be legally institutionalized in ways that compensate for differences in, say, economic and educational advantage. I have in mind the control of campaign financing, the provision of access to the mass media for groups that would not otherwise be able to afford equal time, and the encouragement of civic associations that are formed for the purpose of democratic participation. Given such possibilities, it remains important to formulate the principle of general emancipation so as to permit inequalities that benefit everyone. Nonetheless, the right to public access has its own effect on the inequalities permitted, which are bound to consistency with this democratically prior principle.

[5]For the sake of clarity, let me underscore that maximal equality of public access is not a constitutional principle, because it depends on the substantive principle of justice as general emancipation. The constitution, we might say, stipulates *that* the legal order should be substantively just, in the sense that such an order is anticipated. But the constitution cannot stipulate in what substantive justice consists. Similarly, the constitution stipulates that there should be substantive political equality, but in what this equality consists is an object of the democratic discourse. On some extreme libertarian theories of justice, for instance, the distribution of resources effected by the free market is just and defines substantive equality. Hence, access to the political process that results from the free market distribution of income is political equality. On justice as general emancipation, political equality can mean only equality in political emancipation, and this is what I mean by equality of public access.

The democratic priority of formative rights and, subject to them, of the right to public access is not sufficient to evaluate all competitive relations among the general conditions of emancipation. Within adherence to the prior principles, political decision may require that conditions of health, economic provision, education, cultural context, environmental beauty and integrity, and the pattern of associational life be weighed against each other. So far as I can see, there are no universal principles prescribing for every society the same adjudication of all such competitive relations. In this respect, Habermas is correct in saying that the good is culturally and historically specific, notwithstanding that, against Habermas, it cannot be in *all* respects specific to a given lifeworld. In some societies as compared to others, for instance, relation to the natural environment may be more important than technological advance, or philosophical and artistic pursuits more important than the practice of science, or attachment to local communities in contrast to associational mobility diversely evaluated—and these differences may be consistent with maximizing our common humanity. Within certain limits, in other words, the measure of general conditions of emancipation that is equally available is maximized on any of the alternatives.

Still, there is a further universal principle that governs the relative importance of differing general conditions, and we may approach it through recurring to the project of Alan Gewirth. On his argument, as previously discussed, all human action is bound by a universal and nonteleological principle of equal rights to freedom and well-being, which are "necessary conditions . . . of action and of generally successful action" (1996: 14). Gewirth addresses the problem of conflicts or competitive relations among these conditions in terms of distinctions with respect to their importance for generally successful action. Specifically, he differentiates three kinds of well-being:

> *Basic well-being* consists in having the essential preconditions of action, such as life, physical integrity, mental equilibrium. *Non-subtractive well-being* consists in having the general abilities and conditions needed for maintaining undiminished one's general level of purpose-fulfillment and one's capabilities for particular actions; examples are not being lied to or stolen from. *Additive well-being* consists in having the general abilities and conditions needed for

increasing one's level of purpose-fulfillment and one's capabilities for particular actions; examples are education, self-esteem, and opportunities for acquiring wealth and income (1996: 14).

Conflicts among rights, then, are properly decided by "the criterion of degrees of needfulness for action" (1996: 45, emphasis deleted), such that rights to basic well-being override rights to non-subtractive well-being, and both override rights to additive well-being. Notwithstanding that Gewirth's nonteleological concept of these necessary conditions, as Rawls's notion of primary goods, is not equivalent to the idea of general emancipatory conditions, the articulation of justice as general emancipation can also benefit from Gewirth's analysis of agency's general character.

I have in mind especially his assertion that all significant human achievements, rare exceptions aside, have universal prerequisites. Analogous to Gewirth's "basic well-being" but also extended to embrace in some measure conditions he classifies elsewhere, there is a range of prerequisites I will call basic emancipation. These include, at some basic level, conditions of psychological stability and maturity, economic provision, health care, an orderly and nonthreatening social context, self-respect, and education. Whatever historically and culturally specific character emancipation may properly be said to have, these conditions are so fundamental to human creativity as to be universal. Wherever the resources of a society permit, therefore, the state has a duty to secure basic emancipation insofar as individuals cannot provide it for themselves. To be sure, basic emancipation is also a diversity of conditions between which, conceivably, there may be competitive relations, although I venture that the list I have given ranges them in relative importance beginning with the more essential. In any event, modern societies such as the United States need not adjudicate competitive relations within the conditions of basic emancipation, because these societies do not want for the relevant resources.

At least with respect to such societies, we may speak of a right to basic emancipation and confirm the universality of this right by taking note that the right to public access implies it. The prerequisites of all significant human achievement are also conditions for participation in a democratic association. Indeed, the relation between rights to public access and to basic emancipation is analogous to the relation between rights to public and private liberties. In the substantive case as in the formative one, the practice of democratic discourse implies a wider social practice in which all individuals are treated as potential participants in discourse. Whatever else constitutes this potential substantively, the conditions of basic emancipation are required. This does not mean that these conditions, along with specific institutions designed to control the effects of inequalities on the democratic process, are sufficient to maximize equality of public access. But basic emancipation for all is transparently necessary. Thus, the democratic priority of formative rights and, subject to them, the right to public access can be further explicated by saying that the latter includes the right to basic emancipation. All other political decisions must be consistent with these rights.

We are now in a position to summarize justice as general emancipation in the following set of democratic principles:

1. The political association should be constituted as a full and free discourse, providing equal public liberties and, therefore, equal private liberties.
2. The political order should
   A. maximize equality of public access, providing for all conditions of basic emancipation, and
   B. maximize the general conditions of emancipation to which there is equal access.

The principles are ordered in terms of democratic priority, notwithstanding that 2B, which implies the others and their priority, is the inclusive principle of justice. Also, the difference between 1 and 2 is the difference between formative and substantive principles and defines the character of justice as compound.

Justice as Teleological

Having clarified the priority of formative principles and the principle of public access, we should now attend more fully to the inclusive principle of justice. Democratic politics cannot be indifferent to all political alternatives consistent with the prior principles, since their priority is itself grounded by maximizing general emancipation.

Because it specifies to politics the pursuit of our maximal common humanity and thus maximal creativity in the future as such, the inclusive principle prescribes for the long run. Accordingly, the emancipation to which present purpose should be directed includes that of future generations. Whether a nonteleological theory of justice can consistently prescribe responsibility to future generations has been widely discussed (see, e.g., Jonas 1984; Apel 1987). Advocates of such theories typically argue that the human rights they affirm extend to potential or future human individuals as well as the contemporaries of social action. Having sought in the previous chapter to show that nonteleology is inconsistent with democracy, I will not discuss the specific ways in which differing thinkers defend this extension. But the following summary consideration may be worth mention: Because they do not imply or presuppose any conception of the comprehensive good, the principles of a separationist theory can only assume individuals who have purposes as mere facts, or treat those pursuits as nonmoral except insofar as they affect the nonmoral pursuits of others. But individuals who do not exist have no pursuits that can be affected, so that one may wonder why justice prescribes responsibility to future generations.

Some may respond that decisions to continue the human community are within the rights of contemporary individuals; hence, the rights defined by principles of justice must also be attributed to any children humans choose to have and, by extension, to the children of those children. Given the assumptions of a nonteleological theory, children already born may well be subjects of human rights. But it does not follow that merely potential children and, therefore, future generations have such rights. Beginning with purposes that are nonmoral, one cannot prescribe for action beyond its effects on the individuals who have those purposes, so that present actors cannot have responsibilities to merely potential individuals. To be sure, a nonteleological theory may simply assert that it takes the eventual existence of future individuals and their purposes as a fact. But, clearly, the existence of future humans is not a present necessity, in the sense that they will exist independently of present choices. Whether there will be future humans depends on the decisions, individual and collective, of present individuals. To take future generations as a fact is to endorse the purposes of present individuals in the respect that they do or may lead to that fact, and the endorsement of purposes is or implies a conception of the good. Hence, responsibility to future generations cannot be consistently affirmed without a principle on which the future human community is good, and the latter contradicts a separationist conception of justice.

In any event, maximizing the divine good and thus our common humanity in the long run grounds our responsibility to the human future. Summarily speaking, then, maximizing the general conditions of emancipation to which there is equal access relates the contemporary community to its own future in the following way: Equal access by individuals of future generations to a similar measure of these conditions, insofar as that depends on present decisions, should be protected. Perhaps something like the objection raised against nonteleological theories of justice will seem also to trouble this prescription. The future human community and, therefore, what the prescription implies themselves depend on present decisions. But the telos of our maximal common humanity also defines the principle in relation to which these decisions should be taken: They should be directed to maximizing the distinctively human order in the long run. Applying this principle to particular decisions is, in the nature of the case, subject to the severe limits on human foresight. In the contemporary world, however, the principle prescribes substantial attention to the problem of population growth and identifies the general terms in which deliberation addressed to that problem may proceed.

Our obligation to the human future as such is also a responsibility for the larger natural order as the long-term habitat necessary to our maximal common humanity. In an especially important work, Herman Daly and John B. Cobb Jr. set the human community within "the community of communities . . . extending to the entire biosphere" (1994: 385), indeed to the entire cosmos, and this formulation expresses their conviction that all within the most inclusive or cosmic community have intrinsic worth. In that teleological context, Daly and Cobb press on contemporary public discussion the question of scale in human society, especially the scale of the economic order relative to other human purposes and to the ecosystem. Focusing on the United States, they argue that modern societies are largely driven by economic institutions and purposes. That dominance has prevented serious address to the question of economic scale and, among other consequences, has all but obscured the ecological damage from which future generations will suffer. In contrast to a more or less unconstrained pursuit of economic goals, Daly and Cobb advocate "economics for community" (1994: 138), and the relevant community includes the biosphere in the long run. I will not review the admirable thoroughness and specificity with which Daly and Cobb pursue the question of scale. The point here is that their comprehensive teleology is shared by the conception of justice as general emancipation, and therefore the inclusive principle of justice prescribes a responsibility for the long-term future of the natural context in which our common humanity is set.

As Daly and Cobb also make clear, however, "economics for community" has importance in abstraction from the longer run and the relation of human life to the biosphere. These authors join a considerable company of social critics who censure the dominance of economic purposes in modern social orders for its effects on the contemporary human community itself (see, e.g., Heilbroner 1976, 1985; Habermas 1987; Arendt 1958), and the conception of justice as general emancipation implies a similar set of criticisms. It would be thoughtless and dangerous to ignore the massive advance in human good that modern technology and economic organization have contributed. They have created conditions of health and material provision, including means of transportation and interaction, that massively extend the possibilities of our common humanity. Moreover, scientific pursuits and their technological applications, as well as economic institutions, are themselves important occasions for human communication. But maximal economic growth is not the same as our maximal common humanity, and the general conditions for the former are not at all the same as maximizing the general conditions of emancipation that are equally available.

In part, the issue is that of distributive justice. Due credit to the contribution economic success has made should not obscure the moral issue of proper distribution. Whether or not the current economic inequalities in the United States are, as I judge, far greater than justice as general emancipation permits, the telos of maximal economic growth is no friend of distributive justice. This is because that telos cannot unequivocally commit its adherents to any principle for the social order other than those they simply choose to affirm. I grant that an adequate defense of this criticism requires a detailed discussion with the literature on utilitarianism and welfare economics. Here I will only offer summarily the line of thought that might be developed.

As Daly and Cobb argue, the social dominance of economic growth is culturally authorized by a widely effective set of understandings on which the good realized in an individual's life is equated with the satisfaction of purposes or wants whose content is defined solely by individual choice. Roughly speaking, maximizing economic growth is taken to maximize the satisfaction of these wants, and, accordingly, they are typically taken to be "consumer preferences." Indeed, the persistent public homage paid to economic growth as the inclusive social telos serves to inculcate and reinforce this conception of the good. Thus, the social implications of maximizing economic growth are dependent on the principles that follow from maximizing want satisfaction. To the best of my reasoning, there are no such principles because the maximum in question has no conceptual content.

Considered solely as matters of preference, in other words, wants or purposes have no common character that could be maximized. Purposes are taken to be good by those who choose them; hence, the realization of several purposes can be aggregated only in terms of some variable of the good. If it is said that all wants are equally good, aggregation requires some common feature all objects of purpose equally exemplify. But a preference can have as its object anything the individual chooses. Aside from the fact that all such objects are wanted, the only features they commonly exemplify are metaphysical. Since these define the most general character of any object at all, they could be equally exemplified in all possible objects of preference only if all objects were identical. Focusing on the fact that all objects of preference are wanted, one might now suppose that want satisfaction can be aggregated in terms of its enjoyment, that is, in terms of some subjective form or quality. This means that satisfaction is assumed to have some intersubjective measure that is independent of the things enjoyed. Independently of their objects, however, it is impossible to define subjective qualities. The difference between consciousness of a sunset and consciousness of a stone disappears if one takes away the sunset and the stone—and unless one substitutes some other object, the consciousness itself vanishes.

Given that solely preferential purposes cannot be aggregated in terms of their objects or of some independent subjective form, pursuit of maximal want satisfaction cannot imply moral principles of social order because the concept of that maximum is not coherent. In truth, then, it implies that the measure of aggregation and any distributional consequences it may have are themselves solely matters of choice. This putative social telos means only that each individual is authorized to pursue without constraint the satisfaction of her or his own preferences and, therefore, is not bound by any social prescriptions except those she or he prefers.[6]

Those who advocate maximal economic growth typically attempt to solve the problem of aggregation by measuring in terms of something assumed to be solely instrumental to whatever wants one may have, specifically, measuring in terms of monetary value. Having so

---

[6]Some may respond that this conclusion ignores an insight of common sense: Parties to an informed, voluntary exchange are both better off by virtue of the exchange; otherwise, they would not agree to it. Hence, we can know, without specifying the measure by which satisfaction is aggregated, that a social system in which informed, voluntary transactions are maximized will also maximize the satisfaction of preferences. But if the notion of maximizing preference satisfaction has no conceptual content, then no system can have this effect. Although both parties to an informed, voluntary exchange find it agreeable, in no way does it follow that total preference satisfaction is thereby greater than it would otherwise have been, precisely because there is no sensible aggregation. Perhaps each party believes that her or his realization of the good has been increased, according to her or his preferred variable of the good, but we cannot sensibly speak of total realization having been increased without some variable of the good by which the objects of all purposes can be summated.

If we are now told that a system of informed, voluntary exchanges is one in which each person's realization of the good is maximized, according to her or his own definition of the good, this, too, is a fallacious conclusion. In many cases, a given individual's realization of the good, on her or his conception of it, would be greater if she or he could coerce other individuals. At best, then, voluntary exchange increases each participant's realization of the good, on her or his conception of it, given the prior requirement that the participation of the other person or persons must be voluntary. But this is simply to say that voluntariness, on some understanding of it, is affirmed. The social ethic advanced is now a nonteleological one, since the prescription of universal voluntariness cannot itself be derived from maximizing preference satisfaction. On my reading, Milton Friedman, one of the more noted advocates of the position here criticized, is clear that his principle of freedom is nonteleological (see Friedman 1962). Moreover, the prescription of universal voluntariness itself is vacuous until the meaning of "voluntariness" is clarified, and this concept cannot be defined without a non-teleological stipulation about the conditions under which individuals act voluntarily, this is, without an independent principle for the distribution of resources. I am not sure that Friedman is clear on this point.

assumed, they may argue that certain principles follow from economic maximization; for instance, the social order should maximize informed voluntary exchanges in competitive markets and, on some accounts, distributional considerations are also said to be implied. But if maximal economic growth is authorized by a supposed telos that has no conceptual content, then any principles that follow from measuring the former in terms of a solely instrumental value are groundless. Alternatively stated, an advocate of such principles seeks to maximize an instrumental value for its own sake. Hence, maximizing economic growth can lead to nonpreferential conclusions about the social order only by stipulating or independently affirming conditions that cannot be derived from maximizing preference satisfaction. To be sure, one may incorrectly believe and act on the supposition that the latter implies certain nonpreferential principles. But individuals who do so are, at best, afflicted by ambiguous motivation. The public approval of maximal economic growth can be joined with constraints on an individual's pursuit of her or his own preferences only at the price of being inconsistent with the conception of the good this approval inculcates and reinforces and on which it depends. At least in the sense that adherents of it are motivationally conflicted, then, economic maximization is no friend of justice.[7]

Nonteleological theories of justice also conclude, each in its own way, that the notion of maximal want satisfaction does not imply any acceptable theory of the social order. Accordingly, they assert independent principles of justice that constrain conceptions of the good and to which, therefore, one may appeal to constrain the pursuit of eco-

---

[7]Nothing included or implied in this discussion denies that exchange relationships effected by the use of money can and do occur. I take the use of money to mean that each party to the relationship is unconcerned with the ends pursued by the other, and, taking these ends for granted, seeks a relationship that is mutually instrumental. Social purpose might take such transactions to be the most important form of human relationship, in the sense that public policy is principally designed to maximize their monetary value. Something like this policy is precisely what Daly and Cobb, along with many others, are concerned to criticize. The discussion above is meant simply to show that a social telos conceived in terms of economic goals, however economic achievement might be measured or the relevant public policy might be designed, is nonsensical—because maximizing economic benefits implies a conception of the good that cannot imply any principle for the social order.

nomic growth. Habermas, for instance, argues that systems of strategic action in advanced capitalism have "colonized" realms of social action that are properly coordinated by common values and, thereby, have undermined the associational order required for democratic discourse (see especially 1987). On Gewirth's analysis, the generic goods needful for generally successful action include not only basic and nonsubtractive but also additive goods—such as education, self-esteem, opportunities for acquiring wealth and income, and the sense of belonging; hence, his principle of equal generic rights to these goods significantly circumscribes the pursuit of economic growth. But just because these are separationist principles of justice, they merely constrain economic growth as the inclusive social purpose. In other words, nonteleological theories cannot offer conceptual resources with which to criticize the view that an individual's good, so long as she or he honors the independent principles, consists in the realization of solely preferential purposes. As a consequence, these theories cannot overcome the possible ambiguity in motivation that threatens the pursuit of justice.

The nature of moral motivation on a nonteleological conception of morality has been extensively discussed at least since Kant's assertion that reason can be practical. In his revision of Kant, Gewirth seeks to show that every purposive agent has unambiguous motivation to act in accord with the Principle of Generic Consistency. Because an agent's choice of a purpose and thus its prudential requirements are themselves the endorsement of her or his own rationality, Gewirth argues, the agent is motivated without equivocation to constrain her or his own purposes by the rational requirement that she or he affirm the equal generic rights of all. "By virtue of the PGC's being rationally justified the rational agent is in fact motivated to accept it, since, being rational, he accepts what is rationally justified" (1978: 195). Hence, "the PGC's derivation shows how reason can be practical; but 'reason' now includes not only logical form but also the conative content, . . . , that . . . is necessarily combined with this form" (1978: 196).

But this argument must deny by assumption that the choice of a purpose expresses a conception of the good with which the agent evaluates her or his alternatives inclusively. Given such an evaluation, principles of justice that are not authorized by it would imply ambiguity of motivation. To the best of my reasoning, in other words, Gewirth can reach his conclusion only if it is stipulated in the premises, that is, only if the purposes an individual is permitted to choose are so conceived that they already include the equal generic rights of all agents. On that account, however, the conception of justice depends on a stipulation about the good. Hence, the price of non-teleological principles is that individuals are authorized to pursue as their inclusive end the satisfaction of their own preferences, and this purpose is at odds with any commitment to justice they do not simply choose. In this sense, nonteleological principles subvert the very social order they prescribe. Whatever may be said in defense of separationist principles of justice, people can be motivated to act accordingly only because they so prefer or in spite of their preferential conceptions of the good. Thus, integrity in the commitment to justice requires a teleological criticism of maximal preference satisfaction and, with it, economic growth as the inclusive social telos.

Indifference to distributive justice is only one moral failing of which this telos should be convicted. Even if we assume a distribution in which the measure of economic benefits to which there is equal access is maximized, a legal order directed to maximal economic growth is unjust. Our inclusive telos is the maximal order created by human communication, and economic purposes are properly relativized by or subservient to the purpose of creating our common humanity. Quite apart from questions of the longer run and care for the biosphere, this fundamental point remains in the phrase "economics for community." For Daly and Cobb, the contemporary political debate about alternative economic proposals is typically framed in terms of differences between more libertarian and more equalitarian understandings of economic distribution, thereby begging the question of economic scale in relation to good human purposes as such. Recognizing the "important issues" (1994: 8) in that debate, Daly and Cobb argue that our controlling evaluation should be directed to creating and enhancing human communities themselves.

John Dewey's discussions of democracy seek persistently to make the same point. "Democracy has many meanings, but if it has a moral meaning, it is found in resolving that the supreme test of all political institutions . . . shall be the contribution they make to the all-around growth of every member of society" (1957: 186). The term "growth," on Dewey's intent, is a virtual synonym for human "creativity," as used in the present work, and this is confirmed when Dewey also formulates the meaning of democracy teleologically. Questions of metaphysics aside, he identifies our maximal common humanity: "Every way of life that fails in its democracy limits the contacts, the exchanges, the communications, the interactions by which experience is steadied while it is also enlarged and enriched. Since the task of this release and enrichment is one . . . that can have no end till experience itself comes to an end, the task of democracy is forever the creation of a freer and more humane experience in which all share and to which all contribute" (1951: 394). For Dewey, then, modern society requires "a form of social organization that should include economic activities but yet should convert them into servants of the development of the higher human capacities" (1963: 31–32). The "higher human capacities" are expressed in human association for its own sake, and the emancipation of these capacities depends beyond economic resources on participation in our common humanity itself.[8]

The Possibility of Justice

The contemporary economic system, many have argued, has its own imperatives that influence or condition the beliefs of citizens and, therefore, their political evaluations. At least in part, this is the point Habermas makes in calling the economy a "self-regulating" system of action (1996: 78). Finding, with Habermas, that economic growth does dominate contemporary social purpose, others have been led to pessimism about the political possibilities of relativizing this pursuit prior to the time when its destructive consequences for the environment and social stability become severe (see, e.g., Heilbroner 1980). Most such conclusions express in their own way and with whatever revisions they may add the influence of Marx, especially his conviction that culture is the creation but not the creator of the "forces of production," so that social transformation in modern societies cannot occur without class warfare. Given this context of interpretation, justice as general emancipation, however valid in principle, may seem politically impotent because it requires a transformation in moral beliefs that the dominant institutions of the society prevent.

---

[8]I have offered a more extended reading of Dewey's democratic theory in Gamwell 1984, especially chapter 5.

An address to this sense of futility may be approached by first noting that the problem could be given more radical grounds. The dominance of institutions designed to produce and distribute for the pursuit of preferences is, one might argue, the modern expression of a more profound and abiding feature of the human condition. On this view, humans as such are powerfully tempted by interpretations that attribute inordinate worth to their own futures or the future of some narrow group in which they participate. Something very similar is, we may recall, fundamental to Reinhold Niebuhr's account of sin or duplicity as universally human and to his assertion that self-centeredness is the primary form of sin. In premodern societies, one might continue, the expression of duplicity was typically contained within ascriptive social orders that were themselves taken for granted or sustained by cultural and institutional authority. But historical consciousness in the modern age has released self-centeredness from fixed forms of life, and its expressions have become indistinguishable from the assertion of preferential self-interests.

Given that political deliberation should assume inordinate self-centeredness as an abiding feature of human life, the most one can expect from politics is the achievement of some rough justice among individuals or groups that typically focus on their own perceived advantage. This conclusion cautions against the hope for widespread commitment to some common telos by which the pursuit of narrow or private interests might be controlled. Our political aim, we are counseled, should be confined to an order promoting greater and more equal opportunity to satisfy such interests, perhaps including constraints on the power of some to affect how others perceive their own satisfaction. Realism requires recognition that politics is largely a process of bargaining, and the most that democratic politics can do is enforce conditions on the bargaining process that proscribe coercion and insure a significant measure of fair participation.

"Tyranny and anarchy," Niebuhr writes, "represent the Scylla and Charybdis between which the frail bark of social justice must sail" (1941–43, 2: 258), where "tyranny" in its general sense means the domination of some by others, and "anarchy" in its general sense means the breakdown of a social order that allows mutual advantage, both conceived principally in terms of the private interests individuals assert. As any reader of Niebuhr is sensible, his theism and its supreme "law of love" are expressed, sometimes eloquently, in affirmations that human mutuality or community, as distinct from equality and mutual advantage among perceived interests, is the proper telos of life in this world. As previously cited, he calls "the social substance" the source of human individuality as well as its "end and fulfillment" (1960: 48), and Niebuhr also affirms that the measure of community possible within history is indeterminate: "The achievements of justice in history may rise in indeterminate degrees to find their fulfillment in a more perfect love and brotherhood" (1941–43, 2: 246). But when Niebuhr offers more thorough formulations in political theory, his profound sense of human fault typically leads him to state the problem of justice principally in terms of conflicts among self-centered pursuits. For this reason, his developed political theory is focused on the "balance" or "equilibrium" of power in the larger social order, where "power" means principally the capacity to assert one's own private interests in competition with those of others, and on the "central organizing principle and power" or government, without which the conflicts among self-interests would be anarchical (see 1941–43, 2: chapter 9, especially p. 257).

To be sure, Niebuhr also vigorously defends democratic government, and he insists that democracy is possible only because each individual has the "capacity to consider interests other than his own" (1941–43, 2: 249). To the best of my reading, however, democracy is necessary principally because it prevents the organizing center from becoming the instrument of dominating interests and, thereby, tyrannical, so that Niebuhr's democratic theory is designed to stress that justice requires a more or less equal balance of specifically political power. He persistently criticizes as "foolish" or "sentimental" those democratic theorists, of whom he takes John Dewey to be an exemplar, who think that democratic politics can be based on widespread commitment to a common good and thus can pursue as a worldly possibility the kind of mutuality that, for Niebuhr, exists only in a transcendent "kingdom of God." The absence of "realism" about human possibilities, he believes, always leads one to neglect the importance of balanced power and, thereby, compromises even the rough justice that can be achieved.

Niebuhr is certainly right to insist on the importance of political realism, in his sense. He has instructed many on the injustice that results when the capacity of humans to value inordinately their own narrow self-interests and, having done so, to engage in politics strategically is not taken into account. As previously discussed, the democratic constitution should be realistic in its institutionalization of the democratic decision-making process, recognizing that bargaining will often be in greater or lesser measure involved. It also follows that democratic laws and policies will be naive and, thereby, threaten the realization of justice if they allow the concentration of power and rely on a commitment to the common good among the powerful. But realism in this sense is one thing, and the telos of the democratic process is another; the one counsels lucidity about the means that will serve the end, the other defines what end this lucidity should serve. So far as I can see, Niebuhr's developed political theory so leans on the former that it fails to formulate an end for the social order other than rough equality in the satisfaction of asserted or self-centered interests. In Niebuhr's polemic against John Dewey, then, Dewey's conviction that democracy is meant to serve "the all-around growth" or creativity of every member of society and thus the development of the higher human capacities is equated with naïveté about human self-centeredness. But whether or not Dewey was unrealistic in this sense is independent of the end to which, for him, democratic politics is properly directed. In Niebuhr's more sustained treatment of politics, the issue Dewey raised in his formulation of our maximal common humanity is lost.

We can even say that Niebuhr's developed political theory, notwithstanding its setting within a theistic teleology, becomes in its own way nonteleological. Because the possibility of human mutuality is so thoroughly removed from history to a reality transcendent to the world, principles of justice are formulated as if they were independent of the diverse individual pursuits in the political community and their implied conceptions of the good. This is not to say that Niebuhr fails to relate justice to a transcendent reality. The previous section argued that separating justice from the good subverts the commitment to justice, even in the nonteleological sense of greater equality among diverse preferential interests, and it is just this problem to which Niebuhr's theism offers a religious response: The conviction that politics is included within a transcendent kingdom of God will, he holds, sustain and empower the commitment to justice. This is one way to express what he took to be the paradoxical relation of love to justice or the relevance of a "love commandment" that is "no simple historical possibility" (1941–43, 2: 247) but, rather, an "impossible possibility" (1941–43, 2: 76).

Nonetheless, and quite apart from whether Niebuhr's theistic formulation is convincing, an ideal of mutuality that is merely transcendent and, therefore, historically impossible arrests at least the commitment to democratic discourse, in distinction from the democratic ordering of strategic power or the democratic control of the bargaining process. Commitment to discourse affirms that convincing argument can have its part in determining the associational order and, therefore, that politics in significant measure can both depend on and help to evoke a general commitment to the common good. So understood, participation in discourse assumes that the possibilities of justice in this world are not exhausted by increasing the satisfaction of asserted interests more or less equally but include the pursuit of mutuality or our common humanity. Indeed, this participation assumes that the democratic process itself can be a realization of mutuality.

It is telling, I think, that Niebuhr's famous aphorism, "man's capacity for justice makes democracy possible; but man's inclination to injustice makes democracy necessary" (1960: xiii), does not explicitly assert that our capacity for justice also makes democracy necessary. Saying this would mean that justice is in service to our common humanity, and democratic discourse is required to realize within the political process itself the good that human life as such ought to maximize. The measure in which we may hope that such discourse will occur is not easily determined. But Niebuhr, I am persuaded, finally did not or would not deny its importance to democracy. Without the real possibility of democratic debate, democratic forms for the bargaining process could not themselves be constituted and protected. Further, Niebuhr's own argument for political realism would be politically impotent. In any event, this seems clear: The measure of genuine discourse in contemporary democracies will itself be compromised if those who hold that politics ought to serve our maximal common humanity do not, with whatever realism may be needed, advocate that telos and thus justice as general emancipation.

In the last analysis, this, too, is all we can say to those for whom the imperatives of the economic system prevent the transformation in moral beliefs or in political culture required by justice as general emancipation. The power of those imperatives depends at least in part on whether citizens who are convinced that justice has this character exercise their citizenship by asserting and defending their conviction as effectively as they can. Principles of justice at odds with beliefs widely persuasive within the political community and widely reinforced by its institutions are, in the nature of the case, at a disadvantage in the democratic process. But if the constitution is on the whole democratic, and if the legal order secures in some proximate measure the right to public access, then the possibilities of genuine discourse and the power of good argument cannot be absent, and there is finally no alternative except to do what one can to convince one's fellow citizens. If that effort is futile, so, too, is democracy.

Moreover, those who advocate justice as general emancipation do have this on their side: Their fellow citizens are already attached to our maximal common humanity because the divine purpose is implicitly understood and affirmed by human existence as such. Against all competitors, appeal to this telos has the advantage of coherence with the abiding human passion for authenticity. "Just as love of God includes love of our neighbor," says Aquinas, "so, too, the service of God includes rendering to each one his due" (*Summa Theologica*: 2–2. 58. 1). In our context, adherence to this abiding truth is a commitment to democracy within the reality of God.

Appendix to Part Two
The Democratic Importance of Religion

This work has articulated the relation of justice to the divine purpose principally in contrast to nonteleological or separationist political thought. In that respect, the discussion has engaged contemporary political theories that are, in the most common sense of the term, liberal. But recent political discussion includes other thinkers who are also critical of liberalism in this sense. I have in mind especially some of those who purport to reform and reassert "republican political theory" or "civic republicanism." These names have long histories in political thought and mean differing things to contemporary thinkers who claim them. My interest is directed specifically to those who share the view that democracy is properly constituted as a discourse about the common good and, therefore, is not adequately conceived in terms of independent political principles. On my reading, most recent expressions of republican thought so understood pursue, in contrast to the present work, a conception of democracy that remains independent of any metaphysical or theistic backing. Attention to the difference this difference makes will permit a summary restatement of the present proposal. With this aim in view, I will briefly discuss this alternative mode of contemporary political thought, principally through attention to Michael Sandel's volume, *Democracy's Discontent*.

On Sandel's account, democracy has suffered because "a certain version of liberal political theory" (1996: 4) has been ascendant in

United States politics. The dominance of this "Kantian liberalism," as he calls it (1996: 11), has created a "procedural republic" (1996: 4) in which justice is thought to mean a social or political order separated from and, in that sense, neutral to all conceptions of the good life. For Kantian liberals, "the right is prior to the good" (1996: 10), such that each individual's pursuit of whatever she or he takes to be good is properly restrained by independent principles of justice. This view of politics, Sandel continues, implicates a certain understanding of human persons, on which the identity of each is "independent of the desires and ends it may have at any moment" (1996: 12). The self is "prior to its ends" (1996: 13), in the sense that proper ends are not given to it but are solely the consequence of its choice or decision; the self is "unencumbered by aims and attachments it does not choose for itself" (1996: 12). Political theory, then, is focused by "a framework of rights" (1996: 11) that assures for each individual the liberty or freedom to choose, revise, and pursue her or his own interests.

In truth, however, human persons are "encumbered selves" (1996: 14). Identity is constituted by membership in communities, cultures, and traditions that are "antecedent to choice" (1996: 15). Moral obligations, therefore, cannot be independent of the particular social or communal constitution of the self and, to the contrary, are dependent on some conception of the good in which communal conditions are included. Given this dissonance between the procedural republic and the true nature of human persons, democracy in the later twentieth century is "discontent"; the democratic experience is widely characterized by "two fears—for the loss of self-government and the erosion of community" (1996: 3). The two are inseparable, because self-government is the practice that both expresses and creates the identity of persons as participants in a given political community. When the governance of that community becomes solely procedural, the "qualities of character" (1996: 6) or "habits and dispositions" (1996: 66) of civic virtue are not developed, and the lives of individuals are increasingly at odds with the political community from which their identities cannot be divorced. The loss of self-governing community, then, is also experienced as "a loss of mastery" or "growing sense of disempowerment" (1996: 323). Whatever else may be involved, the sense that "we confront a world governed by impersonal structures of power that defy our understanding and control" (1996: 323) betrays a political culture for which democracy is an instrumental condition and thus not a constitutive part of the good life. Given that view, democratic citizens abdicate creation of the public world, and institutional systems, especially those of the economy, are left in large measure to follow their own internal and imposing logic.

In both thought and in practice, we require a retrieval of republican political theory. So far from "defining rights according to principles that are neutral among conceptions of the good, republican theory interprets rights in light of a particular conception of the good society—the self-governing republic. In contrast to the liberal claim that the right is prior to the good, republicanism thus affirms a politics of the common good" (1996: 25). Among other things, this makes politics a "formative project" (1996: 321), in the sense that it has a stake in and government has a responsibility to help cultivate both the civic virtue "self-government requires" (1996: 6) and the public spaces, formal and informal, in which this virtue can be developed and exercised. "To deliberate well about the common good requires more than the capacity to choose one's ends and respect others' rights to do the same. It requires a knowledge of public affairs and also a sense of belonging, a concern for the whole, a moral bond with the community whose fate is at stake" (1996: 5). The republican view also insists on "substantive moral discourse" (1996: 323). Properly understood, a self-governing community does not impose any good on its citizens. To the contrary, the cultivation of civic virtue opens the possibility of genuine debate about the good. "A successful revival of republican politics would not resolve our political disputes; at best, it would invigorate political debate by grappling more directly with the obstacles to self-government in our time" (1996: 338). At its best, in other words, "political deliberation is not only about competing policies but also about competing interpretations of the character of a community, of its purposes and ends" (1996: 350).

Naturally, this summary review abstracts entirely from the details with which Sandel presents the republican view of politics to United States citizens, especially from the impressive historical argument in which he seeks to show how the procedural republic has become ascendant. Still, enough has been said to suggest the rapport between his republican theory and the conception of justice as general emancipation. The relation between rights and "the self-governing republic" in which substantive moral discourse occurs is at least similar to the derivation of rights from the principle that all should be treated as potential participants in a democratic discourse about the comprehensive purpose and its specification to the activities of the state. Moreover, this similarity reflects a substantially common conception of human persons. The self "encumbered" by or, as Sandel also says, "situated" in associations and communities that help to constitute its moral identity is insofar an individual whose emancipation depends on her or his participation in a distinctively human order having a complex character.

The self-governing community Sandel advocates also has its affinities with the principle of democracy Habermas defends. As might be expected from the previous discussion of Habermas, however, he believes that republican theories like Sandel's compromise the "concept of deliberative politics" by ignoring the respect in which democratic discourse is bound by universal standards. On the republican view, Habermas says, "the only genuinely political discourses are those that have collective self-understanding as their goal," and "where political will-formation is presented as ethical discourse, political discourse must be considered *always* with the aim of discovering, at a given point in time and within the horizon of shared ways of life and traditions, what is best for citizens as members of a concrete community" (1996: 280, 281). As noted above, the term "ethical" here means discourses about the good that are not subject to a universal principle but, rather, seek to clarify the telos of a good life, individual or collective, that is in all respects dependent on some historically specific "lifeworld." For Habermas, then, a republican definition of political discourse in relation to the common good loses the universal character of human rights and moral norms. Politics so conceived has no grounds on which to identify "obligations toward *other* political communities" (1996: 548, n. 76) and, finally, cannot consistently defend "the intrinsically rational character of a democratic process" (1996: 285).

It is not immediately apparent that Sandel's position is subject to this critique. He recognizes that the self is encumbered by many communities, patterned in "sometimes overlapping, sometimes conflicting" (1996: 350) ways, and asserts that "contemporary politics puts sovereign states . . . in question." Hence, "self-government today, . . . , requires a politics that plays itself out in a multiplicity of settings, from neighborhoods to nations to the world as a whole. Such a politics requires citizens who can think and act as multiply-situated selves" (1996: 350). This says or implies that substantive moral discourse is not limited to debate about a good dependent in all respects on "the shared ways of life and traditions, . . . of a concrete community." It is striking, then, that Sandel does not, to the best of my reading, state *his* conception of the good, that is, does not formulate a universal telos for human action and association that might be defended in democratic debate and might ground the moral validity of self-government in the multiplicity of settings that stretches to the universal human community.

To the contrary, Sandel's explicit moral affirmations are limited to the good of self-government itself and, therefore, the good of civic virtue. Read in the context of his book as a whole, his assertion that "republican theory interprets rights in light of a particular conception of the good society—the self-governing republic" (1996: 25) leaves the suspicion that, for him, the only universal feature of a good society is its character as self-governing. In an earlier work, criticizing what he there called "deontological liberalism," Sandel noted that this liberalism is distinctively modern because it depends on "a universe empty of *telos*, such as seventeenth-century science and philosophy affirmed." Only with this nonteleological understanding of the world "is it possible to conceive of a subject apart from and prior to its purposes and ends" or to conceive of "conceptions of the good [left] to individual choice" (1982: 175). But nowhere, to my knowledge, does Sandel reassert a comprehensive telos or an understanding of the world that includes a conception of the comprehensive good.

The suspicion that self-government alone is universally good becomes the more difficult to resist when Sandel discusses the Supreme Court's recent treatments of religious freedom. The Court's decisions, he argues, have frequently understood religious liberty as an aspect of the procedural republic; thus, religious adherence has been included as simply another of the unencumbered self's choices to which the state should be neutral. On the republican view, Sandel continues, "what makes a religious belief worthy of respect is . . . its place in a good life or, from a political point of view, its tendency to promote the habits and dispositions that make good citizens. Insofar as the case for religious liberty rests on respect for religion, it must assume that, generally speaking, religious beliefs and practices are of sufficient moral or civic importance to warrant special constitutional protection" (1996: 66). One might have expected him to say that religious beliefs are, whatever else they are, conceptions of the comprehensive good that are constitutionally protected precisely because self-government means a genuine moral discourse. Reducing the political importance of religion to "its tendency to promote the habits and dispositions of good citizens" at least suggests that sharing in self-rule is itself the only universal good.

But if this is Sandel's intent, one is bound to conclude that political forms and civic virtues necessary for genuine democracy have been confused with what its discourse is about. That conclusion would give Habermas every reason to think that Sandel, too, reduces the object of democratic discussion and debate to a "collective self-understanding" that is in all respects bound by the horizon of a specific lifeworld. Without a comprehensive good, political discourse "about competing interpretations of the character of a community, of its purposes and ends" (1996: 350) can have no grounds that are not historically specific. As a consequence, even the good of self-rule itself has nothing other than the same grounds, because the republican view does not separate justice from a conception of the good—or, to rephrase the point, the good of self-rule is inseparable from identities encumbered by a specific political context. Republican theory itself, then, is reduced to the clarification of a historically specific form of life and, in this respect, shares Rawls's appeal to the specific character of democratic political culture.

As we have seen, Habermas concludes that democracy is one expression of the universal principle of discourse, and historically specific ethical discourses should be consistent with universal and non-teleological moral norms separate from the good. But if, as this work has argued, all nonteleological theories of justice implicitly assert some or other conception of the comprehensive good, the limitations of republican theory cannot be overcome without a comprehensive purpose. Against any conception on which the good is historically specific in all respects, the universal telos modernity has so widely rejected must be reaffirmed. In other words, political theory requires a teleology in which every person is encumbered by a purpose constituting the universal human community, however self-localizing this purpose may be. One is left to wonder whether the explicit absence of a comprehensive telos in Sandel's proposal betrays his own implicit participation in the Kantian tradition—specifically, in its conviction that metaphysical conceptions of the good cannot be validated.

Theories of politics similar to Sandel's have also been called "communitarian" views, although Sandel himself does not use this term. It is appropriate insofar as communitarians, with Sandel, conceive of the self as constituted by its communities, so that justice cannot be separated from participation in communal purposes and, therefore, from the good. In *Justice and the Politics of Difference*, Iris Marion Young is critical of communitarian thinkers, notwithstanding that she also agrees with them on the poverty of what Sandel calls procedural liberalism and she calls "the distributive paradigm" (1990: 15). On her account, neither approach provides the understandings with which adequately to resist injustice, but she appears to believe that a third alternative is available without reassertion of a comprehensive purpose.

Thought exemplifying the distributive paradigm, she argues, typically "ignores or tends to obscure the institutional context within which . . . distributions take place," and that context is "relevant to judgments of justice and injustice insofar as . . . [it conditions] people's ability to participate in determining their actions and their ability to develop and exercise their capacities" (1990: 21–22). On Young's account, justice should be so conceived that it sets the terms with which to assess institutionally structured interaction. Specifically, justice proscribes, insofar as they "are potentially subject to collective evaluation and decisionmaking," the oppression and domination that are effected by "institutional organization, public action, social practices and habits, and cultural meanings" (1990: 9). "Oppression" means "systematic institutional processes" that inhibit the ability of some people "to develop and exercise their capacities and express their needs, thoughts, and feelings" (1990: 38, 40), and "domination consists in institutional conditions which inhibit or prevent people from participating in determining their actions or the conditions of their actions" (1990: 38). People are typically oppressed and dominated as members of a distinct social group, that is, "a collective of persons differentiated from at least one other group by cultural forms, practices, or way of life" (1990: 43). Emancipation, Young concludes, requires the political affirmation of difference, and this is her reason for distance from communitarians.

"A community," she writes, "is a group that shares a specific heritage, a common self-identification, a common culture and set of norms," and "the most serious political consequence of the desire for community, . . . , is that it often operates to exclude or oppress those experienced as different" (1990: 234). Accordingly, Young's critique of communitarian political thought takes for granted that such theories replace "the distributive paradigm" with the encumbrance of some historically specific community or community of communities. By virtue of its specific heritage, self-identification, culture, and set of norms, appeal to the common good or common purpose of any such community will or may serve to oppress some social group or groups. "Liberal individualism denies difference by positing the self as a solid, self-sufficient unity, ... Proponents of community, on the other hand, deny difference by positing fusion rather than separation as the social ideal" (1990: 229). So far as I can see, then, the logic of Young's position requires a common purpose that is universal or a telos that prevents oppression because it relativizes every specific community to the emancipation of all humans.

But Young herself does not explicitly turn to a comprehensive teleology. She "rejects as illusory the effort to construct a universal normative system insulated from a particular society" and pursues a kind of "critical theory" in which "the normative ideals used to criticize a society are rooted in experience of and reflection on that very society" (1990: 5). Correspondingly, she has virtually nothing to say about the place of religious convictions in the pursuit of justice. She does concede that the "emancipatory interest" of her critical theory assumes "the equal moral worth of all persons" and, therefore, two "very general" or "universalist" values: "(1) developing and exercising one's capacities and expressing one's experience, and (2) participating in determining one's action and the conditions of one's action" (1990: 5, 37). At best, however, her formulation leaves uncertain whether the "capacities" of individuals that should be developed and exercised have any universal character. Although the second "very general" value itself implies a universal capacity to participate in determining one's action and its conditions, the affirmation of this participation is, at least roughly speaking, equivalent to Sandel's endorsement of self-governance. With Sandel, then, Young does not say whether there is a universal good by which self-governance ought to be directed and in relation to which other universal human capacities may be defined. On my reading, moreover, her insistence on normative ideals that are "historically and socially contextualized" (1990: 5) precludes the conceptual resources with which to provide that backing to the politics of difference.

Without a universal good, however, the human capacities that should be emancipated must be defined in some solely localized manner—that is, solely in terms of the specific social group or set of social groups of which the individual is a member, or solely in terms of individual choice. In the end, this recourse contradicts Young's persistent and convincing critique of the distributive paradigm. If the politics of difference emancipates differences that are in all respects different because constituted solely by different social groups or individual choices, then justice as a principle or set of principles for the political community must be separated from the good of any group or individual, and Young is driven back to a nonteleological conception of justice. To the best of my reasoning, the distance she not only seeks but develops from both the distributive paradigm and communitarian theories cannot be sustained without a conception of emancipation defined in relation to a comprehensive good.

I expect that Young resists a turn in this direction because she is persuaded that any attempt to articulate it will escalate some historically specific human capacities into universal status and, thereby, compromise the politics of difference. But I also suspect that she shares with Sandel witting or unwitting participation in the agreement that also informs all nonteleological theory, namely, that no claim to truth for a metaphysical understanding of the good can be validated. If this judgment is correct, then the effect of that agreement within a theory that is critical of both separationist and communitarian conceptions of justice betrays how powerful the dominant consensus has become.

In response to this assessment, Young might find common ground with Sandel, who objects that the concept of a universal good has little practical use:

> Most of us find ourselves claimed, at one time or another, by a wide range of different communities, some overlapping, others contend-

ing. When obligations conflict, there is no way of deciding in advance, once and for all, which should prevail. . . . The best deliberation will attend to the content of the claims, their relative moral
weight, and their role in the narratives by which the participants
make sense of their lives. . . . No general principle of much practical
use can rank obligations in advance, and yet some responses to moral
and political dilemmas are better—more admirable or worthy or
fitting—than others. Unless this were so, there would be no point,
and no burden, in deliberation itself (1996: 343–44).

But Sandel's description of "the best deliberation" also does not seem
"of much practical use," since it says nothing about how to assign
"relative moral weight." Perhaps he means to assert that such judgments depend on "the narratives by which the participants make sense
of their lives." If so, he must either introduce a universal narrative that
will be or will include the very kind of general principle he finds
mostly useless or leave his position vulnerable to the criticism of
Habermas and Young.

One may agree that no universal principle can rank obligations, if
this means that diverse human associations and communities can be
ordered in a hierarchy of moral dominance and subservience and
conflicts resolved by appeal to this ranking. But if this is why a
universal principle or purpose seems unimportant to Sandel, we may
urge against him his own affirmation: "Some responses to moral and
political dilemmas" must be "better" if deliberation itself is to have
some point. Since democracy itself presupposes that deliberation does
have some point, democratic theory is incomplete without formulating and defending an understanding of the comprehensive purpose.
To be sure, a given thinker may hold that other tasks in political
thought are more important, for instance, criticizing and proposing
reform in the more specific practices of political communities. It
remains, nonetheless, that these pursuits presuppose or imply a comprehensive good. If a teleological theory denies this implication or
even seeks to beg the question, its proposals are, by implication,
reduced to some historically specific context or to claims for assumptions about the good that cannot themselves be redeemed. So
confined, no such conception of democracy itself and the rights it
includes can receive a convincing defense. Hence, this kind of civic

republicanism can give only aid and comfort to "Kantian liberals," like Habermas, who rightly hold that democratic deliberation has no point in the absence of a universal principle of justice—even if they also contradict their own insight by separating justice from the good.

What is true of the political theorist, moreover, is true of the democratic discourse to which, however indirectly, the theory seeks to contribute. Disagreements about the activities of the state and the principles by which they should be determined cannot be contained short of asking about the comprehensive telos of human life and thus the reason for democracy itself. Because humans live with understanding, they cannot fail to ask and answer, at least implicitly, the question of good as such, so that every moral and political claim implies a claim for some answer to that question. When moral and political claims are contested, nothing other than arbitrariness or coercion can exclude disagreement and argument about the comprehensive purpose. Within democratic discourse, in other words, there is always, at least potentially, a discourse among religions. Political thought in which some conception of the comprehensive purpose and the principles of justice it implies is clarified and argued makes a distinct contribution to a democratic political community. It is, moreover, an essential contribution, because democracy itself has as its telos our maximal common humanity and is authorized only by the divine good.

This means that all democratic theories in which comprehensive teleology is denied are incoherent because they contradict the democratic principle of religious freedom. Because every political claim makes or implies a claim for some understanding of the comprehensive good, no theory that separates justice from the good or confines the good to some historically specific community can be redeemed. By implication, then, any such theory asserts that its own conception of justice should be explicitly endorsed by the political constitution, and the democratic discourse should exclude all religions as illegitimate. Since even the theory in question implies a claim for some understanding of the comprehensive good, the denial of comprehensive teleology is, by implication, the affirmation of religious establishment. Only a comprehensive teleology can articulate consistently a conception of justice as compound. Against both separationist and communitarian theories, democracy is nothing other than political association by the way of reason.

Because religious freedom constitutes democracy, specifically religious associations or communities have a distinct calling within the
democratic process. Their distinct task is to clarify the respects in
which contestation about actual or proposed activities of the state
includes choices between differing understandings of the comprehensive purpose and to advocate within the discourse the understanding
for which truth is claimed. If they withdraw from this task or, what
comes to the same thing, accept the counsel that politics is independent of any comprehensive good, democracy is arrested at its most
fundamental level. Moreover, the religious conviction in question is
itself betrayed, because it purports to represent the purpose in relation
to which all human activity is properly evaluated. On my reading, the
divorce of politics from religion is widely practiced in religious communities of the United States, and this is, perhaps, one reason why the
political process here is too easily controlled by the simple adjudication of conflicts that seeks to avoid an evaluation of the contending
interests or conceptions of the good.

At the same time, distinctively religious contributions will corrupt
the democratic process if they, too, are advanced dogmatically or
without commitment to discourse. The belief that understandings of
reality and human purpose as such are not subject to rational assessment is even more widely present in United States religious communities—virtually to the point of being the one belief they all have in
common. Individuals or groups who do pursue politics as a religious
vocation are generally at a loss to transcend the mere assertion of their
religious convictions, and the logic of that approach reduces the
distinctive contribution of religious communities to another merely
private interest. But a claim to truth for any religious understanding
also issues the promise that it can be redeemed by argument. Hence,
the belief that religious understandings cannot be the object of democratic discourse is inconsistent with the claims to truth we make or
imply for them, including the claim to truth for this understanding of
religious understandings. Against both a divorce of politics from
religion and the authoritarian assertion of religion, democracy includes the question about reality and human purpose as such within
the way of reason.

The promise of modernity for "the rationalization of society," to
call again on Habermas's term, waits on the rationalization of relig-

ion. With Whitehead, the affirmation of democracy divorced from discourse about the comprehensive purpose loses "its security of intellectual justification" (1961: 36). Contrary to the consensus dominating our moral theory, comprehensive teleology is so far from being immune to criticism or validation as to be the presupposition of democracy's way of reason. This work has sought to clarify that presupposition and its meaning for politics. Democracy on purpose is properly directed by our maximal common humanity and, therefore, by the principles of justice as general emancipation. They specify to politics our love of God.

Works Cited

Amar, Akhil Reed. 1998. *The Bill of Rights: Creation and Reconstruction.* New Haven, Conn.: Yale University Press.

Apel, Karl-Otto. 1975. The problem of philosophical fundamental-grounding in light of a transcendental pragmatic of language. *Man and World* 8: 239–75.

———. 1978. Transcendental semiotics and the paradigms of first philosophy. *Philosophic Exchange* 2, no. 4 (summer): 3–22.

———. 1979a. The common presuppositions of hermeneutics and ethics: Types of rationality beyond science and technology. *Research in Phenomenology* 9: 35–53.

———. 1979b. Types of rationality today. *Rationality Today*. Edited by Theodore Gereats. Ottawa: University Press, 307–40.

———. 1980a. C. S. Pierce and the post-Tarskian problem of an adequate explication of the meaning of truth: Towards a transcendental-pragmatic theory of truth, Part I. *The Monist* 63, no. 3 (July): 386–407.

———. 1980b. *Toward a Transformation of Philosophy.* London: Routledge and Kegan Paul.

———. 1982. Normative ethics and strategic rationality: The philosophical problem of a political ethics. *Graduate Faculty Philosophical Journal* 9, no.1: 81–107.

———. 1984. *Understanding and Explanation: A Transcendental-Pragmatic Perspective.* Cambridge, Mass.: The M.I.T. Press.

———. 1987. The problem of a macroethic of responsibility to the future in the crisis of technological civilization: An attempt to come to terms with Hans Jonas' 'Principle of responsibility.' *Man and World* 20: 3–40.

———. 1993. Discourse ethics as a response to the novel challenges of

341

today's reality to coresponsibility. *The Journal of Religion* 73, no. 4 (October): 496–513.

Aquinas, St. Thomas. 1948. *Introduction to St. Thomas Aquinas*. Edited by Anton C. Pegis. New York: The Modern Library.

———. 1957. *The Political Ideas of St. Thomas Aquinas*. Edited by Dino Bigongiari. New York: Hafner Publishing Co.

Arendt, Hannah. 1958. *The Human Condition*. Chicago: The University of Chicago Press.

Aristotle. 1941. *The Basic Works of Aristotle*. Edited by Richard McKeon. New York: Random House.

Barry, Brian. 1995. *Justice as Impartiality*. Oxford, UK: Clarendon Press.

Beyleveld, Derek. 1991. *The Dialectical Necessity of Morality: An Analysis and Defense of Alan Gewirth's Argument for the Principle of Generic Consistency*. Chicago: The University of Chicago Press.

Calvin, John. 1989. *Institutes of the Christian Religion*. Grand Rapids, Mich: Wm. B. Eerdmans Publishing Co.

Daly, Herman E. and Cobb Jr., John B. 1994. *For the Common Good: Redirecting the Economy Toward Community, the Environment, and a Sustainable Future*, second edition. Boston, Mass.: Beacon Press.

Dewey, John. 1951. Creative democracy—The task before us." *Classic American Philosophies*. Edited by Max H. Fisch. New York: Appleton-Century-Crofts, 389–94.

———. 1957. *Reconstruction in Philosophy*. Boston, Mass.: Beacon Press.

———. 1963. *Liberalism and Social Action*. New York: Capricorn Books.

Donagan, Alan. 1977. *The Theory of Morality*. Chicago: The University of Chicago Press.

Dworkin, Ronald. 1981. What is equality? Part 2: Equality of resources. *Philosophy and Public Affairs* 10, no. 4 (fall): 283–345.

Friedman, Milton. 1962. *Capitalism and Freedom*. Chicago: The University of Chicago Press.

Gamwell, Franklin I. 1984. *Beyond Preference: Liberal Theories of Independent Associations*. Chicago: The University of Chicago Press.

———. 1990. *The Divine Good: Modern Moral Theory and the Necessity of God*. San Francisco, Calif.: HarperCollins.

———. 1995. *The Meaning of Religious Freedom: Modern Politics and the Democratic Resolution*. Albany, New York: State University of New York Press.

———. 1996. On the loss of theism. *Iris Murdoch and the Search for Human Goodness*. Edited by Maria Antonaccio and William Schweiker. Chicago: The University of Chicago Press, 171–89.

———. 1997. Habermas and Apel on communicative ethics: Their difference and the difference it makes. *Philosophy and Social Criticism* 23, no. 2: 21–45.

Gewirth, Alan. 1978. *Reason and Morality*. Chicago: The University of Chicago Press.

———. 1996. *The Community of Rights*. Chicago: The University of Chicago Press.

Gilligan, Carol. 1982. *In a Different Voice: Psychological Theory and Women's Development*. Cambridge, Mass.: Harvard University Press.

Greenawalt, Kent. 1995. *Fighting Words*. Princeton, N.J.: Princeton University Press.

Griffin, David Ray. 1998. *Unsnarling the World-Knot: Consciousness, Freedom, and the Mind-Body Problem*. Berkeley and Los Angeles: University of California Press.

Habermas, Jürgen. 1984. *The Theory of Communicative Action, Volume 1: Reason and the Rationalization of Society*. Boston, Mass.: Beacon Press.

———. 1987. *The Theory of Communicative Action, Volume 2: Lifeworld and System: A Critique of Functionalist Reason*. Boston, Mass.: Beacon Press.

———. 1990. *Moral Consciousness and Communicative Action*. Cambridge, Mass.: The MIT Press.

———. 1992. *Postmetaphysical Thinking: Philosophical Essays*. Cambridge, Mass.: The MIT Press.

———. 1993. *Justification and Application: Remarks on Discourse Ethics*. Cambridge, Mass.: The MIT Press.

———. 1996. *Between Facts and Norms: Contributions to a Discourse Theory of Law and Democracy*. Cambridge, Mass.: The MIT Press.

Hartshorne, Charles. 1948. *The Divine Relativity: A Social Conception of God*. New Haven, Conn.: Yale University Press.

———. 1970. *Creative Synthesis and Philosophic Method*. LaSalle, Ill: The Open Court Publishing Co.

———. 1972. *Whitehead's Philosophy*. Lincoln, Neb.: University of Nebraska Press.

Heilbroner, Robert L. 1976. *Business Civilization in Decline*. New York: W. W. Norton and Co.

———. 1980. *An Inquiry into the Human Prospect: Updated and Reconsidered for the 1980s*. New York: W. W. Norton and Co.

———. 1985. *The Nature and Logic of Capitalism*. New York: W. W. Norton and Co.

Held, Virginia, ed. 1995. *Justice and Care*. Boulder, Colo.: Westview Press.

Hobbes, Thomas. 1962. *Leviathan: Or the Matter, Forme and Power of a*

Commonwealth Ecclesiastical and Civil. New York: Collier Macmillan Publishers.

Hume, David. 1975. *Enquiries Concerning Human Understanding and Concerning the Principles of Morals.* Edited by P. H. Niddich. Oxford, UK: Clarendon Press.

Jonas, Hans. 1984. *The Imperative of Responsibility: In Search of an Ethics for the Technological Age.* Chicago: The University of Chicago Press.

Kant, Immanuel. 1949. *Fundamental Principles of the Metaphysic of Morals.* Indianapolis, Ind.: Bobbs-Merrill Educational Publishing.

———. 1956. *Critique of Practical Reason.* Indianapolis, Ind.: Bobbs-Merrill Educational Publishing.

———. 1960. *Religion within the Limits of Reason Alone.* New York: Harper and Row.

———. 1965. *Critique of Pure Reason.* New York: St. Martin's Press.

Kymlicka, Will. 1990. *Contemporary Political Philosophy: An Introduction.* New York: Oxford University Press.

Locke, John. 1952. *The Second Treatise of Government.* New York: The Liberal Arts Press.

Lovin, Robin W. 1995. *Reinhold Niebuhr and Christian Realism.* New York: Cambridge University Press.

MacIntyre, Alasdair. 1967. Egoism and altruism. *The Encyclopedia of Philosophy*, vol. 2. Edited by Paul Edwards. New York: Macmillan Publishing Co., 462–66.

Mead, Sidney E. 1963. *The Lively Experiment: The Shaping of Christianity in America.* New York: Harper and Row.

Mill, John Stuart. 1973. Utilitarianism. *The Utilitarians: Jeremy Bentham, John Stuart Mill.* Garden City, NY: Anchor Press/Doubleday, 399–472.

Moore, George Edward. 1953. *Some Main Problems of Philosophy.* New York: The Macmillan Co.

Murdoch, Iris. 1970. *The Sovereignty of Good.* London and New York: Routledge.

———. 1992. *Metaphysics as a Guide to Morals.* New York: Allen Lane, The Penguin Press.

Murray S.J., John Courtney. 1988. *We Hold These Truths: Catholic Reflections on the American Proposition.* Kansas City, Mo: Sheed and Ward.

Niebuhr, Reinhold. 1941–43. *The Nature and Destiny of Man*, 2 vols. New York: Charles Scribner's Sons.

———. 1942. Religion and action. *Science and Man.* Edited by Ruth Nada Anshen. New York: Harcourt, Brace, and Co., 44–64.

———. 1949. *Faith and History: A Comparison of Christian and Modern Views of History.* New York: Charles Scribner's Sons.

———. 1960. *The Children of Light and the Children of Darkness: A Vindication of Democracy and a Critique of Its Traditional Defense.* New York: Charles Scribner's Sons.

Noddings, Nel. 1984. *Caring: A Feminine Approach to Ethics and Moral Education.* Berkeley and Los Angeles: University of California Press.

Ogden, Schubert M. 1966. *The Reality of God and Other Essays.* New York: Harper and Row.

———. 1992. *Is There Only One True Religion or Are There Many?* Dallas, Tex.: Southern Methodist University Press.

———. 1996. *Doing Theology Today.* Valley Forge, Penna: Trinity Press International.

Plaskow, Judith. 1980. *Sex, Sin, and Grace: Women's Experience and the Theologies of Reinhold Niebuhr and Paul Tillich.* Lanham, Md.: University Press of America.

Plantinga, Alvin. 1993. *Warrant and Proper Function.* New York: Oxford University Press.

Rawls, John. 1955. Two concepts of rules. *The Philosophical Review* 64: 3–32.

———. 1971. *A Theory of Justice.* Cambridge, Mass.: The Belknap Press of Harvard University Press.

———. 1996. *Political Liberalism* (paperback edition). New York: Columbia University Press.

———. 1997. The idea of public reason revisited. *The University of Chicago Law Review* 64, no. 3 (summer): 765–807.

Rorty, Richard. 1979. Transcendental arguments, self-reference, and pragmatism. *Transcendental Arguments and Science.* Edited by Peter Bieri, Rolf Horstman, and Lorenz Kreuger. Dortrect, Holland: D. Reidel, 77–103.

———. 1982. *Consequences of Pragmatism.* Minneapolis, Minn.: University of Minnesota Press.

Sandel, Michael. 1982. *Liberalism and the Limits of Justice.* New York: Cambridge University Press.

———. 1996. *Democracy's Discontent: America in Search of a Public Philosophy.* Cambridge, Mass.: The Belknap Press of Harvard University Press.

Sartre, Jean-Paul. 1957. *Existentialism and Human Emotions.* New York: The Philosophical Library.

Schleiermacher, Friedrich. 1989. *The Christian Faith.* Edinburgh, Scotland: T. and T. Clark.

Schneewind, J. B. 1998. *The Invention of Autonomy: A History of Modern Moral Philosophy*. New York: Cambridge University Press.

Searle, John R. 1983. *Intentionality: An Essay in the Philosophy of Mind*. New York: Cambridge University Press.

———. 1992. *The Rediscovery of the Mind*. Cambridge, Mass: The MIT Press.

———. 1995. *The Construction of Social Reality*. New York: The Free Press.

Silber, John R. 1959. The Copernican revolution in ethics: The good re-examined. *Kant-Studien* (fall): 85–101.

———. 1960. The ethical significance of Kant's *Religion*. Introductory Essay to *Immanuel Kant: Religion within the Limits of Reason Alone*. New York: Harper and Row, lxxix–cxxiv.

Stout, Jeffrey. 1981. *The Flight from Authority*. Notre Dame, Ind.: University of Notre Dame Press.

Sturm, Douglas. 1998. *Solidarity and Suffering: Toward a Politics of Relationality*. Albany: State University of New York Press.

Sunstein, Cass R. 1993. *Democracy and the Problem of Free Speech*. New York: The Free Press.

Taylor, Charles. 1995. *Philosophical Arguments*. Cambridge, Mass.: Harvard University Press.

Tillich, Paul. 1951. *Systematic Theology*, vol. 1. Chicago: The University of Chicago Press.

———. 1952. *The Courage to Be*. New Haven, Conn.: Yale University Press.

Toulmin, Stephen. 1990. *Cosmopolis: The Hidden Agenda of Modernity*. New York: The Free Press.

Whitehead, Alfred North. 1938. *Modes of Thought*. New York: Capricorn Books.

———. 1941. Immortality. *The Philosophy of Alfred North Whitehead*. Edited by Paul A. Schlipp. Evanston, Ill.: Northwestern University Press, 682–700.

———. 1955. *Symbolism: Its Meaning and Effect*. New York: The Macmillan Co.

———. 1961. *Adventures of Ideas*. New York: The Free Press.

———. 1963. *Science and the Modern World*. New York: New American Library.

———. 1978. *Process and Reality*, corrected edition. Edited by David Ray Griffin and Donald W. Sherburne. New York: The Free Press.

Wolterstorff, Nicholas. 1983. Can belief in God be rational if it has no foundations? *Faith and Rationality*. Edited by Alvin Plantinga and Nicholas Wolterstorff. Notre Dame, Ind.: University of Notre Dame Press, 135–86.

————. 1996. *John Locke and the Ethics of Belief*. New York: Cambridge University Press

————. 1997. The role of religion in decision and discussion of political issues. Robert Audi and Nicholas Wolterstorff. *Religion in the Public Square: The Place of Religious Convictions in Political Debate*. New York: Rowan and Littlefield, 67–120.

Young, Iris Marion. 1990. *Justice and the Politics of Difference*. Princeton, N.J.: Princeton University Press.

Index

activities
  divine. *See* God; theism
  human, 34, 35, 57, 59, 105, 107
    as actuality, 115
    as cause and effect, 37
    comprehensive purpose and,
      46–47
    consciousness of reality as such
      in, 32–33
    consciousness of universals and,
      24
    contemplation versus action in,
      70–72
    creativity in, 123
    defined, 17
    freedom of, 38, 39, 56, 131
    happiness and virtue in, 133
    individuals and, 20–21, 26,
      116–17
    love and, 9
    metaphysics and, 52–53, 115
    misunderstandings in, 48n
    moral law and, 51, 283
    past and, 126–27
    relations constituting, 21
    relations to God of, 7, 16, 141
    self-deception in, 72–73
    self-understanding and, 40
    subjectivity and objectivity of,
      36–37
    suicide and, 260n
    temporality of, 108–9, 111,
      119–20, 122
    understanding in, 22
    unity-in-diversity and, 129
    validity claims and, 154

  versus metaphysical activities,
    116
  worth and, 41, 45
  See also actualities; individuals;
    understanding
  metaphysical, 149
    composites and, 116
    defined, 116
    as fragmentary, 141
    versus human activities, 116
    See also actualities
actualities, 147, 149
  as activities, 116
  creativity in, 122, 282
  defined, 114
  metaphysics and, 114–16
  priority and posteriority in, 117n
  as subject of metaphysics, 115, 121
  temporality of, 116, 120, 122
  See also activity, metaphysical
aesthetics, 123–24, 126, 282–83, 256
affirmation-negation contrast, 27. *See
  also* negation; discrimination
aggregates. *See* composites
Amar, Akhil Reed, 217n
anarchy, 194,195, 196, 321–22
animals, nonhuman, 23, 25, 116, 284
Apel, Karl-Otto, 202, 262n
  argument types in, 168
  communicative respect in, 199–200
  criticism of, 170–73
  democracy in, 182
  Kant in, 227
  long-run responsibility in, 312–13
  nonteleology in, 226–28
  pragmatic theory of belief in, 153